Oracle SOA Suite 12*c* Administrator's Guide

A guide to everything an Oracle SOA Suite 12*c* administrator needs to hit the ground running

Arun Pareek

Harold Dost

Ahmed Aboulnaga

[PACKT] enterprise 🕱
PUBLISHING   professional expertise distilled

BIRMINGHAM - MUMBAI

Oracle SOA Suite 12c Administrator's Guide

First published: November 2015

Production reference: 1231115

Published by Packt Publishing Ltd.
Livery Place
35 Livery Street
Birmingham B3 2PB, UK.

ISBN 978-1-78217-086-0

www.packtpub.com

Credits

Authors
 Arun Pareek

 Harold Dost

 Ahmed Aboulnaga

Reviewers
 Pradip Gupta

 Jorge Quilcate

 Chintan Shah

Commissioning Editor
 Erol Staveley

Acquisition Editor
 Meeta Rajani

Content Development Editor
 Athira Laji

Technical Editor
 Pranjali Mistry

Copy Editor
 Neha Vyas

Project Coordinator
 Bijal Patel

Proofreader
 Safis Editing

Indexer
 Monica Ajmera Mehta

Graphics
 Disha Haria

Production Coordinator
 Arvindkumar Gupta

Cover Work
 Arvindkumar Gupta

About the Authors

Arun Pareek is an IASA-certified software architect and has been actively working as an SOA and BPM practitioner. Over the past 8 years, he has worked in the capacity of a consultant and an architect for the implementation of a variety of large-scale SOA and BPM projects for customers across the globe. He has a knack for designing systems that are scalable, performance efficient, and fault tolerant, and he is a keen enthusiast of BPMN, automation, and cloud computing. He is currently employed by Rubicon Red, an innovative IT professional services firm headquartered in Australia, which focuses on enabling enterprise agility and operational excellence through the adoption of emerging technologies, such as SOA, BPM, and cloud computing.

Prior to working with Rubicon Red, Arun worked for companies such as Dell and Accenture, where he successfully executed many Oracle FMW-based projects in the communications and utilities domain.

Arun has also been engaged with Packt Publishing as a technical reviewer for quite some time now, reviewing a few of their books on **Oracle BAM 11g** and the book *Oracle BPM 11g Cookbook*. He is also an active blogger of these technologies and runs a widely popular blog at `http://beatechnologies.wordpress.com`. He can be contacted at his personal e-mail address at `arrun.pareek@gmail.com`.

A large part of the knowledge in this book has come from the numerous great people I have worked with. Not all of them are listed here, but they have certainly influenced me in my life, which has resulted in this work.

I cannot thank my employers, Matt Wright, James Hemmings, and John Deeb, enough for being very appreciative and supportive about me completing this book. All of them are exceptional leaders and have allowed me to focus my energy on writing, and I greatly thank them for that.

Most importantly, I appreciate the encouragement I have received from my parents for helping me achieve many things in my life. Finally, a special note of thanks to my wonderful wife, Karuna, for her constant support, cooperation, and patience without which it would have been impossible for me to manage my work and life together. Thank you for believing that I can write this book when I did not believe it myself and for supporting me even when my already busy schedule only got busier.

I have learned a lot from all of you and have so much more to learn.

Harold Dost III is a Principal Consultant at Raastech who has experience in architecting and implementing solutions that leverage Oracle Fusion Middleware, mostly revolving around products and technologies that include SOA Suite, OSB, BAM, AIA, Java, big data, and mobile development. He is a certified Oracle SOA Foundation Practitioner and has presented on various topics at conferences that include OpenWorld, Collaborate, UKOUG, WMOUG, and MOUS.

Xiomara, I love you, and thank you for being patient.

Ahmed Aboulnaga is a Technical Director at Raastech, a complete lifecycle systems integrator headquartered at Virginia, USA. His professional focus is in technical management, architecture, and consulting within the Oracle Fusion Middleware stack. He has implemented enterprise solutions for commercial, government, and global customers over the years. Ahmed holds an MS degree in Computer Science and is an Oracle ACE, OCE, and OCA. He actively contributes to the online community in the area of Oracle Fusion Middleware. Ahmed is currently the President of the West Michigan Oracle Users Group.

To my father — I am forever indebted to you.

About the Reviewers

Pradip Gupta has over 25 years of IT experience in analysis, design, development, and implementation and testing; over 10 years of experience in Service-Oriented Architecture: SOA Suite, BPM, BPEL, Mediator, OSB, AIA; and over 20 years of experience in RDBMS' such as Oracle. He is also the founder of GTech Solution Services.

Jorge Quilcate is a developer, consultant, and speaker who is mainly focused on Java EE and integration. He is also recognized as an Oracle ACE Associate and specializes in SOA and Middleware.

He is certified as a specialist on WebLogic Server, SOA/BPM Suite, and Java. He also implements and supports open source projects related with DevOps tools and Java EE. He tweets at `@jeqo89`. He is currently working as a senior consultant at Sysco AS, Norway.

Chintan Shah is a well-versed expert in Oracle Fusion Middleware (FMW) and has been working on FMW technologies for over 12 years as a hands-on architect. He is an active member in the FMW community and maintains a highly accessed blog at `chintanblog.blogspot.com`.

www.PacktPub.com

Support files, eBooks, discount offers, and more

For support files and downloads related to your book, please visit www.PacktPub.com.

Did you know that Packt offers eBook versions of every book published, with PDF and ePub files available? You can upgrade to the eBook version at www.PacktPub.com and as a print book customer, you are entitled to a discount on the eBook copy. Get in touch with us at service@packtpub.com for more details.

At www.PacktPub.com, you can also read a collection of free technical articles, sign up for a range of free newsletters and receive exclusive discounts and offers on Packt books and eBooks.

https://www2.packtpub.com/books/subscription/packtlib

Do you need instant solutions to your IT questions? PacktLib is Packt's online digital book library. Here, you can search, access, and read Packt's entire library of books.

Why subscribe?

- Fully searchable across every book published by Packt
- Copy and paste, print, and bookmark content
- On demand and accessible via a web browser

Free access for Packt account holders

If you have an account with Packt at www.PacktPub.com, you can use this to access PacktLib today and view 9 entirely free books. Simply use your login credentials for immediate access.

Instant updates on new Packt books

Get notified! Find out when new books are published by following @PacktEnterprise on Twitter or the *Packt Enterprise* Facebook page.

Table of Contents

Preface

This book touches upon all the core areas of administration that are needed for you to effectively manage and monitor the Oracle SOA Suite environment and its transactions, from deployments to monitoring to performance tuning, and much, much more. With the vast features and capabilities that the product has to offer come numerous complexities and challenges in administration.

We start by introducing SOA technologies and navigating Enterprise Manager Fusion Middleware Control 12c. We then focus on the three most commonly developed object types for SOA Suite 12c: SOA composite applications, OSB services, and BAM artifacts.

Moving on, you will become acquainted with the three areas of monitoring that an Oracle SOA Suite 12c administrator typically focuses on: transactions, instance state and performance, and infrastructure. Towards the end of this book, we'll take a closer look at how to configure and administer various components that are part of a SOA Suite 12c environment. Based on the type of composites deployed to runtime, you will learn to manage composite instances, the service engines they are executed on, and the additional platform components they use.

What this book covers

Chapter 1, SOA Infrastructure Management – what You Need to Know, provides you with an overview of how to monitor and manage Oracle SOA Suite 12c, which ultimately serves as a prelude for the remainder of this book.

Chapter 2, Navigating Enterprise Manager Fusion Middleware Control 12c, presents the Fusion Middleware Control dashboard and also provides you with an overview of consoles, including WebLogic Server, Service Bus Console, BAM Composer, MFT, B2B, and so on.

Chapter 3, Startup and Shutdown, focuses exclusively on the startup and shutdown of the Oracle SOA Service infrastructure and how to verify the completion of each component.

Chapter 4, Managing Services, discusses the concepts that enable you to manage both SOA composites in the first half of the chapter, followed by OSB services in the latter half.

Chapter 5, Deploying Code, focuses on the three most commonly developed object types for SOA Suite 12c: SOA composite applications, OSB services, and BAM artifacts.

Chapter 6, Monitoring Oracle SOA Suite 12c, covers the three areas of monitoring that an Oracle SOA Suite 12c administrator typically focuses on: transactions, instance state and performance, and infrastructure.

Chapter 7, Configuration and Administration, looks closely at how to configure and administer various components that are part of a SOA Suite 12c environment.

Chapter 8, Managing the Database, discusses less frequently used functionalities surrounding partitions and version history, albeit the functionality that every SOA Suite administrator should be familiar with.

Chapter 9, Troubleshooting the Oracle SOA Suite 12c Infrastructure, focuses more on introducing a troubleshooting methodology, which when coupled with the foundational knowledge you learned in the previous chapters will better equip you with the ability to solve most problems.

Chapter 10, Backup and Recovery, covers the key areas of understanding what needs to be backed up, the recommended backup strategy, implementing the backup process, and recovery strategies.

Chapter 11, Introducing Oracle Enterprise Scheduler, concentrates on introducing ESS to SOA Suite 12c administrators and covers the core areas of administration.

Chapter 12, Clustering and High Availability, describes how to set up a two-node Oracle SOA Suite 12c cluster in an active-active mode, wherein if a server fails, the other will continue processing transactions, ensuring a relatively high degree of availability.

What you need for this book

The following is the software that you will require for this book:

- Oracle Fusion Middleware 12*c* (12.1.3.0.0) Infrastructure
- Oracle Fusion Middleware 12*c* (12.1.3.0.0) SOA Suite and Business Process Management
- Oracle Fusion Middleware 12*c* (12.1.3.0.0) Service Bus
- Oracle Java SE 7 Update 55
- Oracle HTTP Server 12.1.3
- Oracle RCU (Repository Creation Utilities) 12.1.3
- Oracle PDB (Pluggable Database) 12*c*

Who this book is for

With topic areas ranging from simple to complex, this book is intended for novice, mid-level, and experienced administrators of the Oracle SOA Suite 12*c* platform, as well as Oracle WebLogic Server and Oracle Database administrators who are interested in diving into the product.

Conventions

In this book, you will find a number of styles of text that distinguish between different kinds of information. Here are some examples of these styles, and an explanation of their meaning.

Code words in text, database table names, folder names, filenames, file extensions, pathnames, dummy URLs, user input, and Twitter handles are shown as follows: "We can include other contexts through the use of the `include` directive."

Any command-line input or output is written as follows:

```
source setAntEnv.sh
export CLASSPATH=${ORACLE_HOME}/wlserver/server/lib/weblogic.jar
java utils.MulticastTest -N [managedServerName] -A [multicastHost] -P
[multicastPort] -T 10 -S
```

New terms and **important words** are shown in bold. Words that you see on the screen, in menus or dialog boxes for example, appear in the text like this: "clicking the **Next** button moves you to the next screen".

> Warnings or important notes appear in a box like this.

> Tips and tricks appear like this.

Reader feedback

Feedback from our readers is always welcome. Let us know what you think about this book—what you liked or may have disliked. Reader feedback is important for us to develop titles that you really get the most out of.

To send us general feedback, simply send an e-mail to feedback@packtpub.com, and mention the book title via the subject of your message.

If there is a topic that you have expertise in and you are interested in either writing or contributing to a book, see our author guide on www.packtpub.com/authors.

Customer support

Now that you are the proud owner of a Packt book, we have a number of things to help you to get the most from your purchase.

Downloading the example code

You can download the example code files for all Packt books you have purchased from your account at http://www.packtpub.com. If you purchased this book elsewhere, you can visit http://www.packtpub.com/support and register to have the files e-mailed directly to you.

Downloading the color images of this book

We also provide you a PDF file that has color images of the screenshots/diagrams used in this book. The color images will help you better understand the changes in the output. You can download this file from: http://www.packtpub.com/sites/default/files/downloads/1453OT_ColorImages.pdf.

Errata

Although we have taken every care to ensure the accuracy of our content, mistakes do happen. If you find a mistake in one of our books—maybe a mistake in the text or the code—we would be grateful if you would report this to us. By doing so, you can save other readers from frustration and help us improve subsequent versions of this book. If you find any errata, please report them by visiting http://www.packtpub.com/submit-errata, selecting your book, clicking on the **errata submission form** link, and entering the details of your errata. Once your errata are verified, your submission will be accepted and the errata will be uploaded on our website, or added to any list of existing errata, under the Errata section of that title. Any existing errata can be viewed by selecting your title from http://www.packtpub.com/support.

Piracy

Piracy of copyright material on the Internet is an ongoing problem across all media. At Packt, we take the protection of our copyright and licenses very seriously. If you come across any illegal copies of our works, in any form, on the Internet, please provide us with the location address or website name immediately so that we can pursue a remedy.

Please contact us at copyright@packtpub.com with a link to the suspected pirated material.

We appreciate your help in protecting our authors, and our ability to bring you valuable content.

Questions

You can contact us at questions@packtpub.com if you are having a problem with any aspect of the book, and we will do our best to address it.

1
SOA Infrastructure Management – what You Need to Know

Every organization faces the need to predict changes in the global business environment, rapidly respond to competitors, and tries its best to utilize its assets to prepare for the growth and changes in the IT landscape. Your enterprise application infrastructure can either help you meet these business imperatives or it can impede your ability to adapt to change.

To proactively respond to these challenges and the dynamics of change, major organizations worldwide are adopting **Service-Oriented Architectures (SOA)** as a means to deliver on these requirements. They are also trying to improve their business-IT alignment by adopting **Business Process Management (BPM)** methodologies, which cannot be successfully realized without a complementing service-oriented architecture infrastructure. The adoption of SOA and BPM methodologies is helping organizations overcome the complexity of their application and IT environments while narrowing the gap between IT and the business. An SOA represents a fundamental shift in the way new applications are designed, developed, and integrated with legacy business applications, and it facilitates the development of enterprise applications as modular business services that can be easily integrated and reused.

Oracle SOA Suite 12c is a comprehensive suite of products that not only includes the **Business Process Execution Language** (BPEL) process manager, human workflow, Mediator, Service Bus, and Web Services Manager, but also components such as business activity monitoring, **Business-to-Business** (B2B), User Messaging Service, Enterprise Scheduler, and event processing — all designed to help us build, deploy, and manage applications based on enterprise grade SOA. The deployment of the Oracle SOA Suite 12c platform within the enterprise is accelerated by the continued alignment of business and IT as a result of the rapid adoption of service-oriented and event-driven architectures and business process management.

While businesses strive to be more agile and dynamic, their dependency on a reliable, robust, and scalable infrastructure is also increasing. The need for proactive administration, management, and monitoring of the underlying SOA infrastructure is essential for business continuity. As a SOA administrator, here are some important considerations that you should look at to provide a stable and dependable environment:

- An essential aspect of any successful SOA deployment is the ability to continuously monitor mission-critical services, business processes, events, and service levels in real time to immediately identify problems and take necessary corrective actions.

- Proper management of **Service-level Agreements** (SLA) is required to define, track, and control appropriate service levels. They provide us with a necessary alert mechanism in the event of an SLA violation.

- SOA infrastructure monitoring provides us visibility of the performance of each individual service transaction across distributed and heterogeneous systems. With this end-to-end visibility, problems can be spotted quickly and corrected to ensure reliable operations.

- The SOA infrastructure is also expected to enforce policies for runtime governance, security, and audit compliance.

- The ability to easily and efficiently automate deployments is equally important as it enables the administrator to rapidly respond to continuous code changes.

In this chapter, we will provide you with an overview of how to monitor and manage Oracle SOA Suite 12*c*, which ultimately serves as a prelude for the remainder of this book. This book describes each of these areas and more, in varying degrees of detail, to arm you with the necessary background and understanding as well as detailed instructions on how to perform key administrative tasks within the Oracle SOA Suite 12*c* product stack. This chapter introduces the following topics:

- Overcoming monitoring and management challenges in a SOA
- Centralized monitoring and management of the SOA platform
- Performance monitoring and management
- Managing composite application lifecycles
- Overview of the Oracle Fusion Middleware landscape
- The Oracle SOA Suite 12*c* infrastructure stack
- The new features of Oracle SOA Suite 12*c*

This book focuses on core Oracle SOA Suite, Oracle Service Bus, as well as Oracle WebLogic Server, but not on Oracle BPM Suite, Oracle **Business Activity Monitoring** (**BAM**), and Oracle B2B, all of which warrant books of their own.

Identifying and overcoming monitoring and management challenges in the SOA

The very nature of an SOA involves the implementation of services that are distributed and loosely coupled, and thus monitoring these services is complex due to the involvement of disparate systems that may include external systems and external resources (for example, messaging queues, databases, and so on). Tracing transactions across a loosely coupled implementation, particularly if it involves invocations to external applications, is extremely complicated.

The reusable nature of a SOA increases the importance of managing availability and performance of these services and greatly increases the need for a closed loop governance. In order to achieve the desired **quality of service** (**QoS**), each service endpoint must literally be managed like a resource. Managed services should have near zero downtime, measurable performance metrics, and a defined service-level agreement. In a composite service infrastructure, it is required that you monitor and manage the end-to-end view of the systems as well as provide detailed information about performance and availability metrics of individual services. Each part of the overall SOA system can appear healthy while individual service transactions can appear like they are suffering.

[
Tracing transactions across a loosely coupled implementation, particularly involving multiple external systems and resources, is extremely complicated.
]

Another important aspect of SOA monitoring is auditing and logging. The distributed nature of SOA makes a standardized auditing/logging approach difficult to implement. In addition to monitoring services in real time, an administrator is also required to perform standard administrative duties such as health checks, taking backups, deploying code, tuning performance, purging old instance data, and more. In general, SOA infrastructure administrators are swamped with the following tasks and activities:

- Performing health checks of servers and infrastructure
- Managing multitier transaction flows some of which are as follows:
  - Spanning shared components/services
  - Deploying multitier transactions across several tiers in different containers
  - Managing multitier transactions across the enterprise

- Obtaining performance metrics and visibility of SOA services:
  - Obtaining performance metrics beyond generic Java classes and methods
  - Obtaining framework and metadata visibility
  - Obtaining specific knowledge of the Oracle platform

- Maintaining control over configuration changes
- Tuning the performance of a service infrastructure
- Performing time-consuming administrative tasks, which include:
  - Setting up, provisioning, and patching environments
  - Code deployments
  - Cloning and scaling up
  - Backups and restores
  - Purging and cleanup

- Troubleshooting faults and exceptions
- Policy and security administration

This book intends to provide a thorough understanding of how to perform each of these tasks and activities as an Oracle SOA Suite 12c administrator.

Centralized monitoring and management of the SOA platform

Monitoring in Oracle SOA Suite 12*c* enables a closed loop governance by connecting design time to runtime. Once the services, their metadata, and the associated policies are deployed, they are automatically monitored and managed by the service infrastructure that regularly updates the management console with a scorecard of the runtime metrics that are collected.

Oracle SOA Suite 12*c* runs on top of numerous infrastructure components that include a variety of operating systems, database management systems, and Java EE compliant application servers. All Oracle SOA Suite 12*c* components have specific functions that are used to administer and manage parts of a SOA infrastructure, each from a different perspective or for a different audience. In order to address the monitoring and management challenges described earlier, several areas need to be considered:

- Monitoring solutions need to be provided at an enterprise level that encompass all the related applications. This can be as fine grained as monitoring composite endpoints to the overall operational health of the infrastructure.

- Real-time monitoring and proactive alerting based on runtime statistics of the configured **Key Performance Indicator** (**KPI**), availability, performance metrics, and service-level agreements should be implemented.

- Reporting important information in the message (that is, payload), captured as a part of the reporting functionality, can aid middleware administrators in better decision making and troubleshooting.

Performance monitoring and management

Performance means different things to different people. For some, it translates to transaction response time, while others view it as the volume of work that can be processed within a given period of time. In order to maximize performance, you will need to monitor, analyze, and tune all the components that make up your application and infrastructure.

The performance of your SOA composites can be directly impacted by the design and implementation of the application code itself, the settings and configuration of the service infrastructure, or the performance of external resources such as queuing or storage systems. Now, the question is, where do you begin to identify a performance bottleneck?

Fortunately, Oracle Enterprise Manager Fusion Middleware Control is a single console that captures and displays key information such as WebLogic Server performance statistics as well as transaction performance details. The following screenshot is simply an overall server-level performance summary:

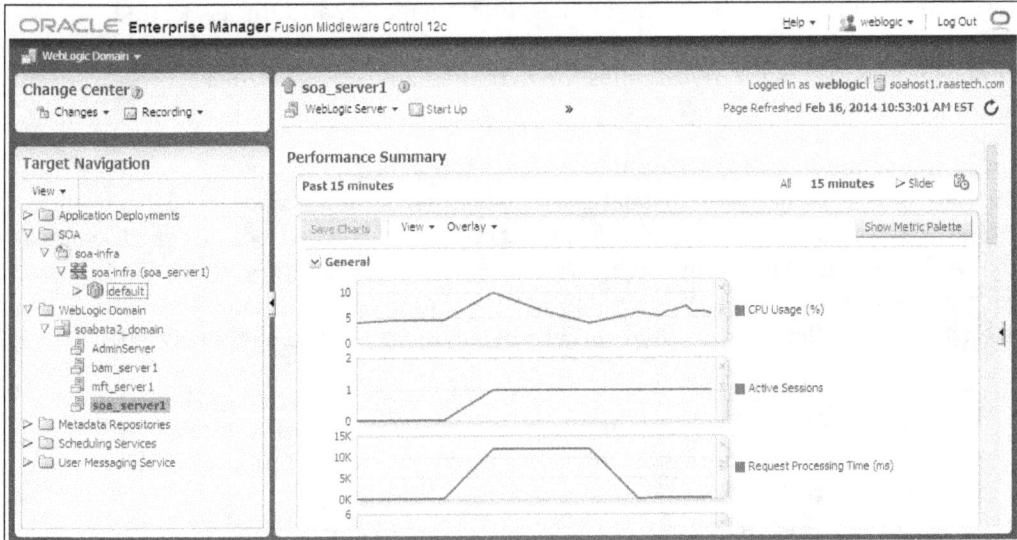

Figure 1.1: Viewing performance snapshots using Oracle Enterprise Manager Fusion Middleware Control

(Later chapters delve into the performance monitoring and tuning aspects of individual components in more detail.)

It is also important to understand that performance tuning is an iterative process. You need to make the adjustments, measure the impact, and then perform an analysis before possibly making further adjustments, and so on. Due to the varying expectations of a performant system, there are no one-size-fits-all solutions that work well in every environment. Improving performance is a process of learning and testing. It is not unusual to obtain considerable performance gains by implementing certain settings or applying specific configurations. Though tuning the service infrastructure is not the only area that impacts performance, it is undoubtedly a key one.

Managing composite application lifecycles

A typical software development lifecycle is comprised of multiple phases such as requirement gathering, analysis, design, development, testing, and promotion. Within the Oracle SOA development lifecycle, deployment and runtime management tend to introduce certain complexities. The following screenshot shows a simple HelloWorld SOA composite application in Oracle JDeveloper 12*c* that is implemented using a BPEL component:

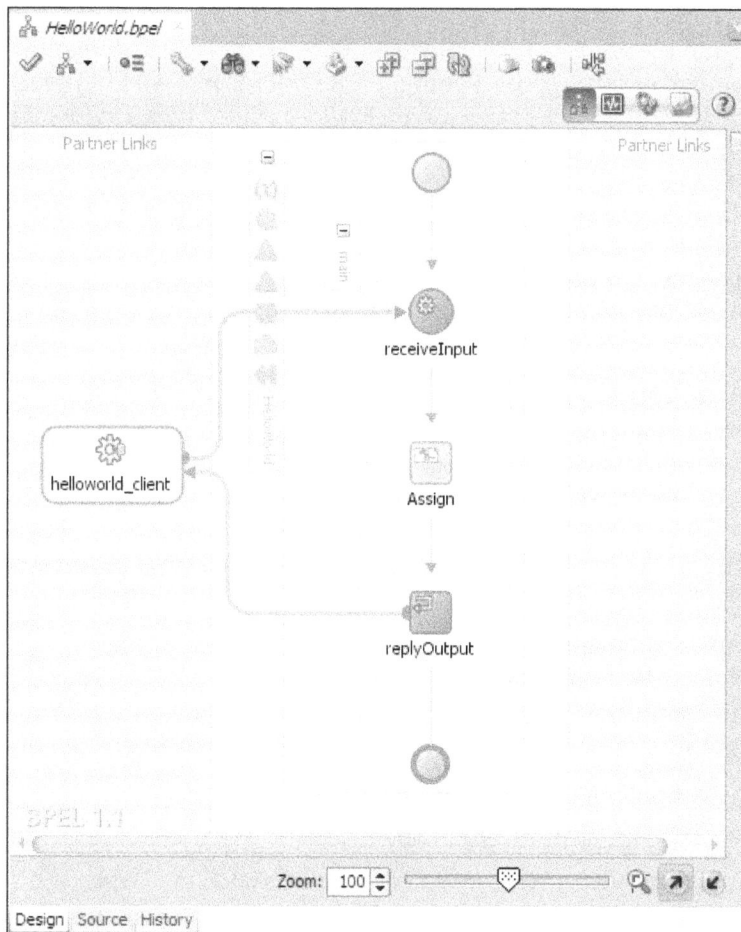

Figure 1.2: Developing a HelloWorld SOA application using BPEL in Oracle JDeveloper

As a SOA composite is being developed, it may reference an endpoint (effectively, a fully qualified URL) on a development server. This reference will need to change when the composite is promoted to higher environments such as test and production.

For example, your developers may have designed a SOA composite that processes payments by calling PayPal's API service. Naturally, they would be referencing PayPal's sandbox server (For example, `https://api.sandbox.paypal.com/2.0`) during development. What happens when this same SOA composite is deployed to production? How are these references automatically updated to utilize PayPal's production servers? How about timeout settings and other properties that differ from environment to environment?

Oracle SOA Suite 12*c* offers comprehensive lifecycle management features starting from development all through packaging, deployment, and post-deployment management:

- The ability to deploy multiple versions of a given composite application and specify a default version from either Oracle JDeveloper, Oracle Enterprise Manager Fusion Middleware Control, or Ant/WLST-based scripts.

- Oracle SOA Suite tooling allows you to make/compile your composite applications and export a deployable **Service Archive (SAR)**.

> A SAR is a deployment unit that describes the SOA composite application. The SAR packages service components, such as BPEL/BPMN processes, business rules, human tasks, and Mediator routing services in a single deployable application.

- Built-in capabilities to connect with versioning systems to version control your composite artifacts.

- Configuration plans that are composite-wide to customize environment-specific values, such as a web service URL that is different in the dev/test environment than in the actual production environment. With configuration plans, many runtime properties can be modified including:
    - Schema references and imports
    - Service endpoints in `composite.xml`
    - Properties of referenced components such as adapters
    - Attaching and detaching security policies to composite endpoints

Figure 1.3 illustrates how a developer IDE such as JDeveloper (top-left corner) is used to build and compile SOA composites that can eventually be packed and deployed as SAR files to the Oracle SOA Suite 12*c* infrastructure for execution. The composites along with their instances can be instantaneously managed and monitored from Oracle Enterprise Manager Fusion Middleware Control (bottom-left corner).

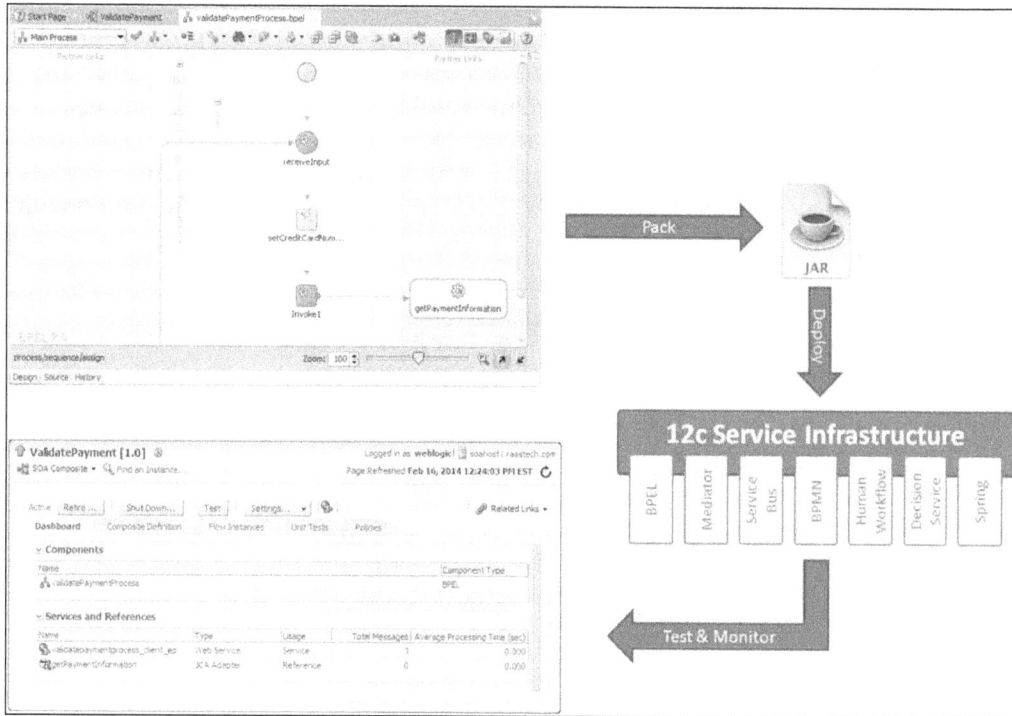

Figure 1.3: A typical Oracle SOA Suite 12*c* application lifecycle

Oracle Service Bus development is now integrated in Oracle JDeveloper 12*c* and no longer requires the separately installed Eclipse IDE for OSB development.

Understanding the Oracle Fusion Middleware landscape

Before examining Oracle SOA Suite 12*c* in more detail, it is important to understand where it lies within the application architecture framework.

Within the Oracle technology stack, Fusion Middleware lies between applications and backend infrastructures such as a database, an operating system, and hardware (refer to *Figure 1.4*). Applications such as Oracle E-Business Suite and Oracle Fusion Applications rely on numerous middleware components to serve several functions. The areas that Oracle Fusion Middleware is meant to address could include reporting. There may be single sign-on requirements. There could likely also be integration with other external applications.

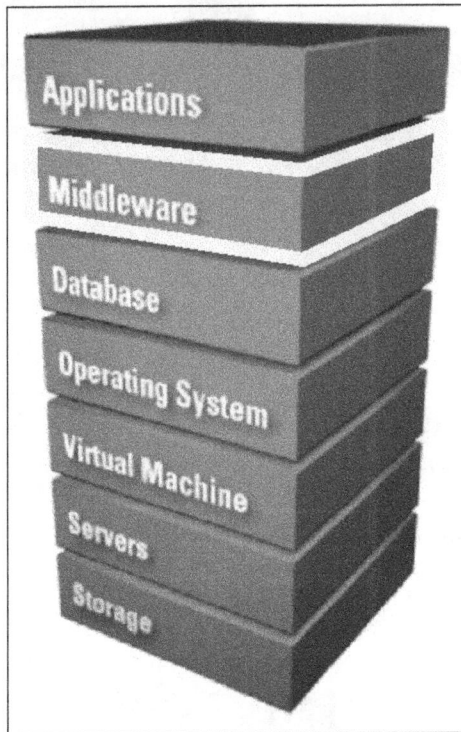

Figure 1.4: Location of the Oracle Fusion Middleware stack within the environment architecture

Unfortunately, many technologists, including Oracle itself, sometimes refer to Oracle Fusion Middleware as a product when in fact it is a collection of software products of which Oracle SOA Suite is a part of. Just to reiterate, despite various press releases or blog post allusions, there is no product called Oracle Fusion Middleware.

Oracle Fusion Middleware encompasses products that service areas of business intelligence, identity management, content management, integration, and more. Products such as **Oracle Business Intelligence Enterprise Edition** (**OBIEE**), **Oracle Access Manager** (**OAM**), Oracle WebCenter Content, and Oracle SOA Suite are all designed to satisfy these various middleware needs, and all of these run on the core application server, Oracle WebLogic Server.

Oracle SOA Suite 12*c* is a middleware component of Oracle Fusion Middleware 12*c* and provides a set of infrastructure services to support SOA composite applications and **Oracle Service Bus** (**OSB**) services. Though this single product can satisfy the overwhelming majority of an organization's SOA needs, it is not the only integration product within the Oracle Fusion Middleware integration stack. Products such as Oracle API Manager, Oracle API Catalog, and **Oracle API Gateway** (**OAG**) cover the governance needs of SOA applications. Oracle SOA Core Extension (formerly known as the Oracle Application Integration Architecture Foundation Pack), an extension to Oracle SOA Suite, provides a framework that is intended to reduce development efforts through the inclusion of templates and methodologies. Tools such as **Oracle Data Integrator** (**ODI**) and Oracle GoldenGate are designed for bulk data transfers. And new tools to Oracle Fusion Middleware 12*c* are Oracle **Managed File Transfer** (**MFT**) and Oracle **Enterprise Scheduler Service** (**ESS**), which are designed to support file transfers and scheduling. The following figure shows Oracle SOA Suite 12*c* at the center of the Oracle Fusion Middleware integration product stack:

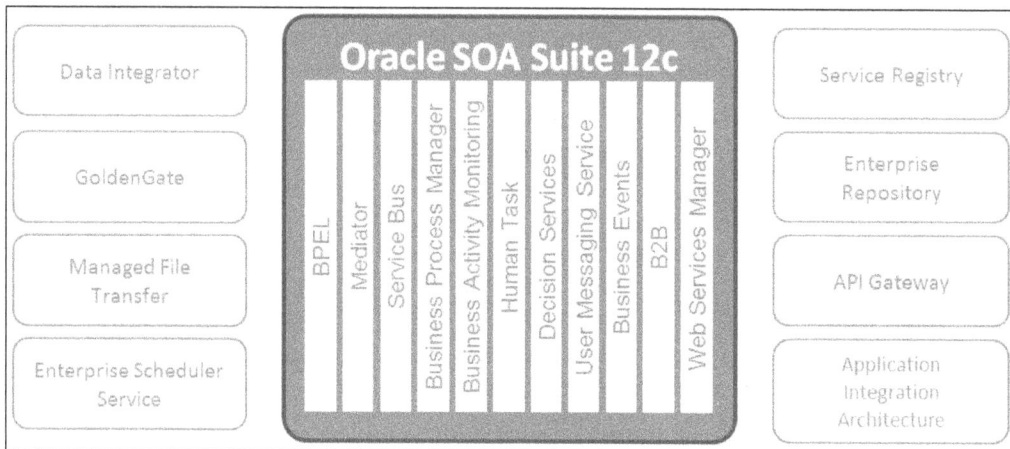

Figure 1.5: Oracle SOA Suite 12*c* at the crux of the Oracle Fusion Middleware integration product stack

Oracle SOA Suite 12*c* is the product of choice for most integration infrastructures, and as shown in *Figure 1.5*, it is the heart of the Oracle Fusion Middleware integration suite of products. It includes numerous subcomponents that include BPEL, Mediator, Service Bus, Business Activity Monitoring, B2B, Web Services Manager, and more. It is not uncommon for Oracle SOA Suite to be deployed and used in conjunction with some of the other integration products described earlier and depicted in *Figure 1.5*.

The Oracle SOA Suite 12c infrastructure stack

As mentioned earlier, Oracle SOA Suite 12*c* is a member of the Oracle Fusion Middleware family of products. Oracle has put in the efforts to make this stack robust, extensible, and agile, in part by including some of the best technologies available in the market. Instead of cobbling together enterprise solutions from disparate vendors and products, Oracle SOA Suite 12*c* provides you with a unified product suite to meet all of your SOA needs. This results in a single design-time experience, single runtime infrastructure, and end-to-end monitoring that greatly simplifies the building, maintenance, and monitoring of distributed SOA implementations. These components include:

- **JDeveloper**: This provides a design and development environment for software developers and architects, using Oracle SOA Suite 12*c* to create standards-based reusable enterprise software assets.

- **Service components**: These can be built as BPEL/BPMN processes, business rules and decision components, human tasks, events and mediators, or a combination thereof. They are the building blocks that are used to construct SOA composite applications. The service infrastructure, comprised of a unified platform for services, processes, and events, provides internal message transport infrastructure capabilities to connect service components and enable data flow. Service engines such as BPEL, Mediator, Human Workflow, Decision Service, and BPMN service engines, process messages received from the service infrastructure.

- **OSB**: This provides a framework for lightweight, scalable, and reliable service orchestration that is designed to connect, mediate, and manage the interaction between heterogeneous systems and services. It is widely adopted in all major SOA implementations and is used to transform protocols and messages between different components. Starting with the Oracle SOA Suite 12*c* release, OSB is built into the suite.

- **Oracle BAM**: This is used to build interactive real-time dashboards and proactive alerts in order to monitor business processes and services, giving business executives and operation managers the information they need to make better business decisions and take corrective actions if the business environment changes.

- **Oracle B2B**: This enables integration between trading partners using industry standard protocols, such as RossettaNet, **Electronic Data Interchange (EDI)**, and so on, to provide a solution for establishing online collaborations and automated processes.

- **Oracle Web Services Manager (OWSM)**: This is used to govern interactions with shared services through security and operational policy management and enforcement to ensure that the service reuse remains under control. Every Oracle SOA Suite 12*c* domain has this component built in by default to facilitate the management of web services.

- **Oracle Enterprise Scheduler**: This provides a scheduling capability to enterprise applications deployed on Oracle SOA Suite 12*c*. It supports many types of jobs including those based on Java, PL/SQL, and web services that can be used to offload larger transactions to run these jobs based on a schedule or automate the execution of maintenance work.

Other binding components and services that would require the knowledge and attention of the administrator include:

- **Java EE Connector Architecture (JCA)** adapters
- HTTP bindings
- REST services
- **Enterprise Java Beans (EJB)** services
- Direct binding services
- **Application Development Framework (ADF)** Business Component services
- Business events
- The **User Messaging Server (UMS)**

SOA composite applications can consist of a variety of components, binding components, references, and services, all of which can be administered from Oracle Enterprise Manager Fusion Middleware Control. A screenshot of Oracle Enterprise Manager Fusion Middleware Control 12*c* is shown here:

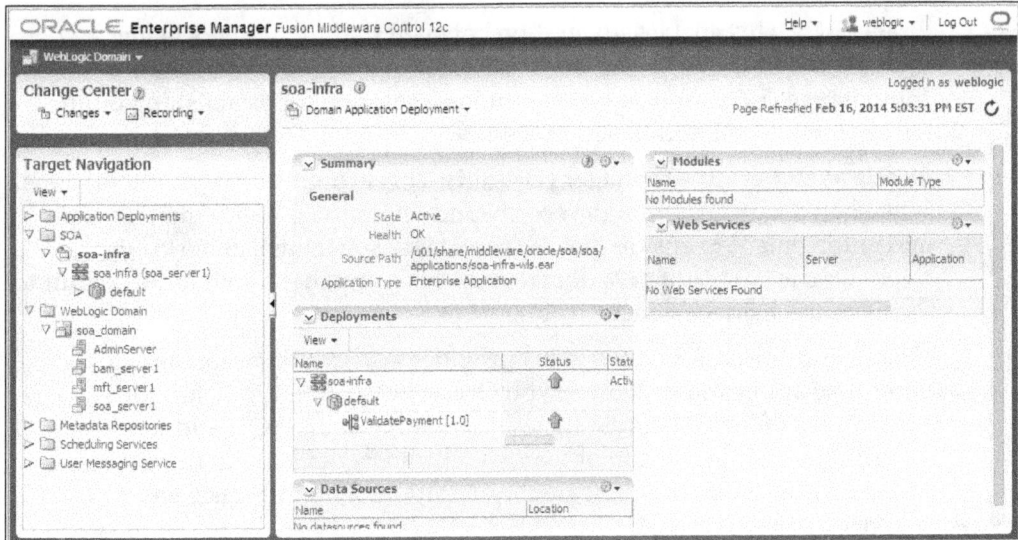

Figure 1.6: A screenshot of Oracle Enterprise Manager Fusion Middleware Control 12*c*

(This will be discussed in much detail in *Chapter 2, Navigating Enterprise Manager Fusion Middleware Control 12c*.)

What differentiates Oracle SOA Suite 12*c* from other comparable products on the market is the consolidation of the stack into a unified service platform that translates to major user benefits. A **Service Component Architecture (SCA)**, a maturing **Organization for the Advancement of Structured Information Standards (OASIS)**, is the key enabler here. SCA enables you to manage versions and deploy components and metadata as a single unit. All artifacts are stored in a single repository, the Oracle **Metadata Services (MDS)**. But, the story doesn't stop here; Oracle SOA Suite 12*c* also consolidates the runtime into a modular architecture of engines plugging into a common service infrastructure. And the engine consolidation naturally leads to a simplified monitoring infrastructure, still maintaining a vendor-neutral Java EE platform! All of this translates into numerous design time, runtime, and monitoring benefits, many of which we will explore throughout this book.

New features of Oracle SOA Suite 12c

What are the benefits of upgrading from Oracle SOA Suite 11*g* to 12*c*? There are numerous, but from an administration standpoint, some of the desirable features introduced with 12*c* include:

- Built-in support for mobile integration. There are improved wizards and adapters that allow easier REST integration; developers can easily expose any reference or service as REST, and support for automated conversion from XML to JSON is now included.

- Cloud integration through newly published cloud adapters, wherein all nuances of interacting with third-party cloud services are handled by these adapters.

- New technology adapters such as the **Lightweight Directory Access Protocol (LDAP)** adapter and Coherence adapter.

- The **Execution Context ID (ECID)** (discussed in detail in *Chapter 6, Monitoring Oracle SOA Suite 12c*) now spans both OSB services and SOA composites, allowing for easier tracing of transactions across both technologies.

- Full **Simple Object Access Protocol (SOAP)** messages are displayed in the instance flow. The following screenshot gives you an example of how this is now viewed in 12*c* compared to 11*g*:

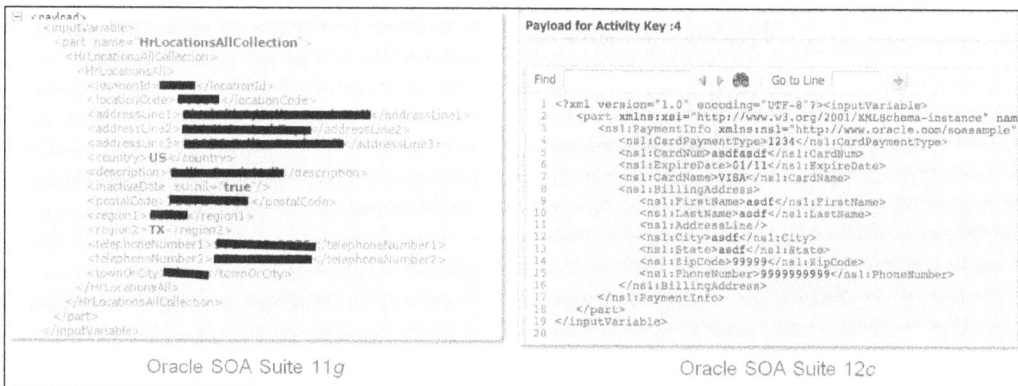

Oracle SOA Suite 11g   Oracle SOA Suite 12c

Figure 1.7: Oracle SOA Suite 12*c* now displays the full payload in the instance trace

- ESS is a powerful new scheduling component that is included in the suite at no extra cost.

> There are too many new features to go through but an exhaustive list can be found in the following Oracle published whitepaper at http://www. oracle.com/technetwork/middleware/soasuite/overview/ wp-soa-suite-whats-new-12c-2217186.pdf.

Summary

In this chapter, we provided a snapshot of some of the important aspects of Oracle SOA Suite 12*c* administration and the capabilities that can be leveraged to effectively manage and monitor the SOA infrastructure.

To summarize this chapter's key takeaways:

- One of the main challenges of monitoring a SOA infrastructure is the need to obtain an end-to-end view of loosely coupled services that may span multiple disparate systems.

- Oracle SOA Suite 12*c* is a complete, integrated, best-of-breed, and hot-pluggable product set that helps to deliver robust, agile, and reliable SOA solutions.

- Oracle SOA Suite 12*c* is a member of the Oracle Fusion Middleware family of products.

- Oracle Enterprise Manager Fusion Middleware Control allows you to both manage and monitor all components and services within the Oracle SOA Suite 12*c* stack from a single web-based console.

- Oracle SOA Suite 12*c* includes many new features such as native support for REST, new cloud and technology adapters, and a new scheduling service.

2
Navigating Enterprise Manager Fusion Middleware Control 12*c*

Oracle Enterprise Manager Fusion Middleware Control 12*c* is a web-based management tool designed to administer the entire Oracle Fusion Middleware product stack, including Oracle SOA Suite 12*c*, and enables a bird's-eye view of your processes and their instances through a centralized management and monitoring console. It organizes a wide variety of performance data and administrative functions into distinct, web-based dashboards. These dashboards make it easy to locate the most important monitoring and performance data and the most commonly used administrative functions for any Fusion Middleware component—all from your web browser!

With Oracle Enterprise Manager Fusion Middleware Control 12*c* (Fusion Middleware Control for short), you can browse running servers, applications, and service engines to easily recognize and troubleshoot runtime problems in the SOA platform. Fusion Middleware Control relies on the power of dashboards, whether at the service engine level or the composite level. From the dashboards, we typically drill down as necessary. The following screenshot shows the dashboard of the SOA composite **ValidatePayment**, where it is possible to obtain all the information pertinent to this composite:

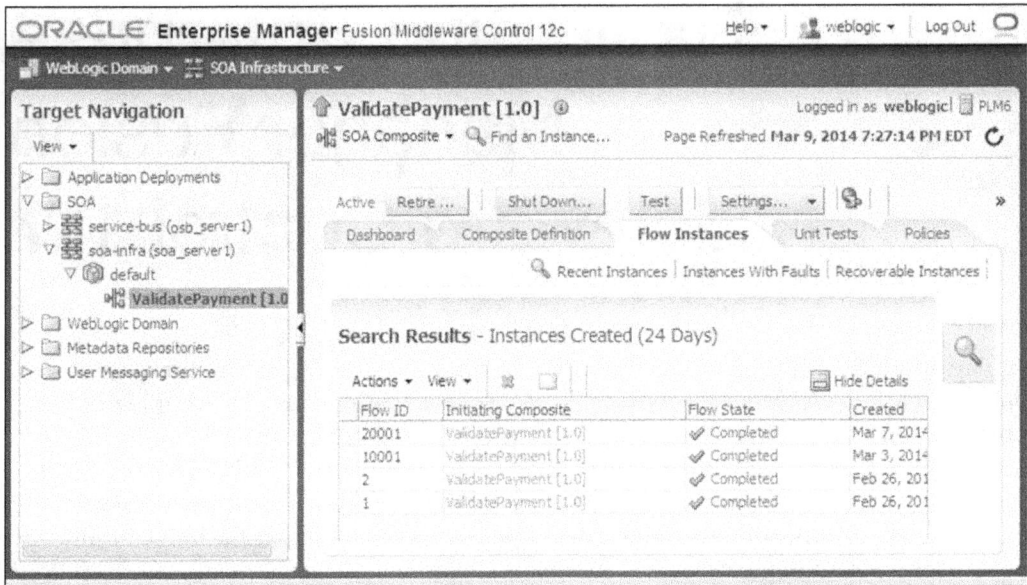

Figure 2.1: A screenshot from Oracle Enterprise Manager Fusion Middleware Control

With out-of-the-box functionality provided by Fusion Middleware Control, you can obtain a real-time, end-to-end view of the business transaction for **Service Level Agreement (SLA)**, fault tracing, and problem determination, including the following information:

- Web service message processing totals and processing times
- Transaction discovery/availability/state/status
- Transaction performance
- Service discovery and relationship/dependency mapping
- Transaction audit trail and flow, faults, and rejected messages
- JMX-based monitoring through MBeans of all components of the SOA infrastructure

If an administrator has a holistic knowledge of looking in the right places on these consoles, no other tool is necessary in order for the administrator to effectively monitor the environment.

Fusion Middleware Control also provides the Oracle SOA Suite 12*c* administrator with management and deployment features. This includes administering areas such as the SOA infrastructure, composite applications, partitions, Java EE applications, and more. Through the console, you can also perform administrative functions that include the following:

- Creating and deleting partitions to provide a logical grouping of composites
- Managing the composite state, including starting, stopping, activating, retiring, and setting the default revision of a deployed composite
- Managing composite instances, including deleting, terminating, and in some cases, recovering instances
- Setting up an error hospital to recover faulted instances and define error notification rules
- Deploying and undeploying composites
- Obtaining performance, metrics, and transaction monitoring
- Exporting a composite or its metadata to a JAR file
- Automating unit testing of composites
- Manually testing composite applications
- Attaching policies to composites, service components, and binding components
- Managing human workflows and notifications
- Publishing or subscribing to business events
- Managing logs
- Performing diagnostics and tuning
- Browsing, viewing, and modifying runtime MBeans
- Implementing security and policy management
- Monitoring and testing OSB services
- Publishing web services to a **Universal Description, Discovery, and Integration (UDDI)** registry such as Oracle Service Registry
- Manage and monitor scheduling components such as jobs, schedules, and job requests

Oracle Enterprise Manager Fusion Middleware Control 12c should not be confused with Oracle Enterprise Manager Cloud Control or the earlier Oracle Enterprise Manager Grid Control, both of which are referred to as **Oracle Enterprise Manager (OEM)**. Oracle Enterprise Manager is a single, central, and comprehensive administration tool used to monitor entire Oracle (and non-Oracle) environments, including multiple Oracle Fusion Middleware installations. Oracle Enterprise Manager Fusion Middleware Control 12c, on the other hand, is deployed and accessible with every installation of Oracle Fusion Middleware and is intended to monitor and manage that domain only.

Oracle Enterprise Manager Fusion Middleware Control 12c provides a comprehensive infrastructure management console that gives an administrator the ability to perform all necessary job functions covering all areas of management and monitoring. The *Oracle Fusion Middleware Administrating Oracle SOA Suite and Oracle Business Process Management Suite 12c Release 1 (12.1.3.0)* documentation does a sufficient job of describing the console, but we present here a rather different approach in introducing it. The console is rich and deep but confusing for the first-time administrator to understand which context menus are used to perform what tasks. Both the remainder of this chapter and subsequent chapters delve into these areas in varying levels of detail.

In this chapter, we will cover the following areas:

- Providing an overview of other related consoles, including WebLogic Server, Service Bus, BAM Composer, MFT, B2B, SOA Composer, and BPM Workspace
- Presenting the Fusion Middleware Control dashboard
- How to navigate Fusion Middleware Control

Discovering the consoles

It is beneficial to understand the various product consoles that may already be deployed in your environment before actually delving deeper into the details Fusion Middleware Control.

A typical SOA Suite 12*c* administrator will undoubtedly have access to and be using the Oracle WebLogic Server Administration Console, as shown in *Figure 2.2*. This console is typically accessed at `http://<adminhost>:7001/console` and is the primary console for everything related to the WebLogic application server. The administrator can create, stop, and start managed servers; administer data sources and connection pools; create and monitor JMS destinations; and perform all aspects of WebLogic Server administration directly from this console.

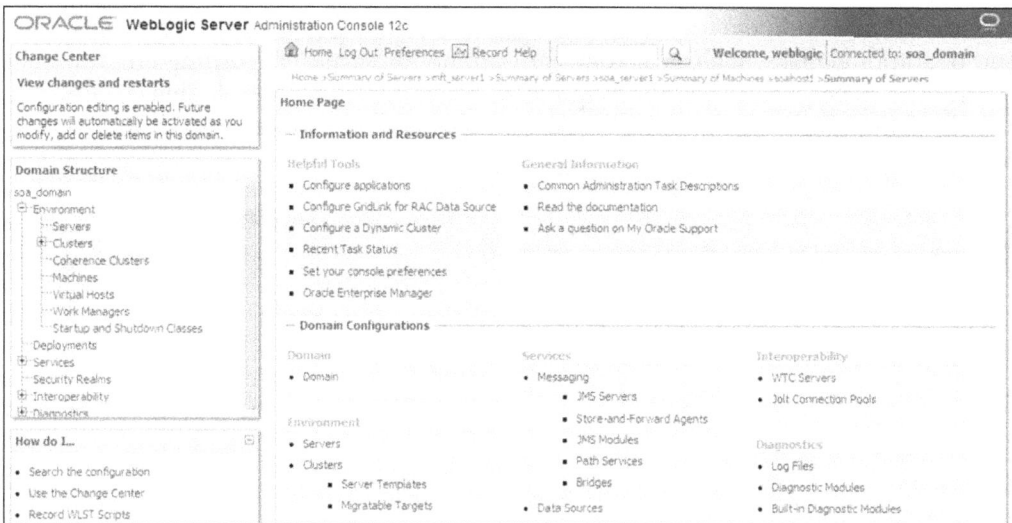

Figure 2.2: A screenshot of the Oracle WebLogic Server Administration Console 12*c*

Though this book does not cover the WebLogic Server Administration Console in detail, it will be something an administrator will definitely be accessing regularly.

In Oracle SOA Suite 12c, OSB is a lot more tightly integrated with SOA Suite compared to the previous 11g release. However, the OSB service engine still runs in a separate container, independent of the other engines such as BPEL and Mediator, and the project console also remains separate in this release. The Oracle Service Bus Console, accessible at `http://<adminhost>:7001/sbconsole`, lists all OSB projects and resources deployed to the server. You can make changes to the OSB projects from here; for example, code changes to the implementation pipelines or protocol changes such as enforcing HTTPS and modifying the endpoint URI of your proxy services (as shown in the following screenshot). However, general administrative and operational tasks, such as enabling/disabling the service or turning on message tracing, are instead performed through Fusion Middleware Control. This is a little confusing at first as you explore the consoles and understand what needs to be performed where.

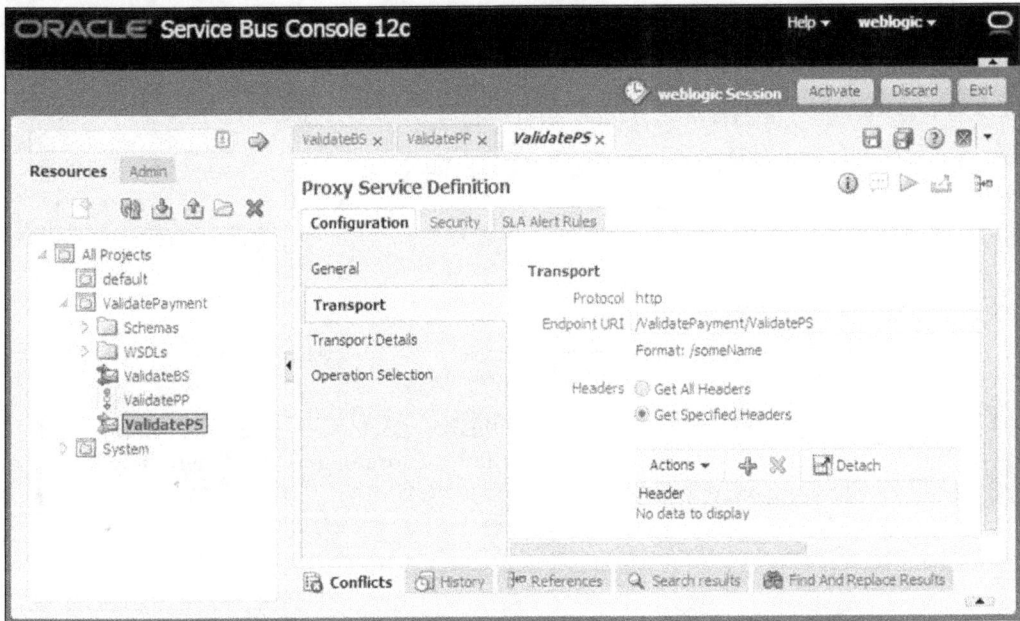

Figure 2.3: A screenshot of the Oracle Service Bus Console 12c

> Generally speaking, any OSB project or code-related changes can be performed within the Oracle Service Bus Console, whereas any runtime and operational changes are performed through Fusion Middleware Control.

The Oracle BAM Composer has also significantly changed from the 11*g* version as it is a completely new product. The complete details of what has changed between 11*g* and 12*c* in BAM is out of the scope of this book but can be accessed in the Oracle documentation at `http://docs.oracle.com/middleware/1213/bam/index.html`. The following screenshot shows a typical BAM Designer dashboard providing access to BAM data objects, dashboards, alerts, business views, users, and more:

Figure 2.4: A screenshot of the Oracle BAM Composer

The BAM landing page console can be accessed at `http://<host>:9001/bam/composer`.

New to 12*c* is Oracle MFT. It too has its own console accessible at
`http://<host>:7020/mftconsole`. The Oracle MFT console is equipped
with the ability to create file transfer jobs, scheduled or manually triggered,
and provides a slew of configuration settings to support encryption/decryption,
streaming, retries, error handling, and much more. The following screenshot depicts
the MFT dashboard:

Figure 2.5: A screenshot of the Oracle MFT console

The Oracle B2B user interface can be accessed at `http://<host>:8001/b2bconsole`
for those projects that require B2B functionality. Configuring and setting up B2B
documents and trading partners warrants an entire book of its own. The home page
is shown in the following screenshot:

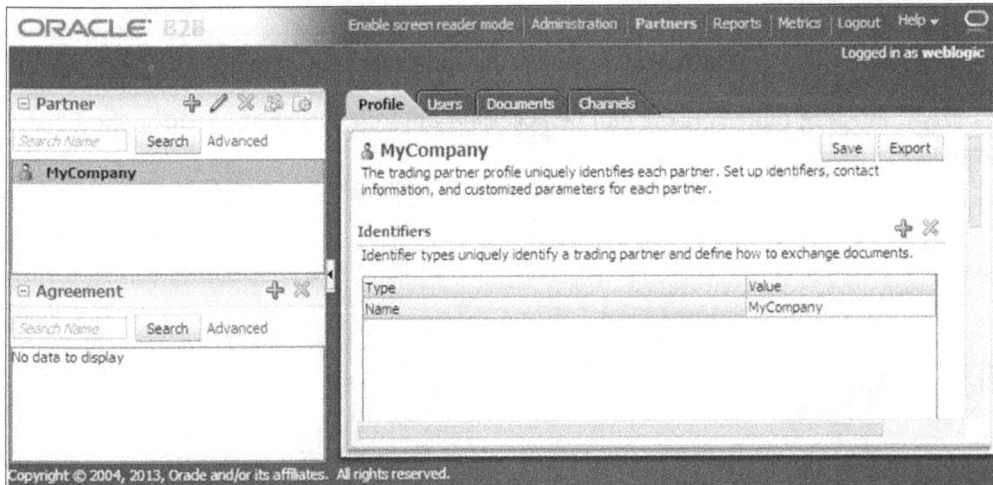

Figure 2.6: A screenshot of the Oracle B2B user interface

Business rules and **Domain Value Maps** (DVM), which are primarily used to provide flexibility to SOA and BPM projects, can be managed via Oracle SOA Composer, accessible at `http://<host>:8001/soa/composer`. Here, shared business rules and DVMs can be modified at runtime, as demonstrated in the following screenshot:

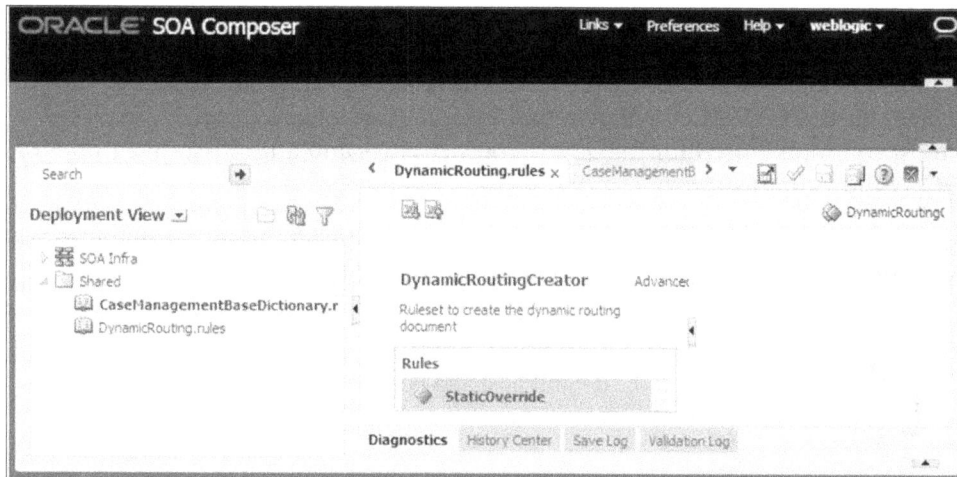

Figure 2.7: A screenshot of the Oracle SOA Composer

The BPM Workspace is tightly coupled with the human workflow components of **Service Component Architecture** (SCA), allowing users to view their workflow tasks and take action accordingly. This console is intended for end user access and is available at `http://<host>:8001/integration/worklistapp`. The following screenshot shows what the end user sees upon logging in to the console:

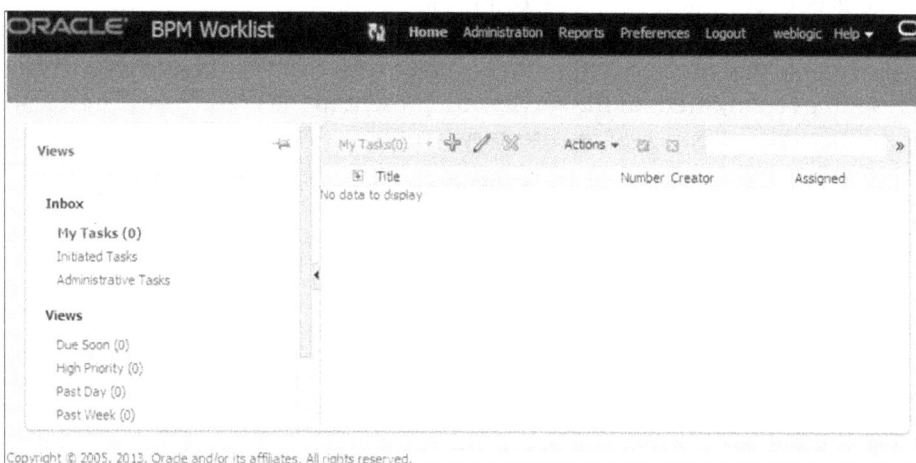

Figure 2.8: A screenshot of the Oracle BPM Worklist upon initial user login

Finally, the ESS Health Check Console is accessible at `http://<host>:8021/ess` and can be used to submit an internal job as well as provide the current status of all ESS servers in the environment. *Figure 11.2* in *Chapter 11, Introducing Oracle Enterprise scheduler*, provides a screenshot of this console.

Each of these consoles is designed to provide deeper and specific capabilities within each of the subcomponents listed previously. Meanwhile, Fusion Middleware Control is designed to be the overarching console for all SOA Suite administrative functions (including other Oracle Fusion Middleware products should they also be installed). Both the WebLogic Server and Fusion Middleware Control consoles are the most commonly used for the day-to-day activities and administrative duties of an SOA Suite administrator.

Once you are logged in to any of the administration consoles, your session is carried over to all others. You need not re-log in to each console subsequently.

> All the hosts and ports provided in the preceding sections assume that the default host and port are used during the platform provisioning.

Accessing Fusion Middleware Control

To log in to Fusion Middleware Control, simply navigate to the following URL in your web browser: `http://<host>:<port>/em`

The default port for HTTP is `7001` and the default port for HTTPS is `7002`, though this depends on the settings used during installation. The default username is `weblogic` and the password is the one provided at installation or subsequently changed. All information related to the ports that the servers run on, the deployments that are targeted to them, along with their deployment orders and other resources configured on the servers are present in the `config.xml` file located under the `$DOMAIN_HOME/config` directory.

Presenting the dashboard

When you log in to Fusion Middleware Control, there are two targets that you will be working most frequently with: **SOA Infrastructure** and **Service Bus**.

By expanding **SOA** in the tree to the left, then clicking on **soa-infra**, you are presented with the `soa-infra` dashboard, as shown in the following screenshot. On the **Dashboard** tab, a consolidated view of various SOA Suite runtime metrics is displayed. It allows you to monitor runtime health, business transaction faults, and composite availability. The dashboard is not particularly useful by itself but provides the tabs **Deployed Composites**, **Flow Instances**, and **Error Hospital**, which you will use often. You can expand `soa-infra` to further drill down to the various partitions and composites.

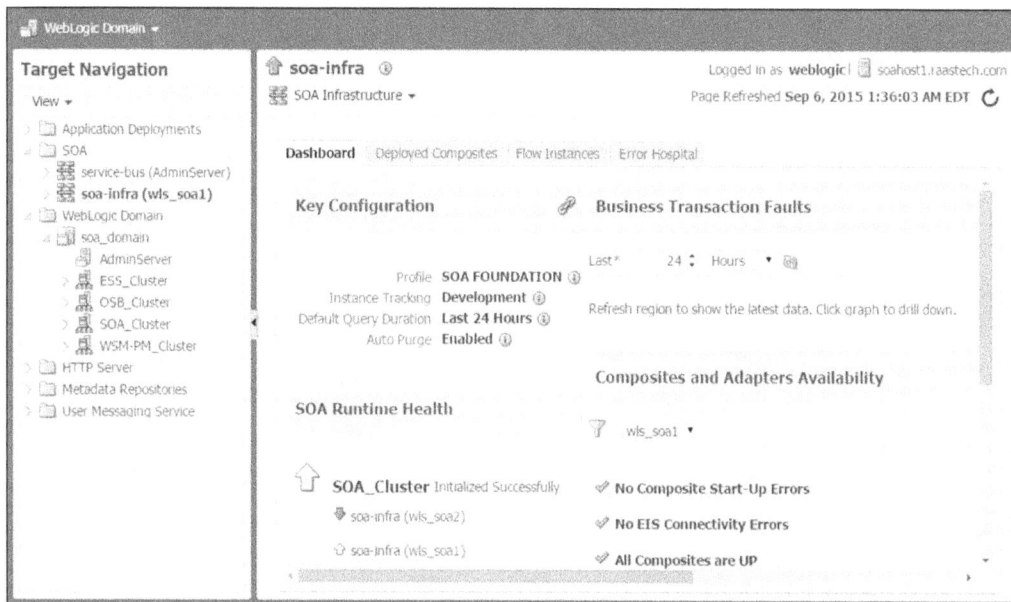

Figure 2.9: The soa-infra dashboard

The OSB engine is a completely separate runtime engine from `soa-infra`. There is no dependency between the OSB and SOA infrastructures; thus, each component can be started up, monitored, and administered separately (though it is entirely possible that OSB services are dependent on SOA composite services and vice versa). Therefore, OSB has its own dashboard, as depicted in the following screenshot:

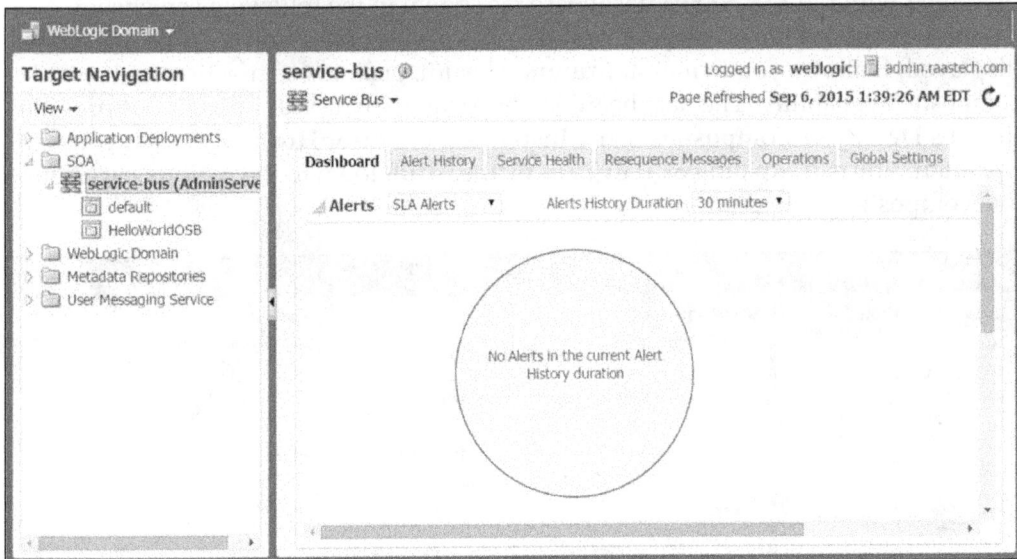

Figure 2.10: The service-bus dashboard

Runtime metrics are shown here with further options available in the **Alert History**, **Service Health**, **Resequence Messages**, **Operations**, and **Global Settings** tabs.

The dashboards are somewhat useful to quickly and immediately obtain a snapshot of the overall health of the system. Later in this chapter, we delve deeper into various navigation menus, while later chapters focus on the actual configuration and monitoring aspects.

> The `soa-infra` and `service-bus` runtime components are only visible when the respective SOA and Service Bus managed servers are in running mode.

Navigating the console through the navigator

The vertical navigation tree on the left, or the **navigator**, is your primary means of navigating to all other areas within the console. Here, you can right-click on many (but not all) menu items to pop up additional submenus. The navigator is the leftmost column, as shown in the following screenshot:

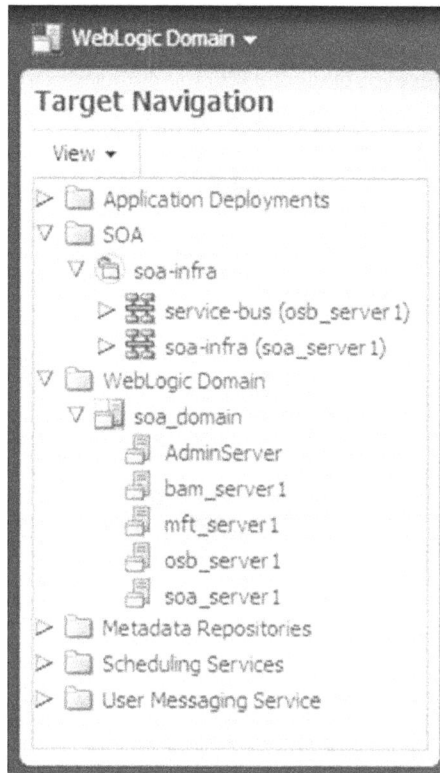

Figure 2.11: The navigator

> Some of the servers or services displayed in the navigator may differ in your installation depending on what you have installed.

Some of the menus are self-explanatory, while others, such as **Metadata Repositories**, are sparingly used. The various menu options are rather confusing for a new administrator, and in this section, we offer a different approach to explaining how to access the various options.

Java EE applications

Expanding **Application Deployments** on the navigator lists all deployed Java EE applications, as shown in the following screenshot:

Figure 2.12: Deployed Java EE applications

These same applications can be managed in the WebLogic Server Administration Console as well. Some of the default applications installed with Oracle SOA Suite 12*c* include:

- `b2bui`
- `DefaultToDoTaskFlow`
- `soa-infra`
- `service_bus`
- `soa-webapps`
- `usermessagingdriver-*`
- `usermessagingserver`
- `worklistapp`
- `ESSAPP`
- `ESSNativeHostingApp`

On expanding **Application Deployments | Internal Applications**, a further list of applications is shown. The default internal applications installed with Oracle SOA Suite 12*c* include these:

- `DMS Application`
- `em`
- `Service Bus LWPF_ConsoleService Bus *`
- `wsil-wls`
- `wsm-pm`

By clicking on any of these Java applications, you can view the source path of the EAR or JAR file, required data sources and modules, and so on.

It is fairly common to deploy additional custom Java applications, such as Java web services designed to supplement your SOA code, and target them to the SOA server (for example, `soa_server1`), although it is generally recommended to dedicate a separate managed server to them. Java applications can be deployed through WebLogic Server Administration Control or Fusion Middleware Control and through Ant scripts, for those interested in a command-line approach.

Service Bus

Expanding **SOA** exposes the `service-bus` infrastructure. Note how right-clicking on the OSB project name (for example, **ValidatePayment**) presents a reduced list of options — those that are only specific to the particular project — compared to right-clicking on `service-bus`. In the following screenshot, the menu on the left is specific to server-wide options:

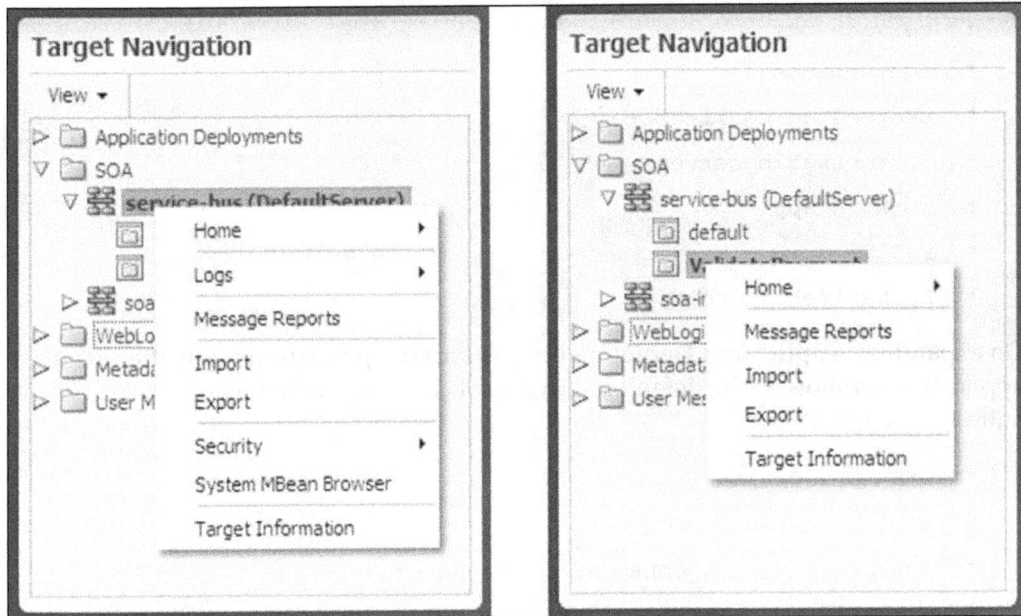

Figure 2.13. Understanding the service-bus menus

When an OSB project is selected, the pane on the right displays the dashboard for that project. The dashboard provides a mechanism to search for existing Service Bus artifacts based on a number of search criteria such as service types, names, paths, and additional metadata. Clicking on **Service Bus Project** displays yet another menu exactly identical to the screenshot on the right of *Figure 2.13*. Direct links to each of the tabs shown are available (for example, **Service Health**, **Operations**, and so on) and access to the **Message Reports**, **Import**, and **Export** menus are provided. As you can see, Fusion Middleware Control provides numerous ways to navigate to the same destination. Later chapters discuss each of these options in more detail.

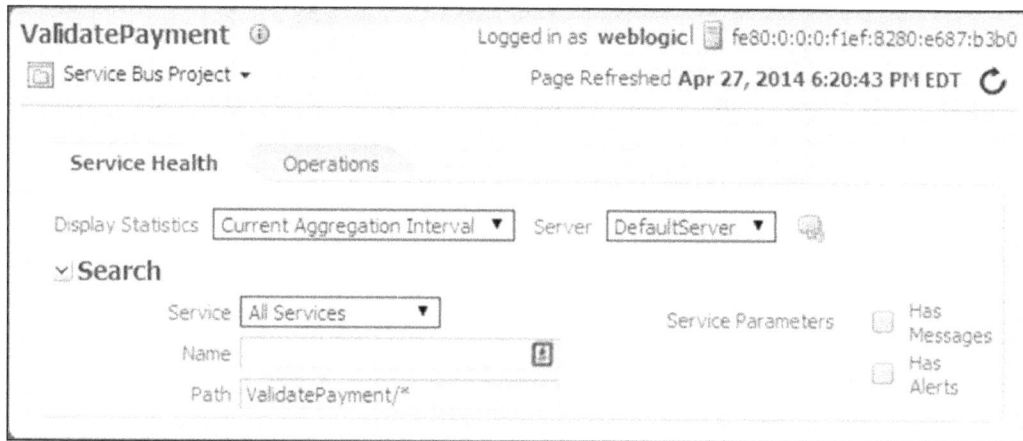

Figure 2.14: An OSB project dashboard

The SOA infrastructure

Expanding **SOA** and right-clicking on `soa-infra` displays the following menu. Everything related to the management of Oracle SOA Suite 12*c* is done through here, as shown in the following screenshot:

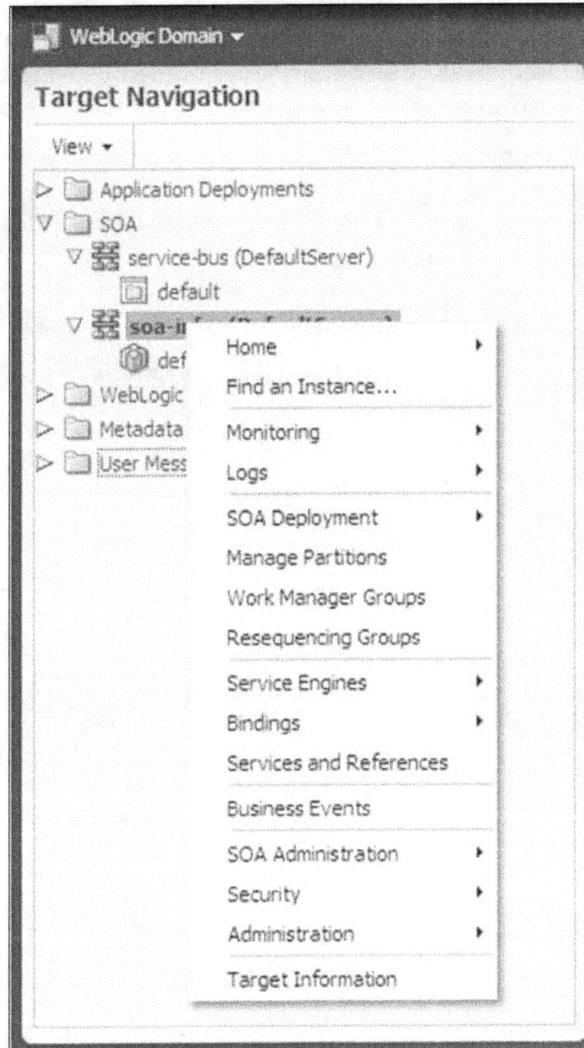

Figure 2.15: The soa-infra context menu

Likewise, when you left-click on the **SOA Infrastructure** link at the top of the page, the same menu options appear (compare *Figure 2.15* and *Figure 2.16*). The **SOA Infrastructure** link appears only when you have selected a SOA composite to work with. The following screenshot depicts the **SOA Infrastructure** drop-down menu:

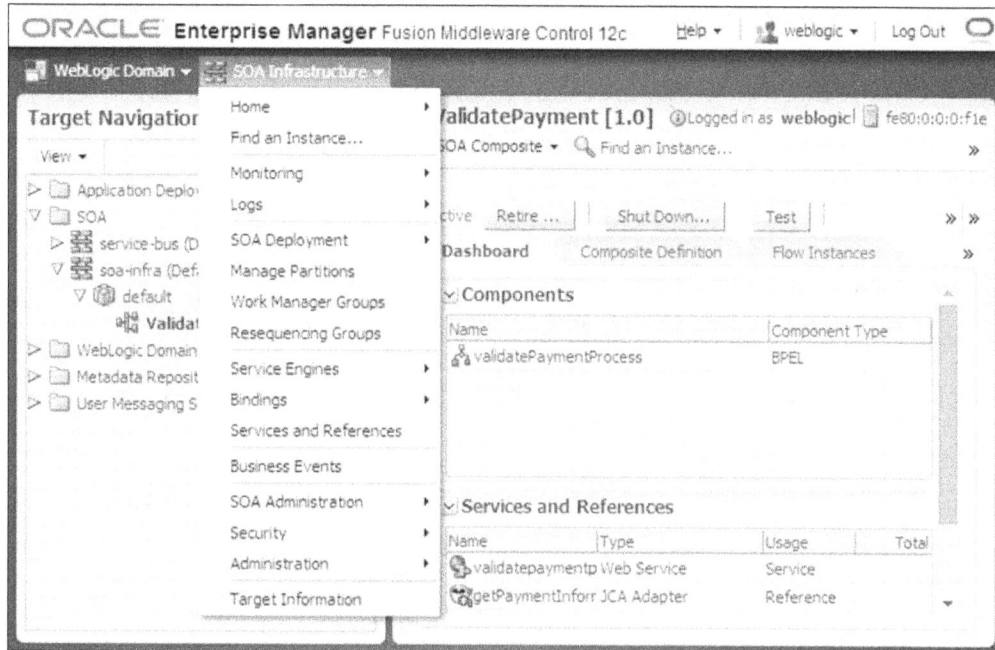

Figure 2.16: The SOA Infrastructure drop-down menu

As with OSB projects, SOA composites have a **SOA Composite** drop-down list that is available when you have navigated to a SOA composite (see *Figure 2.17*). Here, direct links to the tabs shown on the screen are available (for example, **Dashboard**, **Composite Definition**, **Flow Instances**, **Unit Tests**, and **Policies**) and access to other menu items such as **Find an Instance**, **SOA Deployment** (**Undeploy/Redeploy**), **Export**, **Test Service**, and **Service/Reference Properties** are available. This is designed to make it easy for an administrator to quickly access specific functionality without having to navigate through multiple web pages. Observe the following screenshot:

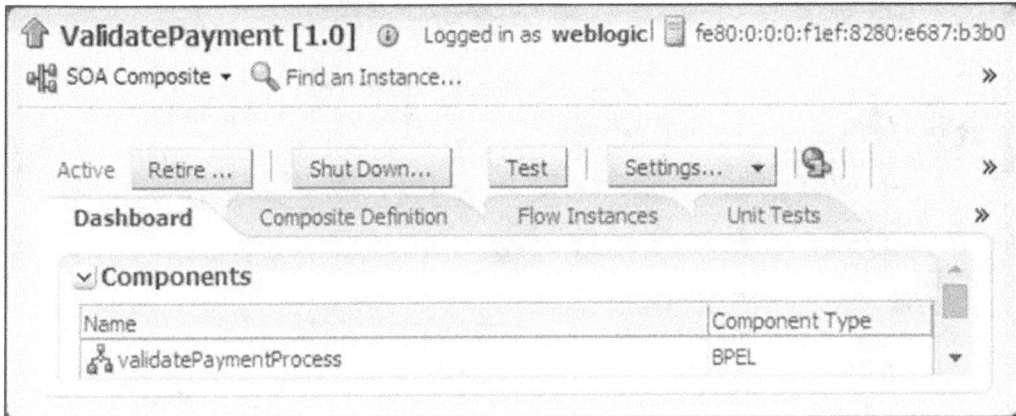

Figure 2.17: A SOA composite dashboard

WebLogic Domain

Expanding **WebLogic Domain** on the navigator and right-clicking on the name of your domain shows the context menu displayed in *Figure 2.18*. Here, key WebLogic Server administration functions are immediately and easily accessible. This includes setups such as data sources, JMS servers and resources, and managed servers. The majority of the functionality here can also be accessed via the WebLogic Server Administration Console, but not all of it. Functions related to Web Services Manager policies, component wiring, and SOA deployments can only be done from this console.

Clicking on **WebLogic Domain** in the top-left corner of the navigator displays the same menu shown in the following screenshot:

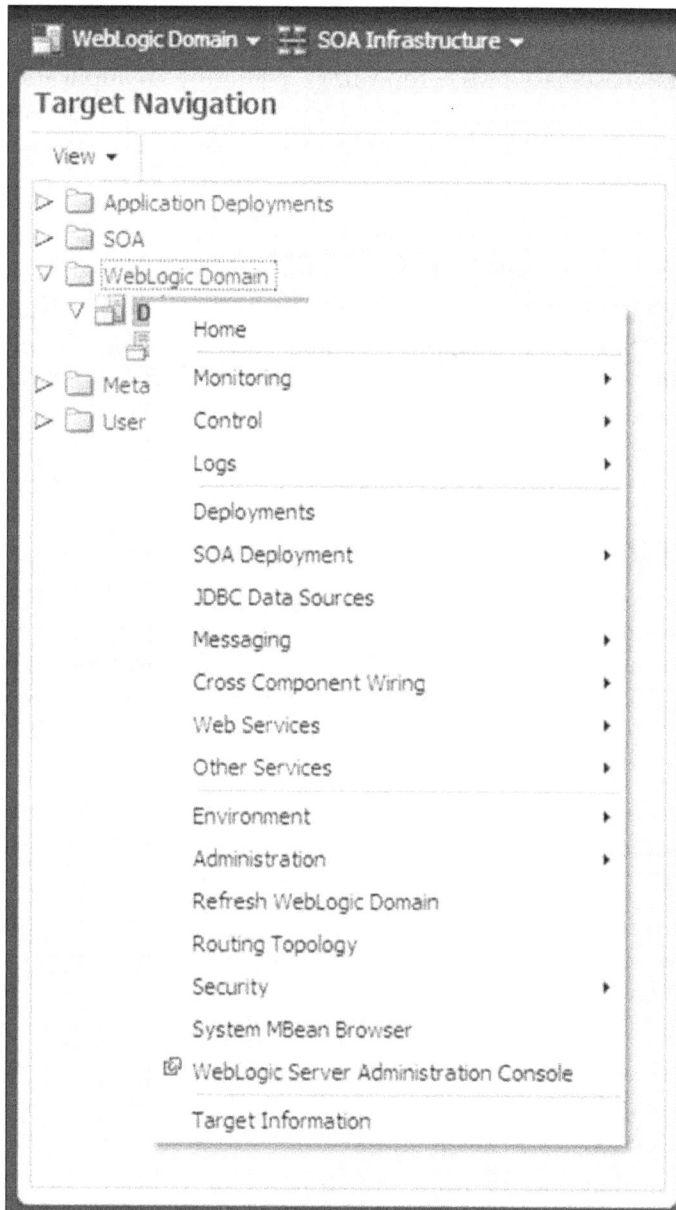

Figure 2.18: The WebLogic Domain menu

Metadata Repositories

Expanding **Metadata Repositories**, also referred to as **MDS**, may display any number of MDS repositories such as mds-mft, mds-owsm, and mds-soa, depending on your installation. This gives the administrator the ability to register and deregister a file-based or database-based MDS repository, configure an application to use a different metadata repository, move from a file-based to a database-based repository, move metadata from a test system to a production system, and manage labels in the MDS repository.

User Messaging Service (UMS)

Expanding **User Messaging Service**, or **UMS**, provides access to various drivers such as e-mail, SMS, Twitter, Google Voice, and more. The administrator can configure, monitor, and manage the various aspects of UMS from here. *Chapter 7, Configuration and Administration*, describes the configuration and setup of UMS in more detail.

Summary

In this chapter, we presented an overview of Oracle Enterprise Manager Fusion Middleware Control 12c and how to navigate the multitude of menus and submenus made available through the console. Accessing a particular function can be done through numerous navigation paths and is sometimes daunting for new administrators.

Here are this chapter's key takeaways:

- Oracle Enterprise Manager Fusion Middleware Control 12c is the primary web-based console of choice for administering all aspects of Oracle SOA Suite 12c.

- Depending on what is installed, secondary consoles that the administrator may have access to include WebLogic Server Administration Console, Service Bus Console, BAM Composer, Managed File Transfer, the B2B user interface, SOA Composer, and BPM Worklist.

- The navigator, the vertical navigation tree on the left, is designed to provide direct and quick access to all monitoring and management functionality through easy-to-use context menus.

- The service-bus and soa-infra infrastructures are the two areas where the administrator will spend most of the time administering the infrastructure.

3
Startup and Shutdown

Oracle SOA Suite 12c provides an administrator numerous ways to start up and shut down various entities and components, which are perhaps a little confusing to new administrators. However, these multitude of options provide power and flexibility in the long run.

This chapter focuses exclusively on the startup and shutdown of the Oracle SOA Suite infrastructure and how to verify the completion of each component. Many cases exist in which the administrator may want to turn off specific services if they are redundant or not being used in order to increase the performance and stability of the environment. Learning how to start up and shut down individual SOA composite applications and OSB services is detailed in *Chapter 4*, *Managing Services*.

The startup and shutdown of the infrastructure holistically or at a component level can be done through Fusion Middleware Control, the command line, or WLST. This chapter will provide you with directions on how to perform each of the following:

- Starting up and shutting down the entire infrastructure using the console
- Starting up and shutting down the entire infrastructure using the command line
- Starting up and shutting down the entire infrastructure using WLST

Once you have familiarized yourself with the various approaches, you can decide to script the startup and shutdown process in a way that is preferable to you. All command-line instructions in this chapter are based on Linux, the recommended operating system for Oracle SOA Suite 12c installations.

Preparing the environment

The SOA infrastructure can be started up and shut down in several ways—through the console, WLST, or the command line, each having their own benefits. All approaches are valid and depend on your standards and preference. However, our recommendation is that you use a set of scripts to make this repetitive process less cumbersome and more consistent. The following figure demonstrates how AdminServer can start up or shut down a remote managed server by issuing commands through Node Manager:

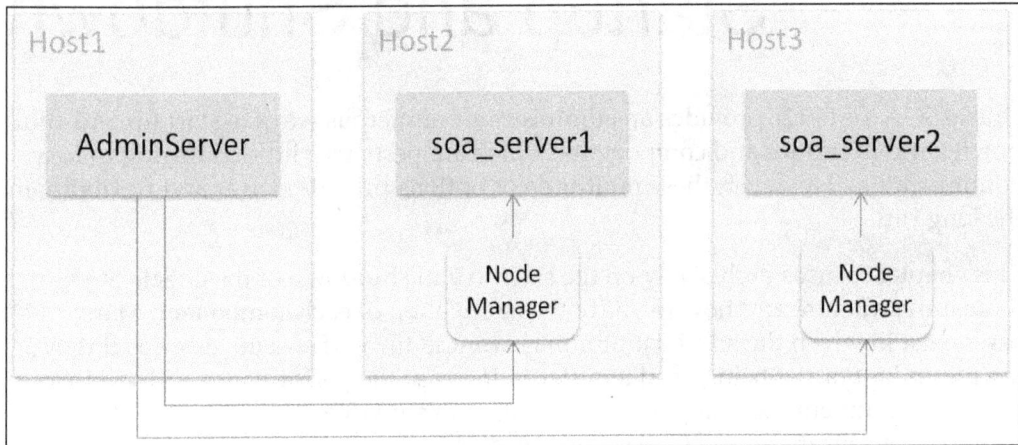

Figure 3.1: AdminServer issues commands to remote hosts through Node Manager

Regardless of the approach you follow, be aware of a few points. You should ideally start up Node Manager first. If you have a clustered installation, then Node Manager should be started up on each host separately. Node Manager serves multiple purposes—it can automatically restart a managed server that has crashed, it provides you the ability to start up or stop managed servers remotely, and it is required for clustered installations. In a clustered installation, AdminServer is started up on only one physical server per entire cluster.

> Node Manager is a Java utility that runs as a separate process from WebLogic Server and allows you to perform common operation tasks for a managed server, regardless of its location with respect to its Administration Server.

Setting up the environment

Setting up the environment simplifies subsequent commands and allows more efficient scripting. To set up the environment, customize the values in the following command lines so that they are reflected in your environment:

```
export ORACLE_HOME=/u01/oracle/products/Oracle_SOA1

export WL_HOME=${ORACLE_HOME}/wlserver

export DOMAIN_NAME=soa_domain

export DOMAIN_HOME=${ORACLE_HOME}/user_projects/domains/${DOMAIN_NAME}
```

Disabling the prompt of the WebLogic password

Whether you are scripting your startup process or using the console to start each component, you will want to disable the prompting of the WebLogic administrator password.

When you start up any managed server, you are typically prompted for the username and password that was used to create the domain. To disable the prompting of these credentials at startup, edit the `boot.properties` file on all managed servers. This is a one-time step that is recommended to be done on every managed server on each node of your cluster.

Prior to starting up the SOA, OSB, BAM, ESS, and WSM managed servers, perform the following steps:

1. Create a `boot.properties` file on each of the managed servers inside the physical servers in the cluster, replacing the username and password with those values that reflect your environment:

   ```
   cd ${DOMAIN_HOME}/servers/soa_server1/security

   echo "username=weblogic" > boot.properties

   echo "password=welcome1" >> boot.properties
   ```

2. Repeat the preceding step on all servers in the cluster.

Now that you have created the `boot.properties` file, after you start up the managed server, both the username and password will be encrypted in this file.

Starting up the infrastructure

We described multiple ways to start up the Oracle SOA Suite 12*c* environment. The command line, WLST, the console, or a combination of these can be utilized for both the infrastructure startup and shutdown.

Using the command line

The command line is possibly the quickest way to start up the infrastructure. It is also the simplest to script. All command-line instructions here are based on Linux but can be adapted to other operating systems with minor modifications.

Starting up Node Manager

Node Manager should be started up once per physical server. The following command dumps the output of both the standard out and standard error to the `NodeManager.out` log file. Log in to each node in your cluster and issue the following commands:

```
cd $DOMAIN_HOME/bin
nohup ./startNodeManager.sh > NodeManager.out 2>&1 &
```

Starting up AdminServer

The AdminServer should be started only on a single host in the cluster and must be started via the command line (or WLST). The following command dumps both the standard output and standard error to the `AdminServer.out` log file. Log in to the server that hosts AdminServer and run the following commands:

```
cd $DOMAIN_HOME/bin
nohup ./startWebLogic.sh > AdminServer.out 2>&1 &
```

Starting up the managed servers

The instructions mentioned in the following sections describe how to start up and shut down the SOA infrastructure in Linux using the bash shell. Your installation may (or may not) consist of multiple managed servers that include the SOA server, OSB server, BAM server, ESS server, and WSM server. Simply skip the components that are not installed in your domain. The instructions to do so are as follows:

Start up the SOA, OSB, BAM, ESS, and WSM managed servers on each node of the cluster, updating the highlighted managed server name, AdminServer hostname and port, and WebLogic username and password to reflect your environment:

```
cd $DOMAIN_HOME/bin

nohup ./startManagedWebLogic.sh soa_server1 http://adminhost:7001
-Dweblogic.management.username=weblogic -Dweblogic.management.
password=welcome1 > soa_server1.out 2>&1 &

nohup ./startManagedWebLogic.sh osb_server1 http://adminhost:7001
-Dweblogic.management.username=weblogic -Dweblogic.management.
password=welcome1 > osb_server1.out 2>&1 &

nohup ./startManagedWebLogic.sh bam_server1 http://adminhost:7001
-Dweblogic.management.username=weblogic -Dweblogic.management.
password=welcome1 > bam_server1.out 2>&1 &

nohup ./startManagedWebLogic.sh ess_server1 http://adminhost:7001
-Dweblogic.management.username=weblogic -Dweblogic.management.
password=welcome1 > ess_server1.out 2>&1 &

nohup ./startManagedWebLogic.sh wsm_server1 http://adminhost:7001
-Dweblogic.management.username=weblogic -Dweblogic.management.
password=welcome1 > wsm_server1.out 2>&1 &
```

> If the -Dweblogic.management arguments are not specified, you will be prompted to manually enter the username and password. If they are specified, be aware that the clear text password can be found logged in to the respective system's out file and process output list (for example, the ps command). If you have created and modified boot.properties in each of the managed servers, then these arguments may be skipped.

These commands dump the output to the respective .out log file, which can be viewed in real time as needed.

You must repeat the preceding commands for the other servers running in the cluster, modifying the managed server name accordingly (for example, soa_server2, soa_server3, and so on). You do not need to be logged in to those hosts as long as Node Manager is running on them, as the commands are sent to AdminServer, which then forwards them along to the appropriate host and managed server.

> The `http://adminhost:7001` argument is an optional argument but is needed if you are running on a nondefault port or are not executing the script on the same server where AdminServer resides.

Using the console

Unfortunately, it is not possible to completely start up the infrastructure through the console. After all, don't you need to start up the console first in order to allow you to bring up the remainder of the environment? Using the console to bring up your infrastructure requires starting up AdminServer and Node Manager on all target hosts.

Starting up Node Manager

Starting up Node Manager is a requirement if you intend to use the console to start up and shut down the managed servers. However, Node Manager must be started up either with the command line or through WLST. Later in this chapter, we will describe how to start up Node Manager through WLST. Simply run the following to start up Node Manager on each host using the command line:

```
cd $DOMAIN_HOME/bin

nohup ./startNodeManager.sh > NodeManager.out 2>&1 &
```

Starting up AdminServer

Likewise, AdminServer must be started up before you bring up the rest of the infrastructure. The WebLogic Server Administration Console, which we utilize to bring up the remainder of the infrastructure, is targeted to AdminServer by default. If AdminServer is up, the WebLogic Server Administration Console is up. Simply run the following commands to bring up AdminServer:

```
cd $DOMAIN_HOME/bin

nohup ./startWebLogic.sh > AdminServer.out 2>&1 &
```

Starting up the managed servers

Now that AdminServer is started, the WebLogic Server Administration Console is accessible. Here, you can manually start up each of the SOA, OSB, BAM, ESS, and WSM managed servers on each node of the cluster in a single shot.

To start up all managed servers, perform the following steps:

1. Log in to the WebLogic Server Administration Console at `http://<adminhost>:7001/console`.

2. Navigate to **Servers | Control**.

3. Select the managed servers that you wish to start up.

4. Click on **Start**. Refer to the following screenshot for an example.

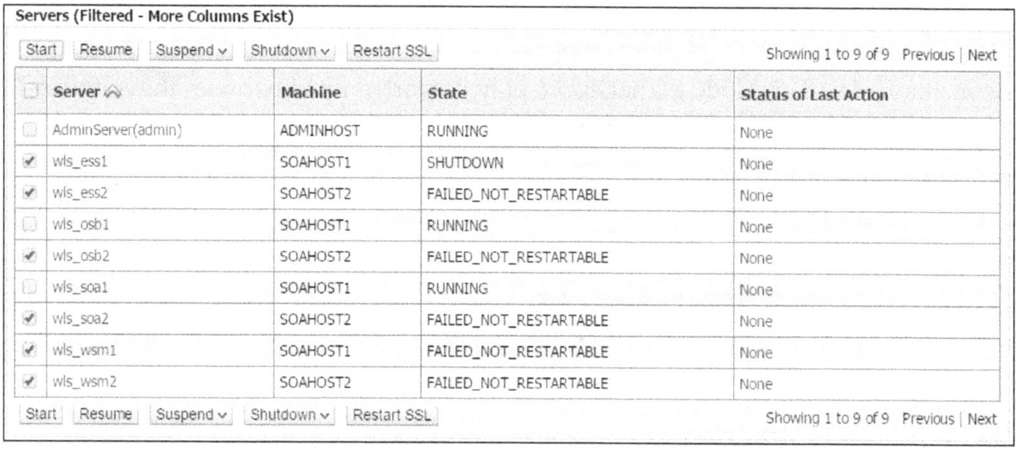

	Server ⌄	Machine	State	Status of Last Action
☐	AdminServer(admin)	ADMINHOST	RUNNING	None
☑	wls_ess1	SOAHOST1	SHUTDOWN	None
☑	wls_ess2	SOAHOST2	FAILED_NOT_RESTARTABLE	None
☐	wls_osb1	SOAHOST1	RUNNING	None
☑	wls_osb2	SOAHOST2	FAILED_NOT_RESTARTABLE	None
☐	wls_soa1	SOAHOST1	RUNNING	None
☑	wls_soa2	SOAHOST2	FAILED_NOT_RESTARTABLE	None
☑	wls_wsm1	SOAHOST1	FAILED_NOT_RESTARTABLE	None
☑	wls_wsm2	SOAHOST2	FAILED_NOT_RESTARTABLE	None

Servers (Filtered - More Columns Exist). Start | Resume | Suspend | Shutdown | Restart SSL. Showing 1 to 9 of 9 Previous | Next

Figure 3.2: Starting up the managed servers on the WebLogic Server Administration Console

Your installation may include MFT, and the instructions to start it up are not described here. Refer to the *Oracle Fusion Middleware Using Oracle Managed File Transfer 12c Release 1 (12.1) for Windows or UNIX* documentation from Oracle for more information.

Using WLST

WLST is another method to start up the infrastructure. Many administrators who come from a BEA background and have extensive experience with Oracle WebLogic Server tend to prefer WLST over the other approaches.

> One clear advantage of using WLST is that the scripts developed are typically cross-platform; that is, they can be executed on different operating systems with minimal to no change.

It is possible to use WLST to connect to and issue the commands to Node Manager or to connect to and issue commands to AdminServer. Both are acceptable, and the following instructions are specific to the latter.

Starting up Node Manager

As mentioned earlier, Node Manager can only be started up either with the command line or WLST. Simply run the following WLST command to start up Node Manager:

```
$WL_HOME/common/bin/wlst.sh
```

```
startNodeManager()
```

Starting up AdminServer

In a clustered installation, AdminServer is started up on only one of the nodes of the cluster. The following WLST command starts up AdminServer:

```
$WL_HOME/common/bin/wlst.sh
```

```
startServer('AdminServer', 'soa_domain', 't3://adminhost:7001',
'weblogic', 'welcome1', '/u01/oracle/products/Oracle_SOA1/user_projects/
domains/soa_domain', 'true', 60000, 'false')
```

Starting up the managed servers

One way to start up the managed servers through WLST is by connecting and issuing the commands to Node Manager. Described in this section though is an alternate approach of connecting to AdminServer and issuing the commands to it instead. Regardless of which of these options you utilize, it is possible to start up all managed servers in a cluster or start up each managed server individually.

To start up any of the SOA, OSB, BAM, ESS, or WSM managed servers, use WLST to connect to AdminServer and then initiate the start commands for each managed server:

```
$WL_HOME/common/bin/wlst.sh
wls:/offline> connect('weblogic', 'welcome1', 't3://adminhost:7001')
wls:/soa_domain/serverConfig> start('soa_server1', 'Server')
wls:/soa_domain/serverConfig> start('osb_server1', 'Server')
wls:/soa_domain/serverConfig> start('bam_server1', 'Server')
wls:/soa_domain/serverConfig> start('ess_server1', 'Server')
wls:/soa_domain/serverConfig> start('wsm_server1', 'Server')
```

Alternatively, you can start up an entire cluster by issuing a single command as shown in the following code. Thus, all managed servers within that cluster are brought up with a single command:

```
wls:/soa_domain/serverConfig> start('soacluster', 'Cluster')
wls:/soa_domain/serverConfig> start('osbcluster', 'Cluster')
wls:/soa_domain/serverConfig> start('bamcluster', 'Cluster')
wls:/soa_domain/serverConfig> start('esscluster', 'Cluster')
wls:/soa_domain/serverConfig> start('wsmcluster', 'Cluster')
```

Verifying server startup

There are numerous ways to verify whether a particular server component of the infrastructure is up and running. This varies by the operating system. The majority of instructions in this book are specific to Linux, the predominant, preferred, and recommended operating system on which Oracle SOA Suite 12*c* is installed.

Verifying Node Manager

You can use one or all of the following approaches to confirm that Node Manager is running. This includes checking the running operating system process, confirming the startup from the log file, and verifying that the port is being listened on.

You can run a simple Linux command to check whether the Node Manager process is running:

```
ps -ef | grep NodeManager | grep -v grep
```

If nothing is returned, then Node Manager is likely not running. Otherwise, you will find two `startNodeManager.sh` processes running and a third child Java process similar to what is shown here:

```
oracle   24081 21990  0 05:38 pts/1     00:00:00 /bin/sh ./
startNodeManager.sh
oracle   24083 24081  0 05:38 pts/1     00:00:00 /bin/sh /u01/share/
middleware/oracle/wlserver/server/bin/startNodeManager.sh
oracle   24122 24083 25 05:38 pts/1     00:00:23
/u01/share/middleware/jdk1.7.0_15/bin/java -client -Xms32m -Xmx200m
-XX:MaxPermSize=128m ... -Dweblogic.nodemanager.JavaHome=/u01/share/
middleware/jdk1.7.0_15 weblogic.NodeManager -v
```

Secondly, you can confirm a log entry similar to the following in the `NodeManager.out` log file confirming that the Node Manager listener process has started:

```
<Aug 25, 2014 5:38:47 AM EDT> <INFO> <Secure socket listener started on
port 5556, host localhost/127.0.0.1>
```

Lastly, you can run the following operating system command to check whether the default Node Manager port `5556` is being listened on:

```
netstat -an | grep LISTEN | grep 5556 | grep -v grep
```

If no output is returned, then either Node Manager is running on a different port or not running at all. An output similar to the following should be displayed if Node Manager is running:

```
tcp   0   0 ::ffff:127.0.0.1:5556     :::*      LISTEN
```

Generally speaking, confirming that the process is running is typically sufficient enough to confirm that Node Manager is running as well.

Verifying AdminServer

The default port for AdminServer is `7001`, and in most installations, this is not changed. Thus, simply running the basic operating system `netstat` can confirm that the port is being listened on:

```
netstat -an | grep LISTEN | grep 7001 | grep -v grep
```

If no output is returned, either AdminServer is not running or it is running under a different port. An output similar to the following should be displayed if AdminServer is running:

```
tcp    0    0 ::ffff:71.178.205.215:7001  :::*    LISTEN
tcp    0    0 ::1:7001                     :::*    LISTEN
tcp    0    0 ::ffff:127.0.0.1:7001        :::*    LISTEN
tcp    0    0 fe80::20c:29ff:fe54:7c:7001 :::*    LISTEN
```

Checking the listening port is not a guarantee that AdminServer is up, but merely an indication that there is some process listening on the `7001` port. Therefore, checking whether the process is running is a natural next step:

```
ps -ef | grep AdminServer | grep -v grep
```

If an output is returned, you can see that a Java process is running, the paths are valid, and the managed server name is correctly set:

```
oracle   24320 24243  3 05:40 pts/1    00:06:00 /u01/share/middleware/
jdk1.7.0_15/bin/java -client -Xms768m -Xmx1536m -XX:PermSize=256m
-XX:MaxPermSize=768m -Dweblogic.Name=AdminServer ...
```

Finally, the `AdminServer.out` log file should have the following entry, confirming that it has started up successfully:

```
<Aug 25, 2014 5:45:11 AM EDT> <Notice> <WebLogicServer> <BEA-000360> <The
server started in RUNNING mode.>
```

Alternatively, bring up the WebLogic Server Administration Console. The console is targeted by default to AdminServer, so if AdminServer is up, the console would be up as well. Now, simply navigate to `http://adminhost:7001/console`.

Some, any, or all of these approaches can be used in conjunction to confirm whether AdminServer is running or not. Usually, accessing the console is sufficient enough for validation.

Verifying the managed servers

Verifying any of the managed servers, such as SOA, OSB, BAM, ESS, or WSM, is relatively identical to how we checked whether AdminServer is running. Each managed server has its own name and port, so simply substitute those when running any of the subsequent commands.

For example, the default port for `soa_server1` is `8001`, and in most installations, this is unchanged. Thus, simply running the basic operating system `netstat` can confirm that the port is being listened on:

```
netstat -an | grep LISTEN | grep 8001 | grep -v grep
```

If no output is returned, then `soa_server1` is either not running or is assigned a different port. Otherwise, an output similar to the following should be displayed:

```
tcp   0   0 fe80::20c:29ff:fe54:7c:8001 :::*    LISTEN
tcp   0   0 ::ffff:127.0.0.1:8001        :::*    LISTEN
tcp   0   0 ::1:8001                     :::*    LISTEN
tcp   0   0 ::ffff:71.178.205.215:8001   :::*    LISTEN
```

Once again, it is best to confirm whether the operating system process is actually up and running, and checking this can be done through a simple `ps` operating system command as follows:

```
ps -ef | grep soa_server1 | grep -v grep
```

If an output is returned, then you should see that a Java process is running, the paths are valid, and the managed server name is set correctly:

```
oracle   28654 28579 12 06:57 pts/1    00:13:14 /u01/share/middleware/
jdk1.7.0_15/bin/java -client -Xms768m -Xmx1536m -XX:PermSize=256m
-XX:MaxPermSize=768m -Dweblogic.Name=soa_server1 ...
```

When a managed server has successfully started, the following message is also printed to the system out file (for example, `soa_server1.out`):

```
<Aug 25, 2014 6:15:08 AM EDT> <Notice> <WebLogicServer> <BEA-000360> <The
server started in RUNNING mode.>
```

For a clustered installation, you must run each of these commands on their respective hosts to confirm that they're running, and for each OSB, BAM, ESS, and WSM, you must substitute the managed server name and port number.

However, by utilizing WLST, you can also confirm whether a server has been started up and can verify all the servers within the cluster without having to log in to each host, since the commands are issued from AdminServer. By issuing the following three commands, you should see RUNNING on the prompt:

```
$WL_HOME/common/bin/wlst.sh
wls:/offline> connect('weblogic','welcome1')
wls:/soa_domain/serverConfig> state("soa_server1")
Current state of "soa_server1" : RUNNING
```

For the SOA managed servers specifically, even if the managed server is up and reporting RUNNING, the SOA server will not be ready to accept requests until all SOA composites are first loaded. Therefore, to truly confirm whether the SOA managed server is up and accepting requests, you must see the following entry in the system out file:

SOA Platform is running and accepting requests

Clearly, logging in to the WebLogic Server Administration Console is sufficient enough to confirm the state of the managed servers. Simply navigate to **Servers | Control** and observe the following screenshot. By this, you can get a unified view of the state of all the managed servers across all nodes of your cluster:

Servers (Filtered - More Columns Exist)

Click the *Lock & Edit* button in the Change Center to activate all the buttons on this page.

New Clone Delete   Showing 1 to 9 of 9 Previous | Next

Name ⌄	Type	Cluster	Machine	State	Health	Listen Port
AdminServer(admin)	Configured		ADMINHOST	RUNNING	✅ OK	7001
wls_ess1	Configured	ESS_Cluster	SOAHOST1	SHUTDOWN	Not reachable	8021
wls_ess2	Configured	ESS_Cluster	SOAHOST2	FAILED_NOT_RESTARTABLE	Not reachable	8021
wls_osb1	Configured	OSB_Cluster	SOAHOST1	RUNNING	✅ OK	8011
wls_osb2	Configured	OSB_Cluster	SOAHOST2	FAILED_NOT_RESTARTABLE	Not reachable	8011
wls_soa1	Configured	SOA_Cluster	SOAHOST1	RUNNING	✅ OK	8001
wls_soa2	Configured	SOA_Cluster	SOAHOST2	FAILED_NOT_RESTARTABLE	Not reachable	8001
wls_wsm1	Configured	WSM-PM_Cluster	SOAHOST1	FAILED_NOT_RESTARTABLE	Not reachable	7010
wls_wsm2	Configured	WSM-PM_Cluster	SOAHOST2	FAILED_NOT_RESTARTABLE	Not reachable	7010

New Clone Delete   Showing 1 to 9 of 9 Previous | Next

Figure 3.3: Viewing the state (health) of the managed servers

Shutting down the infrastructure

Similar to the startup process, shutting down the SOA infrastructure can be done in several ways—through the console, the command line, or WLST. The shutdown process is generally performed in reverse, wherein the managed servers are the first to be brought down, followed by AdminServer, and finally, Node Manager.

Using the command line

The command line can be used to shut down the entire infrastructure. This is both simple and ideal for scripting purposes.

Shutting down the managed servers

To shut down the SOA, OSB, BAM, ESS, and WSM managed servers, simply run the following commands:

```
cd $DOMAIN_HOME/bin
```

```
./stopManagedWebLogic.sh soa_server1 t3://adminhost:7001 -Dweblogic.
management.username=weblogic -Dweblogic.management.password=welcome1
```

```
./stopManagedWebLogic.sh osb_server1 t3://adminhost:7001 -Dweblogic.
management.username=weblogic -Dweblogic.management.password=welcome1
```

```
./stopManagedWebLogic.sh bam_server1 t3://adminhost:7001 -Dweblogic.
management.username=weblogic -Dweblogic.management.password=welcome1
```

```
./stopManagedWebLogic.sh ess_server1 t3://adminhost:7001 -Dweblogic.
management.username=weblogic -Dweblogic.management.password=welcome1
```

```
./stopManagedWebLogic.sh wsm_server1 t3://adminhost:7001 -Dweblogic.
management.username=weblogic -Dweblogic.management.password=welcome1
```

> Either the t3 protocol or the http protocol can be used in the startup and shutdown commands.

In a clustered installation, you can run the commands to start up and shut down all the managed servers from the same host, as the commands are anyway sent to AdminServer for processing, making no difference as to where they are initiated from.

Shutting down AdminServer

Shutting down AdminServer simply involves the execution of the stopWebLogic.sh script as shown via the following commands:

```
cd $DOMAIN_HOME/bin
```

```
./stopWebLogic.sh
```

Shutting down Node Manager

There is no way but through the command line (or WLST) to stop the Node Manager process. This can simply be done by running the stopNodeManager.sh script:

```
cd $DOMAIN_HOME/bin
```

```
./stopNodeManager.sh
```

This can also be done by running the following command to obtain the process IDs of the Node Manager processes and killing them:

```
ps -ef | grep NodeManager | grep -v grep | awk '{print $2}' | xargs kill
-9
```

Using the console

Another easy way to shut down the SOA infrastructure is through the WebLogic Server Administration Console. The console can be used to shut down everything except Node Manager.

Shutting down AdminServer and the managed servers

Simply shutting down one or more of the managed servers, including AdminServer, can be done from the WebLogic Server Administration Console.

To shut down a managed server, go through the following steps:

1. Log in to the WebLogic Server Administration Console at `http://adminhost:7001/console`.

2. Navigate to **Servers | Control**.

3. Select the managed servers you wish to shut down.

4. Click on **Server** and then **Force Shutdown Now**. Refer to the following screenshot.

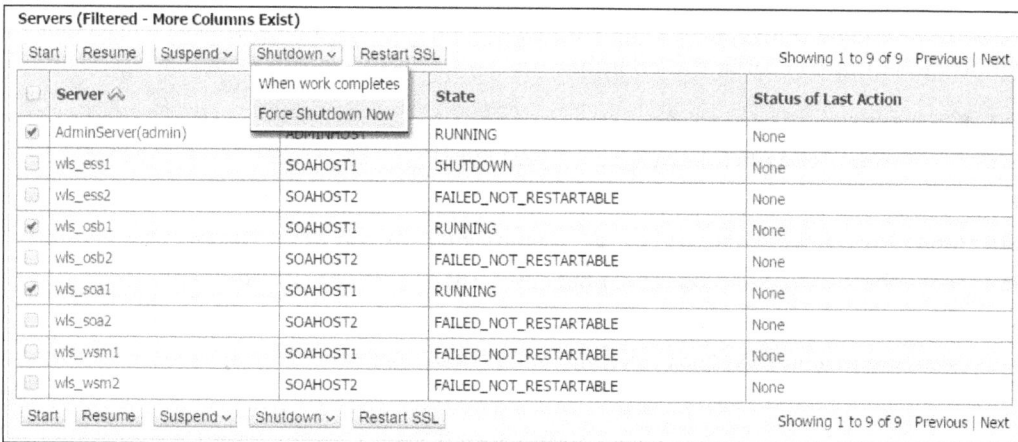

Server ⌃		State	Status of Last Action
AdminServer(admin)	ADMINHOST	RUNNING	None
wls_ess1	SOAHOST1	SHUTDOWN	None
wls_ess2	SOAHOST2	FAILED_NOT_RESTARTABLE	None
wls_osb1	SOAHOST1	RUNNING	None
wls_osb2	SOAHOST2	FAILED_NOT_RESTARTABLE	None
wls_soa1	SOAHOST1	RUNNING	None
wls_soa2	SOAHOST2	FAILED_NOT_RESTARTABLE	None
wls_wsm1	SOAHOST1	FAILED_NOT_RESTARTABLE	None
wls_wsm2	SOAHOST2	FAILED_NOT_RESTARTABLE	None

Servers (Filtered - More Columns Exist)

Start | Resume | Suspend ⌄ | Shutdown ⌄ | Restart SSL — Showing 1 to 9 of 9 Previous | Next

When work completes / Force Shutdown Now

Start | Resume | Suspend ⌄ | Shutdown ⌄ | Restart SSL — Showing 1 to 9 of 9 Previous | Next

Figure 3.2: Shutting down multiple managed servers through the WebLogic Server Administration Console

> Keep in mind that shutting down AdminServer will result in losing the access to the WebLogic Server Administration Console and Fusion Middleware Control, but it will not affect any managed servers that happen to be running.

Shutting down Node Manager

This can simply be done by running the `stopNodeManager.sh` script:

```
cd $DOMAIN_HOME/bin
./stopNodeManager.sh
```

Or, the process can be killed directly:

```
ps -ef | grep NodeManager | grep -v grep | awk '{print $2}' | xargs kill
-9
```

Using WLST

Similar to the startup process, WLST can be used exclusively to shut down the entire infrastructure, including the managed servers, AdminServer, and Node Manager.

Shutting down the managed servers

WLST can be used to shut down the managed servers. The instructions here connect to and issue commands through AdminServer. It is possible to shut down all managed servers in a cluster or each managed server individually.

To shut down any of the SOA, OSB, BAM, or WSM managed servers, use WLST to connect to AdminServer and then initiate the start commands for each managed server:

```
$WL_HOME/common/bin/wlst.sh
wls:/offline> connect('weblogic', 'welcome1', 't3://adminhost:7001')
wls:/soa_domain/serverConfig> shutdown('soa_server1', 'Server')
wls:/soa_domain/serverConfig> shutdown('osb_server1', 'Server')
wls:/soa_domain/serverConfig> shutdown('bam_server1', 'Server')
wls:/soa_domain/serverConfig> shutdown('ess_server1', 'Server')
wls:/soa_domain/serverConfig> shutdown('wsm_server1', 'Server')
```

Alternatively, you can shut down an entire cluster by issuing a single command as shown in the following commands:

```
wls:/soa_domain/serverConfig> shutdown('soacluster', 'Cluster')

wls:/soa_domain/serverConfig> shutdown('osbcluster', 'Cluster')

wls:/soa_domain/serverConfig> shutdown('bamcluster', 'Cluster')

wls:/soa_domain/serverConfig> shutdown('esscluster', 'Cluster')

wls:/soa_domain/serverConfig> shutdown('wsmcluster', 'Cluster')
```

Thus, all managed servers within that cluster are brought down with a single command.

Shutting down AdminServer

AdminServer is stopped no differently than a regular managed server. The following WLST command shuts down AdminServer:

```
$WL_HOME/common/bin/wlst.sh

wls:/offline> connect('weblogic', 'welcome1', 't3://adminhost:7001')

wls:/soa_domain/serverConfig> shutdown('AdminServer', 'Server')
```

Shutting down Node Manager

Stopping Node Manager is done manually on every node of the cluster. Unless you are going through a major upgrade, it is often rare and unnecessary to bring down Node Manager, even when performing regular administrative or maintenance activities. But should you choose to, you must connect to Node Manager before shutting it down through WLST. Execute the following commands to shut down Node Manager:

```
$WL_HOME/common/bin/wlst.sh

wls:/offline> nmConnect('weblogic', 'welcome1', 'soahost1', '5556', 'soa_
domain',
'/u01/oracle/products/Oracle_SOA1/user_projects/domains/soa_domain')

wls:/offline> stopNodeManager()

Verifying server shutdown
```

On Linux, when a managed server is successfully shut down, there are no active processes. Issuing a simple operating system command to check processes should return no active processes. For example, running the `ps` command should return nothing if the server is indeed down:

```
ps -ef | grep soa_server1 | grep -v grep
ps -ef | grep osb_server1 | grep -v grep
ps -ef | grep bam_server1 | grep -v grep
ps -ef | grep ess_server1 | grep -v grep
ps -ef | grep wsm_server1 | grep -v grep
```

Likewise, if AdminServer is down, it should also return nothing:

```
ps -ef | grep AdminServer | grep -v grep
```

Finally, the same applies to Node Manager. No output should be returned if Node Manager is truly down:

```
ps -ef | grep NodeManager | grep -v grep
```

Alternatively, you can observe the last lines of the system out files to confirm whether the server is down or not.

Summary

Starting up and shutting down the entire Oracle SOA Suite infrastructure is quite simple and straightforward once you are familiarized with the commands. It is often performed via the command line, WLST, or the console, and choosing one approach over another is merely a matter of preference and choice for the administrator. Generally speaking, using WLST and Node Manager are the recommended approaches for a production environment.

There are cases when the administrator may want to turn on or off a particular service, such as an SOA composite or an OSB service. This is described in *Chapter 4, Managing Services*.

In this chapter, you learned how to start up and shut down the infrastructure entirely from the command line, mostly from the console, and using WLST. You also learned how to verify that the environment has started up and shut down.

4
Managing Services

Developers can create SOA services by using a number of different technologies. Oracle SOA Suite 12c provides us with the ability to run services that are developed as SOA composite applications (or simply SOA composites) and OSB services. Though both types of services are packaged in single deployable JAR files, they are very dissimilar technologies that are developed differently and are executed and managed in completely separate runtimes. However, the beauty of Fusion Middleware Control 12c is that the administrator is given a single consolidated view of runtime instances of these distinct services. Developers can harness the advantages of each of these separate technologies while the administrator can manage them collectively.

Composites can contain any number of service components, which include BPEL or BPMN processes, mediator services, human tasks and workflows, and business rules. They do not include OSB services, which are separately developed and deployed components. Together, SOA composite applications and OSB services can coexist and include logic that forms the foundation of SOA-based integrations.

Though the design and development of composites and services are not the ultimate responsibility of the Oracle SOA Suite 12c administrator, the deployment, monitoring, and management of their lifecycle are.

In this chapter, we will discuss the concepts that enable you to manage both SOA composites in the first half of the chapter, followed by OSB services in the latter half. The following topics are covered in this chapter:

- Managing SOA composite lifecycles
- Structuring SOA composites with partitions
- Managing OSB service lifecycles

Managing SOA composite lifecycles

Every SOA composite has a state, mode, and associated metadata. The state can be up (started) or down (shut down). The mode can either be active or retired. Metadata is stored in the **Metadata Store** (**MDS**), which is generally a database-backed repository used by Oracle SOA Suite 12*c*, and consists of information that includes the default revision number, last modification date, deployment and redeployment times, and instance runtime information. Before walking through how to manage the state and mode of SOA composites, we will begin by describing composite revisions.

Understanding revisions

When a HelloWorld composite is deployed to on the server, a revision is required during the deployment. Thus, a service's WSDL can be accessed via a URL similar to the following, clearly indicating a revision of 1.0 after the composite name:

```
http://soahost1:8001/soa-infra/services/default/HelloWorld!1.0/
HelloWorld.wsdl
```

However, there may be a case where a new version of the composite needs to be deployed and that this version has a different implementation from the existing one. Overwriting the existing version may not be the right option as it would break all the client applications that are already consuming the service. Thus, it makes sense to deploy the new composite using a different revision, such as revision 2.0, making both versions available simultaneously. The composite would, therefore, be accessible at a different URL, http://soahost1:8001/soa-infra/services/default/HelloWorld!2.0/HelloWorld.wsdl.

Now, the old and new services are both available and accessible. Clients accessing revision 1.0 of the SOA composite may transition to revision 2.0 at their own pace.

If multiple revisions of the same service are deployed, one of them must be specified as the default revision. This can be specified during the deployment time or can be changed at runtime by the administrator. The default revision would thus be accessed at a revision-independent URL, http://soahost1:8001/soa-infra/services/default/HelloWorld/HelloWorld.wsdl.

Typically, client applications will access the default revision. Revisions are advantageous in environments where maintaining old and new versions of the same SOA composite is required, particularly if it involves breaking changes or supporting clients that require backward portability.

As shown in the following screenshot, default revisions are indicated by a green dot in the list of SOA composites for a given partition:

Figure 4.1: Green dots are used to identify default revisions of a SOA composite

Partitions will be explained in detail later in this chapter.

Changing the SOA composite default revision at runtime

If a SOA composite is not the default revision, the **Set As Default...** button will appear in the SOA composite page, as shown in the following screenshot. By clicking on this button, it is possible at this point to set the revision of this composite as the default revision if you want to.

Figure 4.2: The Set As Default button appears for non-default SOA composite revisions

If a default SOA composite application is undeployed, the default revision is automatically changed to the last deployed revision.

Starting up and shutting down SOA composites

SOA composites are automatically started up when they are deployed. If a composite is shut down, all requests to the composite are rejected, including callbacks. New requests are not served and new instances are not created. However, all running instances are allowed to complete.

Though starting up and shutting down SOA composites via the console is extremely easy. If you require to start up or shut down multiple SOA composites, two approaches are available, which are discussed in detail later in this chapter:

- SOA composites deployed on the same partition can all be started up or all be shut down with a single operation
- Ant or WLST can be used to automate the startup and shutdown of SOA composites

Starting a SOA composite

To start up a single SOA composite from the console, proceed with the following steps:

1. Log in to Fusion Middleware Control at `http://<adminhost>:7001/em`.
2. On the navigator, expand **SOA | soa-infra**.
3. Expand the partition (for example, **default**) and click on the SOA composite name and the revision (for example, **HelloWorld [1.0]**).
4. Click on the **Start Up...** button, which will only appear if the SOA composite is already shut down, as shown in the following screenshot:

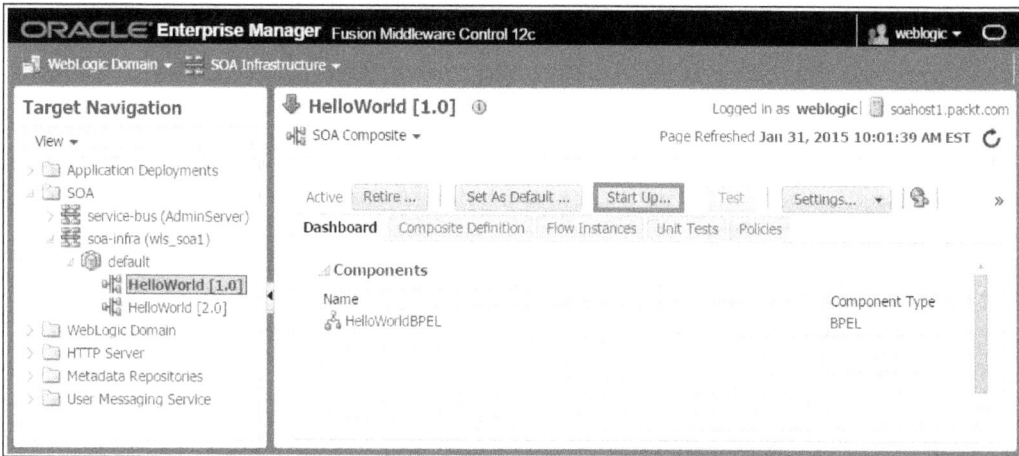

Figure 4.3: Starting up a SOA composite from Fusion Middleware Control

Shutting down a SOA composite

To shut down a single SOA composite from the console, proceed with the following steps:

1. On the navigator, expand **SOA | soa-infra**.

2. Expand the partition (for example, **default**), choose from the deployed SOA composites, and click on the composite name and the revision (for example, **HelloWorld [1.0]**).

3. Click on the **Shut Down...** button, which will only appear if the SOA composite is already started up, as shown in the following screenshot:

Figure 4.4: Shutting down a SOA composite from Fusion Middleware Control

Retiring and activating SOA composites

SOA composites have two modes—active and retired. These are often confused with SOA composite states, which can be up (started) and down (shut down).

SOA composites are automatically activated when they are deployed (in fact, they are also started up as well, so active and started SOA composites are really identical in nature). However, when a SOA composite is retired, new instances cannot be created. Existing instances, however, continue to completion. This includes instances that receive callbacks. The ability to receive callbacks and time-based waits is the primary difference between a retired SOA composite and a SOA composite that has been shut down.

> The only difference between activating a SOA composite and starting up a SOA composite is that activating the SOA composite affects the retired mode, while starting up a composite affects the shutdown state.

Retiring a SOA composite

To retire a single SOA composite from the console, perform the following steps:

1. On the navigator, expand **SOA | soa-infra**.

2. Expand the partition (for example, **default**) and click on the SOA composite name (for example, **HelloWorld**).

3. Click on the **Retire** button, which will only appear if the SOA composite is already active.

Activating a SOA composite

To activate a single SOA composite from the console, go through the following steps:

1. On the navigator, expand **SOA | soa-infra**.

2. Expand the partition (for example, **default**) and click on the SOA composite name (for example, **HelloWorld**).

3. Click on the **Activate** button, which will only appear if the SOA composite is already retired.

Deleting SOA composite instances

Every time a SOA composite application is invoked, a new instance of the composite is created. Every instance has a unique ID and its details can be retrieved from Fusion Middleware Control. All the instance ID types are explained in detail in *Chapter 6, Monitoring Oracle SOA Suite 12c*. Oracle SOA Suite 12c maintains an audit history of the instance that is saved in what is referred to as the dehydration store. Too much instance-related data requires additional storage, but more importantly, it impacts the performance of the console. Administrators are expected to delete completed instances periodically to control growth. We will discuss the management of instance data in *Chapter 8, Managing the Database*, but it may be worth briefly describing how to delete instances, thereby purging all data related to it, manually from Fusion Middleware Control as part of SOA composite management activities. Deleting instances is quite easy, as demonstrated in the following steps:

1. On the navigator, expand **SOA** | **soa-infra**.

2. Expand the partition (for example, **default**) and click on the SOA composite name (for example, **HelloWorld**).

3. Click on the **Instances** tab.

4. At this point, you can delete instances in one of the following two ways:

    ° Highlight the list of instances (press the *Ctrl* key and click on each SOA composite one by one) and click on the **Delete Selected** button.

    ° Click on the **Delete With Options** button. From here, you can delete instances older than a specific time or delete all instances within a time frame that have a certain state.

You can also bulk delete/purge SOA composite instances from the underlying database dehydration store through the use of SQL scripts. Again, this will be covered in more detail in *Chapter 8, Managing the Database*.

Structuring SOA composites with partitions

Partitions provide a mechanism to logically group your SOA composites. Thus, for example, the code for your Human Resources integrations can reside in a partition separate from your EBS integrations, offering better structure and organization. There are a few bulk lifecycle management tasks that can be performed on all SOA composite applications in a partition, as we will describe in this section. For example, all SOA composites within a partition can be shut down with a single operation. The following screenshot shows a list of partitions in the navigator under **soa-infra**:

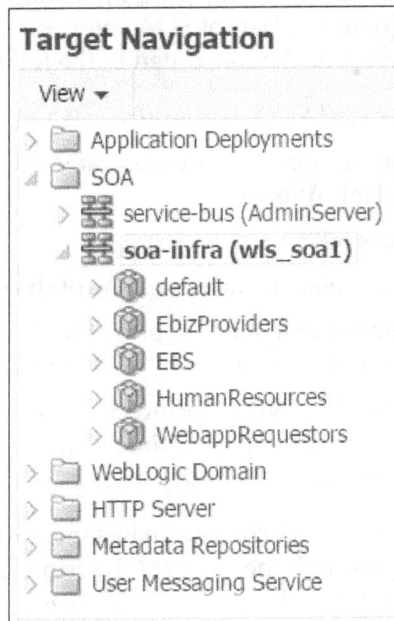

Figure 4.5: Partitions are displayed in the navigator in Fusion Middleware Control

Each partition may have one or more SOA composite applications deployed to it. Partitions in Oracle SOA Suite 12c also provide the ability to set up group-specific or user-specific permissions on each partition, including viewing, deployment, and administration. Partitions cannot be nested (that is, a partition cannot have a child partition). Partitions also do not have their own configuration or logging.

> One advantage of using partitions is the ability to perform bulk lifecycle management tasks, such as starting up or shutting down all SOA composites in a partition with a single operation.

Domain libraries, extension modules, server **Java Naming and Directory Interface (JNDI)**, and infrastructure properties are shared across all partitions.

The default partition

Oracle SOA Suite 12*c* should have, at minimum, one partition. The default partition is created automatically when the product is installed, but it can be deleted afterwards if you choose to do so. You must always have at least one partition to which you can deploy SOA composites.

Managing partitions

You can perform several management tasks pertaining to partitions. These tasks include:

- Creating a partition
- Deleting a partition, including all SOA composites within the partition
- Starting up and shutting down all SOA composites in a partition
- Retiring and activating all SOA composites in a partition
- Undeploying all SOA composites in a partition

The simplest method to manage partitions is via the **Manage Partitions** page. Simply navigate to this page to create, delete, or perform bulk lifecycle management operations on the partitions as follows:

1. Right-click on **soa-infra** and then click on **Manage Partitions** to access the **Manage Partitions** page.

2. At this point, you can do one of the following four things:

   ° Click on the **Create** button to create a partition.

   ° Highlight an existing partition and click on the **Delete** button to delete the partition.

   ° Highlight an existing partition and click on the **Composites Control** button to start up, shut down, activate, or retire all SOA composites within that partition.

   ° Highlight an existing partition and click on the **Deployment** button to undeploy all SOA composites within this partition or to deploy a single composite to this partition.

The **Manage Partitions** page with each of its action buttons is shown in the following screenshot:

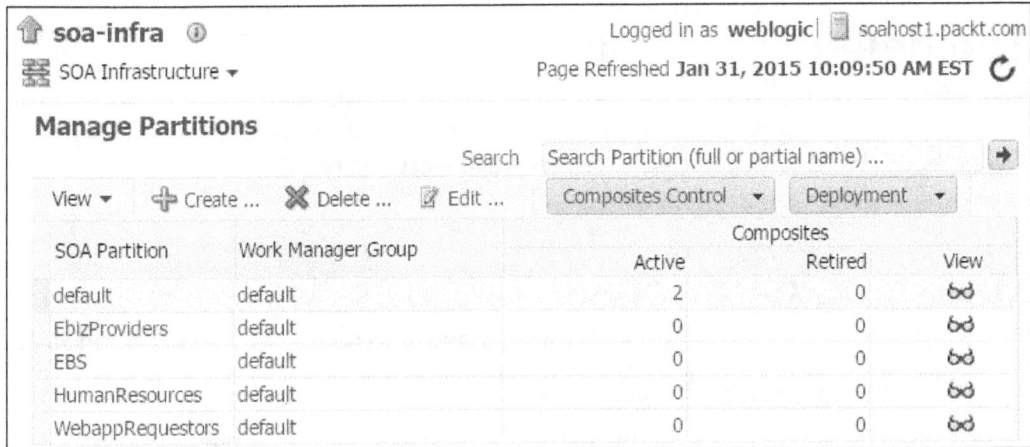

SOA Partition	Work Manager Group	Composites		
		Active	Retired	View
default	default	2	0	👓
EbizProviders	default	0	0	👓
EBS	default	0	0	👓
HumanResources	default	0	0	👓
WebappRequestors	default	0	0	👓

Figure 4.6: The Manage Partitions page

The **Composites Control** and **Deployment** buttons are only activated when a partition is highlighted.

> Partitions do not have a state or mode. Thus, for example, you are not shutting down the partition, you are actually shutting down all the SOA composites within the partition.

Creating a partition

When creating a partition, be mindful of the following naming conventions:

- Letters, numbers, underscores, and hyphens are allowed (hyphens are not allowed as the first character)
- Spaces are not allowed

Partitions cannot be renamed once they are created. Every partition must be assigned to a Work Group Manager, which is described shortly.

Deleting a partition

There should always exist at least one partition. If you delete all the partitions, it will not be possible to deploy any code to the server. If you delete a partition, all the SOA composites within that partition are automatically undeployed.

Grouping SOA composite applications into partitions

Typically, developers choose which partition a particular composite should be deployed to, but as an administrator, you must understand its implications.

When SOA composites are deployed — whether through JDeveloper, the console, Ant, or WLST — a partition name must be specified. Code deployed to the default partition will result in a different WSDL URL than that deployed to, for example, the HumanResources partition, as follows:

- http://soahost1:8001/soa-infra/services/default/HelloWorld/ HelloWorld.wsdl

- http://soahost1:8001/soa-infra/services/HumanResources/ HelloWorld/HelloWorld.wsdl

Considerations for partition management

There are some considerations regarding partition management that you should be aware of:

- Avoid creating partitions called Dev, Test, and Prod. Though possible, partitions are not to be separated by environment.

- Domain libraries and resource adapters (such as DB, MQ, and AQ) are shared by all partitions, so it is not possible to have different versions of these libraries or extensions for each partition.

- Partitions do not provide multi-tenant capabilities in Oracle SOA Suite 12*c* yet. As such, server JNDI names of resources, such as data sources, connection pools, JMS destinations, and so on, are shared by all composites deployed across different partitions.

- Oracle SOA Suite 12*c* configuration parameters such as timeouts, threads, and recovery configurations can only be defined at the WebLogic Server domain level, not by a partition.

- If composites that use inbound adapters (such as the inbound AQ Adapter, in which messages are automatically dequeued from an Oracle AQ) are deployed to multiple partitions, it is not guaranteed which composite will dequeue the inbound message (that is, they will compete with each other).

Updating runtime properties for SOA composites

Once SOA composites are deployed, certain properties can be updated at runtime without the need to redeploy them. All properties can be set at design time (through JDeveloper 12*c*) or at runtime (via Fusion Middleware Control).

Examples of runtime properties include:

- HTTP Read Timeout
- HTTP Connection Timeout
- JCA Retry Count

To update a runtime property for a composite, you can perform the following steps:

1. On the navigator, expand **SOA | soa-infra**.
2. Expand the partition (for example, **default**), choose from among the deployed SOA composites, and click on the composite name and the revision (for example, **HelloWorld [1.0]**).
3. On the **Dashboard** tab, scroll down and locate Services and References.
4. Click on one of the service or reference names.
5. Click on the **Properties** tab.
6. You will find a number of customizable properties, depending on whether you have clicked on a service or reference, and the type of service or reference.

Assigning a partition to a Work Manager Group list

When you create a partition, you must assign it to a **Work Manager Group**, as shown in the following screenshot:

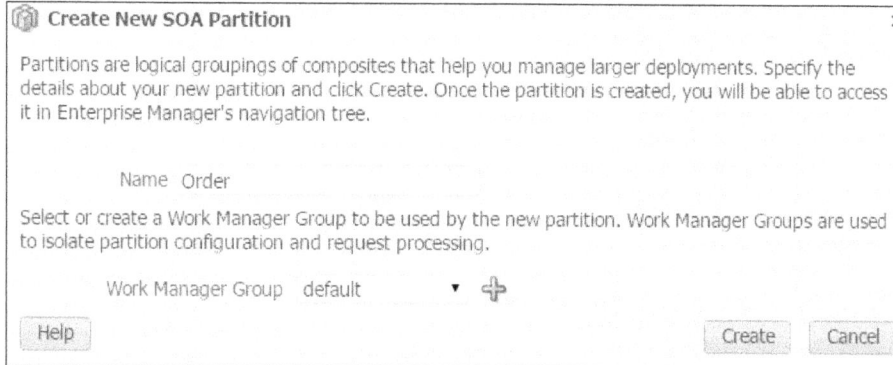

Figure 4.7: Creating a SOA partition requires assigning it to a Work Manager Group list

Work Manager Groups are first created by right-clicking on **soa-infra** then clicking on **Work Manager Groups** (every new installation will have a default Work Manager Group). The following screenshot shows the two custom-created work managers—**HighPriority** and **LowPriority**. On the rightmost column, the partitions assigned to the Work Manager are shown:

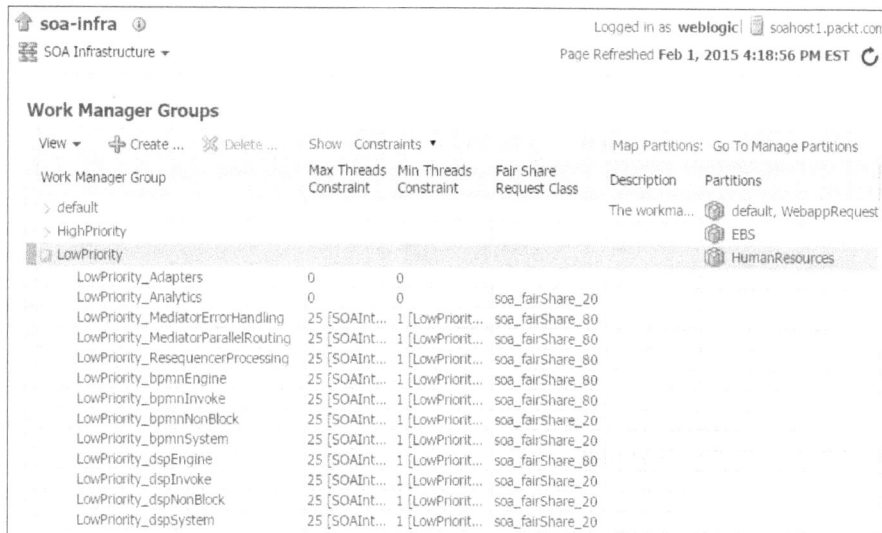

Figure 4.8: The Work Manager Groups page

You may modify the work manager of any partition at any time, but a server restart is required for it to take effect. When you create a Work Manager Group from Fusion Middleware Control, multiple work managers are created in Oracle WebLogic Server. These work managers are entities that represent logical thread pools. For example, after creating the Work Manager Group **LowPriority** and navigating to **[Domain]** | **Environment** | **Work Managers** in the WebLogic Server Administration Console, numerous work managers and constraints that are created are displayed, as shown in the following screenshot:

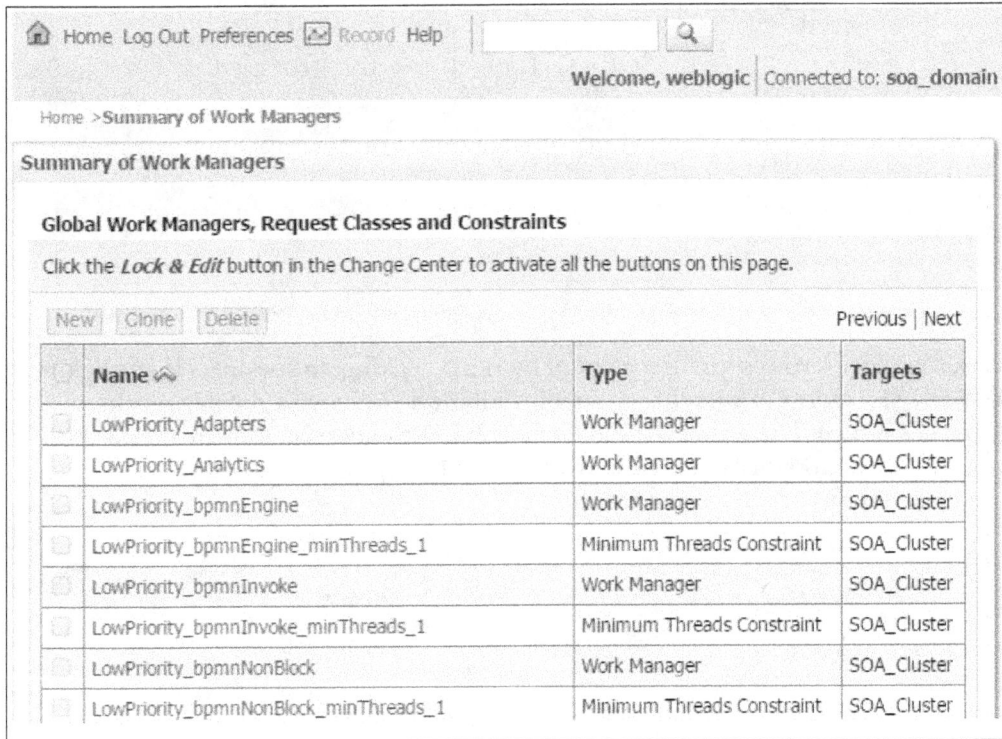

Figure 4.9: Work Managers in the WebLogic Server Administration Console

The priority of these work managers can be customized as needed. However, now it is enough to understand that Oracle WebLogic Server manages the thread pool on behalf of Oracle SOA Suite 12*c*. Multiple partitions can be assigned to a single Work Manager Group that is dedicated to processing background transactions. Certain aspects of Work Managers are further explained in *Chapter 7, Configuration and Administration*.

If you take a look at *Figure 4.9* again, clicking on **LowPriority_Adapters** takes us to *Figure 4.10*. Here, it is shown in the following screenshot that the **Maximum Threads Constraint** type is not defined (in fact, it is defaulted to unlimited):

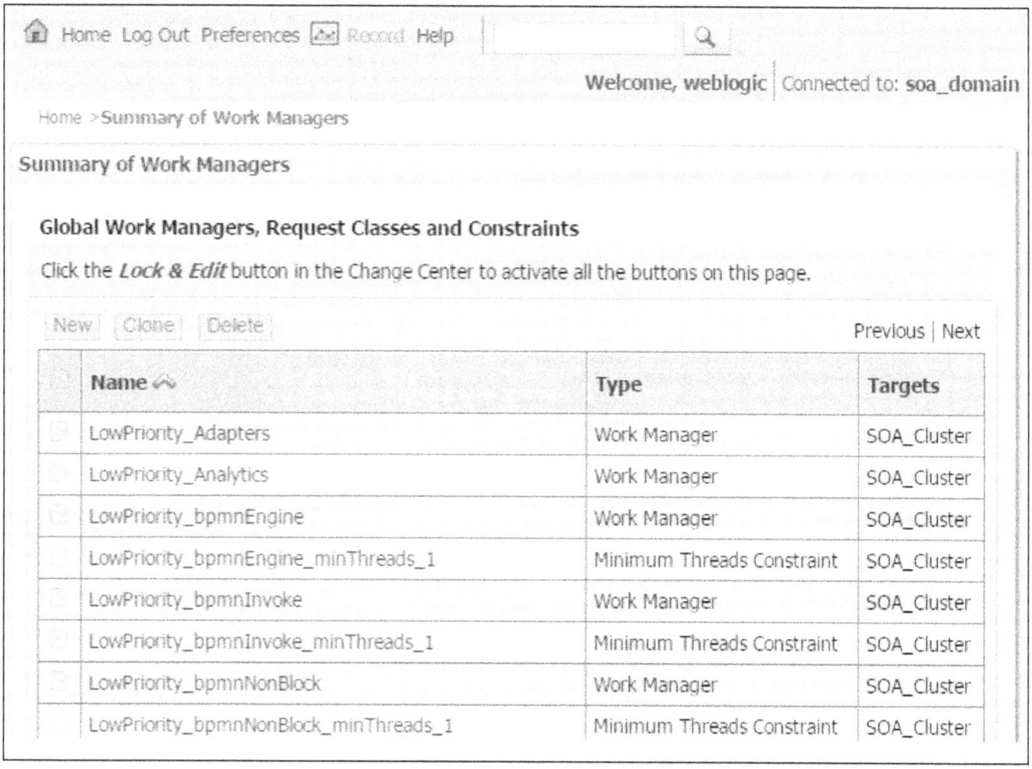

Name	Type	Targets
LowPriority_Adapters	Work Manager	SOA_Cluster
LowPriority_Analytics	Work Manager	SOA_Cluster
LowPriority_bpmnEngine	Work Manager	SOA_Cluster
LowPriority_bpmnEngine_minThreads_1	Minimum Threads Constraint	SOA_Cluster
LowPriority_bpmnInvoke	Work Manager	SOA_Cluster
LowPriority_bpmnInvoke_minThreads_1	Minimum Threads Constraint	SOA_Cluster
LowPriority_bpmnNonBlock	Work Manager	SOA_Cluster
LowPriority_bpmnNonBlock_minThreads_1	Minimum Threads Constraint	SOA_Cluster

Figure 4.10: Viewing the configuration of a WebLogic Server work manager

The **Maximum Threads Constraint** field limits the number of concurrent threads to the value indicated here. By clicking on **New**, you can create a new Maximum Threads Constraint and assign it a value either based on a count or data source. The following screenshot shows us how to set this value to 5:

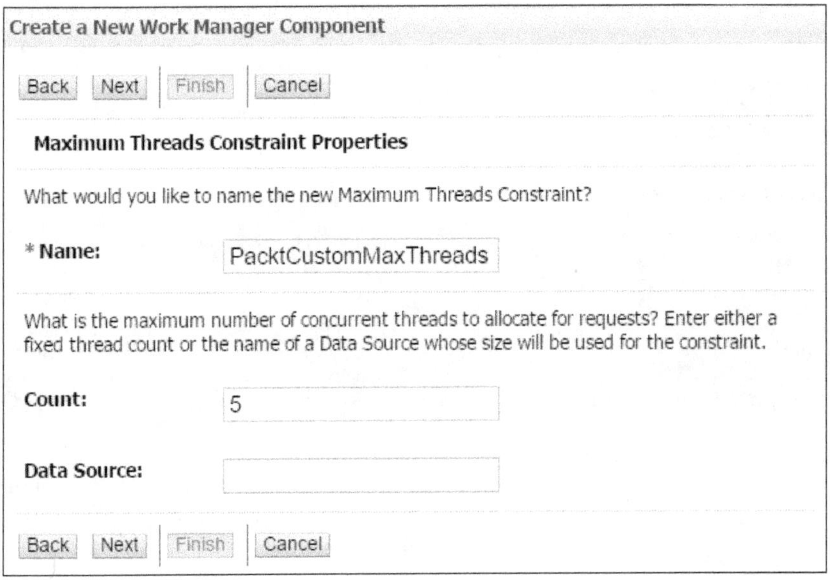

Figure 4.11: Creating a Maximum Threads Constraint in the WebLogic Server Administration Console

Thus, for the Work Manager Group **LowPriority**, the adapter's work manager defined in Oracle WebLogic Server was customized to a maximum concurrent value of 5 threads.

This fine-grained configuration provides the ability to significantly control the behavior of background processes of the code running in your SOA partitions. This is valuable in cases where certain composites that are deployed to specific partitions need to be given higher processing priority and/or concurrency over others.

There are some considerations surrounding the assigning of Work Group Managers to partitions, which are as follows:

- Consider creating separate Work Group Managers for high-priority and low-priority transactions
- Consider assigning partitions that maintain high-priority SOA composites to the high-priority Work Group Manager and likewise, the low-priority ones to the low-priority Work Group Manager

Securing access to partitions

Another new feature introduced by Oracle SOA Suite 12*c* is the ability to control access to SOA partitions. For example, a user logging in to Fusion Middleware Control will only be able to view the partitions and their underlying SOA composites that they have access to.

To restrict a partition to a particular user, the following steps are performed:

1. On the navigator, expand **SOA** and right-click on **soa-infra**.
2. Navigate to **Security | Application Roles**.
3. Click on the **search** icon.
4. For every partition that exists, you will find the following roles:
   - **[PartitionName]_Monitor**
   - **[PartitionName]_Composer**
   - **[PartitionName]_Tester**
   - **[PartitionName]_Deployer**
   - **[PartitionName]_ApplicationOperator**
5. Choose a role and click on **Edit**.
6. Click on **Add** and search for a user to assign this role to.

Managing OSB service lifecycles

The lifecycle of OSB services is rather different from that of SOA composites. Naturally, managing them is also considerably different. At a high level, an OSB service typically consists of one or more proxy services, one or more business services, and pipelines. The **proxy service** is the interface of the OSB pipeline that contains the service orchestration logic, whereas a **business service** is merely a façade of your external services. Think of a proxy service as the input to your OSB service. This could be a simple WSDL interface that is called as a web service on demand or it could be a polling service, wherein the proxy service, for example, polls a particular table or queue to receive its input.

On the other hand, a **business service** is simply a wrapper to the target services, such as a database table, JMS queue, flat file, or another web service, that the OSB components of your projects may call.

Unlike SOA composites, OSB services can be completely manipulated through the console, including updating any business logic, mappings, or flows! In fact, all development can be exclusively done via the Oracle Service Bus Console, and technically, there is no need to develop OSB projects in Oracle JDeveloper 12*c* if you choose not to.

In this section, we describe various settings that can be manipulated at runtime to allow you, the administrator, to manage various OSB service lifecycles.

Managing OSB service operations

All OSB runtime operational settings are manipulated through Fusion Middleware Control (accessible at /em), not the Service Bus Console (accessible at /servicebus or /sbconsole), which is purely dedicated to design-time configuration.

On the navigator in Fusion Middleware Control, expanding **SOA** and then **service-bus** reveals a list of all your deployed OSB services (refer to *Figure 4.12*). Here, you can either navigate to the operational settings of an individual service or view the operational settings for all services. For example:

- Right-clicking on **service-bus** then navigating to **Home | Operations** displays the operational settings of all deployed services

- Right-clicking on a particular service in the navigator, for instance, **CustomerReq**, then navigating to **Home | Operations** displays the operational settings for that individual service only:

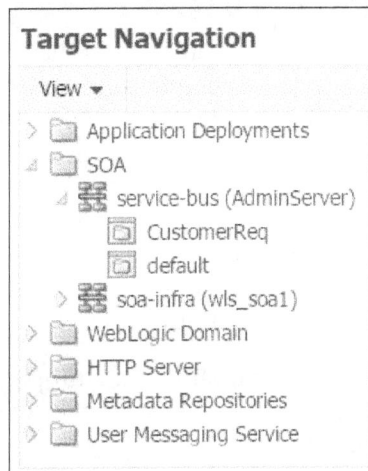

Figure 4.12: All OSB services are listed under service-bus in the navigator

Operational settings let you update configurations such as monitoring, alerts, reporting, logging, message tracing, and business service result caching at runtime. You can specify operational settings for all services, at the service and global levels, and use the global settings to turn on and off monitoring, SLA alerts, pipeline message reporting, and pipeline message logging.

The following screenshot displays all runtime operational settings deployed to our OSB server. If a checkbox is unchecked, for example, it is highlighted in yellow, as shown in the following screenshot, after which you must click on the **Apply** button to commit the change:

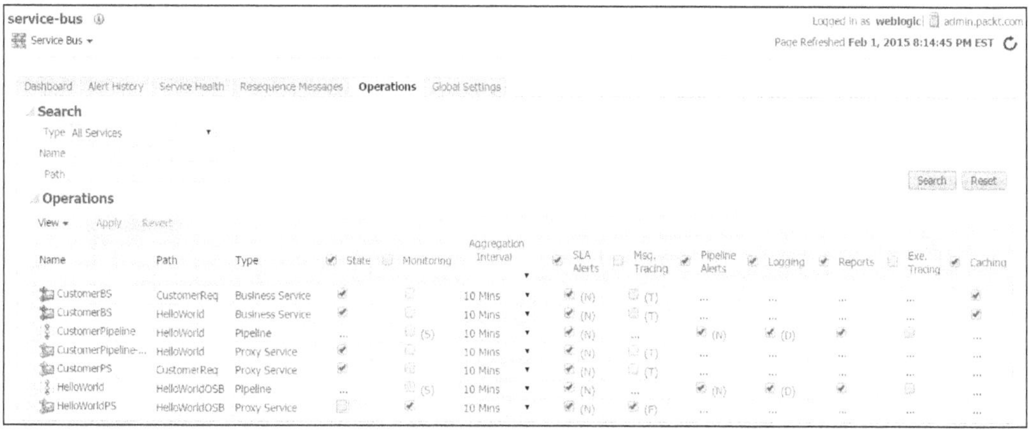

Figure 4.13: Viewing operational settings for all OSB services

The changes take effect immediately. Not all settings are applicable to all OSB component types. For example, **Caching** is only applicable to business services while **Reports** are only relevant to pipelines. Each of the operational settings shown in *Figure 4.13*, also described in more detail in *Chapter 6, Monitoring Oracle SOA Suite 12c*, provide us with further details on the settings that are related to monitoring.

State

Disabling an OSB proxy service essentially stops the OSB service from accepting an input. If the OSB proxy service is a web service, calls to the service will fail with an HTTP 404 error similar to the following:

```
10.4.5 404 Not Found
```

```
The server has not found anything matching the Request-URI. No indication
is given of whether the condition is temporary or permanent.</p><p>If the
server does not wish to make this information available to the client,
the status code 403 (Forbidden) can be used instead. The 410 (Gone)
status code SHOULD be used if the server knows, through some internally
configurable mechanism, that an old resource is permanently unavailable
and has no forwarding address.
```

If the OSB proxy service is a polling service, then polling is suspended. The reverse is true when enabling a proxy service.

> A single OSB project may contain multiple proxy services, so each proxy service must be enabled or disabled separately.

Manipulating the state of a proxy service is the equivalent of turning on or off the service. Similarly, State is applicable to business services.

Monitoring

The Monitoring operational setting enables or disables service monitoring. Certain operational settings, such as Logging and Alerts, rely on monitoring being enabled for them to function. Monitoring is disabled by default for all services.

Aggregation Interval

The Aggregation Interval operational setting defines the aggregation interval for the service. Statistical data for the OSB component is collected and aggregated over the time period selected here. The default interval is 10 minutes.

SLA Alerts

During design time, the developer may have set up **Service-level Agreement (SLA)** Alerts. SLA Alerts can be viewed in Fusion Middleware Control under the **Alert History** tab, as shown in the following screenshot:

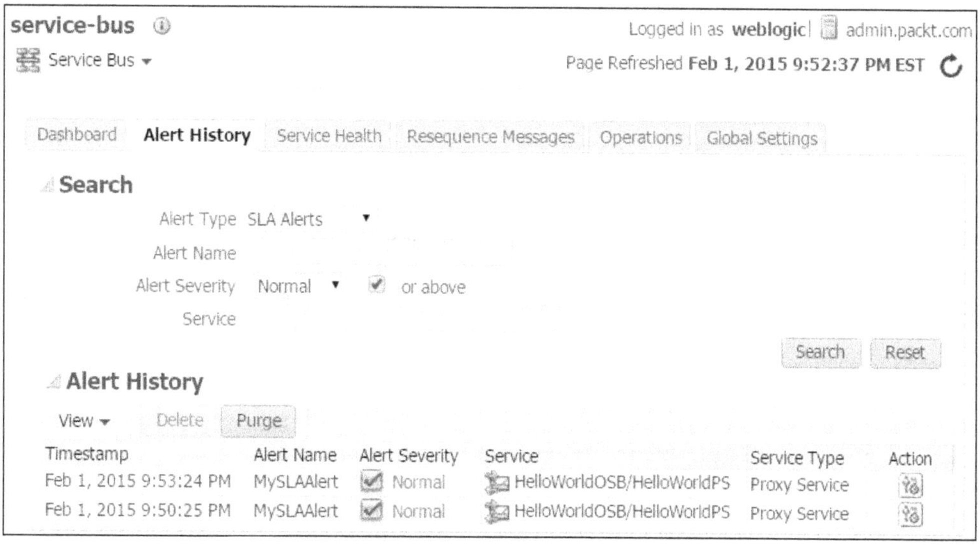

Figure 4.14: Viewing SLA alerts

The SLA Alerts operational setting simply enables or disables this function. SLA Alerting is enabled by default for all services.

Message Tracing

Message Tracing is a feature in OSB that enables us to log pipeline actions in the server log at various levels. It allows administrators to troubleshoot and diagnose a message flow in one or more proxy services. Like other operational settings, Message Tracing can be enabled or disabled. During design time, a developer may choose to configure Message Tracing, as shown in the following screenshot:

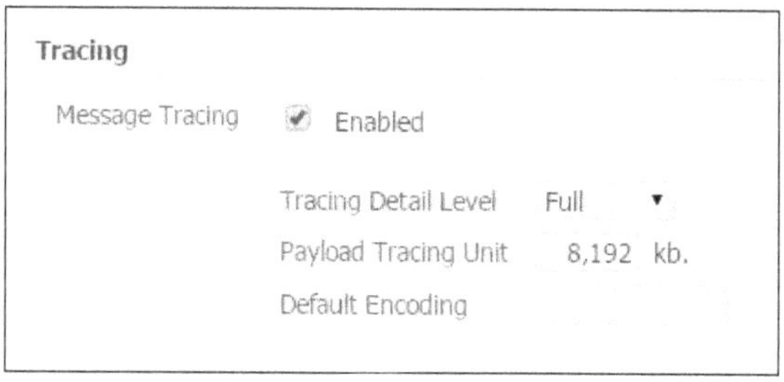

Figure 4.15: Configuring Message Tracing through the Oracle Service Bus Console

This configuration is performed either through JDeveloper or the Service Bus Console. The enablement and disablement of Message Tracing is done through Fusion Middleware Control. Message Tracing is disabled by default.

Pipeline Alerts

The Pipeline Alerts operational setting allows the administrator to enable or disable alerting for pipelines at a specific severity level (or higher). Pipeline alerts are enabled at the normal level or higher by default.

Logging

The Logging operational setting enables or disables logging at a specific severity level for pipelines and split-joins. For example, when logging is enabled and the message tracing detail level is set to **Full** (as in *Figure 4.15*), full logging details can be observed in the `osb_server1-diagnostic.log` log file. This can include request and response payloads and everything in between, as shown in the following code:

```
[2015-02-01T09:34:16.598-05:00] [wls_osb1] [NOTIFICATION] [OSB-398200]
[oracle.osb.resources.service.service] [tid: [ACTIVE].ExecuteThread: '22'
for queue: 'weblogic.kernel.Default (self-tuning)'] [userId: <anonymous>]
[ecid: b136da4e-2d94-4b59-98d5-5291c201bb2b-000592c9,0] [APP: Service Bus
Kernel] [FlowId: 0000Kh5^42J6ATMS6MGNsy1Kl6jH00000D] [[

[OSB Tracing] Inbound request was received.


Service Ref = HelloWorldOSB/HelloWorldPS

URI = /HelloWorldOSB

Message ID = 47b2cdd7.7e483a17.c.14b422bd014.N7fff

Request metadata =

   <xml-fragment>

      <tran:headers xsi:type="http:HttpRequestHeade
rs" xmlns:http="http://www.bea.com/wli/sb/transports/http"
xmlns:tran="http://www.bea.com/wli/sb/transports" xmlns:xsi="http://www.
w3.org/2001/XMLSchema-instance">

         <http:Accept-Encoding>gzip,deflate</http:Accept-Encoding>

         <http:Connection>Keep-Alive</http:Connection>

         <http:Content-Length>252</http:Content-Length>

         <http:Content-Type>text/xml;charset=UTF-8</http:Content-Type>

         <http:Host>osb.packt.com:8011</http:Host>
```

```
        <http:SOAPAction>""</http:SOAPAction>

        <http:User-Agent>Apache-HttpClient/4.1.1 (java 1.5)</http:User-
Agent>

      </tran:headers>

      <tran:encoding xmlns:tran="http://www.bea.com/wli/sb/
transports">UTF-8</tran:encoding>

      <http:client-host xmlns:http="http://www.bea.com/wli/sb/transports/
http">static-71-178-205-210.washdc.fios.verizon.net</http:client-host>

      <http:client-address xmlns:http="http://www.bea.com/wli/sb/
transports/http">71.178.205.210</http:client-address>

      <http:http-method xmlns:http="http://www.bea.com/wli/sb/transports/
http">POST</http:http-method>

    </xml-fragment>
 Payload =
<soapenv:Envelope xmlns:soapenv="http://schemas.xmlsoap.org/soap/
envelope/" xmlns:wss="http://raastech.com/">

   <soapenv:Header/>

   <soapenv:Body>

      <wss:hello>

         <arg0>Jack</arg0>

      </wss:hello>

   </soapenv:Body>

</soapenv:Envelope>


]]

[2015-02-01T09:34:16.663-05:00] [wls_osb1] [NOTIFICATION] [OSB-398201]
[oracle.osb.resources.service.service] [tid: [ACTIVE].ExecuteThread: '18'
for queue: 'weblogic.kernel.Default (self-tuning)'] [userId: <anonymous>]
[ecid: b136da4e-2d94-4b59-98d5-5291c201bb2b-000592c9,0:1] [APP: Service
Bus Kernel] [FlowId: 0000Kh5^42J6ATMS6MGNsy1Kl6jH00000D] [[

 [OSB Tracing] Inbound response was sent.


 Service Ref = HelloWorldOSB/HelloWorldPS

 URI = /HelloWorldOSB

 Message ID = <47b2cdd7.7e483a17.c.14b422bd014.N7fff>

 Response metadata =
```

```
<xml-fragment>

  <tran:headers xsi:type="http:HttpResponseHeaders" xmlns:http="http://
www.bea.com/wli/sb/transports/http" xmlns:tran="http://www.bea.com/wli/
sb/transports" xmlns:xsi="http://www.w3.org/2001/XMLSchema-instance">

    <http:Content-Type>text/xml; charset=utf-8</http:Content-Type>

  </tran:headers>

  <tran:response-code xmlns:tran="http://www.bea.com/wli/sb/
transports">0</tran:response-code>

  <tran:encoding xmlns:tran="http://www.bea.com/wli/sb/
transports">utf-8</tran:encoding>

</xml-fragment>

 Payload =

<?xml version="1.0" encoding="UTF-8"?>

<soapenv:Envelope xmlns:soapenv="http://schemas.xmlsoap.org/soap/
envelope/" xmlns:wss="http://raastech.com/">

  <soapenv:Header/>

  <soapenv:Body>

    <wss:hello>

      <arg0>Hello Jack</arg0>

    </wss:hello>

  </soapenv:Body>

</soapenv:Envelope>


]]
```

Logging is extremely beneficial to troubleshoot issues. Generally speaking, enabling full logging is discouraged in a production environment that is running without any issues.

Reports

Report actions are valuable as they allow specific elements to be captured and displayed through the Oracle Service Bus Console. For example, you may have an order transaction that consists of hundreds of elements in the payload. But for the purposes of monitoring, you simply wish to capture the order number in order to identify its OSB instance. The following screenshot shows an example where we are capturing an order number from the input payload as a Report action:

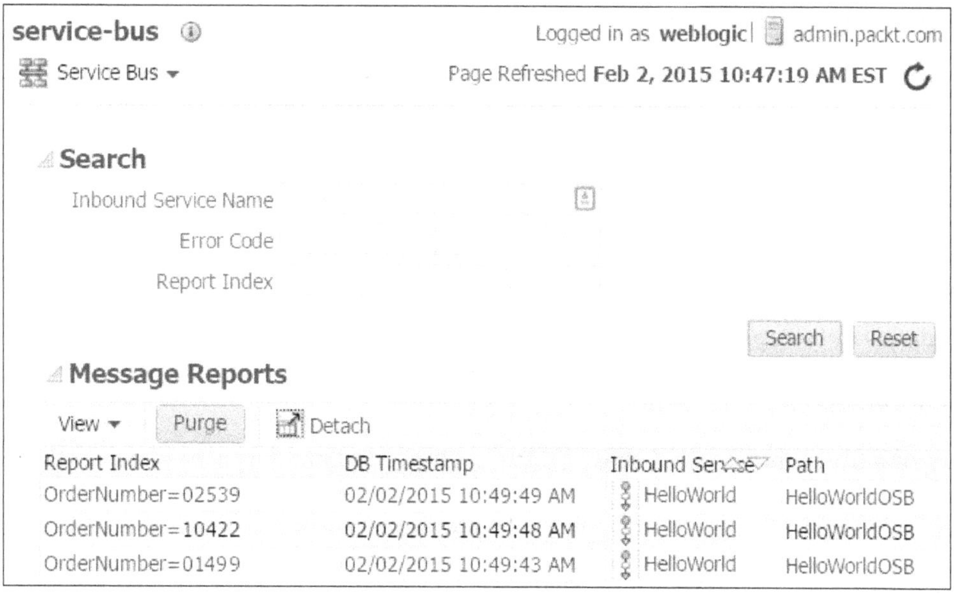

service-bus ⓘ

Logged in as **weblogic**| admin.packt.com

Service Bus ▾

Page Refreshed **Feb 2, 2015 10:47:19 AM EST** ↻

◢ **Search**

Inbound Service Name	
Error Code	
Report Index	

Search   Reset

◢ **Message Reports**

View ▾   Purge   Detach

Report Index	DB Timestamp	Inbound Service	Path
OrderNumber=02539	02/02/2015 10:49:49 AM	HelloWorld	HelloWorldOSB
OrderNumber=10422	02/02/2015 10:49:48 AM	HelloWorld	HelloWorldOSB
OrderNumber=01499	02/02/2015 10:49:43 AM	HelloWorld	HelloWorldOSB

Figure 4-16. Searching through captured Report actions

In Fusion Middleware Control, simply navigate to **SOA | service-bus | Message Reports**, where a list of all Report actions are displayed. In the preceding screenshot, we can also see numerous order numbers. In this example, administrators can search by a Report Index type to locate a specific order number. From there, clicking on **Report Index** unveils additional details surrounding this OSB instance.

The Report operational setting simply enables or disables message reporting for pipelines.

> There is considerable overhead for Report actions for the mere fact that the OSB service is no longer stateless, as this data must be persisted.

Therefore, Report actions may not be ideal for extremely high-volume transactions. The Report operational setting is enabled by default.

Execution Tracing

The Execution Tracing operational setting is also used to enable or disable execution tracing for pipelines and split-joins. Execution tracing is disabled by default, but when enabled, gives the administrator the ability to troubleshoot a message flow. Information, such as a stage name, pipeline or route node name, and the current message context, is captured.

Caching

Caching is only applicable for business services. The Caching operational setting simply enables or disables result caching for a business service at runtime. OSB uses coherence in the backend as its cache.

It is generally recommended that you use caching for data that is not frequently updated. For example, if you are an online retailer, the description of your product being sold rarely changes, and lookups to product descriptions may benefit from the 15% to 25% performance gain achieved by leveraging caching. The normal behavior of the caching feature is that it does not require re-invoking the backend until the data in the cache expires.

Advanced debugging in OSB

Oracle Service Bus also allows advanced debugging by letting you enable and disable debug flags for various modules. These flags are present in either `alsbdebug.xml` (component-related debug flags) or `configwkdebug.xml` (configuration-related debug flags). These files are located in the root directory of the domain where OSB is configured. By default, all component and configuration debug flags are set to `false`. The following XML markup provides a snippet of `alsbdebug.xml` with debugging turned on for the throttling and caching modules:

```
<java:sb-debug-logger xmlns:java='java:com.bea.wli.debug'>

  <java:alsb-throttling-debug>true</java:alsb-throttling-debug>

  <java:alsb-result-caching-debug>true</java:alsb-result-caching-debug>

</java:sb-debug-logger>
```

Changes to debug log configuration files require a server restart to take effect.

Summary

This chapter focused on various functions the administrator can perform through Oracle SOA Suite 12*c* to manage SOA composites and OSB services. Most of these runtime settings are manipulated through Fusion Middleware Control and any change typically takes effect immediately. To summarize, the following management areas were covered:

- Understanding SOA composite revisions and how the endpoint URL is composed as a result
- Setting the default revision for a SOA composite
- Starting up, shutting down, retiring, and activating a SOA composite
- Deleting SOA composite instances
- Best practices for SOA partition management, including assigning partitions to Work Group Managers
- Securing access to SOA partitions
- Manipulating various OSB operational settings at runtime, including monitoring, aggregation interval, SLA alerts, message tracing, pipeline alerts, logging, reports, execution tracing, caching and so on

5
Deploying Code

Oracle SOA Suite 12*c* has grown to include numerous component types and objects, each of these naturally requiring some form of a deployment process. Though developers traditionally use JDeveloper for deployment, this is not ideal in an enterprise with multiple environments. Thus, automating deployments becomes a necessity.

This chapter focuses on the three most commonly developed object types of SOA Suite 12*c*: SOA composite applications, OSB services, and BAM artifacts. We cover multiple ways each of these can be deployed, giving the administrator the flexibility of choosing the option that best suits their environment.

We describe in detail how to automate the deployment of these components:

- Deploying SOA composites, including the use of configuration plans
- Deploying OSB services, including the use of customization files
- Deploying BAM artifacts
- Exporting and importing MDS artifacts

Instructions to deploy components to a single node or clustered environments are generally the same.

Deploying SOA composites

Developers typically create composite applications that are packaged into single deployable JAR files. These applications can contain any number of service components that include BPEL or BPMN processes, mediator services, human tasks and workflows, and business rules. Composites include logic and code that form the foundation of SOA-based integrations.

Deployment tools

There are a number of different tools that can be used to deploy code. However, some are better suited in providing a consistent deployment process. The tools include: JDeveloper, Fusion Middleware Control, Ant, and WLST.

As an administrator performing deployments, JDeveloper and Fusion Middleware Control provide an ancillary role. Developers deploy to certain non-production environments primarily using the former, and the latter should only be used in rare cases, if ever, for production deployments. Knowing how to deploy from Fusion Middleware Control could prove useful in a few cases though.

Path to deployment

To many, the act of deploying code into an environment is a one-step process of deployment. However, in reality, there are a number of phases that take place along the way, some of which could be further broken down, but for our purposes, we will treat them as a single unit. These phases include: setup, customization, compilation, packaging, and deployment.

- **Setup**: This should ideally be done only once. The setup phase guarantees that all the resources you need are available to repeatedly deploy code. It generally involves the installation of a tool that will be used for the deployment. Sometimes, this will involve writing some custom scripts that may be required for your corporate environment.

- **Customization**: This refers to the incorporation of environment-specific values into the code prior to compilation. For example, the code may include references to a development environment that need to be substituted with values of the production environment. Using configuration plans (for SOA composites) or customizations files (for OSB projects) are two fairly common approaches. Leveraging tools such as Ant detokenization is equally acceptable.

- **Compilation**: In this context, compilation is a complex set of operations that interprets developers' code and turns it into commands that the JVM can understand, will produce any of our classes needed, and place most of it into a target folder. Often, however, this step will be wrapped up into the packaging phase since it is largely dependent upon compilation.

- **Packaging**: This takes all of the compiled classes and configuration files and places them into a single JAR file that can then be deployed.

- **Deployment**: This is the final step in our process and also the most pivotal one. This is the last chance to make changes for environment-specific details that can be reproduced for consistency. Any changes made after the deployment won't be guaranteed to be version controlled.

Deploying from Fusion Middleware Control

Composites are deployed (or redeployed) as JAR files. In fact, these deployable JAR files are also referred to as SOA archives or SARs. Oracle Enterprise Manager Fusion Middleware Control provides the ability to deploy, redeploy, and undeploy a SAR from the convenience and simplicity of a web browser. Though deploying via the console is extremely easy, two important points should be considered:

- SARs may include environment-specific information bundled within the JAR file. For example, the composite may include a reference to an external web service. The URL of this web service is hardcoded in to the JAR file; deploying the same JAR file to a development and a production server may not be valid.

- Deploying multiple composites via the console is cumbersome and time consuming. Using Ant is the preferred method to deploy multiple SARs.

Deploying a composite

To deploy a single composite from the console, we can have a look at the following procedure:

1. Log in to Oracle Enterprise Manager Fusion Middleware Control at `http://adminhost:7001/em`.

2. On the navigator, expand **Farm_[Domain]** | **SOA** and right-click on **soa-infra**.

3. Navigate to **SOA Deployment** | **Deploy**.

4. In the field labeled **Archive is on the machine where the web browser is running,** click on the **Choose File** button and locate your SAR file, as shown in the following screenshot (for example, `C:\svn\SOA12c\HelloWorld\ deploy\sca_HelloWorld_rev1.0.jar`):

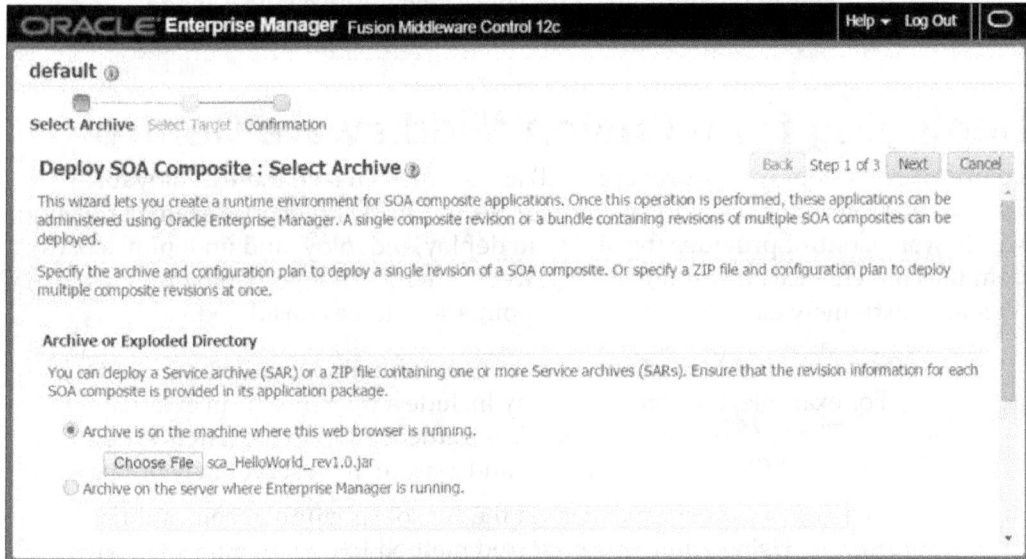

Figure 5.1: Selecting a SAR to deploy

5. Click on the **Next** button.

6. From the drop-down list, select the partition you wish to deploy this composite to.

7. Click on the **Next** button.

8. Choose the **Deploy as default revision** or **Do not change the default revision** radio buttons.

9. Click on the **Deploy** button.

When a composite is deployed, an entry is logged in the `soa_server1-diagnostic.log` file (typically located under `$MW_HOME/user_projects/domains/soa_domain/servers/soa_server1/logs/`) as follows:

```
[2015-02-01T16:13:18.092-05:00] [soa_server1] [NOTIFICATION] []
[oracle.integration.platform.blocks.deploy] [tid: DaemonWorkThread:
'2' of WorkManager: 'wm/SOAWorkManager'] [userId: <anonymous>] [ecid:
9027493d-b37d-4795-a996-331a7c6ae275-00000004,0:513] [APP: soa-infra]
Publishing deploy event for default/HelloWorld!1.0*soa_d91d1c4c-7a7b-
4405-9b6e-6dd5a053bfbb
```

Once it is deployed, the service becomes available immediately. If the composite uses inbound resources, such as an inbound JMS Adapter that consumes from a JMS destination, the consumption begins immediately.

Redeploying a composite

To redeploy a single composite from the console, follow these steps:

1. On the navigator, navigate to **Farm_[Domain] | SOA | soa-infra**.

2. Expand the partition (for example, `default`) and right-click on the composite name you wish to undeploy (for example, `HelloWorld`).

3. Navigate to **SOA Deployment | Redeploy**.

4. In the field labeled **Archive is on the machine where the web browser is running**, click on the **Browse** button and locate your SAR file (for example, `C:\svn\SOA12c\HelloWorld\deploy\sca_HelloWorld_rev1.0.jar`).

5. Click on the **Next** button.

6. Choose the **Deploy as default revision** or **Do not change the default revision** radio buttons.

7. Click on the **Redeploy** button.

Redeploying a composite overwrites the existing revision. The state of the instance of the older revision is changed to stale.

Undeploying a composite

To undeploy a single composite from the console, go through the following steps:

1. On the navigator, expand **Farm_[Domain] | SOA | soa-infra**.

2. Expand the partition (for example, `default`) and right-click on the composite name you wish to undeploy (for example, `HelloWorld`).

3. Navigate to **SOA Deployment | Undeploy**.

4. Click on the **Undeploy** button.

In addition to the service no longer being available, undeploying a composite (or a composite revision) changes the state of all historical instances to stale. If the default revision of the composite is undeployed, the next available revision of the composite becomes the default one.

Deploying with Ant

All component management tasks that can be performed manually through the web-based Oracle Enterprise Manager Fusion Middleware Control console can also be executed with a script through the command-line utility Ant. In this section, we describe how to use Ant to start up, shut down, activate, and retire composites as well as package and deploy them. Oracle SOA Suite 12*c* ships all the necessary Ant scripts to perform these tasks, and they are quite easy to use.

Setting up the environment

Here, we describe how to set up a Linux environment to allow you to run your Ant commands through the command line. The Ant scripts do not have to be installed on the same machine running Oracle SOA Suite 12*c*. In fact, it is not unusual to dedicate a single machine or server that would host your Ant scripts, allowing you to centralize the startup, shutdown, and deployment of your SOA composites to multiple target environments.

Setting up the environment path for Ant

In your environment, we assume that Oracle SOA Suite 12*c* is installed, which is recommended as it will include all the required binaries to run Ant. The Middleware Home, Oracle SOA Suite 12*c* Home, Java Home, WebLogic Server username and password, and SOA server host and port will need to be updated appropriately to reflect your environment. Directory locations and the JDK version may differ depending on the patchset level of your Oracle SOA Suite 12*c* installation. These commands must be executed to set your environment paths before running any Ant command.

In this chapter, we assume that your code resides under $CODE and simply follow the next steps to set up the environment:

1. To set up your environment, we recommend that you first create a setAntEnv.sh shell script with the following content:

    ```
    export USERNAME=weblogic
    export PASSWORD=welcome1
    export SOAHOST=soahost1
    export SOAPORT=8001
    export SOAURL=http://${SOAHOST}:${SOAPORT}
    export CODE=/home/oracle/code
    export MW_HOME=/u01/app/oracle/middleware
    export ORACLE_HOME=$MW_HOME/soa
    ```

```
export JAVA_HOME=$MW_HOME/jdk1.7.0_15

export ANT_HOME=$MW_HOME/oracle_common/modules/org.apache.
ant_1.9.2

export PATH=$JAVA_HOME/bin:$ANT_HOME/bin:$ANT_HOME/lib:$PATH:.
```

2. Make sure to update the parameter values to reflect your actual environment and installation.

3. Change the permissions of the script to **executable**:

```
chmod 750 setAntEnv.sh
```

4. Prior to running any Ant command in the remainder of this section, simply source this shell script once to set the environment for your session as follows:

```
source setAntEnv.sh
```

5. Finally, make sure that you change to the $ORACLE_HOME/bin directory before running any of the Ant commands:

```
cd $ORACLE_HOME/bin
```

All the commands in the remainder of this chapter will be based on Linux.

Packaging a composite

Packaging a SOA composite project effectively involves validating, compiling, and eventually building the project into a single deployable JAR file. To package the HelloWorld composite application in Linux, simply run:

```
ant -f ant-sca-package.xml package -DcompositeDir=$CODE/HelloWorld/SOA
-DcompositeName=HelloWorld -Drevision=1.0
```

If no errors are encountered, you should expect to find the sca_HelloWorld_rev1.0.jar file under the $CODE/HelloWorld/SOA/deploy directory.

Deploying a composite

Now that the composite application is packaged, the SAR (or JAR file) can be deployed. The Ant command references the path to the SAR directly (in Linux), as shown here:

```
ant -f ant-sca-deploy.xml deploy -DserverURL=$SOAURL/soa-infra/deployer
-Duser=$USERNAME -Dpassword=$PASSWORD -DsarLocation=$CODE/HelloWorld/SOA/
deploy/sca_HelloWorld_rev1.0.jar -Dpartition=default -Doverwrite=true
-DforceDefault=true
```

As shown in these examples, the server URL, username, and password to the Oracle SOA Suite 12*c* runtime environment must be supplied. The fully qualified path to the SAR file must be provided in the sarLocation argument. Similar to deploying a composite to the console, you must specify the partition on which you want to deploy. In this example, you can see that we do not provide a revision for the composite. This is because the revision was already specified during packaging time.

The overwrite argument specifies whether you want to overwrite the composite already deployed to the server and the forceDefault argument specifies whether you want this revision to be set as the default revision once it is deployed.

Undeploying a composite

A composite can be undeployed via Ant as well. On Linux, this is done by simply running this command:

```
ant -f ant-sca-deploy.xml undeploy -DserverURL=$SOAURL/soa-infra/
deployer -Duser=$USERNAME -Dpassword=$PASSWORD -DcompositeName=HelloWorld
-Dpartition=default -Drevision=1.0
```

Deploying with WLST

The WebLogic Server Tool, more commonly known as WLST, uses Jython, which allows Python scripts to be executed, but can also be used interactively to issue ad hoc commands. In the transition to WebLogic Server 12*c*, the tool remains largely unchanged. It can, however, provide a valuable asset to administrators who are more comfortable with WLST. Behind the scenes, these WSLT commands actually invoke the Ant scripts.

Setting up the environment

WebLogic Server, SOA Suite, and JDeveloper installations come shipped with a wlst.sh script. To deploy SOA composites using WLST, you must run the script from the bin subdirectory in the Oracle Home directory of the SOA Suite product as follows:

```
export MW_HOME=/u01/app/oracle/middleware
export ORACLE_HOME=$MW_HOME/soa
cd $ORACLE_HOME/bin
$ORACLE_HOME/common/bin/wlst.sh
wls:/offline>
wls:/offline>connect()
```

Once you are connected and in the offline mode, you must connect to the domain by providing your WebLogic username, password, and server URL (for example, `t3://adminhost:7001`).

Packaging a composite

To package the `HelloWorld` composite application in WLST, simply run:

```
sca_package ("/home/oracle/code/HelloWorld/SOA", "HelloWorld", "1.0",
oracleHome="/u01/app/oracle/middleware/soa")
```

The first parameter is the path to the source code of your composite. The second parameter is the name of the composite. The third is the composite revision number, whether it be 1.0, 1.1, and so on. If no errors are encountered, you should expect to find `sca_HelloWorld_rev1.0.jar` under the `$CODE/HelloWorld/SOA/deploy` directory.

Deploying a composite

Now that you have a packaged composite application, the JAR file can be deployed. The WLST command to deploy the composite is:

```
sca_deployComposite("http://soahost1:8001", "/home/oracle/code/
HelloWorld/SOA/deploy/sca_HelloWorld_rev1.0.jar", true, user="weblogic",
password="password123", partition="default")
```

The first parameter is SOAURL, taking the format of `http://host:port`. This is the port of the SOA server, not the AdminServer. The SARFILE parameter should be the absolute path to the JAR file that needs to be deployed.

> The WLST commands actually invoke the underlying Ant scripts and thus should use the HTTP protocol for the SOAURL parameter.

The next parameter is the `overwrite` parameter, a Boolean value that determines whether to overwrite the existing composite or not. The last parameters are simply username, password, and the target partition in which to deploy the composite.

Undeploying a composite

A composite can be undeployed via WLST as well. This is done by running this command:

```
sca_undeployComposite("http://soahost1:8001", "HelloWorld", "1.0",
user="weblogic", password="password123", partition="default")
```

The parameters here are nearly identical to that of the deployment command, with the only difference being the REVISION parameter that identifies which revision to undeploy.

Using configuration plans

Promoting code refers to the activity of taking code from one environment, such as the development environment, and deploying it to the next one, such as the test environment. A typical software development promotion lifecycle sees code move from development to test to QA (quality assurance) to production. As code is successfully tested in one environment, it is deployed to the next.

Why do we need configuration plans?

Unlike Java applications, SOA composite applications do not rely on property files to maintain environment-specific configuration. Many SOA projects may include references to other external services, for example, `http://payment-processing-server-dev:7777/proc/servlet/createCustomer`. As you can see from this example URL, the developer is referencing some external development server as identified by the hostname `payment-processing-server-dev`. This URL is hardcoded within the code and ultimately included within the deployable SAR. Prior to deploying this code to the test environment, the administrator must find a way to ensure that the test URL is referenced instead (which may have a different host, port, and protocol), as shown here: `https://payment-processing-server-test:7778/proc/servlet/createCustomer`.

The SAR may potentially have other environment-specific settings, such as URLs, JNDIs, and hostnames hardcoded in the SAR. One option is to manually extract the contents of the JAR file, manually edit all entries, and re-JAR them. This is a manual, cumbersome, and error-prone process. Another approach is to attach a configuration plan to your composite at deployment.

The configuration plan is a single XML file that is attached to the SAR at deployment time. It is similar to a search-and-replace functionality, ensuring that the references of one environment (such as development) are replaced with the next one (such as the test environment).

Understanding configuration plan contents

The following `cfgplan_test.xml` file is a configuration plan designed to be attached to the SAR at deployment time. It is used when deploying code that is written against a development environment to a test environment:

```xml
<?xml version="1.0" encoding="UTF-8"?>
<SOAConfigPlan xmlns:jca="http://platform.integration.oracle/blocks/
adapter/fw/metadata"
               xmlns:wsp="http://schemas.xmlsoap.org/ws/2004/09/
policy"
               xmlns:orawsp="http://schemas.oracle.com/ws/2006/01/
policy"
               xmlns:edl="http://schemas.oracle.com/events/edl"
               xmlns="http://schemas.oracle.com/soa/configplan">

  <composite name="*">

    <import>
      <searchReplace>
        <search>http://soa12cdev:8001</search>
        <replace>http://soa12ctest:8001</replace>
      </searchReplace>
    </import>

    <service name="readFile">
      <binding type="*">
        <property name="inFileFolder">
          <replace>/u01/input/test</replace>
        </property>
      </binding>
    </service>

    <reference name="*">
      <binding type="ws">
        <attribute name="location">
          <searchReplace>
            <search> http://payment-processing-server-dev:7777/proc/
servlet</search>
            <replace> https://payment-processing-server-test:7778/
proc/servlet</replace>
          </searchReplace>
        </attribute>
      </binding>
    </reference>
```

```
      </composite>

  <wsdlAndSchema name="HelloWorld.wsdl|xsd/HelloWorld.xsd">
    <searchReplace>
      <search>sharedSchemaServerDev</search>
      <replace>sharedSchemaServerTest</replace>
    </searchReplace>
    <searchReplace>
      <search>7777</search>
      <replace>80</replace>
    </searchReplace>
  </wsdlAndSchema>
</SOAConfigPlan>
```

The file contains two main sections: composite and wsdlAndSchema. All entries within the <composite> tags are applied to the composite.xml file in the SOA composite application. In this example, the <wsdlAndSchema> tag is specifically applied to the HelloWorld.wsdl and xsd/HelloWorld.xsd files within the project.

Let's walk through the preceding configuration plan in some detail:

- The <composite name="*"> tag: This indicates that no matter which composite this configuration plan is attached to, the search-replace rules will apply to all, designated by the *. Alternatively, it is possible to create different rules that apply to different composites such as:

```
<composite "HelloWorld1">

  <import>

    <searchReplace>

      <search>http://soa12cdev:8001</search>

      <replace>http://soa12ctest:8001</replace>

    </searchReplace>

  </import>

</composite "HelloWorld1">

<composite "HelloWorld2">

  <import>

    <searchReplace>

      <search>http://soa12cdev:8001</search>

      <replace>http://soa12ctest:8001</replace>

    </searchReplace>

  </import>

</composite "HelloWorld2">
```

The only reason to separate composite configuration as shown here is if the search-replace rules are different for each composite. If you do not envision any difference in the search-replace rules, we recommend that you stick to `<composite "*">` instead in order to maintain simplicity.

- The `<import>` tag: The `import` tag is a sub element of the `<composite>` tag. Essentially, any search-replace rule within the `<import>` tag applies to the `<import>` sections in `composite.xml`. You can have any number of search-replace elements here.

- The `<service>` tag: In this, all composites will likely have a service. A service definition is synonymous with the input of the composite. A composite may have multiple services (for multiple interfaces), where each can be invoked separately.

  In the configuration plan, the `<service>` and `<reference>` tags use similar approaches. In the preceding example, there appears to be an inbound File Adapter that has an `inFileFolder` property. The code may be hardcoded with the folder property `/u01/input/dev`. But here, the configuration plan will overwrite that property with the setting of `/u01/input/test` as the input folder.

- The `<reference>` tag: Composite references refer to other resources such as another web service or an adapter. A composite may have zero references or have many. Often, the reference can be a fully qualified URL to some other service either on the same server or a different one. Here, the configuration plan will replace all references to `http://payment-processing-server-dev:7777/proc/servlet` (the development server) with `https://payment-processing-server-test:7778/proc/servlet` (the test server).

Attaching a configuration plan

Attaching a configuration plan is quite simple. The Ant command to deploy a composite application does not change and only an additional argument is required, which is the reference to the fully qualified path to the configuration plan:

```
ant -f ant-sca-deploy.xml deploy -DserverURL=$SOAURL/soa-infra/deployer
-Duser=$USERNAME -Dpassword=$PASSWORD -DsarLocation=$CODE/HelloWorld/SOA/
deploy/sca_HelloWorld_rev1.0.jar -Dpartition=default -Doverwrite=true
-DforceDefault=true -Dconfigplan=/tmp/cfgplan_test.xml
```

The recommended approach to using configuration plans

The approach to manage code promotion effectively involves following a simple process to maintain consistency and ensure proper substitution of environment-specific settings and deployment to other environments.

The summarized approach we recommend is as follows:

- Developers should ensure that all URLs, JNDIs, hostnames, ports, and so on reference development environments and they should try to remain as consistent as possible.

  For example, if multiple developers are working on multiple pieces of code that reference the same external service, they should try to be as consistent as possible. Say, for example, that the following reference is used:

  ```
  http://payment-processing-server-dev:7777/proc/servlet
  ```

  They should avoid being inconsistent across their code:

  ```
  http://payment-processing-server-dev.somedomain.org:7777/proc/
  servlet
  ```

  ```
  http://PAYMENT-PROCESSING-SERVER-DEV:7777/proc/servlet
  ```

  ```
  https://payment-processing-server-dev:7778/proc/servlet
  ```

  The lack of consistency only means that additional search-replace statements will need to be added in the configuration plans.

- Any environment-specific setting used by developers (such as the service URL in the preceding step) should be communicated to the Oracle SOA Suite 12*c* administrator.

- The Oracle SOA Suite 12*c* administrator should create a configuration plan for every environment:

  - Test – cfgplan_test.xml
  - QA – cfgplan_qa.xml
  - Prod – cfgplan_prod.xml

  The cfgplan_test.xml configuration plan should replace all development environment settings with the test equivalent. The cfgplan_qa.xml plan should, similarly, replace all development environment settings that are QA equivalent. The cfgplan_prod.xml plan should do the same.

Thus, the code will always maintain development environment-specific settings, and it is the configuration plan that will ensure that these settings are replaced appropriately when the code is deployed to the target environment.

- Every time a new environment-specific setting is used, the administrator should ensure that it is added to each of the configuration plans.

- The administrator should always attach a configuration plan to every deployment.

Exemplying the usage of configuration plans

In this example, we will demonstrate the usage of configuration plans in a real-world scenario.

We have a simple HelloWorld BPEL project already deployed to both our development and test servers, as shown in *Figure 5.2*. On our development server, this project is accessible at `http://soa12cDEV:8001/soa-infra/services/default/HelloWorldBPEL/helloworld_client_ep?WSDL`.

On our test server, it is accessible here, with only the hostname being changed:

`http://soa12cTEST:8001/soa-infra/services/default/HelloWorldBPEL/helloworld_client_ep?WSDL`

As shown in the following figure, the developer creates a new Mediator project that invokes this BPEL service and deploys it to the development server:

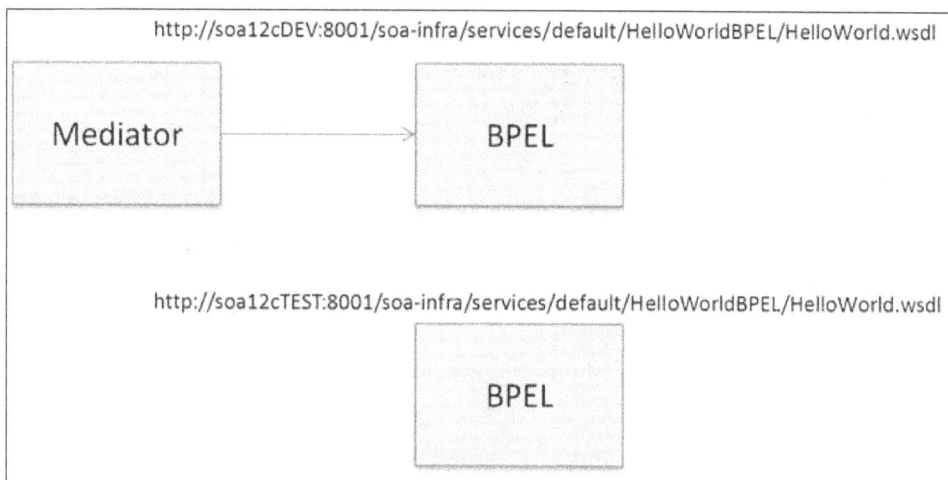

Figure 5.2: The Mediator composite invoking a BPEL composite in a development environment

Our goal, as the administrator, is to deploy this same Mediator project to the test server and change its references to the test environment accordingly.

Once the Mediator project is saved, the project will include two files with hardcoded URLs. The `composite.xml` file has the following code snippet:

```
<reference name="HelloWorldBPEL_BPEL"
            ui:wsdlLocation="http://soa12cdev:8001/soa-infra/
services/default/HelloWorldBPEL/HelloWorldBPEL.wsdl">
   <interface.wsdl interface="http://xmlns.oracle.com/SOA12c/
HelloWorldBPEL/HelloWorld#wsdl.interface(HelloWorld)"/>
   <binding.ws port="http://xmlns.oracle.com/SOA12c/HelloWorldBPEL/
HelloWorld#wsdl.endpoint(helloworld_client_ep/HelloWorld_pt)"
            location="http://soa12cdev:8001/soa-infra/services/
default/HelloWorldBPEL/helloworld_client_ep?WSDL"
            soapVersion="1.1">
     <property name="weblogic.wsee.wsat.transaction.flowOption"
            type="xs:string" many="false">WSDLDriven</property>
   </binding.ws>
</reference>
```

And the `Mediator1.componentType` file in the same project includes the following:

```
<reference name="HelloWorld_BPEL"
            ui:wsdlLocation="http://soa12cDEV:8001/soa-infra/services/
default/HelloWorldBPEL/HelloWorld.wsdl">
   <interface.wsdl interface="http://xmlns.oracle.com/SOA12c/
HelloWorldBPEL/HelloWorld#wsdl.interface(HelloWorld)"/>
</reference>
```

Prior to deploying this to the test server, we first create a `cfgplan_test.xml` configuration plan with the following content:

```
<?xml version="1.0" encoding="UTF-8"?>
<SOAConfigPlan xmlns:jca="http://platform.integration.oracle/blocks/
adapter/fw/metadata"
              xmlns:wsp="http://schemas.xmlsoap.org/ws/2004/09/
policy"
              xmlns:orawsp="http://schemas.oracle.com/ws/2006/01/
policy"
              xmlns:edl="http://schemas.oracle.com/events/edl"
              xmlns="http://schemas.oracle.com/soa/configplan">

   <composite name="*">

     <import>
       <searchReplace>
```

```
      <search>http://soa12cDEV:8001</search>
      <replace>http://soa12cTEST:8001</replace>
    </searchReplace>
  </import>

  <reference name="*">
    <binding type="ws">
      <attribute name="location">
        <searchReplace>
          <search>http://soa12cDEV:8001</search>
          <replace>http://soa12cTEST:8001</replace>
        </searchReplace>
      </attribute>
    </binding>
  </reference>
</composite>


</SOAConfigPlan>
```

The configuration plan replaces all references of `http://soa12cDEV:8001` to the test server's equivalent `http://soa12cTEST:8001`.

We finally deploy the Mediator project to the test environment, attaching the configuration plan that has just been created:

```
cd $ORACLE_HOME/bin

ant -f ant-sca-deploy.xml deploy -Duser=$USERNAME -Dpassword=$PASSWORD
-DserverURL=$SOAURL/soa-infra/deployer -DsarLocation=$CODE/HelloWorld_
Mediator/deploy/sca_HelloWorld_Mediator_rev1.0.jar -Dpartition=default
-Doverwrite=true -DforceDefault=true -Dconfigplan=/tmp/cfgplan_test.xml
```

By attaching the configuration plan, the code originally developed to reference development server-specific URLs is now deployed to the test server that references test-specific URLs.

Deploying OSB projects

With the transition to SOA Suite 12*c*, OSB development is finally supported in JDeveloper. As with SOA composites, JDeveloper has the ability to deploy OSB code, but it is not the recommended method for administrators. Though OSB projects can be deployed through a web-based console, using WLST via the command line allows us to create repeatable scripts for a more expedient and automated deployment process.

[⟋ SOA composites are deployed and undeployed. OSB services are imported and deleted. They essentially mean the same thing.]

Importing from the Oracle Service Bus Console

OSB projects are imported as JAR files. Fusion Middleware Control is unfortunately not used to deploy OSB projects and is instead performed through the Oracle Service Bus Console. It provides the ability to import and delete an OSB project from the convenience and simplicity of a web browser.

[⟋ While SOA composites are deployed through Fusion Middleware Control, OSB services are imported through the Service Bus Console.]

Importing an OSB service

To import a single OSB service from the console, go through the following steps:

1. Navigate to the Oracle Service Bus Console at `http://adminhost:7001/servicebus`.
2. Click on **Create** to create a session.
3. Right-click on **All Projects** and navigate to **Import | Config Jar**.
4. Click on the **Choose File** button and locate the JAR file on your local filesystem; then click on the **Next** button.
5. Click on the **Import** button.
6. Click on the **Close** tab.
7. Click on the **Activate** button and then click on **Activate** again to commit the changes.

Deleting an OSB service

To delete a single OSB service from the console, perform the following steps:

1. Navigate to the Oracle Service Bus Console at `http://adminhost:7001/servicebus`.
2. Click on **Create** to create a session.

3. Under **All Projects**, right-click on the project name you would like to delete and click on **Delete**.

4. Click on the **Yes** tab.

5. Click on the **Activate** button and then click on **Activate** again to commit the changes.

Deploying with WLST

The WLST script to import and delete OSB services is largely similar to those created for SOA Suite 11*g* with some minor differences.

Setting up the environment

WebLogic Server, SOA Suite, and JDeveloper installations come shipped with a `wlst.sh` script. The following environment settings must be set up prior to the execution of the `import` and `delete` commands:

```
export MW_HOME=/u01/app/oracle/middleware

export ORACLE_COMMON_HOME=$MW_HOME/oracle_common

export OSB_HOME=$MW_HOME/osb

export CLASSPATH=$OSB_HOME/lib/modules/oracle.servicebus.kernel-wls.
jar:$CLASSPATH

export CLASSPATH=$MW_HOME/wlserver/modules/com.bea.core.
utils_2.3.0.0.jar:$CLASSPATH

export CLASSPATH=$MW_HOME/wlserver/modules/com.bea.core.utils.
full_2.3.0.0.jar:$CLASSPATH

export CLASSPATH=$MW_HOME/wlserver/server/lib/weblogic.jar:$CLASSPATH

export CLASSPATH=$OSB_HOME/lib/modules/oracle.servicebus.kernel-api.
jar:$CLASSPATH

export CLASSPATH=$OSB_HOME/lib/modules/oracle.servicebus.configfwk.
jar:$CLASSPATH
```

Modify the `$MW_HOME` variable to reflect your environment. These environment settings can be scripted or included in your profile script for reuse.

Creating a customization file

Customization files are used to assign or replace environment values to an OSB deployment after it has been deployed. This feature is similar to the configuration plan for SOA composites and simplifies the deployment of an OSB service to multiple environments without the need to create different versions of the code.

In this section, our customization file will be blank. This means that no assignment or substitution of settings in our code is expected, so the OSB project will be deployed unchanged. Later in this chapter, we explain OSB customization files and describe how to tailor them to suit your needs.

Create the `customize.xml` file with the following content:

```
<?xml version="1.0" encoding="UTF-8"?>
<cus:Customizations xmlns:cus="http://www.bea.com/wli/config/
customizations" xmlns:xsi="http://www.w3.org/2001/XMLSchema-instance"
xmlns:xt="http://www.bea.com/wli/config/xmltypes">
</cus:Customizations>
```

Creating an import configuration file

The `envcode.properties` file is a custom-created file that references both your OSB code and your OSB environment.

Create the `envcode.properties` file with the following content, replacing the highlighted values to reflect the location of your OSB project and environment settings:

```
adminUrl=t3://soahost1:7001
importUser=weblogic
importPassword=welcome1
importJar=/home/oracle/code/HelloWorldOSB.jar
customizationFile=customize.xml
```

Downloading the import.py script

Mark Nelson, an architect in the Fusion Middleware Central Development team at Oracle, had originally written the `import.py` script for OSB 11*g*, which can be run unchanged in the 12*c* version as long as the instructions described earlier are followed.

Download the `import.py` script from:

```
https://redstack.wordpress.com/2011/08/25/getting-started-with-
continuous-integration-for-osb/
```

Importing an OSB service

Ensure that the `customize.xml`, `envcode.properties`, and `import.py` scripts are located in the same directory.

The WLST command to import the OSB service defined in `envcode.properties` is:

```
$ORACLE_COMMON_HOME/oracle_common/common/bin/wlst.sh import.py
envcode.properties
```

Deleting an OSB service

The `import.py` script is specific to deploying OSB services. An additional script modeled from this script called `delete.py` has been created to support the deletion of an OSB service.

Download the `delete.py` script from: `http://www.raastech.com/packt/scripts/delete.py`.

The WLST command to delete the OSB service defined in `envcode.properties` is:

```
$ORACLE_COMMON_HOME/oracle_common/common/bin/wlst.sh delete.py
envcode.properties
```

Using customization files

The OSB project, in the form of a JAR file, may include environment-specific information bundled within it. For example, the service may reference a web service on a third-party external development server. The URL of this web service is hardcoded in the OSB project; importing the same JAR file to a production server would not be valid. Similar to configuration plans in SOA composites, customization files are used in conjunction with OSB services to address this concern.

Generally speaking, the process of deploying any OSB project involves the following steps:

1. The developer creates a deployable OSB project file (for example, `HelloWorldOSB.jar`).

2. The developer includes a customization file (for example, `OSBCustomizationFile.xml`).

3. The administrator creates customization files for each environment, updating each one with the settings specific to that environment. For example:
   - `OSBCustomizationFile_DEV.xml`
   - `OSBCustomizationFile_QA.xml`
   - `OSBCustomizationFile_PROD.xml`

4. The administrator deploys the OSB project in one of two ways:

   ○ Use WLST to deploy the OSB project, attaching the customization file of the particular target environment during the deployment.

   ○ Use the Oracle Service Bus Console to deploy the OSB project, followed by manually importing the customization file through the console.

In either case, the customization file is a necessary element during the process of deployment.

Why do we need customization files?

Unlike Java applications, OSB projects do not rely on property files to maintain environment-specific configuration. Many OSB projects may include references to other external services, for example, `http://payment-processing-server-dev:7777/proc/servlet/createCustomer`. As you can see from this example URL, the developer is referencing some external development server as identified by the `payment-processing-server-dev` hostname. This may be hardcoded in the business service of the OSB project.

Though the administrator can manually update the business service URL at runtime to reflect the next environment, this is not ideal. Fortunately, customization files can be used to indicate that the test environment should be using `https://payment-processing-server-test:7778/proc/servlet/createCustomer` for the business service instead.

The customization file is a single XML file that is either attached to the deployment when using WLST as described earlier or it could be applied via the Oracle Service Bus Console at any time. Customization files may include instructions to replace the properties of multiple OSB projects already deployed to the OSB server. We recommend you to create separate customization files for every environment, for example, `customization_test.xml` for the test environment, `customization_qa.xml` for the QA environment, and so on.

> Customization files may include customizations for one or more OSB services.

The customization file may be quite large and include a large number of settings, but a snippet is shown here:

```
<cus:customization xsi:type="cus:EnvValueActionsCustomizationType">
  <cus:actions>
    <xt:replace>
```

```
        <xt:envValueType>Service URI Table</xt:envValueType>
        <xt:value xsi:type="tran:URITableType" xmlns:tran="http://www.
bea.com/wli/sb/transports">
            <tran:tableElement>
                <tran:URI>jms://soa12cDEV:8001/weblogic.jms.
XAConnectionFactory/jms/CustomerQ</tran:URI>
            </tran:tableElement>
        </xt:value>
    </xt:replace>
    <xt:replace>
        <xt:envValueType>Service Retry Count</xt:envValueType>
        <xt:value xsi:type="xs:string" xmlns:xs="http://www.w3.org/2001/
XMLSchema">3</xt:value>
    </xt:replace>
  </cus:actions>
</cus:customization>
```

The recommended course of action is to simply export the customization file from the OSB console and customize it to your needs, as it will include all the settings that could require modification.

In the preceding snippet, there is a replace action to substitute the `Service URI Table` value, which is essentially the fully qualified URI for a JMS queue. Another replace action is also included that sets the value of `Service Retry Count` to 3. Thus, settings for a development, test, QA, and production environment can be different, and hence the need to maintain customization files for each environment is necessary.

Exporting a customization file through the OSB Console

The simplest way to generate a customization file is by exporting it from the Oracle Service Bus Console. This, of course, assumes that the project already exists on the server, so this action is generally performed on the development server to create this first customization file.

To export a customization file from the Oracle Service Bus Console, perform the following steps:

1. Navigate to the Oracle Service Bus Console at `http://adminhost:7001/servicebus`.

2. Click on the **Admin** tab on the left-hand side of the menu of the Oracle Service Bus Console.

3. Click on **Create Configuration File**.

4. Select the project(s) you would like to export the customization for. As you can see from the example shown in the following screenshot, multiple projects can be selected, allowing the customization file to include settings and actions for one or more OSB services:

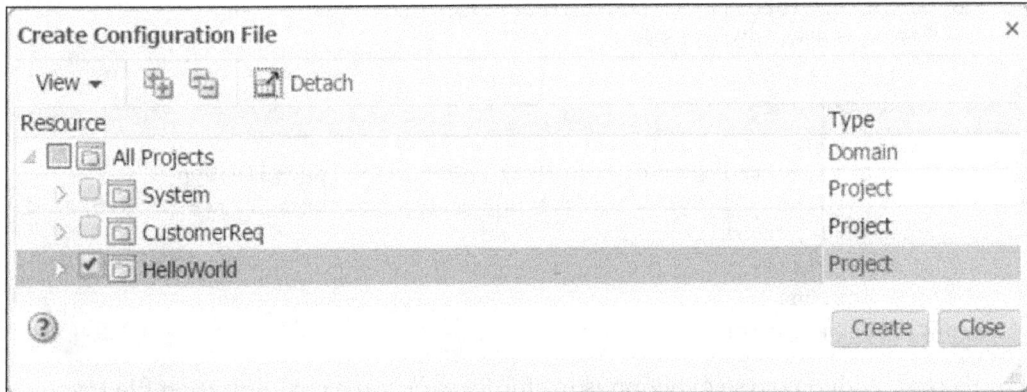

Figure 5.3: Exporting an OSB customization file from the console

5. Click on the **Create** tab.

6. You will be prompted to download a file called `OSBCustomizationFile.xml`.

Applying a customization file through the OSB Console

The customization file can be applied on the server anytime. After multiple OSB projects are imported, you can manually execute the customization file on the server, which will in turn perform all the actions and replacements defined in the customization file.

To apply a customization file from the Oracle Service Bus Console, go through the following steps:

1. Navigate to the Oracle Service Bus Console at `http://adminhost:7001/servicebus`.

2. Click on **Create** to create a session.

3. Click on the **Admin** tab on the left-hand side of the menu.

4. Click on the **Execute Configuration File** option.

5. Click on **Choose File** to locate a customization file in order to upload it from your local machine.

6. You will be shown various actions, replacements, and references. The following screenshot shows an example of the actions that will occur by executing the selected customization file:

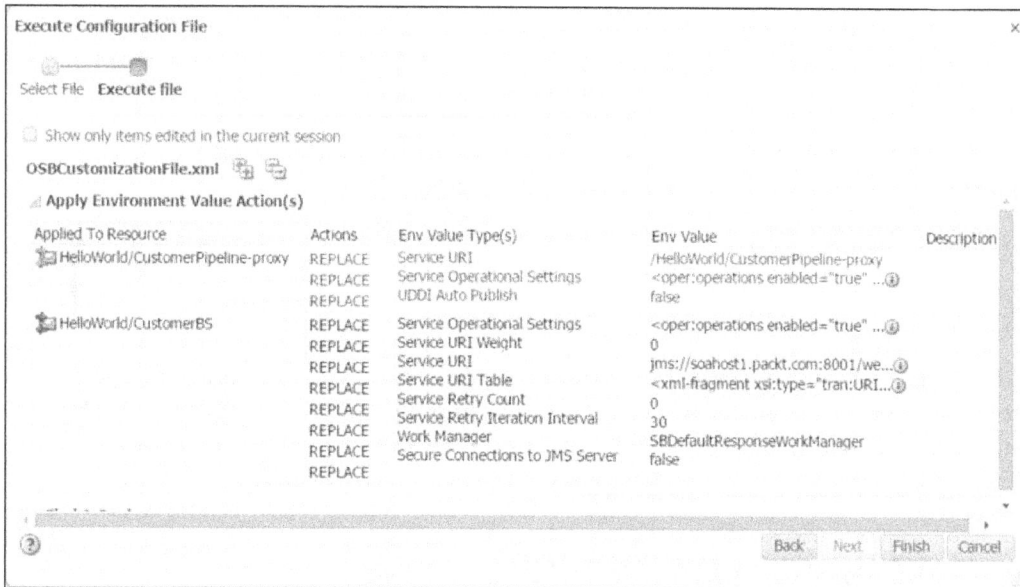

Figure 5.4: Viewing the actions to be performed by the OSB customization file

7. Click on the **Finish** button.
8. Click on the **Activate** button and then click on **Activate** again to commit the changes.

Attaching a customization file when deploying through WSLT

Refer to the section titled *Deploying with WLST* in this chapter for instructions on how to attach a customization file during the deployment of an OSB project through WLST.

Deploying BAM artifacts

Compared to SOA and OSB, BAM is definitely an outlier in terms of functionality as well as a method of migrating code into various environments. To begin with, the development of BAM artifacts is done on the server, whereas SOA and OSB development is primarily done in JDeveloper.

[OSB services can also be developed through the Service Bus Console.   ]

This means that in some ways the deployment process is much easier, since there are really only two steps for exporting and importing BAM artifacts. Both of these steps are accomplished with the same tool, **BAMCommand**.

BAM artifacts, as mentioned earlier, can take the form of **data objects**, **business queries**, **KPIs**, **business views**, **dashboards**, **alerts**, or **parameters**.

[BAMCommand is the successor of ICommand, which was used in the earlier versions of Oracle SOA Suite 10*g* and 11*g*.   ]

It is similar in many respects, but provides some additional commands, making it possible to import artifacts and data from 11*g* into the new 12*c* environment. The full details for migration between the major releases can be found at `http://docs.oracle.com/middleware/1213/core/FUPSS/bam.htm#FUPSS256`.

Setting up the environment

The BAMCommand tool can be used from the middleware installation where BAM exists, but it can also be run remotely. To run it remotely, an installation of BAM or JDeveloper will suffice. In either case, bamcommand (bamcommand.cmd for Microsoft Windows) is located in the `$MW_HOME/soa/bam/bin` directory.

Setting up the environment path

In your environment, we assume that Oracle SOA Suite 12*c* is installed, and more specifically, Oracle BAM 12*c* is installed, as it will include all the required binaries to run BAMCommand.

In this section, we assume that all BAM objects will be imported and exported to a `$CODE` directory. To set up your environment, we recommend you to first create the `setBAMEnv.sh` shell script with the following content:

```
export CODE=/home/oracle/bamcode
export MW_HOME=/u01/app/oracle/middleware
export JAVA_HOME=$MW_HOME/jdk1.7.0_15
export PATH=$MW_HOME/soa/bam/bin:$PATH:.
```

Modify the parameter values to reflect your environment.

Updating the configuration file

BAMCommandConfig.xml is located in $MW_HOME/soa/bam/bin alongside the bamcommand executable. It contains a number of parameters that are used whenever they are not provided in the command line. An example of BAMCommandConfig.xml can be found here:

```
<?xml version="1.0" encoding="UTF-8" standalone="yes"?>
<BAMCommandConfig>
  <host>soahost1</host>
  <port>9001</port>
  <username>weblogic</username>
  <password>welcome1</password>
  <!-- Below fields only needed when using -migrate -->
  <dbusername>DEV_SOAINFRA</dbusername>
  <dbpassword>welcome1</dbpassword>
  <dburl>jdbc:oracle:thin:@soadb:1521:orcl</dburl>
</BAMCommandConfig>
```

Update the settings in this file to reflect your environment. Note that the port number should be that of the BAM managed server and not the AdminServer. Alternatively, you may choose to pass these arguments through the command line.

Exporting BAM artifacts

Since the development process begins on the runtime environment before anything can be deployed, it must first be exported from the existing environment, often a development environment. To export an object, issue the following commands:

```
source setBAMEnv.sh

bamcommand -cmd export -name "Hello/World" -file "$CODE/World.zip
```

The command exports an object named World located in the Hello directory on the server, and the generated output is exported to a file named World.zip. This ZIP file will later be used to import the object into a target server. In Oracle SOA Suite 12*c*, we do not have to explicitly specify the type of this object, whether it is a data object, rule, or otherwise.

Importing BAM artifacts

Once objects have been exported, they can be imported into a target BAM server. This is done with the `import` command after the `-cmd` argument:

```
source setBAMEnv.sh

bamcommand -cmd import -file "$CODE/World.zip"
```

When an import is performed, the fully qualified file path should be provided for the `-file` argument. There are many command-line arguments available that can provide further options and control. Additional information can be found in *Chapter 17, Oracle Fusion Middleware Monitoring Business Activity with Oracle BAM* at `http://docs.oracle.com/middleware/1213/bam/BAMUG/bam-using-commands.htm`. Using the command file to perform multiple operations

The command file can make it easy to perform many operations on objects consistently within BAM. However, the command file is limited to the `<Export>`, `<Delete>`, and `<Rename>` commands. Within each of these commands, it is possible to provide most of the options, including **continue on error**, as if they were being called individually. The `bamcommand` argument can make a very handy tool when you want to clone a BAM environment, since once all the objects are listed, then they can be exported into an archive or series of files.

An example `command.xml` file is shown as follows:

```xml
<?xml version="1.0" encoding="utf-8"?>
<OracleBAMCommands continueonerror="1">
  <Export name="Test/Hello World" file="Hello World.xml" contents="0" />
  <Rename name="Test/Foo" newdisplayname="Bar" />
  <Delete type="EMS" name="ApacheLog" />
</OracleBAMCommands>
```

In this command file, we are performing three functions: exporting a BAM artifact, renaming a BAM artifact, and deleting a BAM artifact.

We can reference the BAM command file through the `-cmdfile` argument. An example is shown using our previous example, `command.xml`:

```
source setBAMEnv.sh

bamcommand -cmdfile "command.xml"
```

Deploying MDS artifacts

The MDS, or Metadata Store, is a database-based repository that stores various artifacts that can be referenced from within your SOA code. This can include schemas (XSD files), WSDLs, fault policies and bindings, **Domain Value Maps** (**DVMs**), configuration files, and more. The beauty of MDS is that all these artifacts can be shared between your SOA and OSB code, thus taking advantage of reusability.

Often, it is needed to export the contents of MDS either for backup, export, or management purposes. Fortunately, Oracle has provided an Ant target that allows the easy export of all or portions of the MDS into a single JAR file. Once the JAR file is exported, it can be unzipped to your local filesystem and browsed using any file browser. Similarly, it is possible to take a packaged MDS JAR file and import it to any environment.

Exporting MDS artifacts with Ant

This command demonstrates how to execute Ant to export the contents of your MDS to a single JAR file:

```
source setAntEnv.sh
cd $ORACLE_HOME/bin
ant -f ant-sca-deploy.xml exportSharedData -DserverURL=$SOAURL/
soa-infra/deployer -Duser=$USERNAME -Dpassword=$PASSWORD
-DjarFile=SOAMetaData.jar -Dpattern=**
```

The `SOAMetaData.jar` JAR file can now be unzipped and browsed through the filesystem. When extracted to a temporary folder such as `/tmp/svn`, it may extract the following files:

```
/tmp/svn/SOAMetaData/faultPolicies/fault-bindings.xml
/tmp/svn/SOAMetaData/faultPolicies/fault-policies.xml
```

These files can now be navigated through the filesystem.

The `pattern` argument can be used to filter the contents you wish to export, allowing you to pick and choose what you want to export should you choose not to export the entire MDS content. For example, specifying a pattern of `/apps/SOAMetaData/dvm/**;/apps/SOAMetaData/faultPolicies/**` will only export the artifacts under those two subfolders within the MDS.

Importing artifacts to the MDS with Ant

Since MDS artifacts and contents are exported as JAR files, it makes sense for artifacts to be imported in the same manner.

For example, you may have the following files that you just updated on your local filesystem and wish to import them to the MDS. This may include fault policies, DVMs, and schemas located in the following local directory structure:

```
/tmp/svn/SOAMetaData/faultPolicies/fault-bindings.xml
/tmp/svn/SOAMetaData/faultPolicies/fault-policies.xml
/tmp/svn/SOAMetaData/dvm/CurrencyCode.dvm
/tmp/svn/SOAMetaData/xsd/ErrorHandling/errorEvent.xsd
```

Firstly, you should zip up the contents of the ~/SOAMetaData subfolder, generating a single SOAMetaData.jar file:

```
cd /tmp/svn
zip -r SOAMetaData.jar SOAMetaData
```

The JAR file is now ready to be imported to the MDS, maintaining the same directory structure:

```
source setAntEnv.sh
cd $ORACLE_HOME/bin
ant -f ant-sca-deploy.xml deploy -Dwl_home=/u01/app/middleware/
wlserver_10.3 -Doracle.home=$ORACLE_HOME -DserverURL=$SOAURL/soa-
infra/deployer -Duser=$USERNAME -Dpassword=$PASSWORD -Doverwrite=true
-DforceDefault=true -DsarLocation=SOAMetaData.jar
```

Summary

This chapter was exclusively dedicated to the deployment of code to the Oracle SOA Suite 12c infrastructure, covering areas of SOA composite applications, OSB services, BAM artifacts, and MDS artifacts. We specifically focused on the following topics:

- Deploying and undeploying SOA composite applications from Fusion Middleware Control

- Using both Ant and WLST to deploy and undeploy SOA composite applications

- Understanding the purpose of SOA configuration plans and how to use them

- Importing and deleting OSB projects through the Oracle Service Bus Console

- Importing and deleting OSB projects through WLST

- Understanding the purpose of OSB customization files and how to use them

- Exporting and importing BAM artifacts using the BAMCommand tool
- Using a command file to simplify BAM deployment of multiple artifacts
- Importing and exporting shared MDS artifacts

This chapter does not cover all deployment configurations, arguments, or settings, but it is thorough enough to provide you, the administrator, with most of what you need to automate your SOA, OSB, BAM, and MDS deployments.

6
Monitoring Oracle SOA Suite 12*c*

There are three areas of monitoring that an Oracle SOA Suite 12*c* administrator typically focuses on. They are as follows:

- Transactions
- Instance state and performance
- Infrastructure

This chapter covers these three areas in detail, providing a comprehensive handle on all aspects of environment monitoring in general. The ultimate goal as an administrator is to ensure that the infrastructure executes transactions reliably and efficiently.

Transactional monitoring involves the following:

- Reviewing faulted instances to take action (retry, replay, or ignore).
- Searching log files for additional log information on faulted instances.
- Searching through composite sensors if the end user complains of a particular business transaction not going through (if composite sensors are implemented in the code).
- Enabling selective tracing, which allows you to change the trace level for a defined scope. Examples of a scope are a particular logged-in user, deployed application, or BPEL composite.

Monitoring instance state and performance involves the following:

- Reviewing the **Performance Summary** and **Request Processing** pages on the console to graphically display specific metrics on selected composites
- Running SQL queries to retrieve summary and detailed performance information on composite instances

Infrastructure monitoring involves the following:

- Reviewing filesystem log files for system and application errors
- Monitoring the Oracle WebLogic Server managed servers for the overall health
- Monitoring the JVM for appropriate sizing and garbage collection frequency
- Monitoring **Java Message Service** (**JMS**) destinations, such as queues and topics to ensure that messages are being processed
- Monitoring data sources to preemptively identify any issues
- Monitoring threads
- Monitoring operating to system-level parameters

Once you understand all areas of monitoring, it might make sense to invest in a tool that helps with the automation of the monitoring activities, an area we do not discuss in this book as there are many options available on the market. Oracle's standard monitoring solution for Oracle SOA Suite 12c is Oracle Enterprise Manager Cloud Control with the SOA Management Pack.

SOA transaction monitoring

When monitoring instances, the goal is to achieve two purposes: to identify transactions that have not been completed successfully to determine further action and ensure that the transactions do not experience poor performance.

When a message is received by the SOA Infrastructure, it may pass through multiple components within your infrastructure and may even traverse multiple external systems as well. For example, an order may be received by an OSB service which then passes it on to a BPEL process for further processing before finally placing it into a queue. Afterwards, it may be consumed by a third-party application that processes this order before sending it back to a Mediator service that routes it to the final order management application.

If one of the six steps in this particular integration fails, how can you identify the location of the message? It would also be important to know the duration of execution by the component to determine whether they are within the defined SLAs.

In this section, which focuses primarily on SOA composites (not OSB services), we provide you with the tools necessary for effective transaction monitoring across the server. OSB monitoring is described later in the chapter.

Monitoring composite instances

To monitor SOA composite instances, you should first understand a few key concepts, which are as follows:

- Every instance displayed on Fusion Middleware Control is a **composite instance**. Each composite instance is designated a unique **composite instance ID**.

- Every SOA composite may consist of one or more **components** (for example, BPEL, BPMN, human workflow, Mediator, and so on). You must navigate to the composite instance and drill down to the component to view its details. Every component has its own component instance ID.

- The **Flow ID** is the ID that is used throughout SOA Suite to tie together all composite and component instances. Related to this, though not the same, is the **Execution Context ID (ECID)**, a global, unique identifier of a particular transaction. It is injected into the header of the payload when the instance is first created and is included throughout the lifecycle of the payload. Thus, the ECID may appear in multiple composites and components. The ECID should not be confused with any of the instance IDs described earlier.

- Every composite instance and component instance has metadata that includes the creation time, last updated time, and state of the instance.

Faulted instances

One of the more common activities that an administrator performs is retrieving a list of faulty or rejected SOA composite instances and getting the necessary information to troubleshoot them.

In SOA Suite 12*c*, this has been simplified. To access the new fault screen, click on **soa-infra** and then click on the **Error Hospital** tab. This screen provides a unified method to review and recover the faulted instances. Faults can be searched for based upon instance start times and fault times. Additionally, they can be grouped by **Composite**, **Partition**, and **Fault Code** to name a few. This can be helpful for getting a quick glance at issues that occur in the infrastructure and sometimes provides the ability to act on them.

Unfortunately, the fault shown on the console may not contain enough information to effectively handle the error and a review of the log files may be necessary. Later in this chapter, we discuss how to identify and view log file information as well as how to increase the logger levels to provide more details.

Searching composite sensors

Composite sensors are added to the SOA composite at design time by the developer. They are not specific to BPEL or Mediator but are instead captured at the composite level. They provide a method of implementing traceable fields on messages.

For example, composite sensors can be used to capture business indicators, such as a customer ID or an order number, and persist this data in the database, which then becomes searchable via the Fusion Middleware Control console.

If the composite is not designed to capture composite sensors, you will not be able to search on them. Refer to the following screenshot to get a look at a composite sensor:

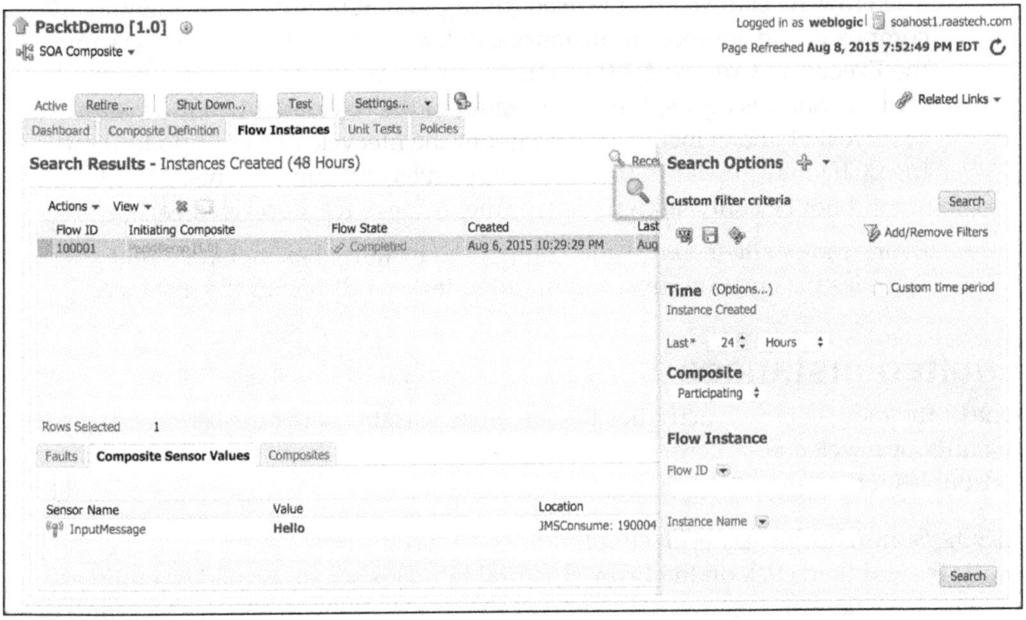

Figure 6.1: Searching by composite sensors

To search for a composite sensor, perform the following steps:

1. Click on the **Flow Instances** tab and confirm that the **Flow Instance** header exists. If it does not, then click on **Add/Remove Filters**, check the box next to **Flow Instance**, and click on the **OK** tab.

2. Now, click on the **Add Sensor Values** tab, and you should be able to choose a **Sensor Name** field and corresponding value. *Figure 6.1* shows that the **PacktDemo[1.0]** composite has an **InputMessage** sensor name with the value **Hello**.

3. When selected, a new search field is added, allowing you to search by that particular composite sensor on this page.

Remember, composite sensors can technically capture any type of data defined by the developer at design time. When searching by a particular composite sensor, a list of instances will be retrieved that contain that particular sensor value.

You can view all composite sensors and their values for an instance by clicking on an instance row and then clicking on the **Composite Sensor Values** tab, as shown in the previous screenshot.

> You can query the COMPOSITE_SENSOR_VALUE table in the database to retrieve composite sensor data.

Developers are encouraged to implement composite sensors. This allows the administrator to search a particular business field such as an order number or customer ID. There is also no limit on the number of composite sensors that can be added to a composite. You can also query the COMPOSITE_SENSOR_VALUE table in the database to retrieve composite sensor data.

> All of this information is unencrypted so precautions should be taken to ensure that **Personally Identifiable Information** (**PII**), such as social security number, date of birth, or bank information, are not used as composite sensor fields.

Searching BPEL process sensors

Another useful set of information is available from the **Sensors** tab of your BPEL process. BPEL process sensors are somewhat similar in concept to composite sensors, though they come in three types. BPEL sensors capture the values of activity, variables, and fault sensors, if any, that are configured at design time.

Sensors are very important means of instrumentation in business processes as they record key business or process analytics information. Take a look at *Figure 6.2* and you will see how a **Variable Sensors** field records the value of the **MessageID** variable.

Sensors are another means of making sure that business processes are executed with all the checks and balances in place. Only sensors with a Sensor action of the **Publish Type** field of **Database** will appear on the page.

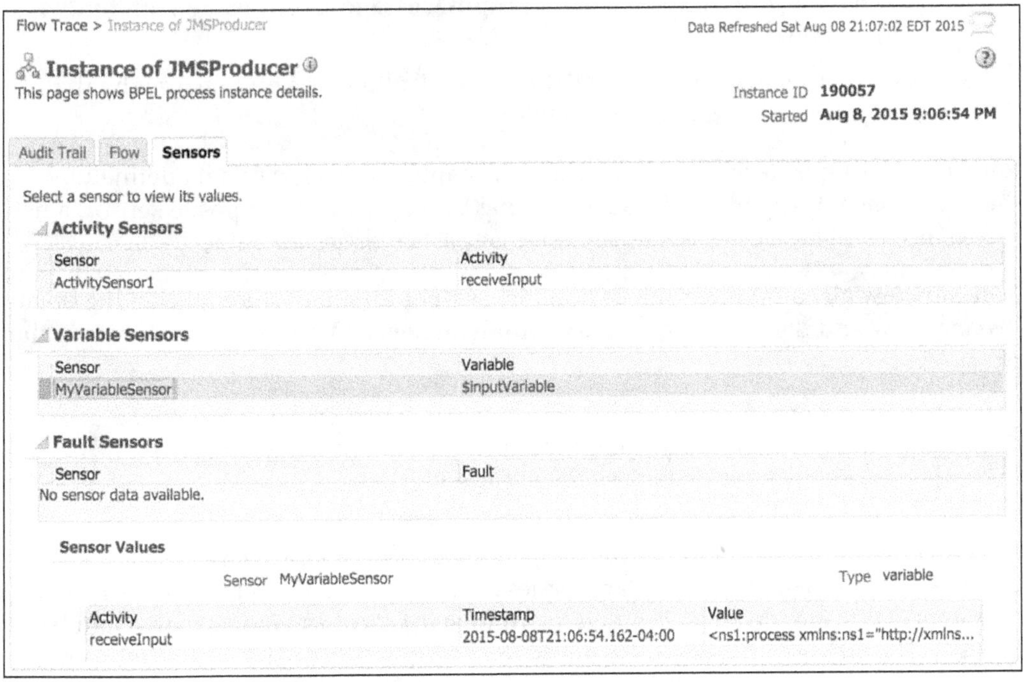

Figure 6.2: Viewing the sensors defined in a BPEL process

The metadata information for process sensors is stored in the dehydration store database. You can find the sensor configuration information for each type in their corresponding dehydration store tables ACTIVITY_SENSOR_VALUES, VARIABLE_SENSOR_VALUES, and FAULT_SENSOR_VALUES in the [PREFIX]_SOAINFRA schema. The data in these tables is also stored in clear text.

Understanding Flow IDs, Instance IDs, and ECIDs

To effectively perform transaction monitoring, it helps to understand the difference between the various IDs. Every individual component instance has an Instance ID, and these are largely inconsequential. The exception is when you hunt down the correct execution, for example, in the event of a transactional JMS execution where a single component may be executed multiple times due to connectivity failures.

Every composite instance has a unique Instance ID, which is commonly referred to as the composite instance ID. The Flow ID, on the other hand, is a sequential numeric identifier and is the primary means of navigating instances through the console. It is also the internal way that SOA Suite 12*c* ties all individual component executions together in a single transactional flow.

Finally, the ECID is a global, unique identifier of a particular transaction. It has a one-to-one correlation with the Flow ID, making it relatively unused for internal purposes. However, as a message is passed from a composite to another, the ECID is passed with each message. This allows the correlation of a message across different components, even when the message leaves Oracle SOA Suite 12*c* and comes back!

An ECID is generated when Oracle Fusion Middleware first processes the request. If it exists in the message header, no new ECID is generated. The following is an example of an ECID:

```
00575SHJjdD5e_xaw9rY6G0000QD0004Sq
```

In the following sample integration design, we have a BPEL process that produces a message in to an external JMS queue. Afterwards, this message is consumed asynchronously by another BPEL process that passes it on to a Mediator service, which in turn invokes a final BPEL process.

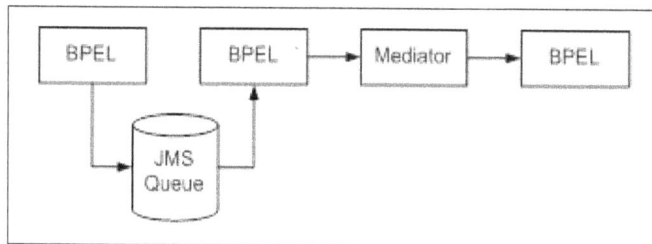

Figure 6.3: The design of our sample integration

Each component instance has its own Instance ID (refer to the Instance IDs `190057`, `190060`, `190061`, and `190062` in the flow in *Figure 6.4*). Upon the instantiation of the first composite, an ECID is generated. As shown in the figure, the first composite instantiated includes the BPEL component **JMSProducer** with an Instance ID of `190057`.

The Flow ID is shown in the top-right corner of the flow trace of the figure. The ECID related to this Flow ID is inserted as a property in the message as it is passed onto the next composite. What does that do you may ask? All composites and components within this single flow maintain the same ECID, allowing us to tie the execution of the transaction into a single flow, as shown in the following screenshot:

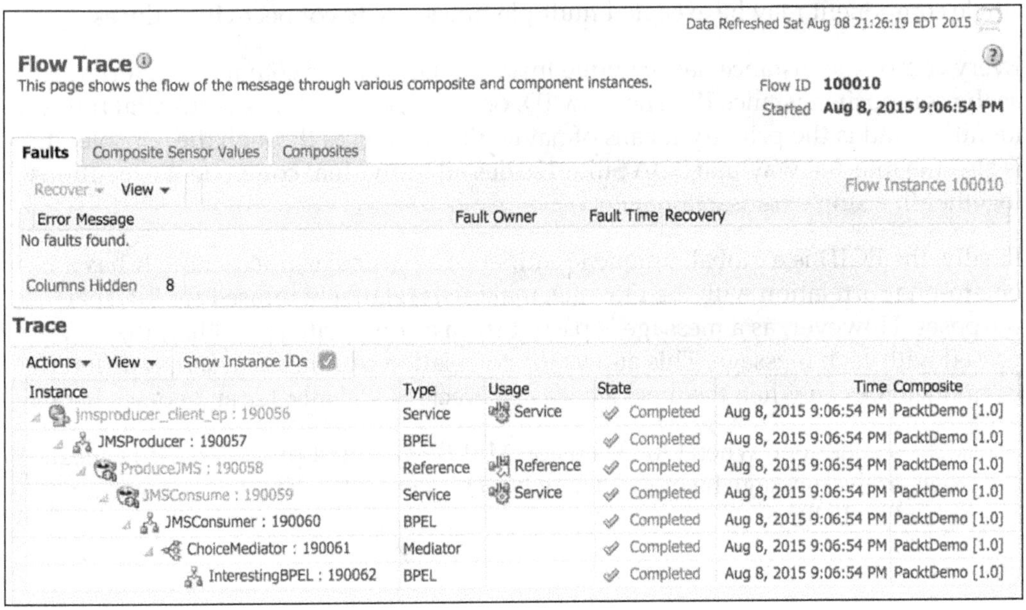

Figure 6.4: Composite instance correlation is achieved by the ECID

Querying the database also confirms this. We can query the SCA_FLOW_INSTANCE table for this particular Flow ID:

```
SELECT flow_id, ecid, created_time
FROM   sca_flow_instance
WHERE  ecid = '0000KwiWDQP5e_xaw9rY6G1Ln9XS00000M';
```

The following screenshot shows two composite instances associated with this ECID:

FLOW_ID	ECID	CREATED_TIME
130012	0000KwiWDQP5e_xaw9rY6G1Ln9XS00000M	15-AUG-15 07.17.27.379000000 PM
130011	0000KwiWDQP5e_xaw9rY6G1Ln9XS00000M	15-AUG-15 07.17.27.378000000 PM

Figure 6.5: Querying the SCA_FLOW_INSTANCES table

Each of these composites has a single component. Thus, we can query the CUBE_INSTANCE table to also retrieve a similar flow, but at the component level:

```
SELECT flow_id, composite_name, component_name, componenttype, state, and
creation_date

FROM    cube_instance

WHERE   ecid = '0000KwiWDQP5e_xaw9rY6G1Ln9XS00000M';
```

Once again, the two components are displayed alongside their types, states, and creation times, as shown in the following screenshot:

FLOW_ID	COMPOSITE_NAME	COMPONENT_NAME	COMPONENTTYPE	STATE	CREATION_DATE
130011	ESSDemoApp	ESSBPEL1	bpel	5	15-AUG-15 07.17.27.419000000 PM
130012	ESSDemoApp	ESSBPEL2	bpel	5	15-AUG-15 07.17.27.429000000 PM

Figure 6.6: Querying the CUBE_INSTANCE table

Querying the product database tables is perhaps the quickest and simplest mechanism to retrieve detailed instance information. *Chapter 8, Managing the Database* will cover more details about the key database tables that maintain runtime data.

Monitoring composite instance performance

There are several means available to help you assist in the viewing of SOA composite instance performance. You can view the details of a single instance through the console or you can rely on several out-of-the-box graphs and metrics. In this chapter, you will also have access to key SQL queries to obtain more detailed performance metrics.

Last update time of instances

What is often confusing about the console is that most of the timestamps shown are actually the last update time of the transaction and not the time it was created. Keep this in mind as sometimes the timestamps may appear out of order, particularly in flows that are linked together via the ECID and are completed at different times.

Let's say that in *Figure 6.4*, you clicked on the JMSProducer BPEL component. You will then be taken to the BPEL component details, as shown in *Figure 6.7*. Timestamps can often give you a good idea on the duration time to execute specific activities. For example, the **Wait** activity shown in the following screenshot took 3 seconds to complete, indicated by having started at **11:44:14 AM** and ended at **11:44:17 AM**:

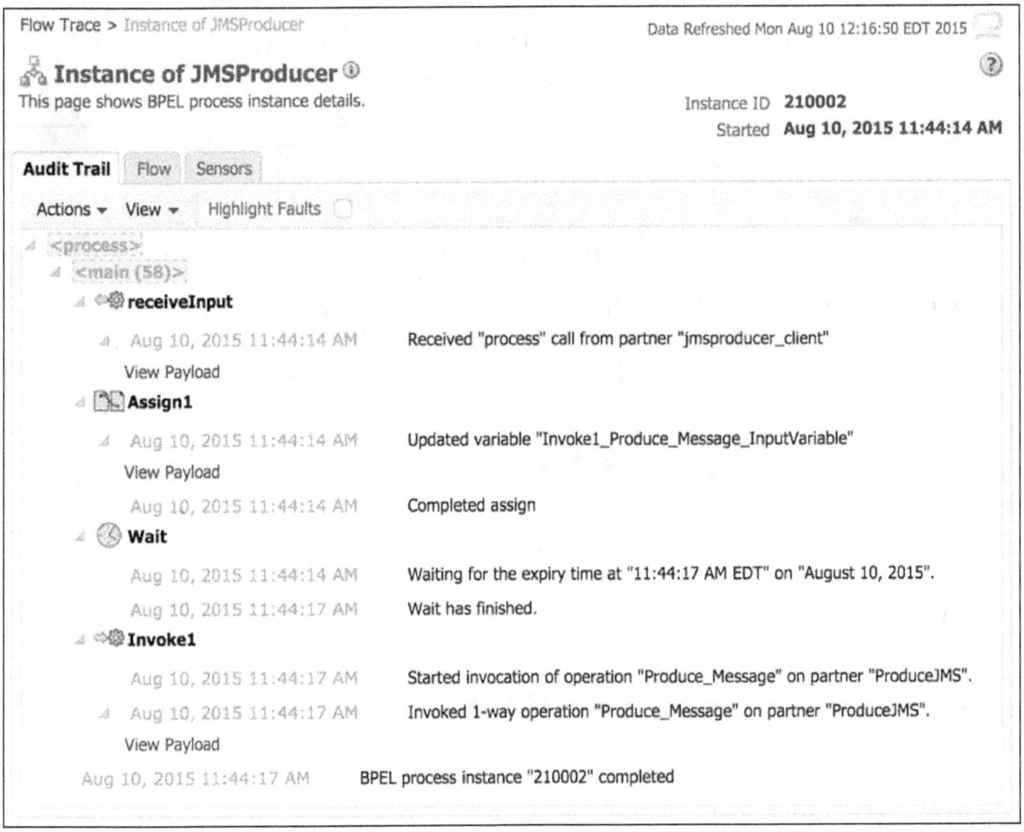

Figure 6.7: The BPEL component audit trail

By clicking on the **Flow Trace** link on the top-left side of *Figure 6.7*, you are taken back to the flow trace shown in *Figure 6.4*. Clicking on the **Mediator** component named **ChoiceMediator** gives you *Figure 6.8*. Likewise, the difference in timestamps can give you an idea of how long a specific routing rule, transformation, assignment, or invocation has taken. For example, the entire execution of the Mediator has taken 4 seconds, as indicated by the start time of **11:44:14 AM** and end time of **11:44:18 AM** in the following screenshot:

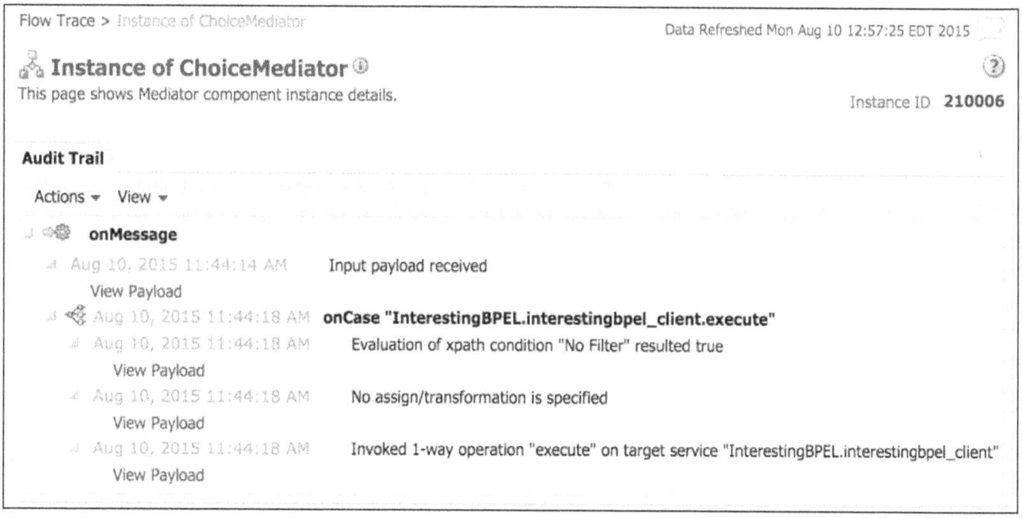

Figure 6.8: The Mediator component audit trail

Performance summary graphs and request processing metrics

On the navigator, expand **SOA**, right-click on **soa-infra**, and navigate to **Monitoring | Performance | Summary**. The **Performance Summary** page is displayed, as shown in *Figure 6.9*. On the right-hand side of this page is the **Metric Palette** section where you can pick and choose the metrics you want to display. We have chosen the following metrics to be displayed for the composite named `PacktDemo`:

- Average processing time for successful instances
- Average incoming message processing time

As you can see in *Figure 6.9*, the average processing time for successful instances (but not failed instances) is steady at the subsecond time: 0.004 seconds for the **InterestingBPEL** BPEL component and just a shade over 0.15 seconds for the **JMSConsumer** BPEL component.

However, we see that the average incoming message processing time, which is the time it took for the BPEL process to consume the message from the JMS queue, experienced a slight dip from over 0.02 seconds to around 0.015 seconds, potentially indicating that our system has seen a reduction in the overall load, as shown in the following screenshot:

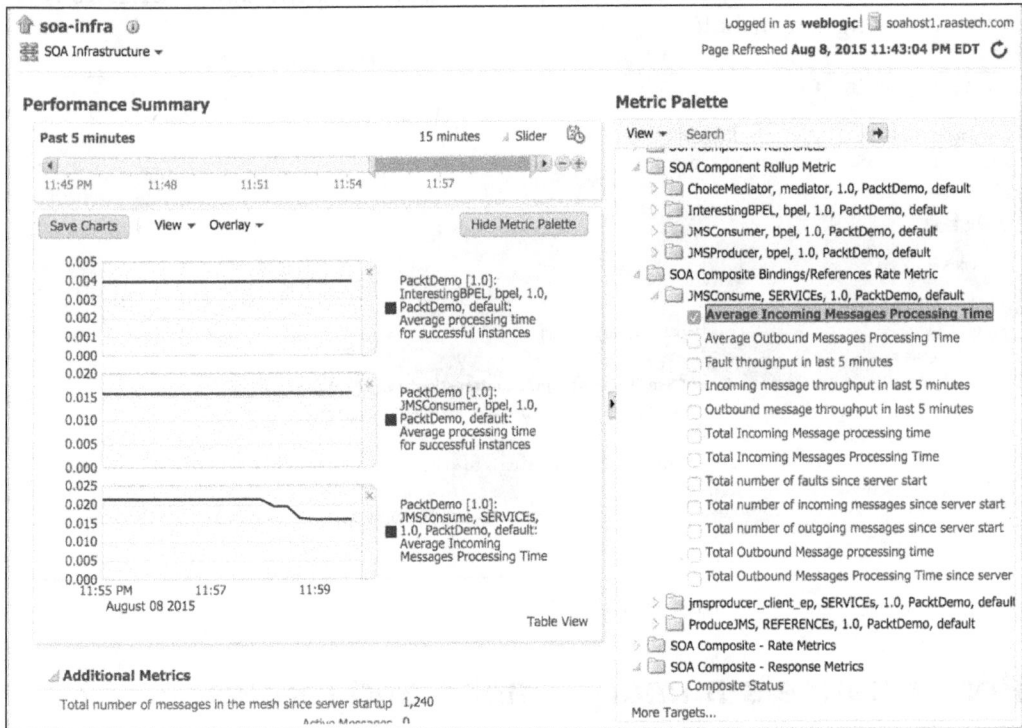

Figure 6.9: The Performance Summary page

On the navigator, expand **SOA**, right-click on **soa-infra**, and navigate to **Monitoring | Request Processing**. The **Request Processing** page is displayed, revealing the **Service Engines**, **Service Infrastructure**, and **Binding Component** metrics. The following screenshot shows the **Service Engines** metrics on this page. These are high-level metrics at the service engine level. Clicking on the service engine **Name** takes you to the service engine home dashboard, allowing you to drill down the statistics, instances, faults, deployed composites, and recovery of the service engine.

⊿ **Service Engines**				
Service engines are containers that host the business logic or processing rules of service components.				
Name	Average Request Processing Time - Synchronous (ms)	Average Request Processing Time - Asynchronous (ms)	Active Requests	Requests Processed
BPEL Engine	0.000	110.167	0	6
Mediator Engine	0.000	134.000	0	1
Human Workflow Engine	0.000	0.000	0	0
Business Rules Engine	0.000	0.000	0	0
Spring Engine	0.000	0.000	0	0

Figure 6.10: The Service Engines metrics on the Request Processing page

SQL queries for BPEL and BPMN metrics

The CUBE_INSTANCE table can be queried to obtain performance metrics on BPEL and BPMN processes, specifically the duration that each component took. *Figure 6.11* shows you the output of the following query, which displays a list of all BPEL component instances, their state, average, minimum, and maximum durations, as well as total count:

```
SELECT domain_name,

       component_name,

       state,

       TO_CHAR(AVG((TO_NUMBER(SUBSTR(TO_CHAR(MODIFY_DATE-CREATION_
DATE),12,2))*60*60) + (TO_NUMBER(SUBSTR(TO_CHAR(MODIFY_DATE-CREATION_
DATE),15,2))*60) + TO_NUMBER(SUBSTR(TO_CHAR(MODIFY_DATE-CREATION_
DATE),18,4))),'999990.000') Avg,

       TO_CHAR(MIN((TO_NUMBER(SUBSTR(TO_CHAR(MODIFY_DATE-CREATION_
DATE),12,2))*60*60) + (TO_NUMBER(SUBSTR(TO_CHAR(MODIFY_DATE-CREATION_
DATE),15,2))*60) + TO_NUMBER(SUBSTR(TO_CHAR(MODIFY_DATE-CREATION_
DATE),18,4))),'999990.000') Min,

       TO_CHAR(MAX((TO_NUMBER(SUBSTR(TO_CHAR(MODIFY_DATE-CREATION_
DATE),12,2))*60*60) + (TO_NUMBER(SUBSTR(TO_CHAR(MODIFY_DATE-CREATION_
DATE),15,2))*60) + TO_NUMBER(SUBSTR(TO_CHAR(MODIFY_DATE-CREATION_
DATE),18,4))),'999990.000') Max,
```

```
        COUNT(1) count
FROM    cube_instance
GROUP BY domain_name, component_name, state
ORDER BY component_name, state
```

In the following screenshot, we can see that there are three successfully completed instances of the **BPELProcess1** BPEL process in the default partition. These three instances took an average of **202.6** seconds and a maximum of **606.9** seconds to complete.

DOMAIN_NAME	COMPONENT_NAME	STATE	AVG	MIN	MAX	COUNT
default	BPELProcess1	0	202.600	0.400	606.900	3
default	BPELProcess1		0.060	0.000	0.500	10
default	ESSBPEL	0	0.050	0.000	0.100	2
default	HelloWorld	0	0.000	0.000	0.200	93322
default	InterestingBPEL	0	0.000	0.000	0.000	64
default	JMSConsumer	0	0.000	0.000	0.000	64
default	JMSProducer	0	0.004	0.000	0.300	92

Figure 6.11: Performance metrics obtained from the CUBE_INSTANCE table

This query provides a single, consolidated snapshot of all BPEL/BPMN high-level performance metrics.

Monitoring OSB instances

To those who are familiar with Oracle Service Bus 11*g*, using 12*c* for the first time will seem a little different when trying to monitor OSB instances. While the concept is the same, Oracle is increasingly bringing OSB more into the fold in terms of how to monitor it. The monitoring functions of OSB have all been moved into Fusion Middleware Control.

Because OSB is designed to be a stateless system, no instance states are captured and maintained unlike SOA composite instances. In fact, no runtime data is stored in the database except for reporting and resequencing functionality (if enabled). Thus, the reliance on the filesystem log files becomes necessary when monitoring OSB instances.

Chapter 4, Managing Services, highlighted some of OSB's operational settings, but here we will delve into several of them in a little more detail, namely:

- Monitoring
- Message tracing
- SLA Alerts

- Reports
- Logging
- Execution tracing

On the navigator in Fusion Middleware Control, expand **SOA** and then **service-bus** and click on the OSB service you would like to monitor.

In the following screenshot, we navigated to our **HelloWorldOSB** service. Click on the **Operations** tab. The settings described earlier can be changed dynamically at runtime from here:

Figure 6.12: Manipulating the operation settings of on OSB service

> The majority of the OSB operational settings will have varying degrees of negative impact on both the performance and log growth of the service.

All the captured information described in the remainder of this section is logged to the `osb_server1-diagnostic.log` file located under the `$DOMAIN_HOME/servers/osb_server1` directory.

Monitoring

When the **Monitoring** operational setting is enabled, if you click on the service's **Service Health** tab, it begins to reveal statistics related to that OSB service (as shown in the following screenshot) such as the average response time, the number of invocations (via the **Messages** column), errors, SLA alerts, and pipeline alerts. Detailed information on the OSB service is not provided here aside from counts and average response time.

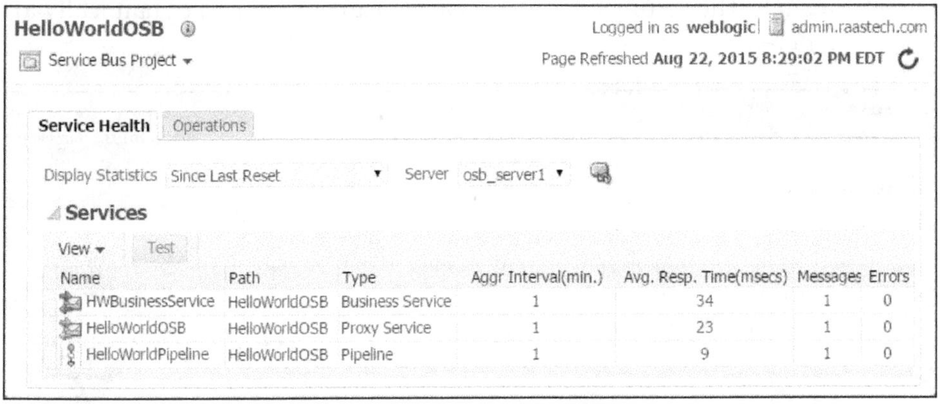

Name	Path	Type	Aggr Interval(min.)	Avg. Resp. Time(msecs)	Messages	Errors
HWBusinessService	HelloWorldOSB	Business Service	1	34	1	0
HelloWorldOSB	HelloWorldOSB	Proxy Service	1	23	1	0
HelloWorldPipeline	HelloWorldOSB	Pipeline	1	9	1	0

Figure 6.13: Reviewing the OSB service's health after enabling monitoring

> OSB monitoring statistics are not maintained between server restarts.

Message tracing

Message tracing is only enabled at either the proxy service or business service levels. Enabling it on the business service, for example, reveals a little bit more information, namely ECID, Flow ID, and URI, as shown in the logs:

```
[2015-08-22T20:39:32.643-04:00] [osb_server1] [NOTIFICATION] [OSB-398202]
[oracle.osb.resources.service.service] [tid: [ACTIVE].ExecuteThread: '4'
for queue: 'weblogic.kernel.Default (self-tuning)'] [userId: <anonymous>]
[ecid: abc31d2b-f294-4f7c-9a35-a05f988ff385-0002e6a7,0] [APP: Service Bus
Publish] [FlowId: 0000KxNzjjo5e_xaw9rY6GlLoe2z000013] [[

[OSB Tracing] Outbound request was sent.


Service Ref = HelloWorldOSB/HWBusinessService

URI = http://soahost1.packt.com:8001/soa-infra/services/default/
HelloWorldSOA/client_ep
]]
```

SLA Alerts

Refer to the section titled *Managing OSB service operations* in *Chapter 4, Managing Services.* SLA Alerts are defined at design time and can be enabled/disabled at runtime.

Reports

Refer to the section titled *Managing OSB service operations* in *Chapter 4, Managing Services.* **Reports** are defined at design time and can be enabled/disabled at runtime. Reports can only be defined within a pipeline.

Logging

Logging is an activity that can be defined at design time. The following screenshot shows that a variable is configured to be captured and an annotation with the text **My Input Element** is also logged. The developer can also define the severity level at which this log should take effect.

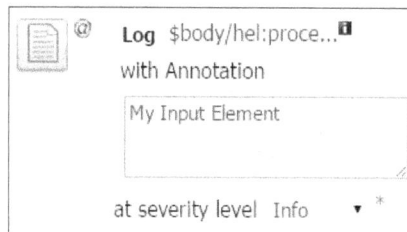

Figure 6.14: Setting logs during OSB design time

When the logging operational setting is enabled, the following entry is shown in the diagnostic log. The ECID and Flow ID are shown as well as the annotation and variable being defined at design time:

```
[2015-08-22T20:40:28.490-04:00] [osb_server1] [NOTIFICATION] []
[oracle.osb.logging.pipeline] [tid: [ACTIVE].ExecuteThread: '21' for
queue: 'weblogic.kernel.Default (self-tuning)'] [userId: <anonymous>]
[ecid: abc31d2b-f294-4f7c-9a35-a05f988ff385-0002e6b4,0] [APP:
Service Bus Logging] [FlowId: 0000KxNzxOT5e_xaw9rY6G1Loe2z000016]
[PipelinePairNode1, PipelinePairNode1_request, stage1, REQUEST] My
Input Element: < hel:input xmlns:hel="http://xmlns.oracle.com/Packt/
HelloWorldSOA/HelloWorld" xmlns:soapenv="http://schemas.xmlsoap.org/soap/
envelope/">Florapaz</hel:input>
```

Logging is an action that can only be defined within a pipeline.

Execution tracing

Execution tracing can only be applied at the pipeline level, and this is perhaps the most valuable troubleshooting setting available for OSB instances.

> Of all the OSB operational settings, the execution tracing setting is the most valuable in troubleshooting OSB instances, but log growth is considerable.

In our simple `HelloWorldOSB` example, execution tracing created 497 extra lines in the log file for a total of 28 KB of additional log data for a single instance! So, exercise caution when enabling this setting.

The value of execution tracing is that every step is captured in detail, allowing us to perform thorough monitoring and troubleshooting. We have taken the entire dump of our log and filtered it to list the `[OSB Tracing]` entries only for the purpose of identifying the steps being logged:

```
[OSB Tracing] Entering proxy HelloWorldOSB/HelloWorldPipeline with
message context:
[OSB Tracing] Entering pipeline pair PipelinePairNode1 with message
context:
[OSB Tracing] Entering pipeline PipelinePairNode1_request with message
context:
[OSB Tracing] Entering stage stage1 with message context:
[OSB Tracing] Exiting stage
[OSB Tracing] The following variables are added:
[OSB Tracing] The following variables are changed:
[OSB Tracing] Exiting Pipeline
[OSB Tracing] Exiting pipeline pair
[OSB Tracing] Echoing request
[OSB Tracing] Exiting HelloWorldOSB/HelloWorldPipeline
```

We now display a condensed snippet of only one of the preceding trace entries. Here, the actual step we are in is shown (for example, `Entering pipeline pair PipelinePairNode1`), and the invoked URI (for example, `/HelloWorldOSB`), the operation called (example, `process`), and the entire payload is logged including all its header information:

```
[2015-08-22T20:41:41.861-04:00] [osb_server1] [NOTIFICATION] [OSB-382162]
[oracle.osb.pipeline.kernel.router] [tid: [ACTIVE].ExecuteThread: '9'
for queue: 'weblogic.kernel.Default (self-tuning)'] [userId: <anonymous>]
[ecid: abc31d2b-f294-4f7c-9a35-a05f988ff385-0002e715,0] [APP: Service Bus
Kernel] [FlowId: 0000KxO0FIo5e_xaw9rY6G1Loe2z000017] [[
```

```
[OSB Tracing] Entering pipeline pair PipelinePairNode1 with message
context:

 [MessageContextImpl  body="<soapenv:Body xmlns:soapenv="http://schemas.
xmlsoap.org/soap/envelope/" xmlns:hel="http://xmlns.oracle.com/Packt/
HelloWorldSOA/HelloWorld">

  <hel:process>

    <hel:input>Florapaz</hel:input>

  </hel:process>

</soapenv:Body>"

 operation="process"

 messageID="N53e0d4be.N7b469f38.12.14f57e189f6.N7ffc"

 attachments="<con:attachments xmlns:con="http://www.bea.com/wli/sb/
context"/>"

 outbound="null"

 fault="null"

 inbound="<con:endpoint name="ProxyService$HelloWorldOSB$HelloWorldOSB"
xmlns:con="http://www.bea.com/wli/sb/context">

  <con:service>

    <con:operation>process</con:operation>

  </con:service>

  <con:transport>

    <con:uri>/HelloWorldOSB</con:uri>

    <con:mode>request-response</con:mode>

    <con:qualityOfService>best-effort</con:qualityOfService>

    <con:request xsi:type="http:HttpRequestMetaData" xmlns:http="http://
www.bea.com/wli/sb/transports/http" xmlns:xsi="http://www.w3.org/2001/
XMLSchema-instance">

      <tran:headers xsi:type="http:HttpRequestHeaders"
xmlns:tran="http://www.bea.com/wli/sb/transports">

        <http:Accept-Encoding>gzip,deflate</http:Accept-Encoding>

        <http:Connection>Keep-Alive</http:Connection>

        <http:Content-Length>310</http:Content-Length>

        <http:Host>admin.raastech.com:4011</http:Host>

        <http:SOAPAction>"process"</http:SOAPAction>

      </tran:headers>

      <http:http-method>POST</http:http-method>

    </con:request>

]

]]
```

The DMS Spy Servlet

The DMS Spy Servlet is a small web-based application that displays metrics related to **Dynamic Monitoring Service (DMS)**, which are built-in metrics that are automatically collected by the server. Simply navigate to the following URL on the AdminServer (`http://adminhost:7001/dms/Spy`) and log in using the administrator account (for example, `weblogic`).

You can retrieve an immediate snapshot of everything from running JDBC statements to JVM threads to MDS repository configuration to numerous Oracle WebLogic Server metrics, as shown in the following screenshot:

Metric Tables	Logout	JDBC_Statement								Logout
Text		Name	Host	Process	Execute	Fetch	SQLText	JDBC_Connection	JDBC_DataSource	JDBC_Driver	JDBC_Ser
DMS Metrics		Statement	soahost1. raastech. com	wls_ soa1: 8001	active, threads	0 active, threads	0 SELECT 1 FROM DUAL	CONNECTION_ 5	SOADataSource	wls_
WebLogic Metrics										
Aggregated Metrics					avg, msecs	0.475 avg, msecs	0			
DMS Metrics					completed, ops	219833 completed, ops	0			
ADF					maxActive, threads	1 maxActive, threads	0			
DFW_DiagnosticDumpSamplingInfo										
DFW_Dump					maxTime, msecs	125 maxTime, msecs	0			
DFW_Incident					minTime, msecs	0 minTime, msecs	0			
JDBC_Connection										
JDBC_DataSource					time, msecs	104332 time, msecs	0			
JDBC_Driver										
JDBC_Statement										

Figure 6.15: Using the DMS Spy Servlet to view currently running JDBC statements

The DMS Spy Servlet is perhaps the easiest way to quickly get instant monitoring information, but it does not maintain history. These DMS metrics can be retrieved using the command line as well.

Identifying and viewing log file entries

When you install Oracle SOA Suite 12*c*, you are likely to have four managed servers: AdminServer, wls_wsm1, wsm_soa1, and wsm_osb1 (or whatever names you happen to configure). In a cluster, the number of managed servers may increase with incrementing numerals at the end (for example, wls_soa2, wls_osb2, and so on). Each of these managed servers has several log files that include the following:

- A managed server log file (for example, wls_soa1.log)
- A diagnostic log file (for example, wls_soa1-diagnostic.log)
- A server startup standard out log file (for example, wls_soa1.out)
- A HTTP access log (access.log)

Fortunately, Fusion Middleware Control provides a means to access and search several of these log files. To download the managed server log and diagnostic log files, perform the following steps:

1. Log in to Oracle Manager Fusion Middleware Control.
2. Right-click on **soa-infra** and then navigate to **Logs | View Log Messages**.
3. Click on the **Target Log Files** button.
4. Select wls_soa1.log (or any other log file) and then click on the **Download** button.

In some cases where the composite instance faults do not offer enough information to help with the troubleshooting efforts, it may be necessary to search for the logs for a particular ECID to retrieve additional information. To search for a particular ECID in the log file, go through these steps:

1. Log in to Oracle Manager Fusion Middleware Control.
2. Right-click on **soa-infra** and then navigate to **Logs | View Log Messages**.
3. Select the **Date Range** (for example, Most Recent 1 hour).
4. Select all Message Types: **Incident Error, Error, Warning, Notification, Trace**, and **Unknown**.
5. Click on the **Add Fields** button and add ECID.
6. Enter an ECID in the field and click on the **Search** button.
7. Review the output.

The following screenshot shows the results of a search through the log for a particular ECID. Rows relevant to this ECID are displayed, and in this case, we see several notifications showing work item expirations for the BPEL engine.

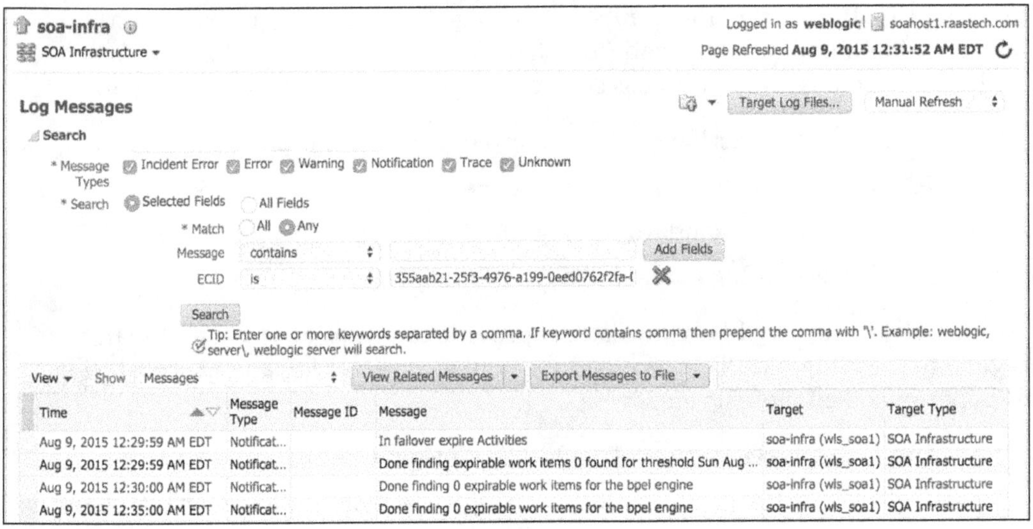

Figure 6.16: Searching the logs for a particular ECID through the console

Unfortunately, searching log files through the console is slow and cumbersome, and we recommend you to access the logs themselves directly through the filesystem instead.

Another important mechanism available to monitor and troubleshoot information from log files is to enable **Selective Tracing** in Fusion Middleware Control.

This can be configured by expanding **Weblogic Domain**, right-clicking on your domain name, and then navigating to **Logs | Selective Tracing**. This will bring you to a screen where you can configure your **Selective Tracing** session. The following screenshot shows how you can select **Add Fields** to choose the scope of your trace session, trace level, duration of trace, and also specify a custom Trace ID:

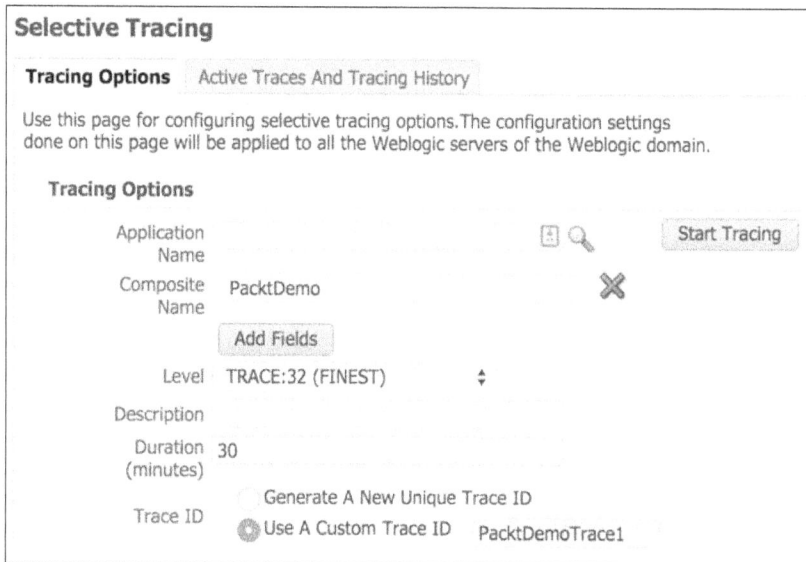

Figure 6.17. Configuring Selective Tracing

You may select the loggers that you want to be active for your tracing session by expanding the **Loggers** icon. All loggers are enabled by default and there is the option to both sort them by the available columns as well as search. You can enable the configured Selective Tracing session by clicking on the **Start Tracing** button.

By selecting the **Active Traces And Tracing History** tab, you will see your tracing session listed. If you now complete the run (success or failure) of the composite for which the tracing session is enabled, you will see that the **Log Viewer** field presents a filtered search on the **Trace ID**. You can now export only the trace entries to a new file. Your trace session will expire at the end of the specified duration or you may manually disable it in the **Active Traces And Tracing History** tab by highlighting the session and clicking on the **Disable** button. Selective Tracing is currently available only at the domain level.

Relevant log files

In a standard installation, the key log files are located in the following locations on the filesystem:

```
$MW_HOME/user_projects/domains/[Domain]/servers/[server_name]/logs/
[server_name].log
```

```
$MW_HOME/user_projects/domains/[Domain]/servers/[server_name]/logs/
[server_name].out
```

```
$MW_HOME/user_projects/domains/[Domain]/servers/[server_name]/logs/
[server_name]-diagnostic.log
```

```
$MW_HOME/user_projects/domains/[Domain]/servers/[server_name]/logs/
access.log
```

The `wls_soa1.log` file logs entries that are specific to both the infrastructure and transaction. In the event that an unclear error is found in a composite instance, locate the timeframe of that instance and search this log file. Here, for example, we can see the details of the error related to the initialization of `MQSeriesAdapter`:

```
####<Sep 28, 2015 10:08:00 PM EST> <Error> <Deployer> <soahost1>
<wls_soa1> <[ACTIVE] ExecuteThread: '0' for queue: 'weblogic.kernel.
Default (self-tuning)'> <<WLS Kernel>> <> < a0e9ac28-7d27-4253-
9d5f-0ddaf5ce2da0-00005a7b> <1325128080369> <BEA-149205> <Failed to
initialize the application 'MQSeriesAdapter' due to error weblogic.
application.ModuleException: The ra.xml <connectionfactory-impl-
class> class 'oracle.tip.adapter.mq.ConnectionFactoryImpl' could not
be loaded from the resource adapter archive/application because of the
following error: java.lang.NoClassDefFoundError: oracle/tip/adapter/api/
OracleConnectionFactory.
```

The `wls_soa1.out` file is generated when you start up the managed server via Node Manager or the Oracle WebLogic Server Administration Console. Review this log for server startup issues. For example, it may include startup information such as JVM heap and CLASSPATH settings as well as runtime infrastructure issues errors:

```
*********************************************************
** SOA specific environment is already set, skipping...
*********************************************************

.

JAVA Memory arguments: -Xms1536m -Xmx1536m -Xgcprio:throughput
-XX:+HeapDumpOnOutOfMemoryError -XXtlasize:min=16k,preferred=128k,wasteLi
mit=8k

.
```

```
WLS Start Mode=Production
.

CLASSPATH=/u01/app/oracle/middleware/oracle_common/modules/oracle.
jdbc_12.1.3/ojdbc6dms.jar:/u01/app/oracle/middleware/Oracle_SOA1/soa/
modules/user-patch.jar:/u01/app/oracle/middleware/Oracle_SOA1/soa/
modules/soa-startup.jar:...


<Jan 1, 2015 2:59:42 PM EST> <Error> <oracle.sdp.messaging.engine> <SDP-
25088> <Unable to refresh the driver locator cache, due to the following
error: EJB Exception: : Local Exception Stack:

Exception [TOPLINK-4002] (Oracle TopLink - 12g Release 1 (12.1.3) (Build
10305)): oracle.toplink.exceptions.DatabaseException

Internal Exception: weblogic.jdbc.extensions.ConnectionDeadSQLException:
weblogic.common.resourcepool.ResourceDeadException: 0:weblogic.common.
ResourceException: Could not create pool connection. The DBMS driver
exception was: IO Error: Socket read timed out
```

The `wls_soa1-diagnostic.log` file writes entries in the **Oracle Diagnostic Logging (ODL)** format. The following figure provides the prototype of a log message in the ODL format. This is a text file, and the entries in this file conform to an Oracle standard that includes information such as the timestamp, server name, error type, component ID, user, and other log information.

Figure 6.18: The anatomy of an ODL log file

In the following log snippet, the entry in the file shows the `CustomerProduce` operation, which inserts a message into a JMS queue, failing due to a connection issue:

```
[2015-10-01T17:12:05.211-05:00] [wls_soa1] [ERROR] [] [oracle.soa.
adapter] [tid: [ACTIVE].ExecuteThread: '2' for queue: 'weblogic.kernel.
Default (self-tuning)'] [userId: <anonymous>] [ecid: cb680017c6a0acfe:-
606797c4:134357968da:-8000-00000000000011fa,0:2] [WEBSERVICE_PORT.name:
CustomerJMSProduce_pt] [APP: soa-infra] [composite_name: JMSProducer]
[component_name: CustomerJMSProduce] [component_instance_id: 12] [J2EE_
MODULE.name: fabric] [WEBSERVICE.name: customerjmsproduce_client_ep]
[J2EE_APP.name: soa-infra] JCABinding=> JMSProducer:CustomerJMS [
CustomerProduce_ptt::CustomerProduce(opaque) ]  Could not invoke
operation 'CustomerProduce' against the 'null' due to: [[

BINDING.JCA-12511

JCA Binding Component connection issue.
```

By right-clicking on **soa-infra** and navigating to **Logs** | **Log Configuration**, you will be taken to the page that allows you to configure the logger levels. This is shown in the following screenshot:

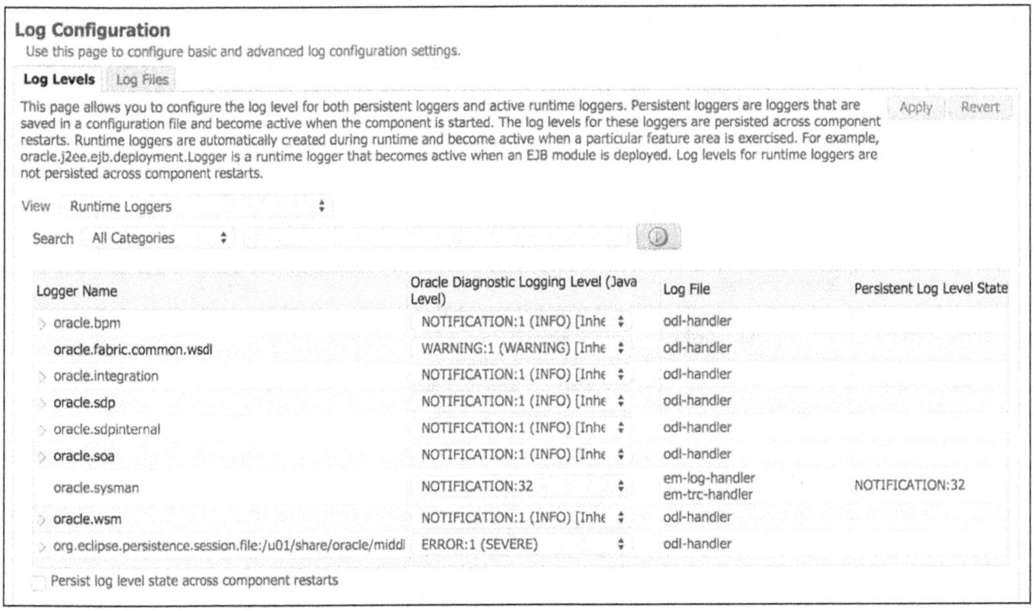

Figure 6.19: Reviewing and modifying logger levels

Navigate to **oracle.soa** | **oracle.soa.bpel** | **oracle.soa.bpel.engine** | **oracle.soa.bpel. engine.deployment** and set the logging level from **NOTIFICATION:1 (INFO)** to **TRACE:1 (FINE)**.

Now, rerun the JMSProducer composite results with considerably more information in the `wls_soa1-diagnostic.log` file, including the payload:

[2015-10-01T22:35:56.144-05:00] [wls_soa1] [TRACE] [] [oracle.soa.
adapter] [tid: [ACTIVE].ExecuteThread: '2' for queue: 'weblogic.kernel.
Default (self-tuning)'] [userId: <anonymous>] [ecid: cb680017c6a0acfe:-
3f1527ec:13487d1ea4c:-8000-0000000000000fe1,0:2] [SRC_CLASS: oracle.
integration.platform.blocks.adapter.fw.log.LogManagerImpl] [WEBSERVICE_
PORT.name: CustomerJMSProduce_pt] [APP: soa-infra] [composite_name:
JMSProducer] [component_name: CustomerJMSProduce] [component_instance_id:
30005] [J2EE_MODULE.name: fabric] [SRC_METHOD: log] [WEBSERVICE.name:
customerjmsproduce_client_ep] [J2EE_APP.name: soa-infra] JMS Adapter
JMSProducer:CustomerJMS [CustomerProduce_ptt::CustomerProduce(body)
] JmsProducer_execute:[default destination = jndi/CustomerJMSQueue]:
Successfully produced message.

[2015-10-01T22:35:56.256-05:00] [wls_soa1] [NOTIFICATION] [] [oracle.
soa.adapter] [tid: weblogic.work.j2ee.J2EEWorkManager$WorkWithLi
stener@16bc6851] [userId: <anonymous>] [ecid: cb680017c6a0acfe:-
5675273b:1348cccad75:-8000-0000000000055743,0] [APP: soa-infra]
JMSAdapter JMSConsumer JMSMessageConsumer_consume: Got message with ID
ID:<458362.1325475356144.0> from destination jndi/CustomerJMSQueue

[2015-10-01T22:35:56.261-05:00] [wls_soa1] [TRACE] [] [oracle.
soa.adapter] [tid: weblogic.work.j2ee.J2EEWorkManager$WorkWithLi
stener@16bc6851] [userId: <anonymous>] [ecid: cb680017c6a0acfe:-
5675273b:1348cccad75:-8000-0000000000055743,0] [SRC_
CLASS: oracle.integration.platform.blocks.adapter.fw.log.
LogManagerImpl] [APP: soa-infra] [SRC_METHOD: log] JMS Adapter
JMSProducer:CustomerJMS [CustomerProduce_ptt::CustomerProduce(body)
] XMLHelper_convertJmsMessageHeadersAndPropertiesToXML:
<JMSInboundHeadersAndProperties xmlns="http://xmlns.oracle.com/pcbpel/
adapter/jms/">[[

    <JMSInboundHeaders>

        <JMSCorrelationID></JMSCorrelationID>

        <JMSDeliveryMode>2</JMSDeliveryMode>

        <JMSExpiration>0</JMSExpiration>

        <JMSMessageID>ID:<458362.1325475356144.0></JMSMessageID>

        <JMSPriority>0</JMSPriority>

        <JMSRedelivered>false</JMSRedelivered>

        <JMSType></JMSType>

        <JMSTimestamp>1325475356144</JMSTimestamp>

    </JMSInboundHeaders>

    <JMSInboundProperties>

```
        <Property name="tracking_ecid" value="cb680017c6a0acfe:-
3f1527ec:13487d1ea4c:-8000-0000000000000fe1"/>

        <Property name="tracking_compositeInstanceId" value="30006"/>

        <Property name="tracking_parentComponentInstanceId"
value="bpel:30005"/>

        <Property name="tracking_conversationId" value="urn:E115FC7034F211E
1BF23313DB35B2981"/>

        <Property name="JMSXDeliveryCount" type="integer" value="1"/>

    </JMSInboundProperties>

</JMSInboundHeadersAndProperties>
```

The `access.log` file logs all HTTP requests to the internal web server following the standard Apache HTTP Server log format. Reviewing this may help in identifying all the SOAP requests that have hit your managed server, as this is the first touch point of the server. This is an example of an entry in the `access.log` file:

```
192.168.97.111 - - [18/Oct/2015:12:12:59 -0500] "POST /soa-infra/
services/default/HelloWorld/helloworld_client_ep HTTP/1.1" 200 466
```

> The same message may be duplicated across many of these log files, so you should gain familiarity with each of them; after this, you will know what to look for.

Monitoring Service Engine instances and faults

As an administrator, you will sometimes need to monitor the recent instances and faults of the different components running in the SOA Infrastructure. The execution status and metrics for an instance in a particular engine can be monitored from the Fusion Middleware Control console by right-clicking on **soa-infra** and navigating to **Service Engines | [Component] | Statistics**.

Once you are there, you can observe high-level statistics for the selected component engine. The four component engines you can choose from are BPEL, Mediator, human workflow, and Business Rules. Each of their pages display statistics differently, depending on the engine. The following screenshot shows an example of the statistics for the **Mediator Engine** information.

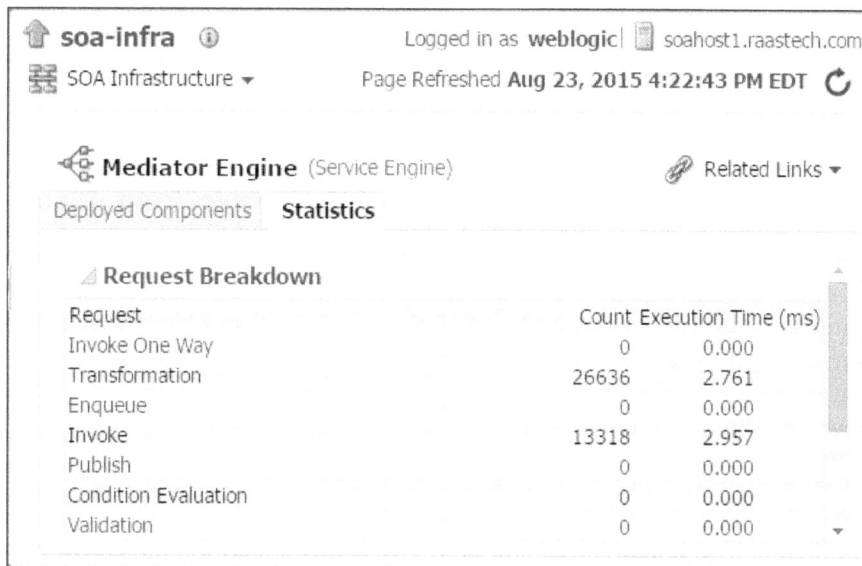

Figure 6.20: Monitoring at the service engine level, in this case, the Mediator Engine

Here, you can see that the majority of processing is roughly divided between transformations and invocations. The BPEL Engine statistics page, on the other hand, lists the total number of active threads and the total number of active and pending requests.

This service engine statistics page is merely a snapshot but provides a quick insight into the overall performance of the engine and the types of request that burden it.

Monitoring Event Delivery Network

Oracle SOA Suite 12*c* has an out-of-the-box EDN that allows you to publish and subscribe to business events. The EDN framework creates the messaging plumbing out of the box so you will not have to create any backend queues in the infrastructure. The default EDN is configured on the database and this uses Oracle **Advanced Queuing (AQ)** behind the scenes. You can also have an EDN based on JMS that uses the JMS API. In the development and testing stages, access to the EDN logs will be of great help to identify and troubleshoot issues with your EDN implementation. You can change the EDN logging level by following the steps listed here:

1. Log in to Oracle Manager Fusion Middleware Control.

2. Right-click on **soa-infra** and then navigate to **Logs | Log Configuration**.

3. Expand the logger nodes to **oracle.integration.platform.blocks.event** or enter `blocks.event` in the search box and press the **Search** button to filter the view.

4. Change the log level of **oracle.integration.platform.blocks.event.saq** to `TRACE:32`. Configuring the logging at this level will ensure that the body of the event message is available in the EDN trace.

5. Check the **Persist log level state across component restarts** box and click on the **Apply** button. This will let the log level survive the managed server restarts.

In addition to configuring the EDN runtime Java loggers as discussed before, you can also enable the debug flag when using the default EDN implementation based on the database. The value of the `ENABLED` column in the `EDN_LOG_ENABLED` table in the dehydration store can be set to `1` to make the EDN logs available for review and configuration in a browser console at `http://<soahost>:<soaport>/soa-infra/events/edn-db-log`.

This page displays the event payload and status (`Enqueing event`, `Enqueing Complete`, `Dequeing Complete`, and so on.). The logging is disabled by default. However, it can be enabled by clicking on the `ENABLE` link on the page. You can also CLEAR the debug table or RELOAD logs from the same page.

Oracle WebLogic Server monitoring

From an infrastructure monitoring perspective, ensuring that Oracle WebLogic Server and all its underlying components are functioning should be your primary concern. In this section, we describe the monitoring of some core areas that have the largest influence on Oracle SOA Suite, namely managed servers, JVM, JMS destinations, and data sources.

Managed servers

As long as your managed servers are reported as healthy, there is usually not much to worry about. A warning state does not necessarily indicate that the managed server is unresponsive, but the cause of the warning should be investigated nonetheless. One of the key issues to managed server monitoring is ensuring the appropriate monitoring of threads.

To view the state of the managed servers, perform the following steps:

1. Log in to the Oracle WebLogic Server Administration Console.

2. On the home page, click on **Servers**.

3. A list of all your managed servers will appear, as shown in the following screenshot:

New Clone Delete						Showing 1 to 9 of 9 Previous | Next
Name ⌃	Type	Cluster	Machine	State	Health	Listen Port
AdminServer(admin)	Configured		adminhost	RUNNING	✅ OK	7001
wls_ess1	Configured	ESS_Cluster	soahost1	RUNNING	✅ OK	8021
wls_ess2	Configured	ESS_Cluster	soahost2	SHUTDOWN	Not reachable	8021
wls_osb1	Configured	OSB_Cluster	soahost1	RUNNING	✅ OK	8011
wls_osb2	Configured	OSB_Cluster	soahost2	SHUTDOWN	Not reachable	8011
wls_soa1	Configured	SOA_Cluster	soahost1	RUNNING	✅ OK	8001
wls_soa2	Configured	SOA_Cluster	soahost2	SHUTDOWN	Not reachable	8001
wls_wsm1	Configured	WSM-PM_Cluster	soahost1	RUNNING	✅ OK	7010
wls_wsm2	Configured	WSM-PM_Cluster	soahost2	SHUTDOWN	Not reachable	7010
New Clone Delete						Showing 1 to 9 of 9 Previous | Next

Figure 6.21: Viewing managed server state and health

Ensure that the managed servers are running and are in a healthy state as designated by the green checkbox with **OK**. In *Chapter 9, Troubleshooting the Oracle SOA Suite 12c Infrastructure*, we have discussed the approaches to troubleshooting warnings or failed managed server states.

JVM

Although there are too many areas surrounding JVM monitoring to describe here, three of the more important ones include ensuring that the heap allocated on the JVM is appropriately sized (that is, comparing heap versus non-heap usage), that there is not excessive garbage collection, and that JVM thread performance is acceptable. Perform the following steps for the garbage collection information:

1. Log in to the Oracle WebLogic Server Administration Console.

2. On the home page, click on **Servers**.

3. Click on one of the server names.

4. Navigate to the **Monitoring | Performance** tab.

5. Here, the total heap size and the percentage of the free heap are displayed.

6. Click on the **Garbage Collect** button. Observe how much **Heap Free Current** is freed before and after the garbage collection.

Oracle WebLogic Server 12c also provides a dashboard that provides real-time monitoring of many metrics, including the JVM runtime heap. This is helpful for reviewing the server while there is a heavy load on the system as it allows you to view the current and free heap size.

Go to `http://adminhost:7001/console/dashboard`. Select **JVM Runtime Heap** and click on the **start** button. **Heap Size Current** and **Heap Free Current** are graphically displayed, as shown in *Figure 6.22*.

If the free heap hovers around zero for a considerable time, this is an indication that the heap size may be configured too small. If repeated and frequent garbage collections occur without much memory being freed up, additional JVM monitoring may be required at that point.

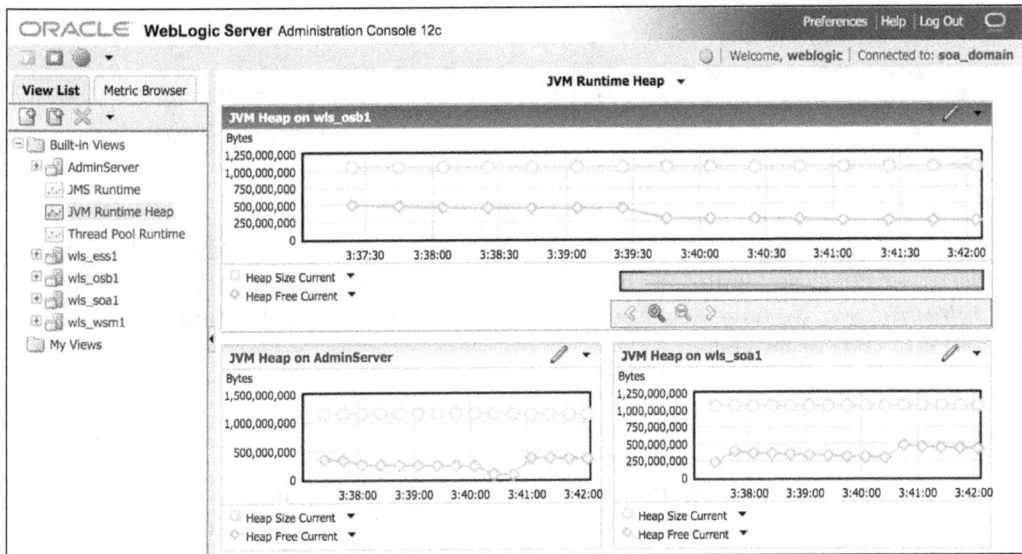

Figure 6.22: The Oracle WebLogic Server Monitoring Dashboard

From the Oracle WebLogic Server Monitoring Dashboard, the **Thread Pool Runtime** can also be monitored in real time. The key is to monitor the **Hogging Thread Count** and the **Pending User Request Count**. In a low-usage environment, these should hover around zero. From the Oracle WebLogic Administration Console, navigate to **Servers** | **[wls_soa1]** | **Monitoring** | **Threads** to view similar information. Various thread pool metrics are displayed there. Everything from **Active Execute Threads** to **Hogging Thread Count** is shown on this page.

The **Throughput** shown on this page is a single value that denotes the mean number of requests completed per second. The higher this value, the better. But the thread pool changes its size automatically to maximize the throughput, so in normal cases, there is nothing you need to do aside from monitoring it to understand the behavior of your server under different types of load.

JMS destinations

More often than not, many of the integrations that run on top of Oracle SOA Suite 12*c* may leverage JMS destinations to support asynchronous integrations. These destinations can be JMS queues (for point-to-point integrations) or JMS topics (for publish-subscribe integrations). Oracle WebLogic Server 12*c* provides a way to easily create these JMS destinations that become accessible via a JNDI lookup in the code.

As an administrator, you must be aware of all queues and topics created, as there are many reasons why you would want to monitor them:

- Ensure that messages in the queues and topics are being produced and consumed without error and/or delay.
- Ensure that poison messages (messages that can never successfully be processed) are not persisted in the queue or topic.

To monitor your JMS destinations, perform the following steps:

1. Log in to the Oracle WebLogic Administration Console.
2. Click on **JMS Modules**.
3. Click on the JMS module name that is hosting your queue/topic.
4. Click on the queue or topic name.
5. Click on the **Monitoring** tab. Here, you will see a summary of statistics regarding your JMS destination such as current, pending, and total messages.

6. If the JMS destination already has subscribers, click on the checkbox beside your destination name and then click on the **Show Messages** button. From here, you can export some or all of the messages to an XML file should you choose to (for either backup purposes or with the intention of importing them into a different environment).

7. Click on the JMS message ID. The following screenshot displays the result of this. Details of the message are displayed as part of the JMS header, including the ECID, composite instance ID, and the payload of the message:

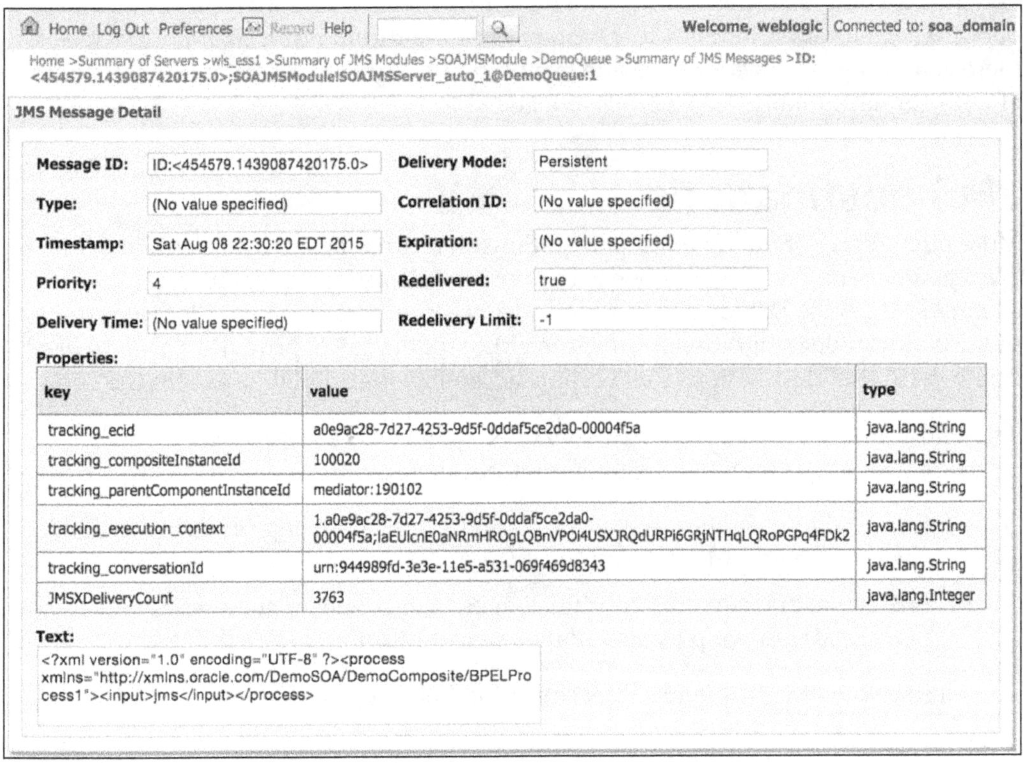

Figure 6.23: Viewing the details of a JMS message

Data sources

For data source monitoring, usually all that is needed is the connection pool configuration to be valid (that is, there are no connectivity issues to the database) and the number of active connections does not approach or exceed the maximum configured connections. There are cases, such as where the time it takes to establish a connection is long (refer to the **Connection Delay Time** column), but these are not common and usually appear in inadequately sized environments.

To check the JDBC Data Source Runtime Statistics, go through the following steps:

1. Log in to the Oracle WebLogic Administration Console.

2. Click on **Data Sources**.

3. Click on the **Monitoring** tab. Here, the state of the data sources (for example, running), as well as the average, current, and high active connection counts are displayed.

4. Click on **Customize this table**. From the **Column Display Available** table, select **Current Capacity**, **Leaked Connection Count**, **Number Available**, and **Active Connections Current Count** and move them under **Chosen Column**.

5. Click on **Apply**.

6. The **Monitoring** tab of the data source will look as shown in the following screenshot. The key is to ensure that the sum of **Active Connections Current Count** and **Leaked Connection Count** does not exceed the connection pool's Current Capacity. If they do, then it is either time to fix the leaked connections or increase the pool's capacity.

7. To get the maximum capacity to determine how to appropriately size your connection pool, perform the following steps:

    1. Click on the data source name (for example, mds-soa).

    2. Navigate to **Configuration** | **Connection Pool**.

    3. Note the setting of the **Maximum Capacity** parameter.

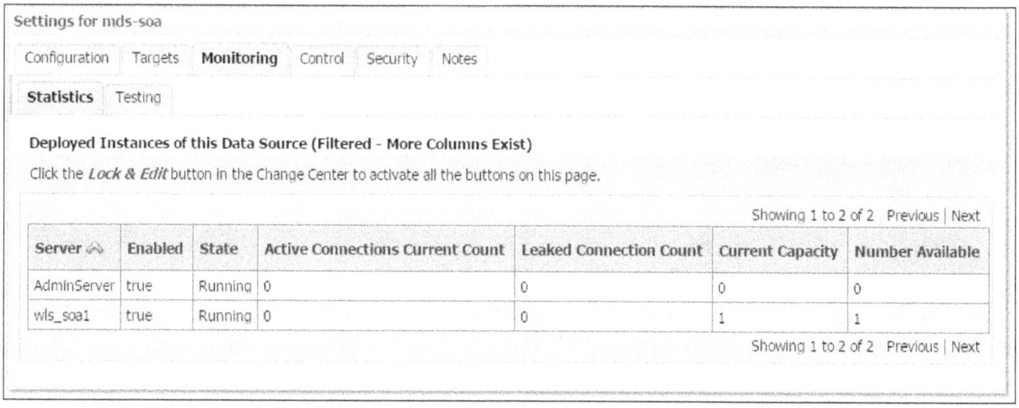

Settings for mds-soa

Configuration   Targets   **Monitoring**   Control   Security   Notes

Statistics   Testing

Deployed Instances of this Data Source (Filtered - More Columns Exist)

Click the *Lock & Edit* button in the Change Center to activate all the buttons on this page.

Showing 1 to 2 of 2   Previous | Next

Server	Enabled	State	Active Connections Current Count	Leaked Connection Count	Current Capacity	Number Available
AdminServer	true	Running	0	0	0	0
wls_soa1	true	Running	0	0	1	1

Showing 1 to 2 of 2   Previous | Next

Figure 6.24: Monitoring data sources

In cases where the database may not be accessible or is down, the database password used for the connection pool has had its password reset, network-related issues occur, or data source-related errors begin appearing in the logs, it may be worth testing to ensure that the data source is working properly by performing the following steps:

1. Log in to the Oracle WebLogic Administration Console.

2. Click on **Data Sources**.

3. Click on the data source name (for example, `mds-soa`).

4. Navigate to **Monitoring | Testing**.

5. Select the radio button and click on the **Test Data Source** button.

6. If the connection is working (that is, the data source is able to access the database at the host, port, database name, username, and password), the following message will appear at the top of the page:

```
Test of [mds-soa] on server [wls_soa1] was successful.
```

OEM Cloud Control and the SOA Management Pack

The latest **Oracle Enterprise Manager (OEM)** Cloud Control 12*c* is Oracle's monitoring and management product of choice for the majority of Oracle software and applications. By leveraging OEM Cloud Control, you can monitor and manage all your Oracle and non-Oracle software through a single centralized console.

OEM Cloud Control should not be confused with Oracle Enterprise Manager Fusion Middleware Control and especially with Oracle Enterprise Manager, which is a console shipped with the Oracle Database and older versions of the Oracle Application Server.

An agent (specifically, the Oracle Management Agent) is installed on every server you wish to monitor, and the data on that system is collected and reported back to the central repository (specifically, the Oracle Management Server) at regular intervals. It is through the **Oracle Management Server (OMS)** that you can log in via a web browser to view the server status and performance, configure alerts, and perform administrative tasks.

For environments with a large number of applications, systems, and servers, we recommend you to use a monitoring tool such as OEM Cloud Control to simplify the monitoring and management functions of the administrator. Some key benefits of OEM Cloud Control include the following:

- Centralized monitoring and management of both Oracle and non-Oracle applications and software

- Preconfigured alerts

- Out-of-the-box support for targets such as applications (for example, Oracle E-Business Suite and Oracle Fusion Applications), middleware (for example, Oracle WebLogic Server and Oracle SOA Suite), databases, operating systems (for example, Windows, Linux, AIX, and Solaris), virtual machines, and more

- The ability to perform administrative functions such as start up/shut down, patching, cloning, provisioning, capturing diagnostic information, and much more

- The following screenshot provides information about component instances:

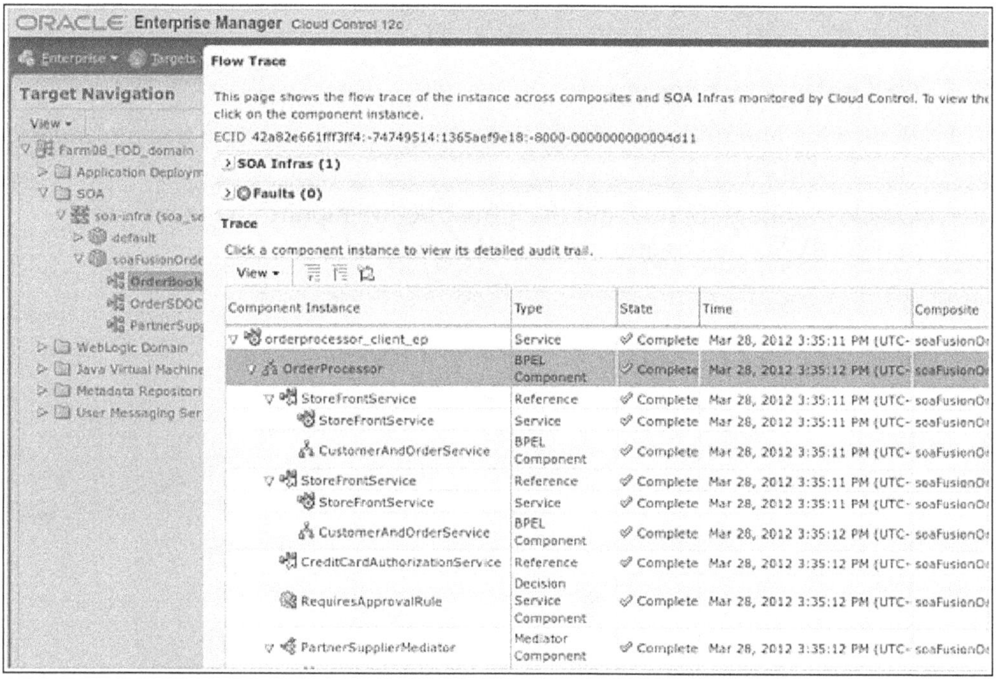

Figure 6.25: SOA composite instance search and trace (image courtesy of Oracle Corporation)

The Oracle SOA Management Pack Enterprise Edition is a separate license, which extends OEM Cloud Control to provide additional functionality such as visibility into complex SOA orchestrations, monitoring of security policies, performance monitoring of Oracle SOA Suite and Oracle Service Bus, and tracing of end-to-end transactions across tiers.

Though *Figure 6.25* looks very similar to what we are accustomed to seeing in Oracle Enterprise Manager Fusion Middleware Control, imagine performing these functions for all your environments from a single, centralized console!

Summary

As an Oracle SOA Suite 12c administrator, you must be comfortable with the monitoring of both the infrastructure as well as transactions. In this chapter, we covered the following topics:

- SOA composite instance monitoring
- Performance of composite instances through the console and SQL queries
- Service engine monitoring
- OSB instance monitoring
- Reviewing and understanding relevant logs, using selective tracing, and the structure of a log entry
- Oracle WebLogic Server and the infrastructure monitoring of managed servers, JVM, queues and topics, and data sources

7
Configuration and Administration

By far, this book has covered several topics in detail, describing many ways to monitor and tune your Oracle SOA Suite 12*c* infrastructure. This chapter will focus on configuring and administering various components that are part of a SOA Suite 12*c* environment. Depending upon the type of composites deployed to the runtime, you as an administrator would need to manage the composite instances, the service engines they execute on, and the additional platform components they use.

The Oracle SOA Suite 12*c* infrastructure provides a rich user interface with access to all deployed composite applications, service engines, service components, business events, notifications, and other platform components. You can also perform a range of administrative tasks such as managing composites and their individual instances, taking corrective actions for faulted and rejected messages, setup auditing, securing composites or components within them by attaching/detaching security policies, and much more. To start with and be able to successfully take up common management tasks of your environment, it is important to be conversant with the methods of navigating to these administration task consoles in Oracle Enterprise Manager Fusion Middleware Control 12*c*.

Navigating key administration areas

In Oracle Enterprise Manager Fusion Middleware Control 12*c*, dashboards have been revamped to focus on quick views of health checks, alerts, and access to faults and saved searches. The landing page is divided into a navigator pane on the left and a dynamic, content-driven dashboard on the right. The navigation tree can be expanded to configure and manage the WebLogic domain, admin and running managed servers, the SOA and OSB infrastructure, metadata repositories, and so on. The following figure shows the navigator view along with the common domain-level dashboard:

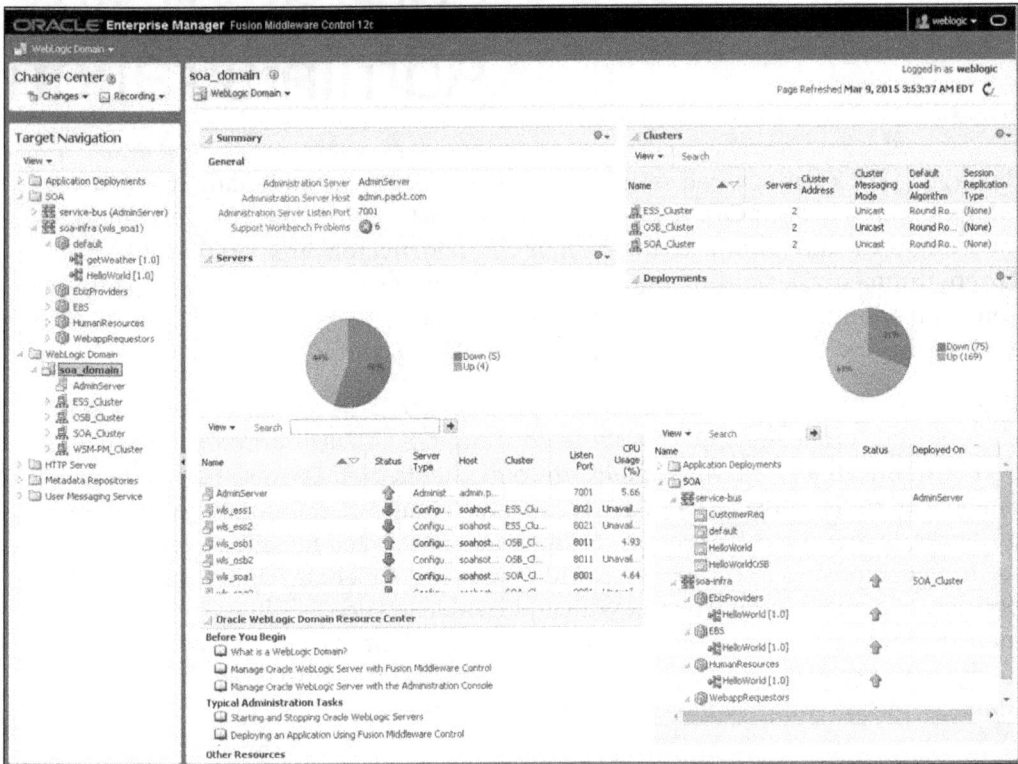

Figure 7.1: Key administration tasks for SOA Infrastructure

The following instructions will help you familiarize yourself with the new dashboards at the SOA domain level:

1. Log in to Oracle Enterprise Manager Fusion Middleware Control.

    ° The domain-level dashboard is displayed as shown in the preceding figure.

    ° The **Deployments** section shows the status of the deployed projects.

    ° The dashboard also shows a summary of admin and managed servers and their statuses.

    ° A brief help section and link to common administration tasks is provided under the Oracle WebLogic Domain Resource Center.

2. Under the **Target Navigation** panel on the left, right-click on the **SOA** folder.

3. From the drop-down menu, select **Expand All Below**. Expanding the SOA folder will show a tree structure with the OSB and SOA engine along with all deployed SOA and OSB projects.

4. Select the **soa-infra (soa_server1)** node to display the SOA infrastructure dashboard at the domain level, as shown in *Figure 7.2*, depicting various summary sections such as:

    ° **Key Configuration**: This section shows default key configurations and provides links on the right for more information and links to change these configuration parameters.

    ° **SOA Runtime Health**: This section shows the initialization status of the infrastructure.

    ° **System Backlogs**: This section provides a snapshot of transactions that are currently being processed in internal system queues.

    ° Oracle SOA Suite 12*c* provides improved performance and responsiveness of Fusion Middleware Control. It does not load all the metrics at once but instead has users define a query window to display the relevant metric.

    ° **Business Transaction Faults**: This section shows a bar graph depicting the states of different types of transaction faults. The graph has hot spots that administrators can click to drill down to an out-of-the-box error hospital.

    ° **Search**: This section provides the ability to find instances based on common search parameters in addition to saved searches. Clicking on **Search Instances** after providing the query parameters will give the control to the **Flow Instances** tab.

○ **Fault Alerts**: This section shows any alerts that have been generated.

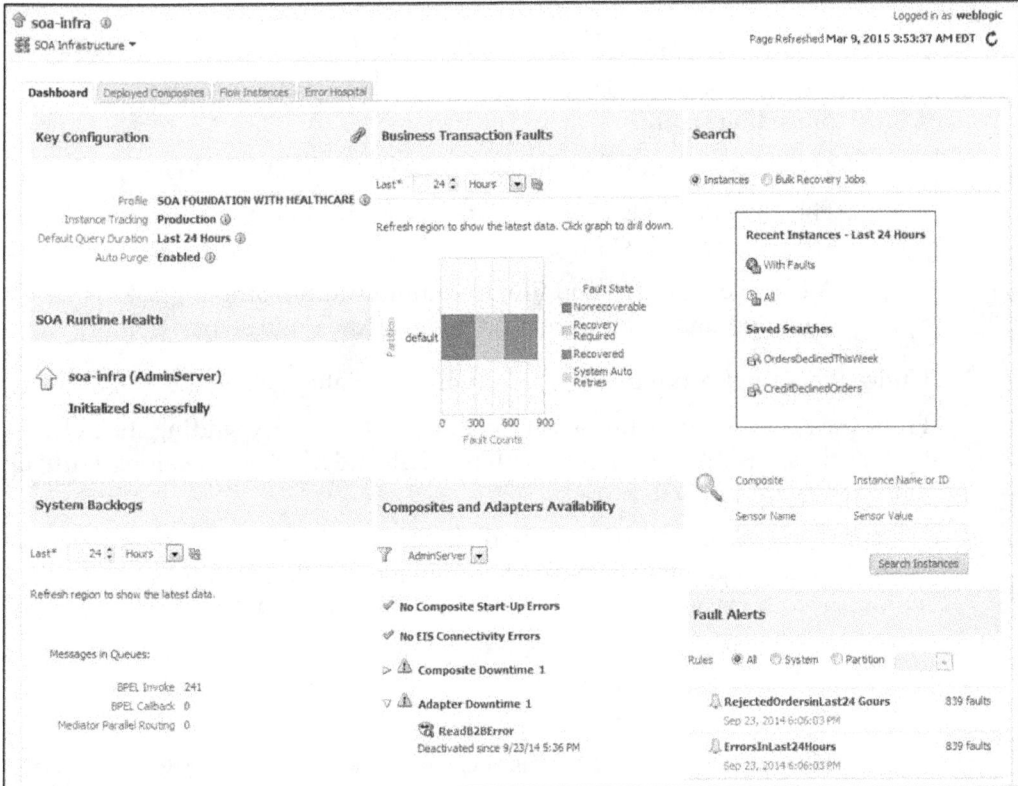

Figure 7.2: Key administration tasks for SOA Infrastructure

> This dashboard is at the domain level and shows information for all the partitions. A partition-level dashboard can be viewed by navigating to **soa-infra** | **SOA Infrastructure** | **Manage Partitions** | **[partitionName]**. The information shown is identical although at the partition level.

5. Clicking on the **SOA Infrastructure** target menu reveals a host of common administration and configuration activities that you can perform (see *Figure 7.3*), such as:

  ° Obtaining a snapshot of the SOA infrastructure and the components deployed to it, such as deployed composites, adapter and enterprise information system configurations, system and business transaction faults, and so on

  ° Monitoring Performance Summary and Request Processing statistics for binding components, service infrastructure, and service engines

  ° Viewing and editing Log Configuration for runtime loggers

  ° Managing composite deployments and their configuration plans from the **SOA Deployment** link

  ° Managing running and faulted instances of deployed composites by expanding **Service Engine** and clicking on a particular engine

  ° Administering endpoint and adapter properties post composite deployment from the **Services and References** link

  ° Configuring and managing business events, current event subscribers, and event fault details from the **Business Events** link

  ° Configuring engine properties for service components that make up the Oracle SOA Suite 12*c* runtime by expanding **SOA Administration**

  ° Using **Define Schedules** to execute a periodic or background job configured using Enterprise Scheduler service

  ° Using **Error Notification Rules** to send notifications (emails, short messages, and so on) for specific errors

Many other SOA Infrastructure configurations and properties are available to edit at runtime by navigating to the **System MBean Browser** under **Administration**.

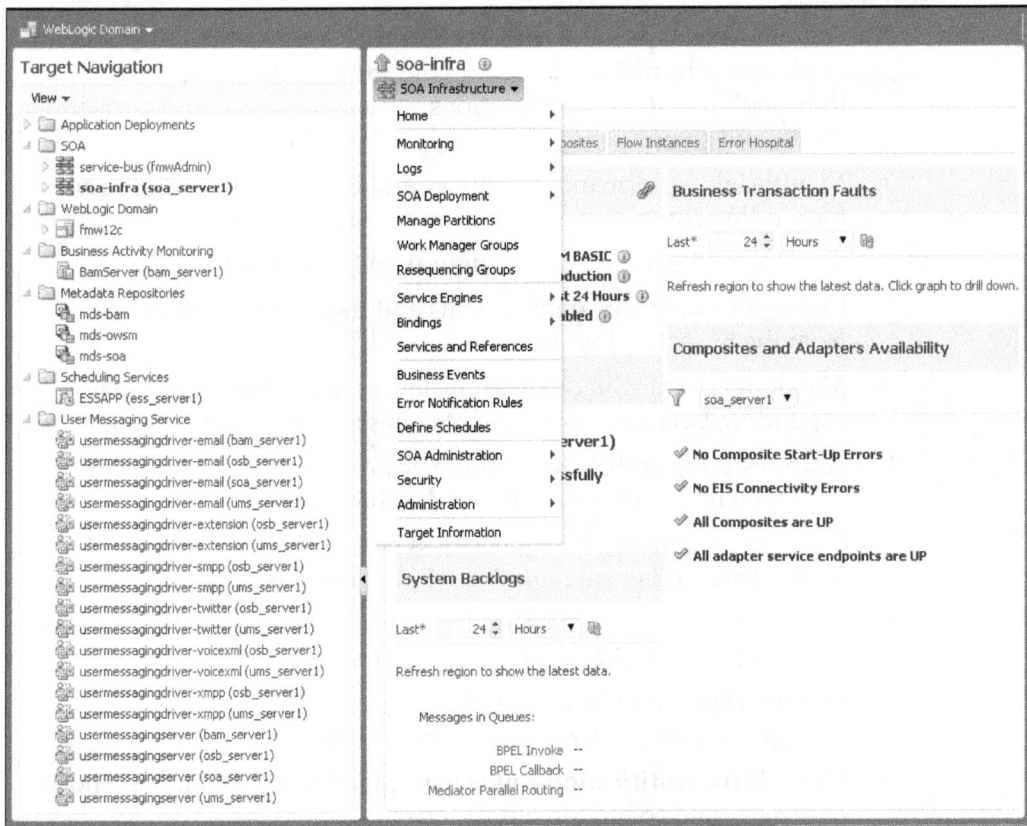

Figure 7.3: Key Administration Tasks for SOA Infrastructure

Having familiarized yourself with navigating to key administration dashboards within the Oracle Fusion Middleware Enterprise Manager Control console, it is time to get ready to execute key management tasks available from these pages. The chapter, in its course, provides details about the following tasks:

1. Introduction to Change Center.
2. Configuring Infrastructure Properties.
3. Managing composites.
4. Configuring and administering JCA adapters and binding components.
5. Configuring and administering BPEL Process Engine and components.
6. Administering the Mediator Service Engines.
7. Administering Oracle User Messaging Service.

8. Administering Human Workflow Service Engines.

9. Administering and configuring Business Activity Monitoring.

10. Administering and configuring Event Engine and Business Events.

11. Administering Domain Value Maps and Cross References.

12. Starting up and shutting down the Infrastructure.

13. Configuring infrastructure resources for developers.

As an administrator of Oracle SOA Suite 12*c*, your responsibility to manage the infrastructure and lifecycle of SOA composites is greatly simplified by the fact that a composite is composed of various components and bindings that execute on individual service engines. Rather than searching for places to manage, you can zero in on a specific engine and administer the instances that have executed on it. In the forthcoming sections of this chapter you will see exactly how to achieve this.

Introduction to Change Center

With this new release, property configurations in Oracle Enterprise Manager Fusion Middleware Control 12*c* are controlled through Change Center, similar to the one available on WebLogic Server Administration Console previously. The Change Center allows recording changes made to the console as a WLST output script, reviewing the change list, and activating/discarding changes.

Configuring infrastructure properties

The infrastructure property settings are properties that apply to all composites running on the SOA infrastructure. Configuring these properties ensures that you have some sort of global setting applied to your environment. You can configure them from by navigating to **Administration | System MBean Browser | Application Defined MBeans | oracle.as.soainfra.config**. Infrastructure properties can be altered at runtime by entering a value in the **Value** text box for the read-write MBeans, as shown in *Figure 7.4*. There is an option to even validate your modifications by invoking the validate function from the **Operations** tab. Key infrastructure properties that can be configured from MBeans include:

- Infrastructure profiles
- Lazy loading and lazy deployment parameters
- Tuning thread pool changes
- Global logging levels, audit, and cache configuration

- Callback server endpoint and dehydration data source JNDI
- JMS or database-based mode for **Event Delivery Network (EDN)** framework
- Global transactions and fatal connection retry settings
- Universal schema validation
- UDDI registry and HTTP server connections
- Infrastructure keystore locations
- Search criteria for the retrieval of recent instances and faults

Take a look at the following screenshot:

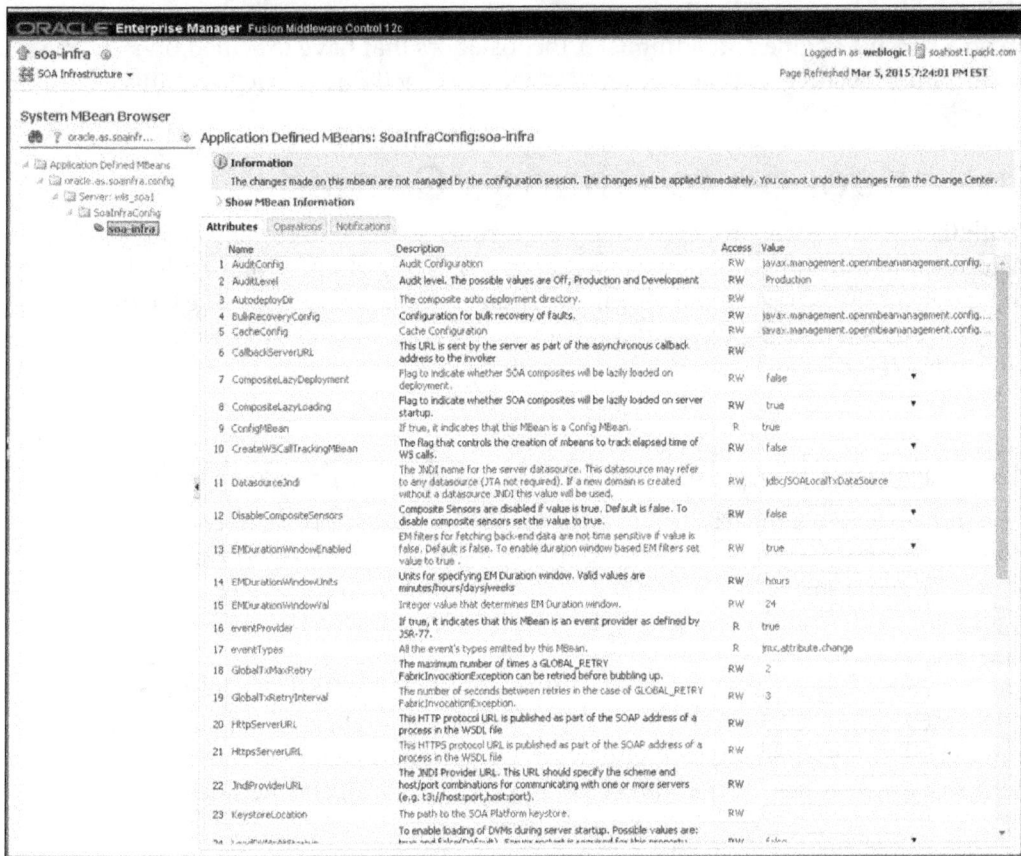

Figure 7.4: Configuring SOA Infrastructure Properties

Apart from configuring the System MBeans from a web browser, their configuration override can also be scripted with the help of **WebLogic Scripting Tool (WLST)**. This is helpful when you are in charge of managing multiple SOA infrastructures and want similar configurations applied across them all by executing a handful of scripts. These WLST scripts can be executed from the WLS offline prompt (wls:/offline>) by running wlst.sh (or wlst.cmd in Windows) under $MW_HOME/wlserver/common/bin. Configuration properties for the SOA infrastructure are available as part of a custom tree. The following WLST script connects with a running SOA server, enters its custom tree, and changes the existing directory to oracle.as.soainfra.config. You can view all MBeans under this by executing the ls() command. The common infrastructure properties can be changed by simple set([propertyName],[property Value]) statements, as shown in the following command snippet:

```
connect('<username>','<password>','<soahost>:<soaport>')
custom()
cd('oracle.as.soainfra.config/oracle.as.soainfra.config:name=soa-infra
,type=SoaInfraConfig,Application=soa-infra')
ls()
set('ValidateSchema',true)
exit()
```

Configuring and managing the infrastructure properties is just the beginning of a long journey.

Managing server profiles

Oracle SOA Suite 12*c* is comprised of different engines and numerous deployment components. As such, the memory utilization can be a problem. Some current challenges with memory utilization with Oracle SOA Suite are:

- Multi-functional capabilities of a middleware platform mean packaging multiple engines together.

- Not all engines are always needed, thereby taking up memory that can be used elsewhere.

- Expanding business means adding more composites and integration points.

- Additional composites add additional resources, adding to server startup times.

With Oracle SOA Suite 12*c*, administrators now have the choice of a number of configuration profiles which control the available functionality, modularity, and consequently, resource consumption. Modularity profiles allow for enabling only necessary components, optimizing memory. These profiles can be configured post installation through Fusion Middleware Control. Currently, there are seven different types of modularity profiles available in Oracle SOA Suite 12*c*. For example, the lightest is probably **BPEL Only**, which is BPEL, core SOA infra, and a partial set of adapters; **SOA FOUNDATION ENTERPRISE** is pretty much everything excluding B2B, Healthcare, and BPM; and **SOA CLASSIC** is everything, that is, including BPM.

To give a comparative analysis there is a 30 percent memory usage difference between BPEL Only and SOA CLASSIC profiles.

Infrastructure profiles can be viewed and modified from Oracle Enterprise Manager Fusion Middleware Control. Navigate to see the currently set profile as follows:

1. Log in to Oracle Enterprise Manager Fusion Middleware Control.

2. Right-click on **soa-infra** and navigate to **SOA Administration | Common Properties**.

3. Under **SOA Infrastructure Common Properties** the currently set profile is visible.

4. To set a different profile, use the **Change Profile** button.

5. Note that changing profiles require, a server restart to take effect.

Configuring composite lazy loading

As an Oracle SOA Suite administrator, you will realize that starting a SOA managed server is very slow. Often, the server startup logs indicate that the SOA server is up and ready to receive requests but composites are still not ready to accept requests and messages are rejected, causing end applications to error out. Beginning with the 12*c* release, this behavior can be somewhat controlled. **Lazy loading** prevents this problem by ensuring composites are ready to receive messages as soon as the SOA server is up. It loads composites minimally, thus improving the availability of the SOA servers. Lazy loading is turned on by default for the domain but can be turned off for composites that have high SLA expectations to avoid delay in processing the first message. Oracle estimates that lazy loading can start the SOA managed server give times faster when loading hundreds of composites.

To modify the lazy loading parameters, follow these instructions:

1. Log in to Oracle Enterprise Manager Fusion Middleware Control.

2. Right-click on **soa-infra** and navigate to **Administration | System MBean Browser**.

3. In the system MBean browser, expand **Application Defined MBeans | oracle.as.soainfra.config | [soa_server] | SOAInfraConfig | soa-infra**.

4. The **CompositeLazyDeployment** and **CompositeLazyLoading** properties can be changed to set or unset lazy loading of composites during either deployment or server startup, respectively (as shown in the *Figure 7.5*).

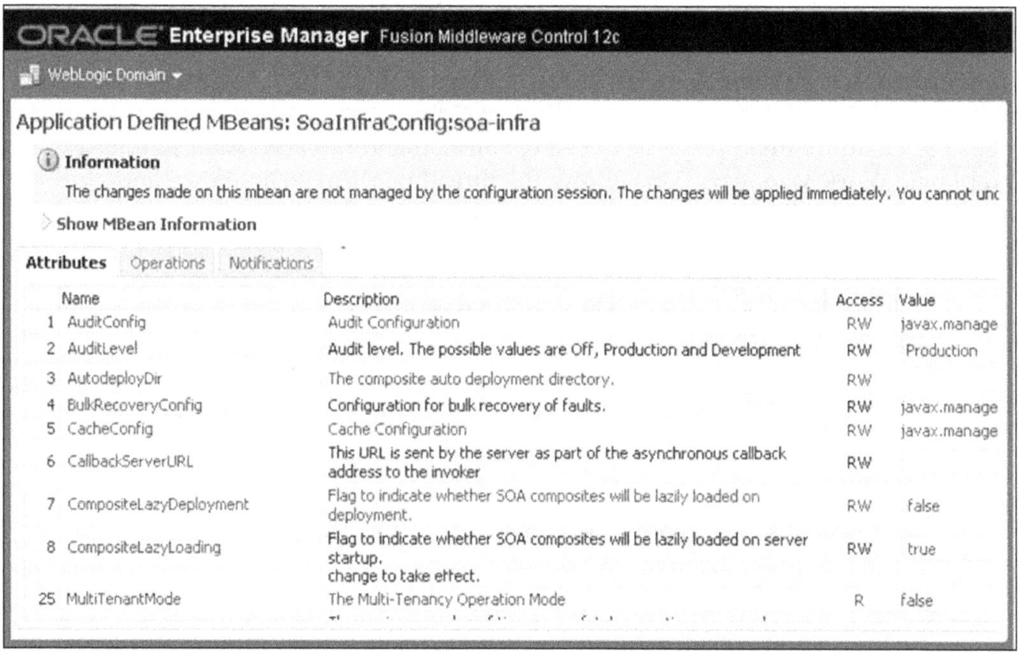

Figure 7.5: Configuring composite lazy loading

Configuring infrastructure thread pool

Though lazy loading is on by default at the domain level, it is not enabled by default for upgraded domains. It is recommended to always enable lazy loading. Despite the composites being loaded minimally, there are no concerns with their behavior. Inbound adapters still listen for messages and inbound web services can be invoked. Generally the first instantiations are a little slower as the composite artifacts are fully loaded. Lazy loading can also be controlled at the composite level, but this is done at design time by updating `composite.xml`.

Oracle SOA Suite 12*c* has redefined the model for thread pool management. In 11*g*, individual engines such as BPEL, BPMN, and Mediator had their respective thread pools that could be configured using the Fusion Middleware Control console. Dispatcher, invoke, and engine threads needed tuning adjustment relative to the infrastructure. Also there were no thread settings to control the number of incoming requests as they were handled by standard WebLogic execution threads. Beginning with 12*c*, custom thread pools have been abolished and replaced with standard WebLogic Work Managers. This allows the thread pools to be managed and monitored in a much more consistent and standard manner. A few benefits of using work managers instead of engine threads are listed here:

- Tuning for service engines is simplified as there are no individual thread based configurations.
- The self-tuning model of work managers means optimal distribution of threads across all the components based on utility and peak periods.

There are three more important changes in addition to these:

- Addition of a new Work Manager for incoming requests to that they can be limited to prevent server overload.
- Thread Constraints in the Work Managers are matched to the total number of connection pool objects on the `SOADataSource`. This minimizes the risk of threads running out of database connections.
- The self-tuning model of work managers means optimal distribution of threads across all the components based on utility and peak periods.

The Oracle SOA Suite 12*c* infrastructure now has a large number of work managers, thread constraints, and request classes with appropriate prefixes. The default configuration has each Work Manager configured to use its corresponding minimum and maximum thread constraints. For instance, SOA_Request_WM uses the SOAIncomingRequests_maxThreads constraint for handling incoming web service requests.

> Oracle SOA Suite 12*c* also allows administrators to create their own Work Manager groups. Each Work Manager is associated with its own min/max thread constraints and fair share request class. A partition in Oracle SOA Suite 12*c* has to be associated with a Work Manager group. All composites deployed to a partition thus have a share of the threads and resources defined for the associated Work Manager group.

Also, by default the SOADataSource is set to a maximum of 50 connections. Of these, 20 percent are allocated to incoming requests, 50 percent to internal processing, and 30 percent to internal buffer. By default calculations, this would result in SOAIncomingRequests_maxThreads being set to 10 threads and SOAInternalProcessing_maxThreads set to 25 threads.

Thread pool tuning is as such simplified. To change the number of threads allocated to a work manager, change the number of data source connection pool objects and/or the thread appropriation ratio. The latter can be configured from Fusion Middleware Control via the Common Properties MBeans as follows (see *Figure 7.6*):

1. Log in to Oracle Enterprise Manager Fusion Middleware Control.

2. Right-click on **soa-infra** and navigate to **Administration** | **System MBean Browser**.

3. In the **System MBean Browser**, expand **Application Defined MBeans** | **oracle.as.soainfra.config** | **[soa_server]** | **SOAInfraConfig** | **soa-infra**.

4. Click on **SOAMaxThreadsConfig** MBean. This will allow the thread appropriation to be set as percentages between internal, buffer, and incoming request processing threads.

Let's have a look at the following screenshot:

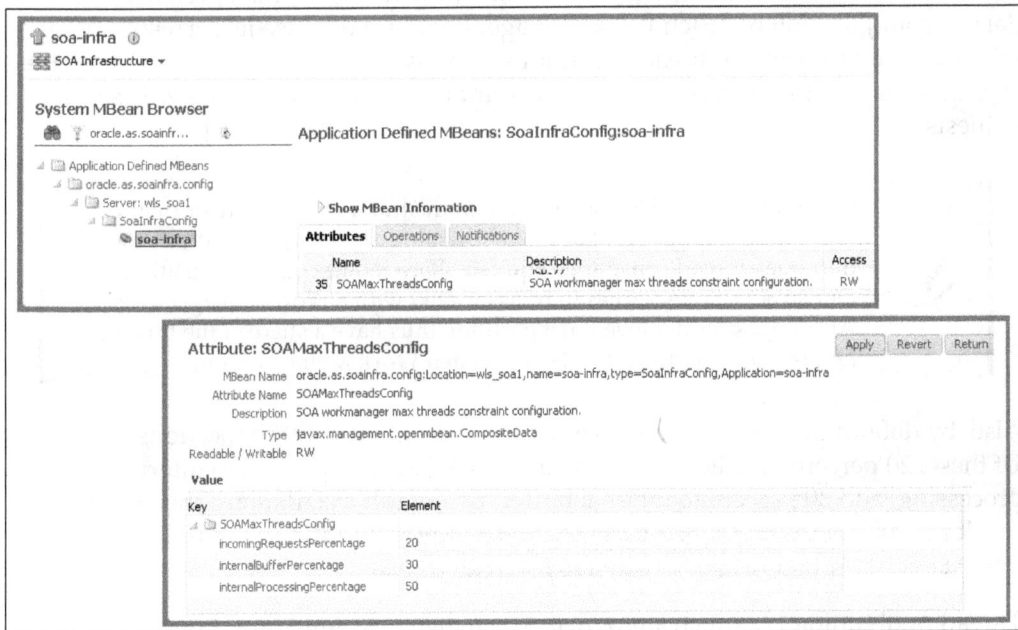

Figure 7.6: Middleware thread pool appropriation

Configuring the Global Transaction Retry settings

When the middleware infrastructure detects errors due either to faults with synchronous messages or components throwing non-recoverable error and/or transaction problems, these errors are retried before being passed for error hospital-based recovery. By default, both the default retry count and retry interval set for the platform are set to small values. The attributes controlling the number and interval of retries the infrastructure will perform when an error is returned from the downstream service engine behavior are `GlobalTxMaxRetry` and `GlobalTxRetryInterval`. These values can be changed by updating their values from the Fusion Middleware Control console.

To modify `GlobalTxMaxRetry` and `GlobalRxRetryInterval`, follow these steps:

1. Log in to Oracle Enterprise Manager Fusion Middleware Control.

2. Right-click on **soa-infra** and navigate to **Administration | System MBean Browser**.

3. In the **System MBean Browser**, expand **Application Defined MBeans | oracle.as.soainfra.config | [soa_server] | SOAInfraConfig | soa-infra**.

4. The attribute values can be overridden from the form by entering them and clicking **Apply**.

Configuring and administering SOA composites

Oracle Enterprise Manager Fusion Middleware Control 12*c* also provides further drilldown into a context-specific administration panel to manage and administer individual composites and their instances within the infrastructure. You can navigate directly to administration tasks for a specific composite by clicking on the **Deployed Composites** tab. The following screenshot shows the dashboard view of **OrderBookingComposite**:

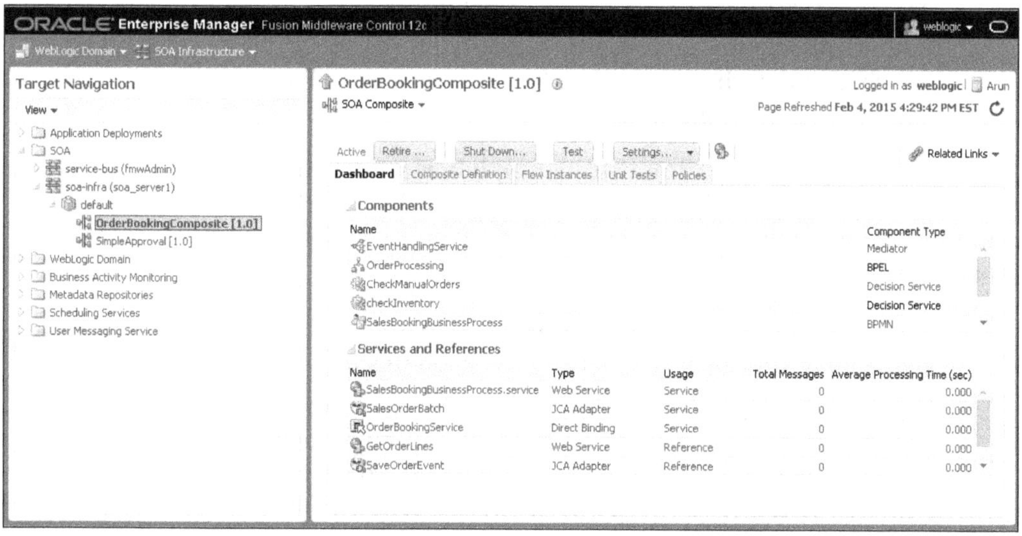

Figure 7.7: Composite dashboard view

As shown in the preceding screenshot we can observe that:

- The **Retire** and **Shut Down** buttons on the dashboard allow the composite to switch the mode and the state of the composite.

- Clicking on the **Test** button provides a list of all service bindings that are exposed from the composite. This enables manual initiation of an instance of this composite through the Test Web Service page.

- The **Settings** menu can be expanded to turn off or on composite payload validations, enable or disable sensors, and change the audit levels.

- A new feature of Oracle SOA Suite 12*c* is the ability to see the composite assembly from the composite dashboard at runtime. This can be viewed from the **Composite Definition** tab.

- The **Unit Tests** option allows you to run test cases that simulate interaction between the composite and its references before deployment to a production environment.

- The **Oracle Web Service Manager** (**OWSM**) based policies for authentication, authorization, message integrity, identity propagation, and so on, can be attached or detached at runtime from the policies link to services, references, or components in a composite.

Additionally, many of the administration activities specific to the current composite are available from the **SOA Composite** menu, which appears below the selected composite. Some of the common and important ones are described here, as also shown in *Figure 7.8*:

- The SOA Deployment menu allows you to undeploy the composite from the partition or replace it with a newer version through the Redeploy action.

- Deployed Composites can also be exported as compressed archives through the Export facility. Composites can be exported to include all runtime changes, only the runtime changes, or just the originally deployed package. The exported archive can be used to promote the composite to other environments through a corresponding Import mechanism.

- A composite typically comprises of exposed services and external references that are bound to change at runtime after the composite is deployed to the infrastructure. Runtime properties of binding components can be updated by expanding the **Service/Reference Properties** section.

Let's have a look at the following screenshot:

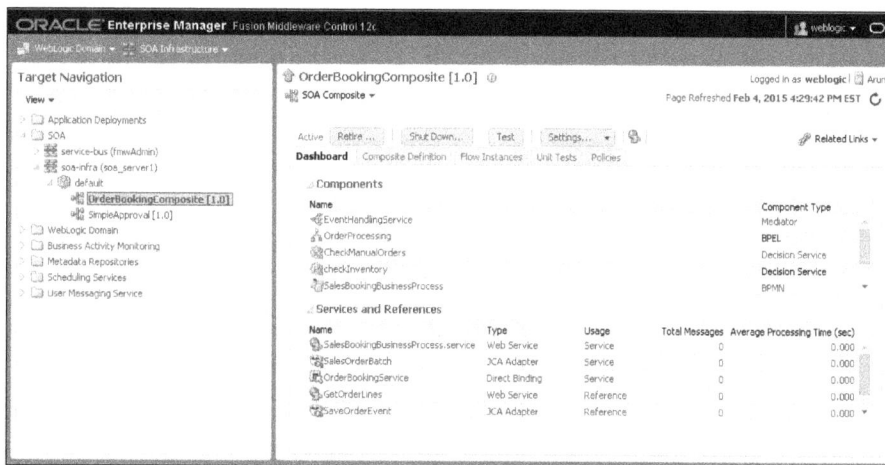

Figure 7.8: Administration tasks for a SOA composite

The composites and service engine dashboard also includes a **Related Links** menu that provides relevant additional links depending on the current context. *Figure 7.9* shows the **Related Links** menu on the **BPEL Service Engine** page, from where you can navigate directly to the SOA Infrastructure home page, the **BPEL Properties** page (to configure engine properties), the Oracle WebLogic Server Administration Console, or the page for viewing **BPEL Engine** log files.

All service engines, SOA Infrastructure Common Properties, and business event dashboards provide access to the **WebLogic Server Console** under the **Related Links** list. Clicking on the ⬏ icon will take you to the a SOA composite in a new tab or browser window:

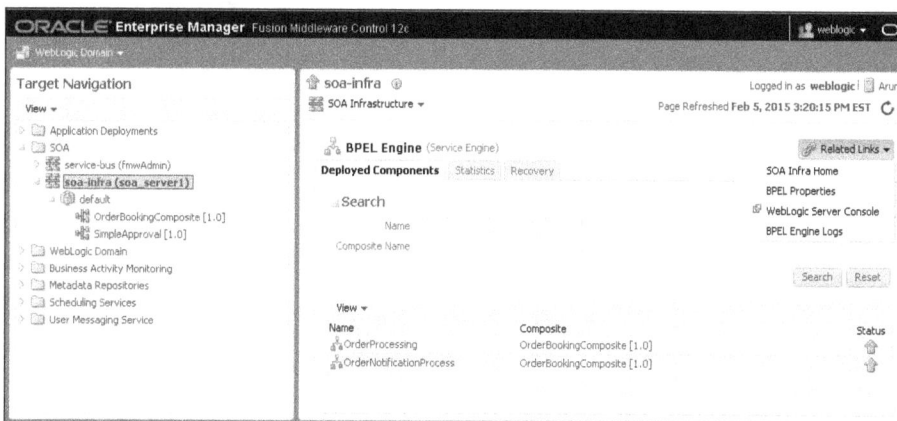

Figure 7.9: The Related Links menu

To make sure you have a better grasp of learning to manage and administer the lifecycle of an Oracle SOA Suite 12*c* environment in production, we introduce in this chapter a brief case study of a composite (having multiple services, references, and components) that is deployed to the infrastructure. You, as the SOA administrator, are responsible for its management. The composite can be invoked over a standard web service protocol or over **Remote Method Invocation (RMI)**. A provision is also made such that it can read batches of orders stored in some file-based directory. Once the composite receives an order or an order collection in any of the ways just described, the composite execution is initiated. It requests additional details for the order from backend systems, runs a set of fulfillment and approval rules, publishes status updates, and eventually sends out an email notification. The approval rules determine whether a particular order should be processed automatically or needs manual approval, in which case human intervention is sought.

Now imagine that you are relied upon to manage this critical business process of your organization and need to ensure that you have a good handle on configuring and administering various engines that instances of this composite run on. It may also be required of you to manage or bulk manage live/completed instances, handle faulted messages (setting up manual and automatic retries), set up notification channels, ensure that the external references are not timing out or unavailable, allow for business rules to change dynamically at runtime, and so on and so forth. Don't feel lost! This chapter will address this in detail, step by step, and arm you with sufficient knowledge to handle all these tasks with ease and effectiveness. The following figure shows a typical composite developed to automate the processing of sales orders:

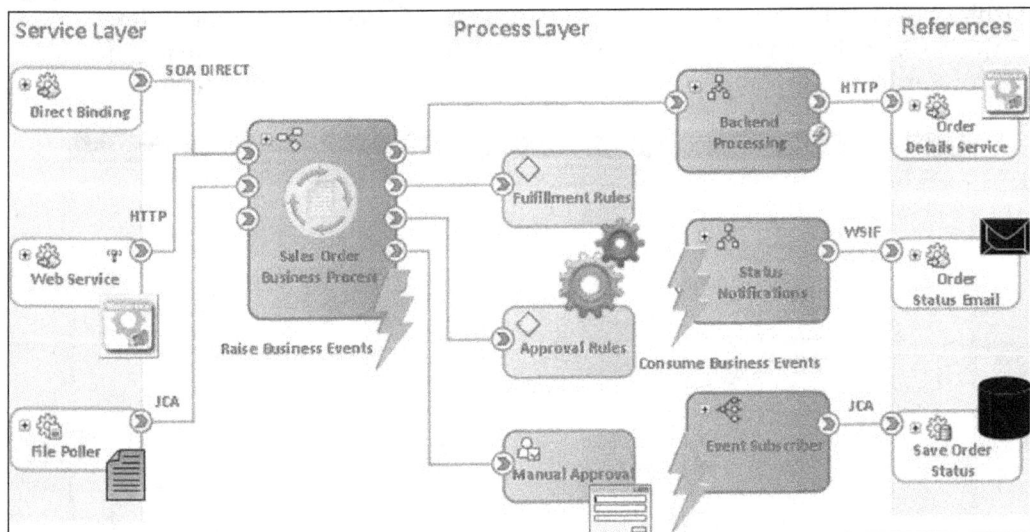

Figure 7-10. A typical sales order composite application [case study]

Composite instance tracking and flow instances

A major enhancement in Oracle SOA Suite 12*c* instance administration is the improvement to the instance tracking experience. Not merely providing better usability, the instance tracking feature has undergone an underlying architectural improvement to deliver better performance, visibility, and traceability of composite transactions. It is integrated with the composite dashboards. The following section will help familiarize administrators with navigating around instance tracking and its various features. The example used here will again be the `OrderBookingComposite` depicted in *Figure 7.10* earlier:

1. Log in to Fusion Middleware Control and navigate to the composite dashboard (for example, `OrderBookingComposite`).

2. Click on the **Flow Instances** tab from the tabbed menu. This will pop up a **Search** section on the left. Also notice that no instances are displayed under **Search Results**. This is significantly different from the behavior observed in 11*g*. Instead of loading instances upon navigating to the **Flow Instances** tab, administrators in 12*c* will need to provide specific search criteria and search before instance information is available.

3. Click on the **Search Instances** button in the **Search** section to execute the default search query.

Observe *Figure 7.11*. The default query duration parameter defined in the common MBean properties for instance search is 24 hours. If there are no search results on the Flow Instances page, this could be because no flow instances were created in the last 24 hours.

The **Search Options** palette provides the ability to define a number of search parameters to control the flow instances to be displayed, including:

- Access to some very common quick searches (Recent Instance, Instances with Fault, Recoverable Instances) and any saved searches.

- The ability to reset the search fields, save a customized search, and create a bookmarkable link of the customized search to share with others.

- The ability to add **State-**, **Fault-**, **Composite-**, and **Time-**based search parameters.

- The ability to add up to six Sensor-based fields to filter instances based on sensor values defined in the composites.

Let's have a look at the following screenshot:

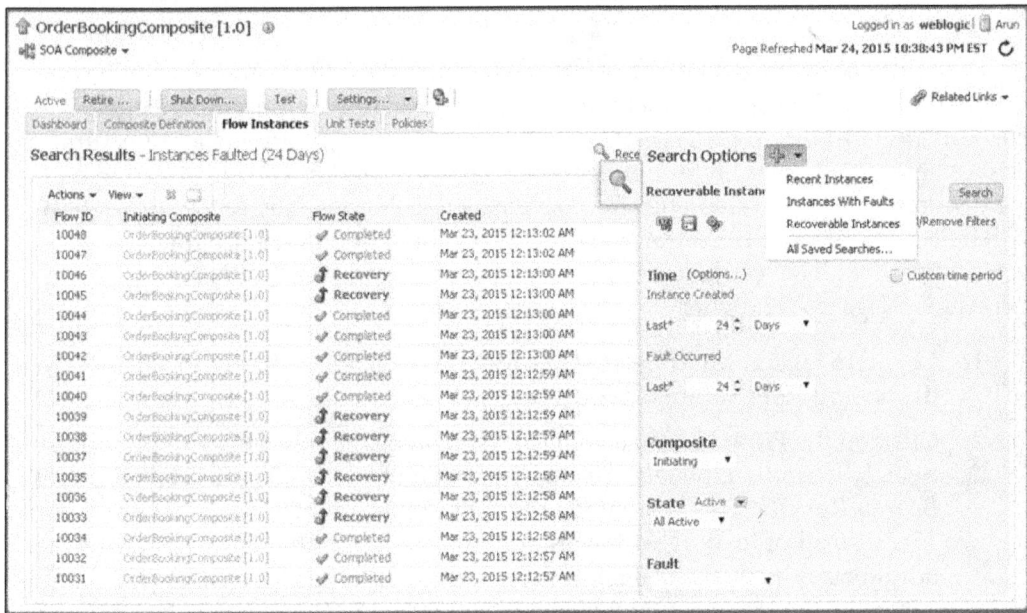

Figure 7.11: Instance Tracking dashboard

Additional information about the instance can be viewed by clicking on the instance in a couple of different ways (see *Figure 7.12*):

- Click on the small space in the row header before the **Flow ID**. This populates summarized information about the composite instance. The **Faults** tab displays faults in the message, if any. The **Composite Sensor Values** tab shows the sensor values for the instance if sensors are configured for the composite.

- Clicking on **Flow ID** for each instance will open up a **Flow Trace** pop-up window with a detailed flow trace for the instance. The flow trace provides detailed auditing and status for each individual component in the composite. If the instance propagates through multiple composites or components deployed to the same domain, the flow trace is able to unify it as a single trail. Clicking on an individual component within the audit trail will drill down into the activities executed within the component. The status of the components and the activities within them can help administrators identify the exact failure point. The **Flow Trace** window, shown in the following screenshot, also has tabs to view alerts, sensor values, and composites, similar to the details pane in the **Flow Instances** page:

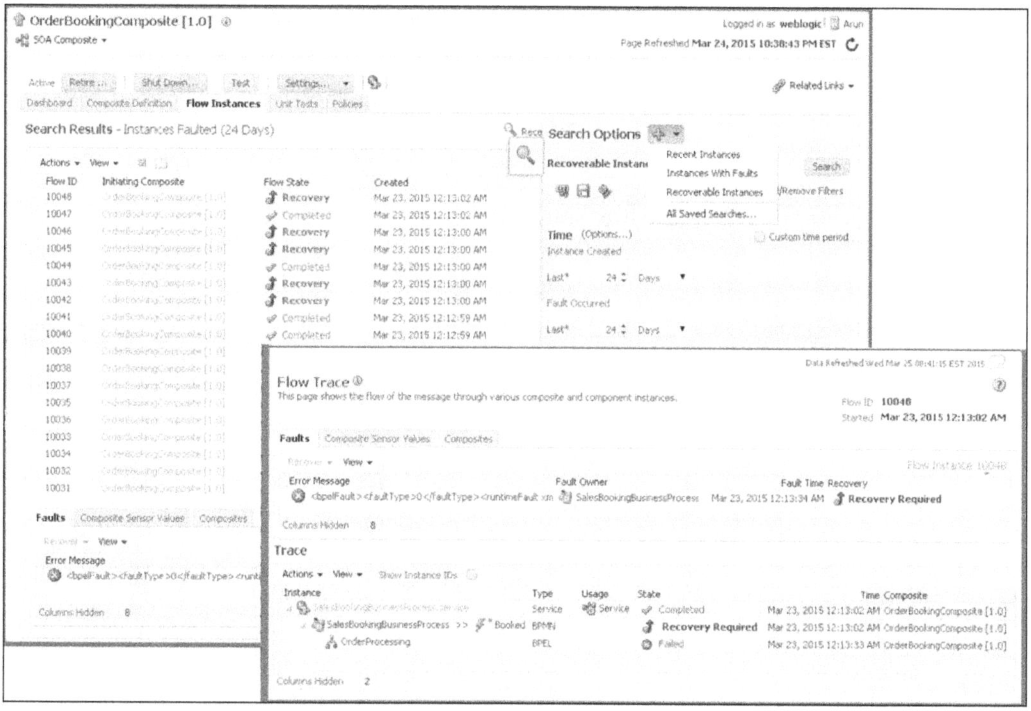

Figure 7.12: Instance Tracking dashboard

Managing and recovering composite instance faults

Oracle SOA Suite 12*c* has introduced a fault management module called **error hospital**. It is used to aggregate transactions that have generated errors and can be used to perform actions such as recovery, abortion, and deletion on transactions with common errors collectively. The aggregations can be based on various criteria based on fault types, names, or at a composite level. Administrators also have the ability to schedule bulk operations to optimize server resources so that they can be executed when business transactions are not.

The SOA Infra dashboard in Fusion Middleware Control provides a summarized view of all faults in the environment based on a specified time period. *Figure 7.13* shows the **Business Transactions Fault** section that displays a chart providing a snapshot on the nature of faults/fault handling in a given period. The following section provides instructions on how administrators can drill down into details of these reported faults and take corrective action:

1. In the **Business Transaction Faults** regions, select an interval from the available dropdowns and click on the refresh icon. This will present a stacked chart of the failed messages grouped by fault states.

2. Click on the chart to navigate to the **Error Hospital** tab page. The page opens with the same query selection from the dashboard. This page has access to the search palette similar to the one used in the **Flow Instances** tab page.

The fault messages are grouped based on various criteria. These criteria can be changed by choosing a value from the **Group By** drop down box. The total faults and their current state for each category are also displayed.

Clicking on **Total Faults** and **Recovery Required** will drill into the **Flow Instances** tab where details of the faults can be viewed:

- Bulk actions can also be performed on groups of messages by clicking on either the **Bulk Recovery** or **Bulk Abort** options on the top menu bar.

Let's have a look at the following screenshot:

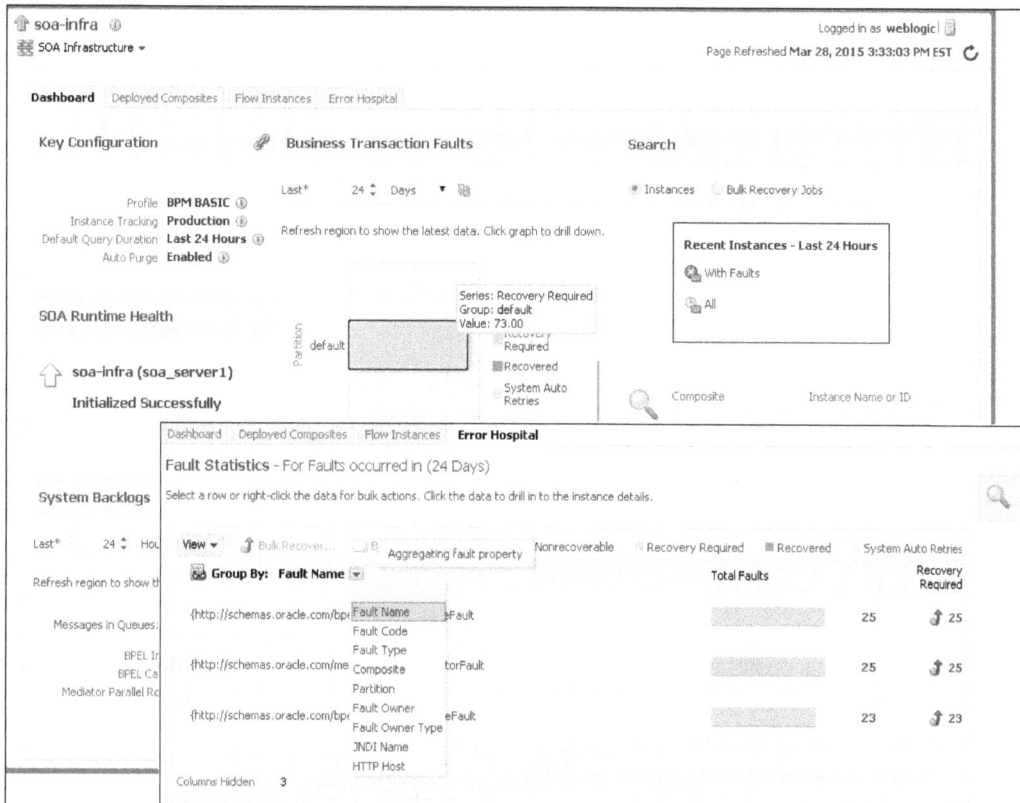

Figure 7.13: Error hospital in Oracle SOA Suite 12*c*

Managing and recovering instance faults

Recovering faulted instances is a crucial administrative function, especially in long-running and durable processes where the process instance has faults after performing a set of activities. If the process is stateful, then in most cases when a fault occurs at a step, it is desirable to perform a recovery from the point of failure. Enterprise Manager Fusion Middleware Control can display detailed audit logging of an instance execution, providing valuable information such as the point of failure, nature of fault, fault details, and remediation options.

The following *Figure 7.14* shows a faulted instance of the **OrderProcessing** BPEL component that failed due to a remote exception (endpoint unavailable) and was marked as **Recovery Required**. Once the target system is available, the fault can be recovered by retrying it. Let's have a look at the following screenshot:

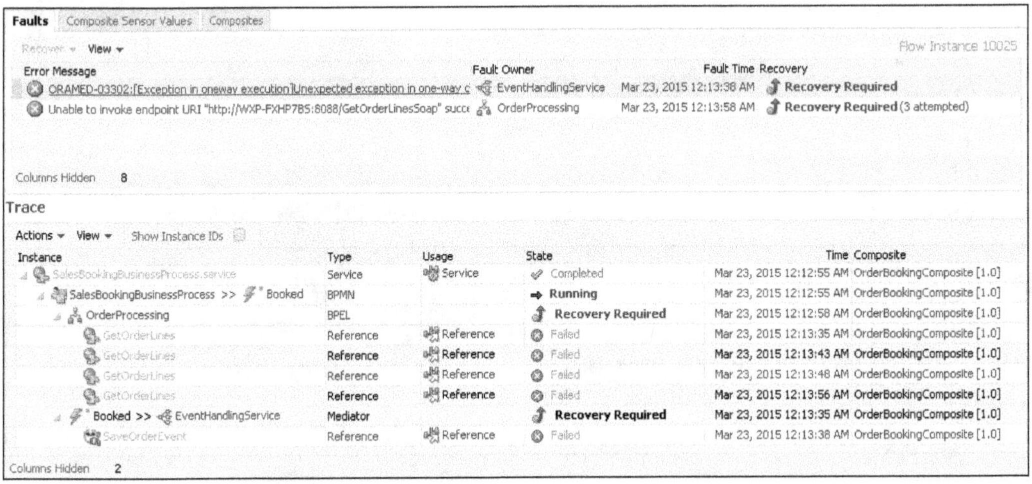

Figure 7.14: Recovering individual instances with the Retry Action

The **Error Message** panel inside the instance audit trail shows distinct faults, and also provides the ability to recover them. Clicking on the 🛠 **action** button drills down to show the **Fault Details and Recovery Options** screen as shown in *Figure 7.15*. A Retry Recovery option can be used to recover this fault once the endpoint is available to resume its processing from the point of failure. If the fault is due to an incorrect message being sent to the target service, the fault recovery console also provides the ability to fix the payload before retrying.

It is important to note that recovery always does not necessarily mean retrying. Depending upon the nature of the processing logic, sometimes other recovery actions, such as Replay and Continue, may also be used. The recovery options available in Oracle SOA Suite 12*c* are briefly described as follows:

1. **Retry**: This action immediately retries the instance from the point of failure.

2. **Abort**: This terminates the entire instance and marks the instance as **Terminated**.

3. **Replay**: This replays the entire scope activity in which the fault occurred. It is only applicable for faults in a BPEL component. Fault recovery using the Replay action is required in scenarios where maintaining the transactional integrity of the process is mandatory. Imagine a BPEL process that inserts order information in three systems via three different invoke operations. Now if these three invokes are defined in a single scope, and any one of the invokes fails, the transaction is rolled back from the previous systems. When performing a recovery for such faults, if the **Retry** option is chosen, it would be incorrect as it will lead to inconsistent updates across different systems.

4. **Rethrow**: This rethrows the fault and propagates it to BPEL fault handlers (that is, Catch branches). By default, all exceptions are caught by the fault management framework unless an explicit Rethrow fault policy is provided.

5. **Continue**: This ignores the fault and continues processing. Again, this option should be chosen with proper consideration. If the subsequent processing of the instance is dependent on the faulted action, performing a recovery with the Continue action will again lead to errors.

There is a certain limitation to this approach as bulk fault recoveries cannot be performed at this level. Also, the message recovery information available on the instance's **Flow Trace** page depends upon the `AuditConfig` property set for the environment. Accessing this MBean from the **Common Infrastructure MBean Properties** page will reveal that the default value of element `bpelRecoveryStatus` is set to `All`. This is how recovery information is made available. To prevent it from being displayed, set the `bpelRecoveryStatus` key to `Off`.

Let's have a look at the following screenshot:

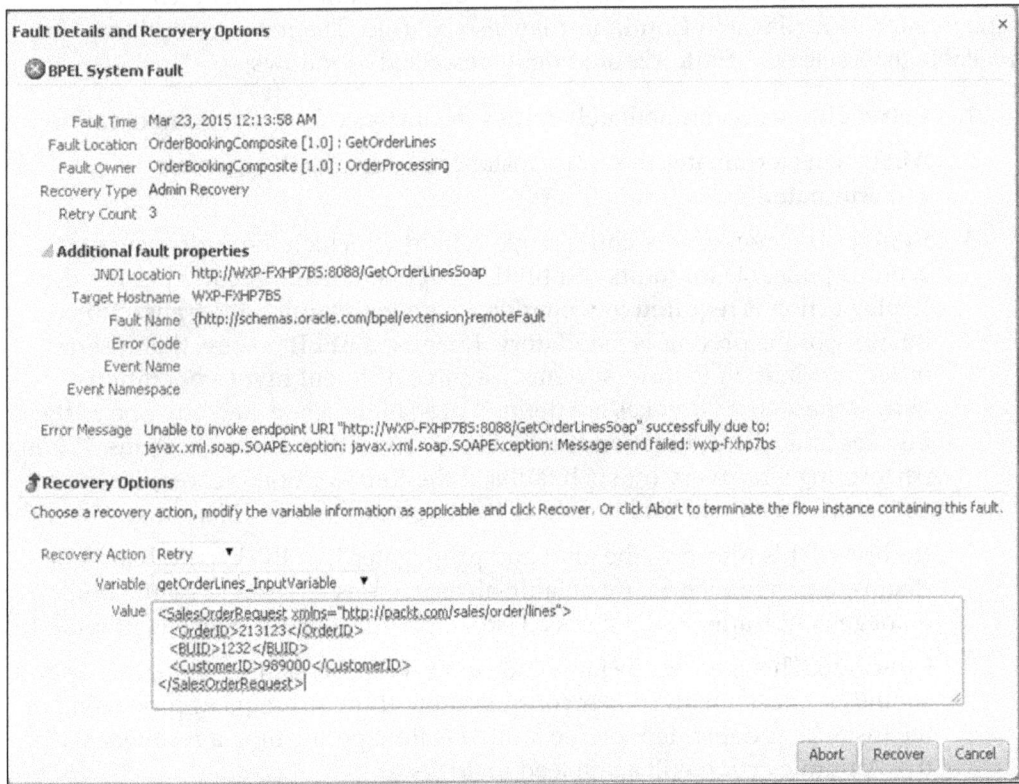

Figure 7.15: Recovering individual instances with Retry Action

Bulk recovery of instance faults

So far you have seen how individual faulted instances can be recovered. Recovering individual faulted instances, though necessary in some cases, may prove to be cumbersome and time consuming. Enterprise Manager Fusion Middleware Control allows administrators to perform both manual and automatic bulk recovery of faulted and recoverable messages. *Figure 7.16* shows how the composite error hospital displays different fault types associated with the instances and a mechanism to recover them in bulk.

For instance, for faults to be identified as recoverable, a fault policy must be defined at design time and bound to the composite. The fault policy should be able to categorize faults and bubble them up to the Enterprise Manager console for manual recovery. In the absence of any fault policies, the fault takes its standard course and it is left to the judgment of the SOA Suite 12*c* infrastructure engines to determine whether it is recoverable or not. It is also important to note that not all faults are recoverable. The following transaction errors will generally not have the option to be recovered:

- Messages with payload errors
- Synchronous messages that have exhausted the retry count
- Messages that triggered a component to throw a non-recoverable error

The bulk recovery commands can be issued by clicking on the **Bulk Recover** icon ($\circlearrowright$) to perform a remedial action as shown in *Figure 7.16*. This will pop up a **Recovery Request** window where scheduling (when to start and end the recovery process) and throttling (how many instances to require at a time and frequency) parameters can be provided. Leaving the default values will execute the recovery immediately. Oracle SOA Suite 12*c* introduced a first-class scheduling component called **Enterprise Scheduler (ESS)**, covered in detail in *Chapter 11, Introducing Oracle Enterprise Scheduler*. Bulk recovery of faulted instances is managed by ESS in 12*c*. Let's have a look at the following screenshot:

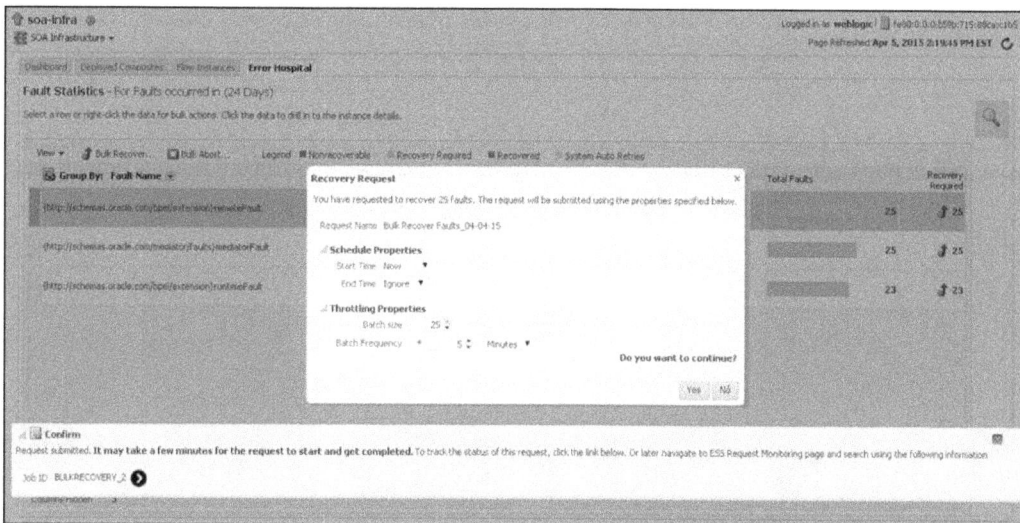

Figure 7.16: Bulk Recovering composite instances with a Bulk Recovery Job

When a bulk recovery request is submitted, it creates an ESS job and provides a job creation confirmation link. This link can be clicked and administrators can view details of the job on the ESS console. The status of the recovery job can be checked by refreshing the console shown in *Figure 7.17*. ESS provides a very powerful tool for Oracle SOA Suite 12*c* administrators to automate the fault recovery process by scheduling bulk recovery jobs to execute during non-business hours or when the server resources are under considerably less duress. Let's have a look at the following screenshot:

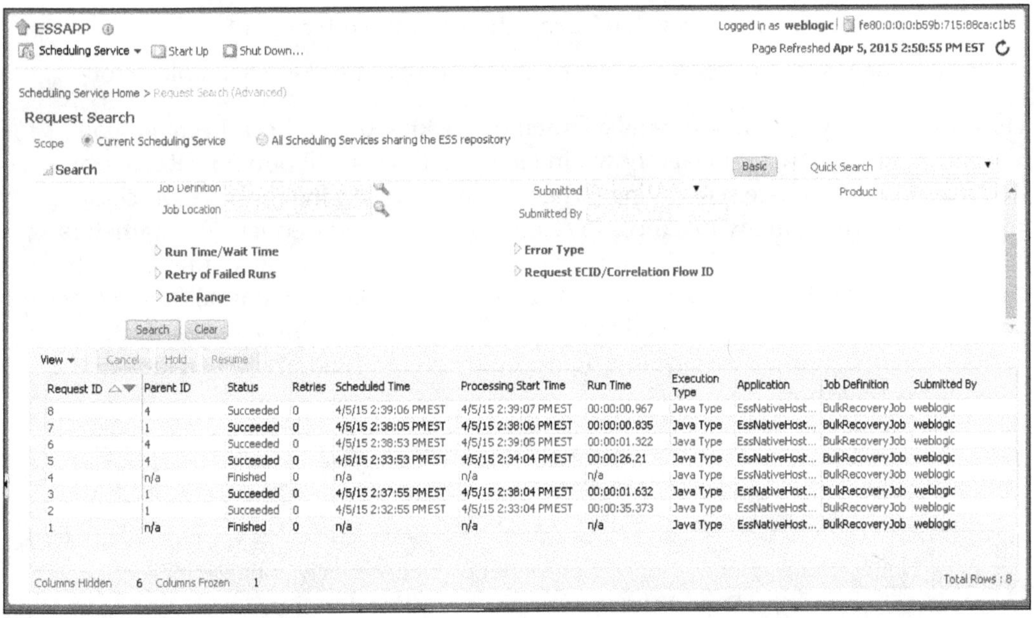

Figure 7.17: ESS Console for viewing Bulk Recovery Jobs

Once the job is completed, checking on the status of the messages that were marked for recovery will show them as **Recovered**, as shown in *Figure 7.18*. Click on the link in the **Total Faults** field to view them on the **Flow Instances** page. If the fault was recovered successfully, the flow state will show as **Completed**. This state represents the final state of the instances and not the intermediate states that it assumed during the execution. Intermediate states can be viewed by launching the flow trace by clicking on the **Flow ID** of one of the messages. The message audit trail shows the state adjusted to **Recovered** from **Recovery Required**. Let's have a look at the following screenshot:

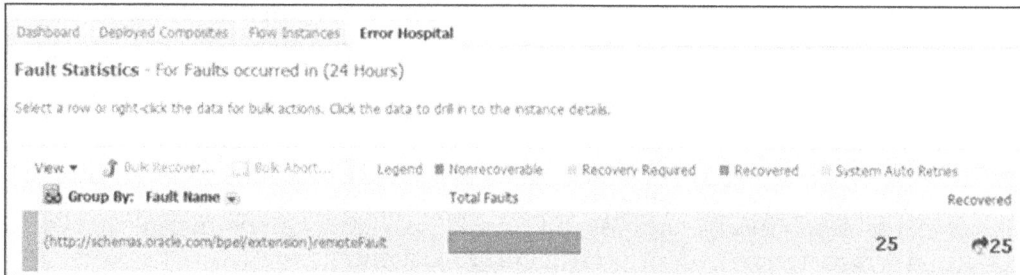

Figure 7.18: Recovered instances after a Bulk Recovery Job

Configuring automatic message recovery through MBeans

Administrators who wish to not use ESS for scheduling fault recoveries can leverage the auto-recovery feature of Oracle SOA Suite 12c. This is, however, only applicable for faults that are encountered in the BPEL engine. The auto-recovery feature is controlled through an MBean property that allows recovery of messages either at the time of restarting the SOA servers or a scheduled recovery during off-peak hours. Messages being recovered can be throttled by limiting the number of messages picked up on each run. *Figure 7.19* shows the `RecoveryConfig` configuration dashboard in System MBean Browser along with the property settings to schedule automatic recovery. The steps to do so are listed here:

1. Log in to Oracle Enterprise Manager Fusion Middleware Control.

2. Right-click on **soa-infra(soa_server1)** and navigate to **SOA Infrastructure | SOA Administration | BPEL Properties | More BPEL Configuration Properties**.

3. Click on the `RecoveryConfig` MBean.

   ° The `RecurringScheduleConfig` MBean allows configuring a time window, preferably non-peak production hours when automatic recovery through retry can be scheduled.

   ° The `maxMessageRaiseSize` property controls the number of messages recovered in one go.

- ° `StartupScheduleConfig` on the other hand instructs the engine to recover faulted messages on server startup.
- ° The amount of time allocated by the engine for recovery is determined by `startupRecoveryDuration`.

However, it is not always possible to recover everything automatically. Auto-recovery is subject to some conditions. Consider the two scenarios explained here:

1. **Scenario 1**: If the BPEL component uses a fault policy and the fault is handled using the `ora-human-intervention` action, the fault is marked as `Recoverable` and the instance state is set to `Running`. In this scenario, such faults marked as `Recoverable` cannot be auto-recovered.

2. **Scenario 2**: If the fault policy applied to a BPEL component catches a fault and rethrows it using the `ora-rethrow-fault` action, the fault is marked as `Recoverable` and the instance state set to `Faulted`, provided the fault is a recoverable one (for example, in the case of a destination system not being available). In this scenario, such `Recoverable` faults can be auto-recovered on server startup and/or prescheduled recovery.

Let's have a look at the following screenshot:

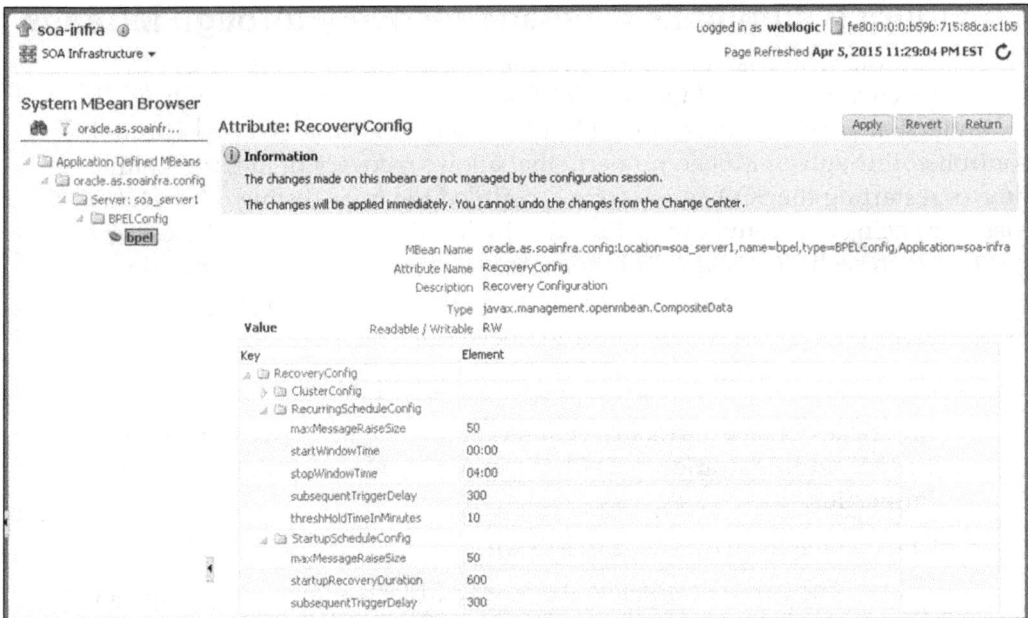

Figure 7.19: Scheduling automatic bulk retries for BPEL engine faults from the RecoveryConfig MBean

Configuring error notification rules

Oracle SOA Suite 12*c* also introduced a new feature allowing administrators to create error notification rules at the SOA infrastructure level or at the individual partition level. Error notification rules can cause alert messages to be triggered when specific fault criteria are met. Alerts can be directed to the Enterprise Manager dashboard and viewed under the Fault Alerts section. Alternatively, communication channels such as e-mail, SMS, or IM can be used for sending notifications. Error notifications provide a very useful means for administrators to create alerts on critical fault conditions that require immediate/proactive monitoring and remediation.

> Error notification rules can only be created when ESS is deployed to the SOA infrastructure.

Error notifications can be scheduled. For example, an alert can be sent every day at 7:00 pm if a fault criterion is met. They can also be sent when an error occurs on an individual instance through fault policy actions, or an aggregated notification can be sent for faults occurring at an infrastructure or partition level. The following steps provide an example of how error notification rules can be configured:

1. Log in to Oracle Enterprise Manager Fusion Middleware Control.

2. Right-click on **soa-infra (soa_server1)** and navigate to **SOA Infrastructure | Error Notification Rules**. This will open the **Error Notification Rules** creation dashboard.

3. Click on the **Create** button to define a new error notification rule. An error notification can be defined by providing information such as the rule metadata (name and description), schedule (frequency), and condition (what criterion caused the trigger).

4. As pointed out before, ESS is required to configure an **Error Notification Rule**. A schedule has to be created beforehand so that it can be selected during error notification rule creation.

5. Right-click on **soa-infra (soa_server1)** and navigate to **SOA Infrastructure | Define Schedules**.

6. The package name for the schedule must be **/oracle/apps/ess/custom/soa** so that it is accessible on the **Error Notification Rule** page.

7. A schedule can be created by providing information such as the schedule metadata (name, description, and package), frequency, and duration. Refer to the following screenshot:

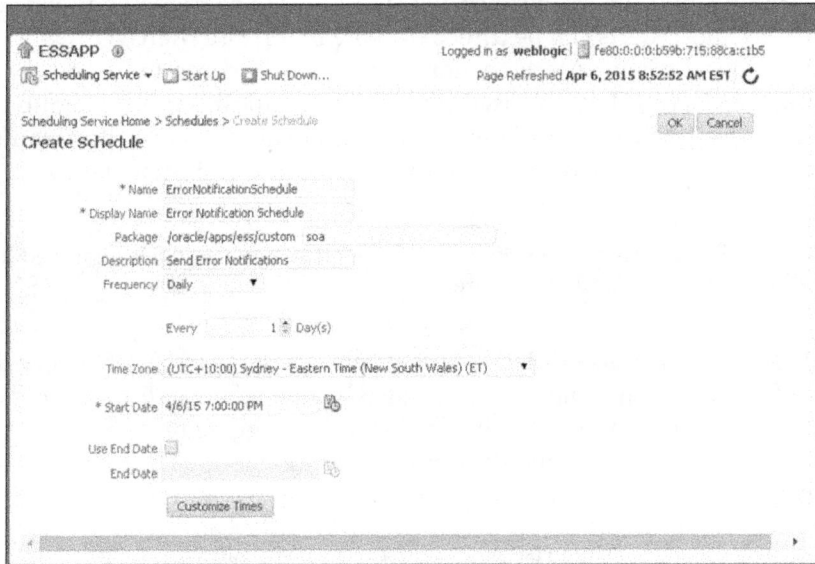

Figure 7.20: Defining a schedule for an error notification rule

8. Once a **Schedule** is created it can be selected in the dropdown when creating the Error Notification Rule as shown in the following screenshot:

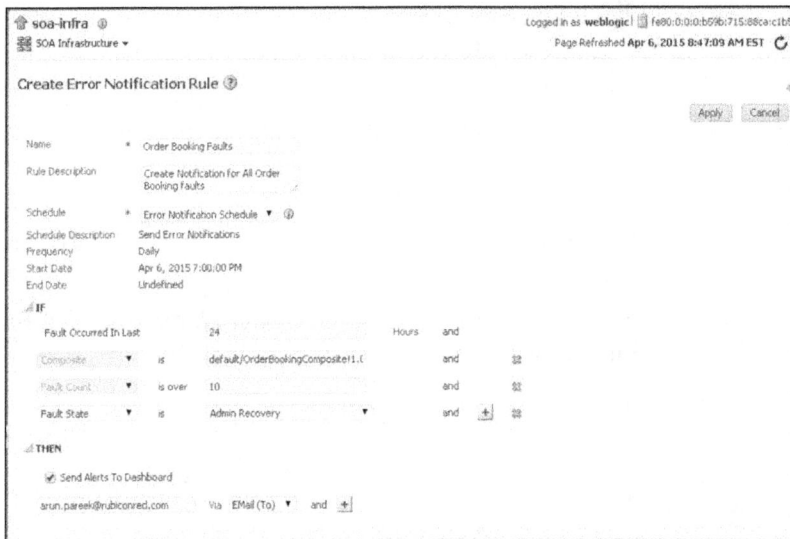

Figure 7.21: Defining a new error notification rule

9. By default, newly created error notification rules are set to **Enabled**. They can be disabled by selecting the alert on the **Edit Notification Rules** page and clicking on **Disable**.

10. When error notification rule criteria are met, the alert is triggered and displayed in the **Fault Alerts** section of the **SOA Infra** dashboard. The frequency with which a rule is invoked is based upon the selected **Schedule**.

Configuring and administering JCA adapters and binding components

After deploying the composite to the SOA infrastructure, one of the main things to address is how to manage and configure properties for binding components packaged inside. Binding components are network protocols and mechanisms connecting your composite to external services, applications, and technologies (such as messaging queues, databases, web services, and so on.). Binding components in Oracle SOA Suite 12*c* are of two kinds:

- **Services**: Services provide an entry point to the composite and advertise their capabilities to external applications by exchanging their service metadata information through a **WSDL (Web Service Definition Language)** file. The service bindings define how client applications can invoke a composite. Examples of service bindings from the sales order composite in *Figure 7.10* are an HTTP-based web service, **JCA (Java EE Connector Architecture)** based file polling service, and a Direct Binding service.

- **References**: References enable message exchanges between composites and externally deployed services. Examine the sales order composite diagram in *Figure 7.10* to see how an HTTP-based, third-party web service; a JCA based database adapter; and a **Web Service Invocation Framework (WSIF)** type notification service act as reference bindings in the composite assembly.

Configuring and managing service bindings

Oracle Enterprise Manager Fusion Middleware Control allows you to perform service binding administration tasks, such as attaching policies, managing errored-out messages, and setting binding properties. Depending upon your preference, there are two available mechanisms to configure binding properties. *Figure 7.22* shows the property configuration screens for a service (`SalesBookingBusinessProcess.service`) in a composite application (`OrderBookingComposite`).

Service binding properties can be accessed by either navigating to **SOA Composite | Service/Reference Properties | [Service] | Properties** or to **Application Defined MBeans** via **oracle.soa.config | Server: soa_server1 | SCA Composite | [Composite] | SCAComposite.SCAService | [Service]**. The System MBean Browser dashboard enables you to modify some advanced properties that aren't available under the **Properties** tab.

The following screenshot displays the MBean attributes for a particular service:

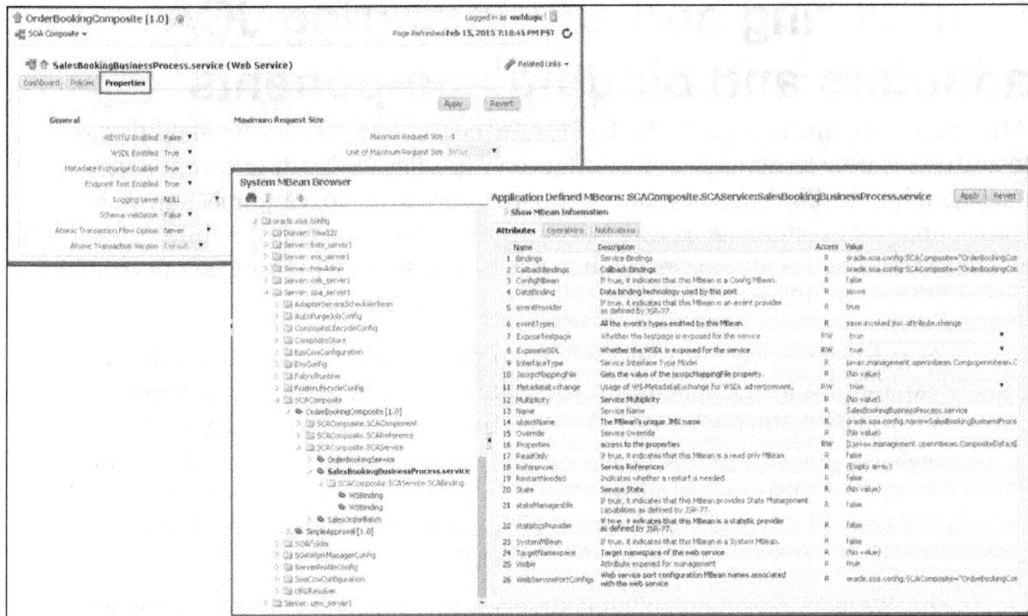

Figure 7.22: Configuring service binding properties

You can configure activation specifications of a service binding component. For example, you can enable REST support by enabling its WSDL support for MTOM (a method of efficiently sending binary data to and from Web Services), set finer logging levels, and enable incoming message semantic validation, among other things.

> You can read more about **Message Transmission Optimization Mechanism (MTOM)** at http://ww.w3.org/TR/soap12-mtom/.

That's not all. If you wish to save yourself from the painful navigation on the consoles, here are the WLST commands to configure them:

```
connect('<username>','<password>','<soahost>:<soaport>')
custom()
cd('oracle.soa.config/oracle.soa.config:name=SalesOrderBatch,revision=
1.0,partition=default,wsconfigtype=WebServiceConfig,SCAComposite="Orde
rBookingComposite",label=soa_54cfa256-b86a-4eec-8503-020ac5a12f5a,j2ee
Type=SCAComposite.SCAService,Application=soa-infra')
ls()
exit()
```

In case you are wondering where to get the directory path to the MBean, *Figure 7.23* shows how it is made available by expanding the ⊞ icon beside **Show MBean Information**:

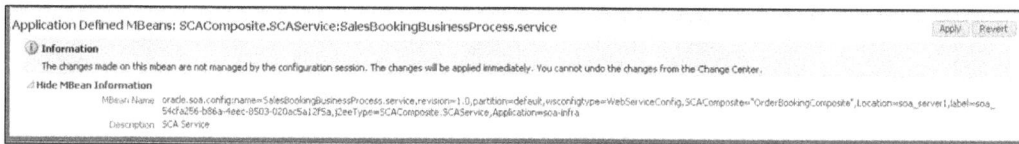

Figure 7.23: Viewing MBean metadata information in System MBean Browser

Our case study has multiple entry points to the composite. The business process, in here, is also initiated when a certain file is available in a certain polling directory. It is very common that the nature of the file being polled or the polling directory itself needs to be changed upon composite deployment. Let's assume that the `PhysicalDirectory` path specified by the developer was `C:\soa\salesorder\file` for a Windows-based development environment. This might need to be changed once the composite is deployed to a Linux server. One way to do this is by overriding the polling directory location during composite deployment using a configuration plan as discussed in *Chapter 5, Deploying Code*.

The *Figure 7.24* depicts another way to modify properties for the JCA file adapter on the OrderBookingComposite, which is from its **Properties** tab at runtime. You can manually edit the adapter binding properties to change the polling directory, polling frequency, batch size, setting for whether to delete the file once it is read, and many other properties related to adapter activation specifications. Depending upon the JCA adapter (file, database, JMS, and so on), different properties are displayed for configuration. Apart from what is displayed on the screen you can also add more properties by clicking the ➕ icon. This will pop up additional properties for the selected service binding as shown in the following screenshot:

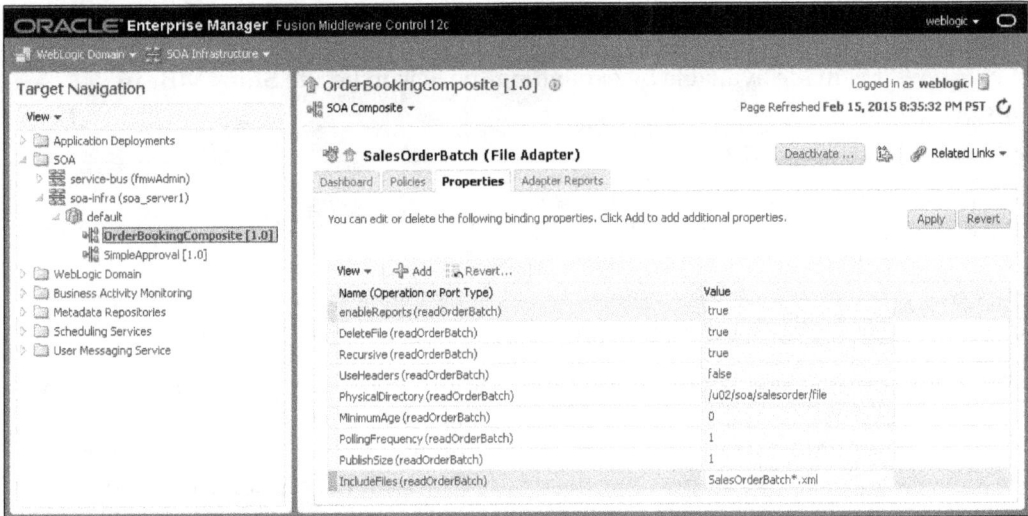

Figure 7.24: Activation Specification Properties dashboard of Inbound JCA File Adapter

Configuring and managing reference bindings

Administering reference bindings is absolutely vital as impeding or slowly responding endpoints can induce latency in your entire infrastructure. It is often better to configure a timeout setting with a scheduled retry when interacting with external systems as there is little or no control over them. If the endpoints are unavailable or perform poorly, discontinue processing the instance rather than keep the thread hanging. Such faulted instances can then be recovered automatically or manually when the external systems are up and running again.

The OrderBookingComposite application in our case study interacts with an external web service and a database. You can also administer interaction specifications (for references) and endpoint properties, such as timeouts, thresholds, retry intervals, and more, for the JCA-based database adapter and web service bindings.

The reference **Properties** tab even has an **Endpoint Address** property field. Setting a value for an endpoint here will override the one configured in the WSDL. *Figure 7.25* shows the Reference Home page in which you can override this and other properties. There are, however, a few important things to keep in mind while configuring these properties:

- If `jca.retry.*` based endpoint properties are added or removed, the composite application containing them needs to be redeployed for changes to take effect.

- If the non-registered JCA binding level properties are manually added in the `composite.xml` file, these and other registered properties for that reference cannot be edited from Oracle Enterprise Manager Fusion Middleware Control.

- There are no restrictions on adding, removing, or changing JCA endpoint properties at runtime if not specified at design time. Adapters get notified of the changes automatically and the composite does not require redeployment.

The following screenshot displays the properties for a composite reference:

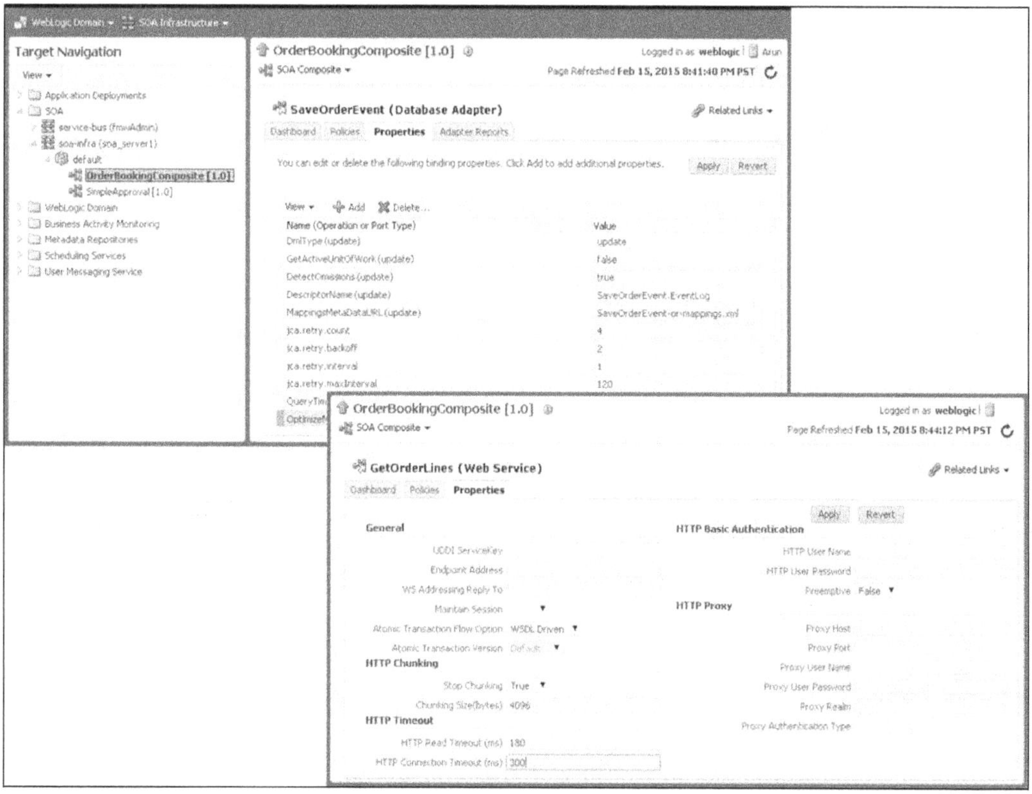

Figure 7.25: Configuring Interaction Specification Properties for references

Resource adapters are defined and deployed at the domain creation/configuration stage and by default always start up within the J2EE container on the relevant target by default. All resource adapters, barring the file adapter, are referenced from a composite by way of a JNDI location that is part of its design time configuration. This JNDI location references the WebLogic Server layer via JCA. At runtime, the deployment descriptor of an adapter must associate the JNDI name with configuration properties (such as the host and port of a socket adapter, the channel and host of an MQ Server, the directory on the filesystems for a file adapter, and so on) required by the adapter to access the backend information source.

Monitoring these resource adapters is critical to ensuring that the deployed composites can execute process instances without errors. Oracle Enterprise Manager Fusion Middleware Control provides the ability to configure diagnostic reports at an individual adapter configuration used within a composite either as a service or reference. Upon enabling diagnostics for adapter references, administrators are able to view their real-time status as well as obtain snapshot information of its behavior over a period of time. The report also shows message statistics providing key insight into the performance of the adapter reference. To enable and obtain diagnostics metrics for adapter references used within a composite, follow the steps outlined here:

1. Navigate to the composite dashboard by clicking on a particular composite (`OrderBookingComposite`, in this example). The composite dashboard reveals all components, services, and references used in it.

2. Click on any resource adapter configuration that is of JCA adapter type.

3. Click on the **Adapter Reports** tab.

    ◦ Enable the **Enable Reports** checkbox to see configuration, real time monitoring, and snapshot reports for the adapter configuration.

    ◦ The **Configuration Reports** provide connectivity information, adapter definition, and tuning properties.

    ◦ The **Monitoring Reports** show the real-time statistics for the adapter endpoint, such as the connection status of the adapter along with its `threadpool` metrics.

    ◦ The **Snapshot Reports** provide historical connectivity and message statistics aggregated over a period of time.

The following screenshot shows a snapshot of the adapter reports as available on the Fusion Middleware Control:

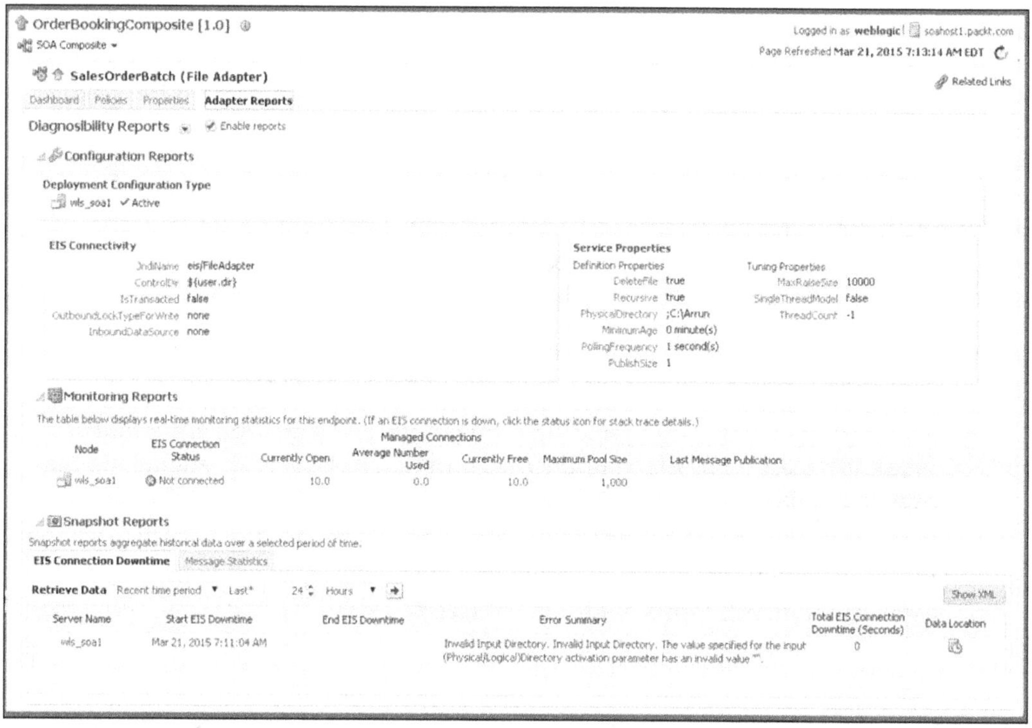

Figure 7.26: Adapter configuration report for EIS connections

Administering BPEL process engine

Oracle BPEL process engine is a container that provides standards for assembling, developing, and executing synchronous as well as asynchronous services into end-to-end business processes in the SOA Infrastructure. When the `soa-infra` application is started, it initializes the BPEL engine in a stateless manner and loads composites from the MDS repository. If the composite contains any BPEL components, it targets them to the BPEL engine. At runtime, the BPEL engine waits for requests from different channels, such as messaging sources, databases, web services, and so on, and uses a `Dispatcher` module that maintains an in-memory logical queue containing units of work to process the incoming messages from these binding components. The BPEL process engine saves the process execution state in the dehydration store through a persistence module based on Oracle TopLink and hence there is no in-memory state replication required. The audit framework` continuously audits the work being processed by storing process execution information in the database.

Oracle Enterprise Manager Fusion Middleware Control allows you to perform key administration tasks, such as monitoring instances, recovering from faults, manually recovering (BPEL) failed messages, and configuring properties for the BPEL Service Engine. It also provides useful statistics and performance monitoring metrics for the engine. *Figure 7.27* shows a typical BPEL Engine landing page that can be accessed by navigating to **SOA Infrastructure** | **Service Engines** | **BPEL**. Note that the engine executes the `OrderNotificationProcess` and `OrderProcessing` components that are part of the `OrderBookingComposite` application. The service engine dashboards have changed in Oracle Enterprise Manager Fusion Middleware Control 12*c*. Instead of showing a view of all instances and faults, it only shows a summarized view of deployed components, statistics of the components, and recoverable instances. Key administration tasks performed from the BPEL service engine dashboard include:

- Displaying of details such as component name, current status, and the composites they belong to via the **Deployed Components** tab.

- Monitoring of active and pending requests, thread statistics, and request breakdown for all BPEL components running on the service engine via the **Statistics** tab.

- Performing a bulk manual recovery of undelivered invokes or callback messages due to a transaction rollback in the process instance for asynchronous BPEL processes via the **Recovery** tab.

Let's have a look at the following screenshot:

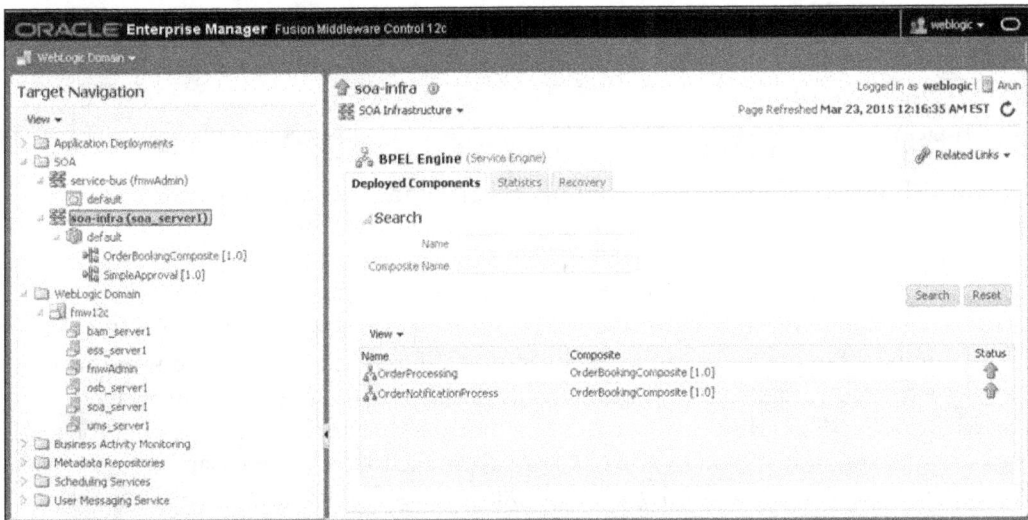

Figure 7.27: The administration dashboard for the BPEL Service Engine

Configuring BPEL service engine properties

The BPEL service engine is the heart of the Oracle SOA Suite infrastructure. The runtime behavior of the engine and the instances executing on it largely depend on its property configurations. It is therefore essential for administrators to understand their functions and be able to alter them when needed. Configuration properties such as audit level and audit trail threshold, automatic recovery for BPEL processes, master node recovery scheduling, automatic recovery attempts for invoke and callback messages, and callback message order preservation are all used by the BPEL process service engine during processing of BPEL process service components. These properties can be accessed and modified by navigating to **soa-infra (soa_server1)** | **SOA Infrastructure** | **SOA Administration** | **BPEL Properties**.

A few of the BPEL service engine properties are described in the following table:

Property	Category	Description
Audit Level	Logging and Auditing	This property controls the level of information collected by the instance tracking infrastructure. The different values for this property are: • Inherit: Same as the infrastructure level. • Off: No flow tracking and payload tracking is collected. • Minimal: Instance tracking information is logged without payloads. • Production: Instance and payload information is collected except for assign activities. • Development: Instance and payload information is collected without any restriction. This may impact performance and should be used for debugging purposes.

Property	Category	Description
AuditDetailThreshold	Logging and Auditing	Defines the maximum size in bytes an audit trail details string can be before it is stored separately from the audit trail. If a details string is larger than the threshold it will not be immediately loaded when the audit trail is initially retrieved; a link will be displayed with the size of the details string.
AuditStorePolicy	Logging and Auditing	This is a very important flag that determines the audit store strategy as one of the following three: • syncSingleWrite: Audit data is stored synchronously when instance data is stored in the cube instance table using the same thread. • syncMultipleWrite: Audit data is stored synchronously when instance data is stored in the cube instance table using a different thread. • AsyncsyncSingleWrite: Audit data is stored asynchronously using an in-memory queue and pool of audit threads.
DisableSensors	BPEL Engine	This flag switches the call to the sensor framework. The default value is false.
ExpirationMaxRetry	Message Retry	This controls the maximum number of times a failed expiration call on activities such as wait/on Alarm is retried before failing. If the activity or instance the expiration call is targeting cannot be found, the call will be rescheduled.
ExpirationRetryDelay	Message Retry	This flag sets the delay between the expiration retries.

Property	Category	Description
LargeDocumentThreshold	Dehydration	Large XML documents severely impact the performance of the BPEL server if they are constantly read in and written out during instance processing. This property controls the maximum size in bytes of a variable before it is stored in a separate location from the rest of the instance data.
MaximumNumberOf InvokeMessagesInCache	BPEL Engine Memory	This property specifies the number of invoke messages that can be kept in the in-memory cache. Once the engine hits this limit, messages are saved in the database and can be recovered using the recovery job. Setting this value to -1 will disable messages being saved to the database. Each invoke message takes about 300 bytes in memory.
MinBPELWait	Dehydration	This property specifies the minimum amount of time that the engine will wait for before involving instance dehydration. If the wait duration is set less than or equal to this value, BPEL engine will execute the subsequent activities in the same thread/transaction.
OneWayDeliveryPolicy	BPEL Engine Memory	This controls how the one-way invocation messages such as invokes and callbacks are delivered. The supported values are: • async.persist: Messages are persisted in the delivery service persistence store. • async.cache: Messages are kept only in memory in delivery service. • Sync: Messages are processed by the same thread synchronously.

Property	Category	Description
QualityOfService	BPEL Engine Memory	This flag enables or disables the Coherence cache for the service engine. If the value is set to CacheEnabled the engine will use Coherence.
InstanceKeyBlockSize	BPEL Engine Memory	Instance IDs for instantiating instances are preallocated from the dehydration store and kept in memory. This property sets the size of the block of instance IDs to allocate from the dehydration store during each fetch.
SyncMaxWaitTime	BPEL Engine	The maximum time a request/response operation will take before it times out. The default is 45 seconds.
ExecuteCallbacksInOrder	BPEL Engine	In order to main transactional integrity across, there is often a need to ensure that the callback message execution order is preserved. Setting this property to true will force the engine to ensure callback messages are picked up in the order in which they were received by the BPEL process service engine for a given business flow instance. This setting impacts all SOA composite applications deployed on the BPEL engine.
RecoveryConfig	Message Recovery	The recovery configuration properties control automatic message recovery during server startup or within a predefined window.
RecurringMaxMessageRaiseSize	Message Recovery	This property defines the number of messages to recover during recurring recovery.
StartupMaxMessageRaiseSize	Message Recovery	This property defines the number of messages to recover during startup recovery.

Property	Category	Description
MaxRecoverAttempt	Message Retry	This property specifies the maximum number of times an invoke or callback activity is attempted for recovery. Once the number of recovery attempts exceeds this count, it is marked as Exhausted.

Administering the Mediator service engine

In properly constructed composites, all service entry points to the different components such as BPEL, BPMN, Business Rules, and so on, are fronted by a mediator. The mediator component of Oracle SOA Suite 12*c* is intended to serve as an intracomposite router that handles interactions between its components. It therefore has the potential to become a constraint in infrastructure setups that involve a high volume of message processing. Fortunately, the Mediator engine dashboard provides a snapshot of processing statistics for various metrics such as count and execution times for one-way invokes, transformations, validations, condition evaluations, and so on. The Mediator engine dashboard also shows all the mediator components deployed to the infrastructure along with their statuses. The dashboard can be viewed by navigating to **soa-infra** | **SOA Infrastructure** | **Service Engines** | **Mediator**.

Configuring Mediator service engine properties

As with the BPEL engine, the performance of the Mediator engine and the components deployed to it depends on the configuration of engine properties. There are five groups of properties available to configure within the Mediator service engine:

- **Logging**: This affects log-related settings.
- **Mediator engine**: This affects engine-specific settings and likely impacts throughput and performance.
- **Custom**: This is used to specify custom properties.

- **Health Check**: This affects the frequency in which the heartbeat framework checks and announces the availability of the server.

- **Resequencing**: This affects all resequencing functionality, which is the ability of Oracle Mediator to resequence incoming messages in a user-specified order.

These properties can be accessed by navigating to **soa-infra | SOA Administration | Mediator Properties**. The following table describes each of the configurable properties available:

Property	Category	Description
Audit Level	Logging	Setting this property to Inherit will use the same audit level settings as the SOA Infrastructure. In all other cases, this property overrides the value of the global SOA Infrastructure audit level property.
Metrics Level	Logging	This property determines whether **Dynamic Monitoring Service (DMS)** metrics should be collected for Mediator services. DMS metrics are used to measure the performance of application components. See *The DMS Spy Servlet* in *Chapter 6, Monitoring Oracle SOA Suite 12c,* for more details.
Parallel Worker Threads	Mediator Engine	This property sets the number of outbound threads for parallel processing. This does not impact sequential services.
Parallel Maximum Rows Retrieved	Mediator Engine	This specifies the number of rows to retrieve per iteration for parallel processing. Oracle documentation recommends setting this value to 50 to 100 times that of the Parallel Worker Threads property. Setting this too high can result in increased memory consumption.
Parallel Locker Thread Sleep	Mediator Engine	This specifies the idle time (in seconds) between two successive iterations for retrieving rows when there is no message for parallel processing. We almost always recommend setting this to 1.

Property	Category	Description
Error Locker Thread Sleep	Mediator Engine	This is similar in concept to `Parallel Locker Thread Sleep`, except that it is specific to errored-out messages.
Parameters	Custom	This allows you to specify custom configuration properties. For example, in resequenced messages, it is possible to configure the buffer window for the time window in best-effort resequencing by adding the `buffer.window=20` custom parameter, which means that 20% of the length of the time window is added as a buffer.
Container ID Refresh Time	Health Check	This is the interval (in seconds) in which the heartbeat thread checks the status of the Mediator Service Engine and announces its presence to other servers in the cluster. This is internally accomplished by updating the timestamp of the unique identifier maintained in each Mediator Service Engine. The default setting is 60 seconds.
Container ID Lease Timeout	Health Check	This is the interval (in seconds) in which the heartbeat thread checks if there are other unique identifiers that have not been updated.
Resequencer Locker Thread Sleep	Resequencing	This specifies the sleep time (in seconds) for a deferred locker when there is no message in the database.
Resequencer Maximum Groups Locked	Resequencing	This specifies the maximum number of group rows retrieved for each locking cycle.
Resequencer Worker Threads	Resequencing	This specifies the number of resequencer threads.

Administering Oracle User Messaging Service

Oracle **User Messaging Service (UMS)** enables two-way communications between actors in processes such as human users or automatic activities and deployed applications. UMS has support for a variety of messaging channels, such as e-mail, IM, SMS, and text-to-voice messages. Any process components, such as BPEL/BPMN, Human Workflow, or BAM, can leverage UMS to send notifications and alerts to user mailboxes. The Oracle SOA Suite 12*c* UMS infrastructure provides a range of features such as:

- Support for multiple messaging channels such as email, **instant messaging (IM)**, **Extensible Messaging and Presence Protocol (XMPP)**, **short message service (SMS)**, Twitter, and voice. Actionable e-mail messages can also be delivered to a process user's inbox.

- Two-way messaging allows sending messages from applications to users (referred to as outbound messaging) who can then initiate messaging interactions (inbound messaging).

- User messaging preferences provide process users with a web interface to define preferences for how and when they receive messaging notifications, allowing applications to become immediately more flexible. Rather than deciding whether to send to a user's e-mail address or IM client, the application can simply send out the message and let UMS route the message according to the user's preferences.

Describing UMS architecture and components

UMS in Oracle SOA Suite 12*c* is made up of a layer of clients, servers, and drivers. The UMS server consists of EJB interfaces, standard web services, and a stateless session bean to provide business logic to client applications. The UMS architecture heavily relies on JMS queues used to buffer content between clients, servers, and drivers. The UMS server layer has JAX-WS servlets to implement web services and also the simple Oracle ADF Faces UI component for managing end-user messaging preferences. The UMS drivers contain JCA resource adapters to interface with external gateways. There is also a database in which the UMS messaging states are stored.

Configuring UMS for Human Workflow and BPEL process components

The `OrderBookingComposite` application that we are managing in the infrastructure has to send status emails to process users configured to receive notifications. All that developers need to do is simply add an e-mail activity in their BPEL process and populate its e-mail details or enable notifications for human worfklow tasks. It is your job as an administrator to configure e-mail drivers to both send and receive messages. E-mail drivers send messages over `SMTP` and use either `IMAP` or `POP3` for receiving incoming messages.

Configuring the e-mail messaging driver and notifications

In the following section, you will learn to configure and set up e-mail driver properties by specifying connection parameters of the e-mail messaging server. This is shown in *Figure 7.28*:

1. Log in to Oracle Enterprise Manager Fusion Middleware Control.

2. On the navigator, expand **User Messaging Server**.

3. Right-click on **usermessagingdriver-email** and navigate to **Email Driver Properties**.

4. Click on the **Create** button to set up a new driver configuration by providing a name and properties for outgoing/incoming mail servers.

5. For outgoing notifications, enter the **Outgoing Mail Server** and **Outgoing Mail Server Port** properties of your SMTP server as well as **Outgoing Default From Address**, **Outgoing Username**, and **Outgoing Password**.

6. For incoming notifications, enter values for a POP server that requires properties such as **Incoming Mail Server**, **Incoming Mail Server Port**, **Incoming Mail IDs**, **Incoming User IDs**, and **Incoming Password**.

7. Click on **OK** to save the configuration.

This screenshot shows the email configuration settings being set:

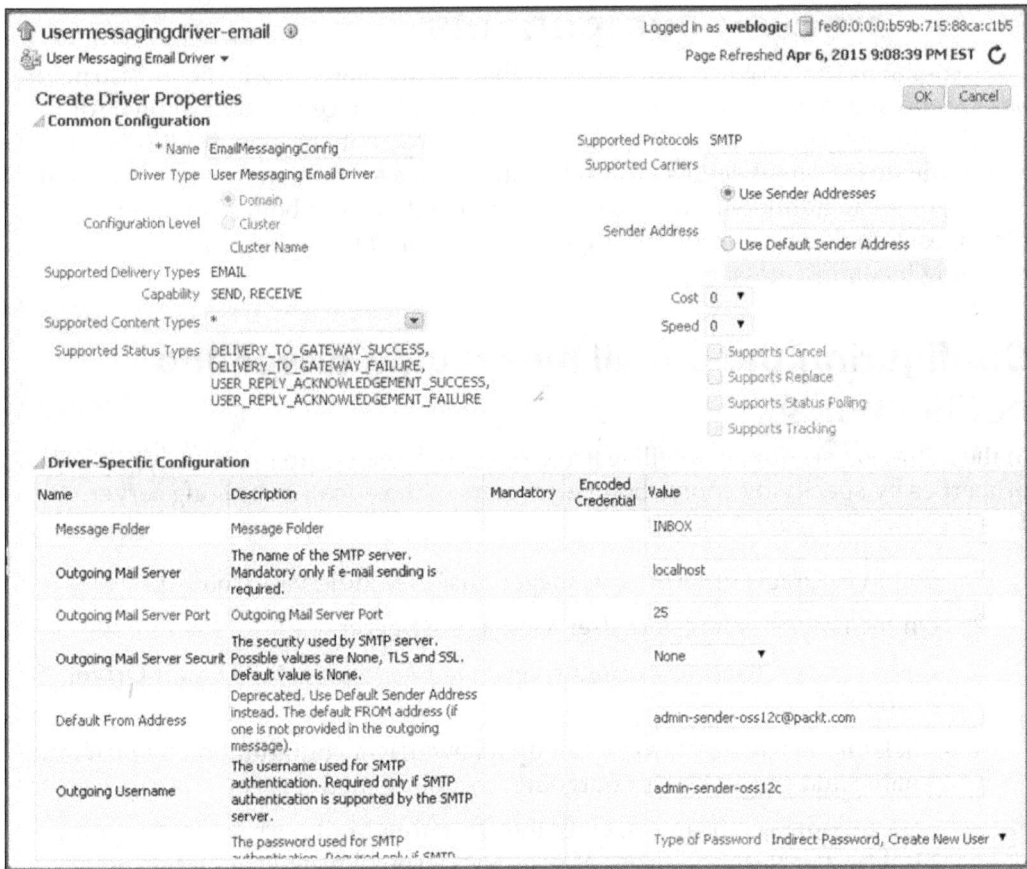

Figure 7.28: Configuring Email driver properties for UMS

The messaging driver configuration as described earlier is a generic user messaging service configuration. For human workflow engine to process notifications through UMS, the workflow notification properties must be configured as well. This can be done by following these steps:

1. Right-click on **soa-infra** and navigate to **SOA Infrastructure | SOA Administration | Workflow Properties** to view the configuration screen of the Workflow Notification properties see *Figure 7-29*.

2. Change the **Notification Mode** to **All** or **Email**.

3. Click on the **More Workflow Notification Configuration Properties** link to view additional MBean properties for configuring workflow notification settings.

4. Enter the **From Address**, **Actionable Address**, and **Reply To Address** of your mail server.

5. Click on **Apply** and then restart all servers on which the UMS drivers are targeted. In a cluster, these properties are automatically propagated to the other servers.

> The hostname and IP address of the inbound (IMAP) e-mail server and outbound (SMTP) e-mail server which are to be configured for UMS must be added to the /etc/hosts file of the server on which Oracle SOA Suite 12c infrastructure is running. A restart of all managed servers on which UMS is targeted is necessary for the setting to take effect.

The property configuration changes for human workflow notifications can also be altered using WLST scripting, which is preferred by administrators who wish to automate configuration changes. Launch the WebLogic scripting tool console from $ORACLE_COMMON_HOME/common/bin/wlst.sh. An example script is provided here:

```
connect('<username>','<password>','<soahost>:<soaport>')
custom()
cd ('oracle.as.soainfra.config/oracle.as.soainfra.config:name=human-wo
rkflow,type=HWFMailerConfig,Application=soa-infra')
set('ASNSDriverEmailFromAddress', 'admin-oss12c@packt.com')
set('ASNSDriverEmailReplyAddress','no.reply@packt.com')
set('ASNSDriverEmailRespondAddress',' admin-oss12c@packt.com ')
set('HWFMailerNotificationMode','ALL')
disconnect()
```

The resultant changes is shown in the following screenshot:

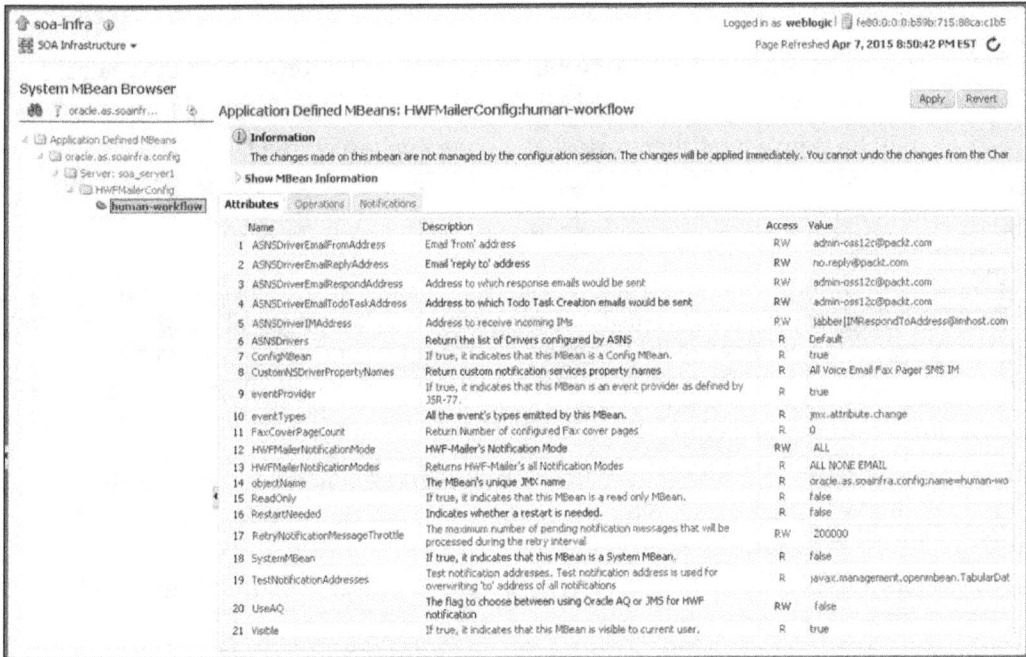

Figure 7.29: Configuring workflow notification properties

Testing UMS notifications from Enterprise Manager

This is it! You have now configured the UMS e-mail driver and Workflow Notification to integrate with the e-mail server. To test whether e-mail notifications are working, perform the following steps:

1. Log in to Oracle Enterprise Manager Fusion Middleware Control.

2. Right-click on **soa-infra** and navigate to **Service Engines | Human Workflow**.

3. Click on the **Notification Management** tab and then on the **Send Test Notification** button.

4. Enter a valid e-mail address under **Send To** and set **Channel** to **Email**.

5. Hit the **Send** button to send a mail to the given e-mail address.

Figure 7.30 shows the **Notification Management** dashboard and the result of testing the e-mail driver configuration via the **Send Test Notification** button. If the e-mail is sent successfully, a **SENT** response output is seen immediately.

The **Notification Management** dashboard also displays all notifications sent from various components along with their delivery status and also offers the ability to resend undelivered notifications. You can select an individual outgoing notification and click on the **Resend** button to resubmit it. Optionally, you can also select a single notification column with **Status** set to **Failure** and click on **Resend All Similar Notifications** to resubmit all such kinds in one go.

This screenshot demonstrates sending a test notification:

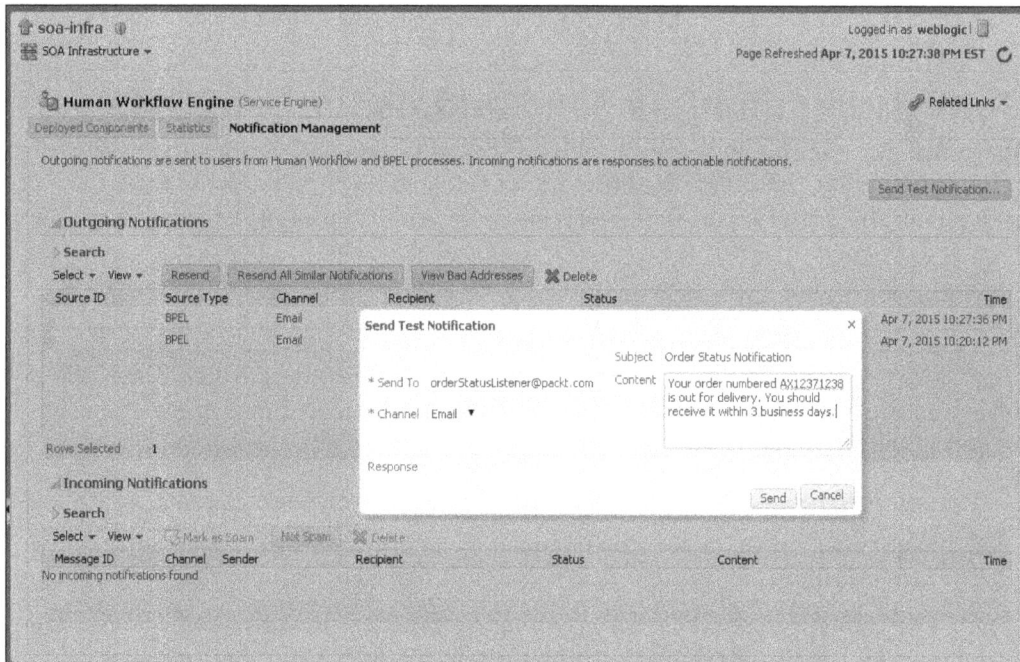

Figure 7.30: Sending test notifications from the Notification Management dashboard

The UMS queues that are used to store messages intermittently can be managed from the WebLogic Server Administration Console by navigating to **JMS Modules** | **UMSJMSSystemResource**. The database schema used to store the UMS messaging state is [PREFIX]_ORASDPM. Connect to this schema and execute the following query to get the list of all UMS messages that are in the faulted state along with the fault reasons:

```
SELECT S.TYPE, M.CHANNEL,M.SENDER, M.STATE, S.CONTENT FROM STATUS
S, (SELECT A.VALUE SENDER, A.DELIVERY_TYPE CHANNEL, D.DELIVERY_
STATE STATE, D.ADDRESS_ID FROM ADDRESS A, DELIVERY_ATTEMPT D WHERE
A.ADDR_ID =D.ADDRESS_ID) M WHERE S.ADDRESS_ID=M.ADDRESS_ID AND
M.STATE<>'SUCCESS';
```

Figure 7.31 shows an example of the output of the preceding query:

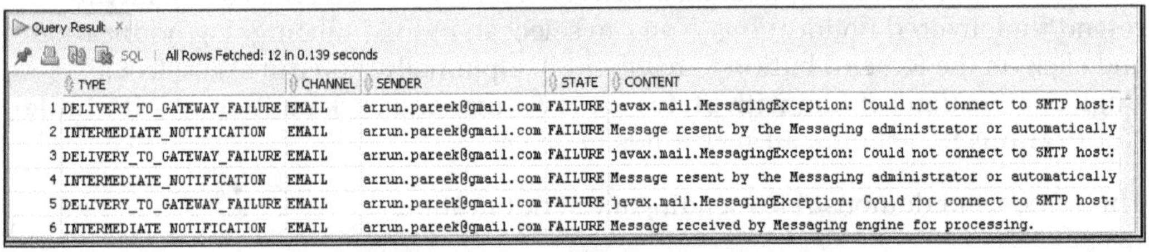
Query Result
SQL | All Rows Fetched: 12 in 0.139 seconds

	TYPE	CHANNEL	SENDER	STATE	CONTENT
1	DELIVERY_TO_GATEWAY_FAILURE	EMAIL	arrun.pareek@gmail.com	FAILURE	javax.mail.MessagingException: Could not connect to SMTP host:
2	INTERMEDIATE_NOTIFICATION	EMAIL	arrun.pareek@gmail.com	FAILURE	Message resent by the Messaging administrator or automatically
3	DELIVERY_TO_GATEWAY_FAILURE	EMAIL	arrun.pareek@gmail.com	FAILURE	javax.mail.MessagingException: Could not connect to SMTP host:
4	INTERMEDIATE_NOTIFICATION	EMAIL	arrun.pareek@gmail.com	FAILURE	Message resent by the Messaging administrator or automatically
5	DELIVERY_TO_GATEWAY_FAILURE	EMAIL	arrun.pareek@gmail.com	FAILURE	javax.mail.MessagingException: Could not connect to SMTP host:
6	INTERMEDIATE_NOTIFICATION	EMAIL	arrun.pareek@gmail.com	FAILURE	Message received by Messaging engine for processing.

Figure 7.31: SQL query result showing failed UMS message information

Configuring multiple send addresses with UMS

There will most definitely be practical scenarios where e-mail notification needs to be distinguished based on the From address information in the e-mail. To understand this better, assume there is one order confirmation BPEL process sending e-mails with **From Address** set to `OrderStatus@yourcompany.com`; a customer rewards process may need to send e-mails with a different From address, such as `Customerservice@yourcompany.com`.

There is just one default From address configured for the e-mail driver in the infrastructure. Configuring multiple send addresses is tricky, but you may do it by following the steps given here (also illustrated in *Figure 7.32*):

1. Log in to Oracle Enterprise Manager Fusion Middleware Control.
2. Right-click on **soa-infra** and navigate to **Administration** | **System MBean Browser**.
3. Expand **Application Defined MBeans** | **oracle.as.soainfra.config** | **Server: server_name** > **HWFMailerConfig** | **human-workflow**.
4. Click on the **Operations** tab and then on **setASNSDriver**.
5. The `propertyName`, `propertyValue`, and `driverName` values have to be entered in the form. Enter `EmailFromAddress`, `OrderStatus@yourcompany.com` (replace with actual email address), and `OrderStatus` respectively in each of these fields.
6. Click on the **Invoke** button to add the entry and repeat from step 4 to add another set of properties (for the Customer Service From Address).
7. Other properties such as `EmailToDoTaskAddress`, `EmailReplyToAddress`, and `EmailRespondToAddress` can similarly be added by providing property name/value combinations against the same driver name.

8. Click on the **Operations** tab and invoke the `getASNSDriverAddresses` operation by passing a driver name. This will return all the addresses being used for the specified driver.

9. Similarly, another `ASNS` driver address can be created, albeit with different e-mail notification properties.

10. In order to now use these different sender addresses, the value specified in the `driverName` attribute has to be used in the **From Account** field of the Email activity during design time. For example, if you need to send an e-mail from the `OrderStatus@yourcompany.com` account name, the **From Account** field needs to have a value of `OrderStatus`.

This screenshot shows where the multiple From addresses are configured:

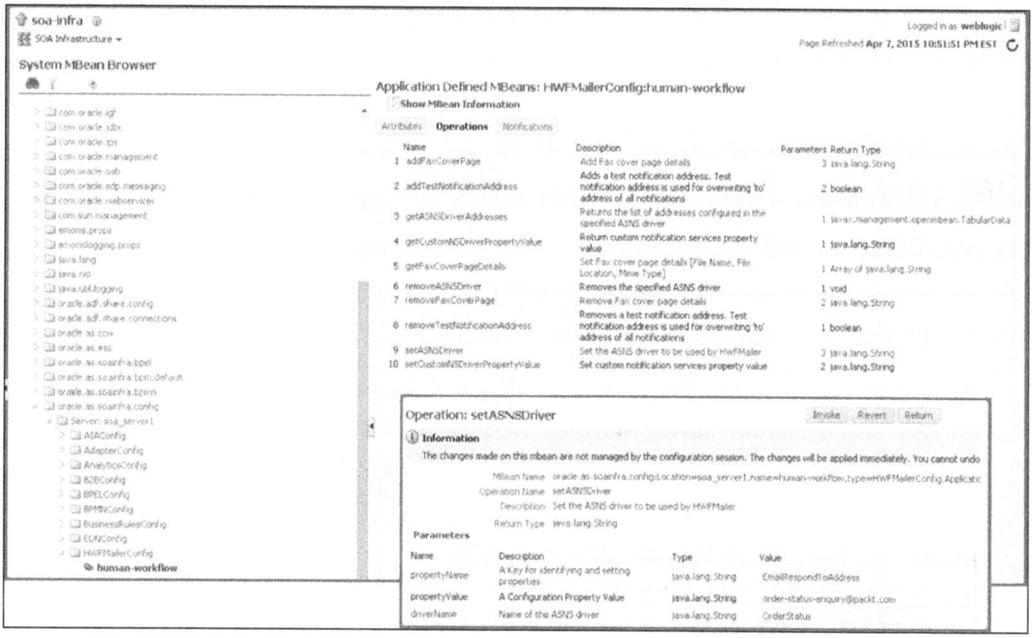

Figure 7.32: Configuring multiple default From addresses for Email activity

Administering human workflow service engines

The human workflow service engine runs as a separate engine in the Oracle SOA Suite 12*c* service infrastructure providing human task execution functionalities to both BPEL and BPMN processes. The human workflow component consists of a number of services that handle various aspects of human interaction with a business process such as task approvals, rejections, reassignments, delegation, and so on.

An instance of the human workflow service engine can be initiated by an invocation from another service component such as the BPEL or BPMN engines. The message is routed to the engine by the SOA service infrastructure and is persisted by the workflow engine in dehydration store schema. Once an invocation transaction is committed, the instance becomes available for human interactions through a thin client such as a browser or mobile-based user interface. Each update on the instance or the runtime state through a user action is then handled by the engine in a separate transaction.

Describing human workflow components and applications

The human workflow engine allows defining to-do tasks that can be assigned to users or groups of users, giving business users more flexibility and a centralized approach for task management. Workflow tasks can be assigned to application roles and then, at runtime, real users or groups from your enterprise repository defined within your organization can be mapped to these application roles. In this section, you will learn ways to integrate your company's directory server with the service infrastructure and pull organizational users to associate them with application or logical business process roles.

An important feature of the Human Workflow Service Engine is a worklist application built on top of ADF-rich client components. The worklist application is accessible via a web browser, giving business users a common look and feel and developers a standardized approach for building user interfacing applications that are flexible and customizable. Business process users can define their own work queues and share these views with other users and groups. All human workflow data definitions and custom task views can be shared across members within an organization. Logging in to the worklist application is role based and the interface is accessible via the following URL:

```
http://<soahost>:<soaport>/integration/worklistapp
```

The human workflow engine leverages the UMS framework deployed in the infrastructure for its notification needs. The UMS engine allows process participants to customize their messaging channels and even set preferred mechanisms of being notified. These preferences, such as the mode to receive notifications (for example, e-mail and SMS), and which devices need to be used, can all be configured from the following address:

```
http://<soahost>:<soaport>/sdpmessaging/userprefs-ui
```

Administration of human task instances, workflow service engine configuration, notification setup, and fault management are performed from the Oracle Enterprise Manager Fusion Middleware Control console. It also provides a mechanism to detect and handle auto-reply messages, poisoned responses, and spam in the workflow engine.

Managing workflow task configuration at runtime

Part of Oracle SOA Suite 12*c*'s design is to allow for as much flexibility and agility as possible by enabling runtime changes to various components, such as business rules, domain value maps, and certain aspects of human workflow task configurations. However, business users may still not be prepared to modify these configurations at runtime. For on-demand, human-task-related configuration changes, the onus is then on administrators to edit task assignment and routing policies, modify approval group settings, change business rules responsible for dynamic task allocation, and so on, to enable a change. Human task runtime configuration changes post deployment of composites can be done by following the steps provided here:

1. Log in to the SOA Composer at `http://<soahost>:<soaport>/soa/composer`.

2. Any configuration changes made to resources such as DVMs, tasks, composite sensors, and rules have to be performed within a session. Click on **Create Session** to initiate a change window.

3. By default, the SOA Composer organizes resources by **Deployment View** (that is, by deployed composites that they are packaged into).

4. Change this to **Types View** by clicking on the ⌄ icon.

5. Expand **Human Tasks** and then click on the task definition you want to edit.

6. *Figure 7.33* shows the task configuration page. This page allows for runtime changes to task routing policies, expiration and escalation policies, and notification settings for a human task after it is deployed to the infrastructure.

7. After finishing the changes, click on the **Publish** button for the changes to take effect.

8. The console will prompt for a session comment to be provided to maintain a change history record.

The following screenshot demonstrates the task configuration page:

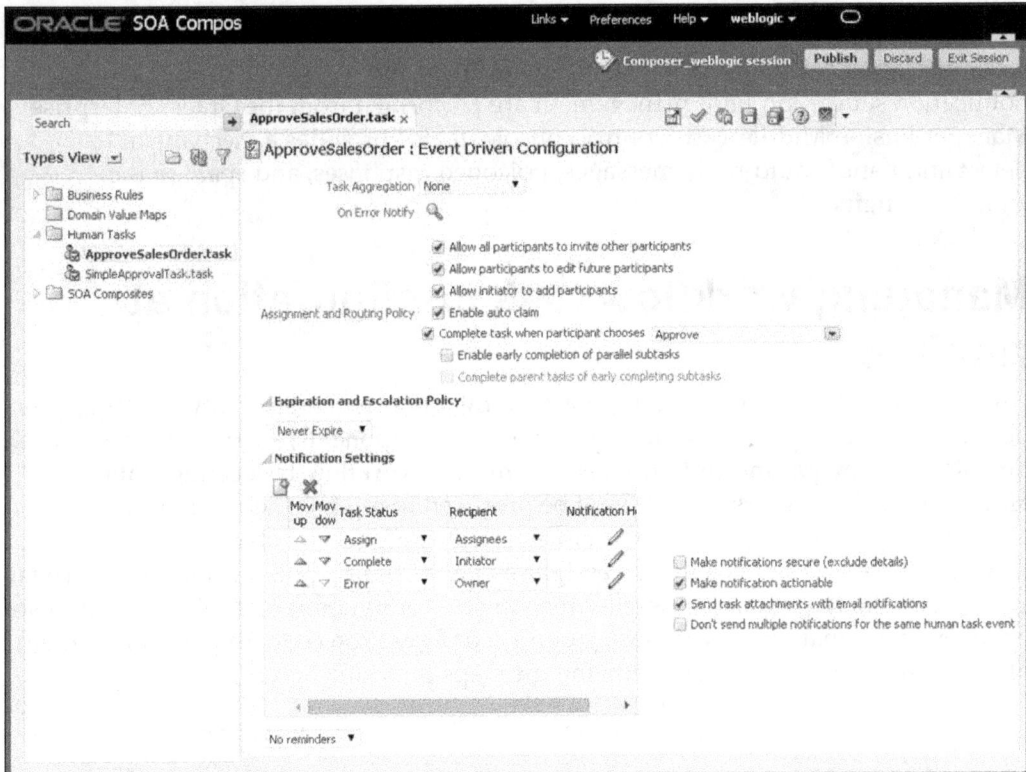

Figure 7.33: Configuring Human Task policies from SOA Composer

Managing human task service component address

A human task component in a composite has an associated user-defined task details interface executing on the worklist application. Configuration of the human task service component task detail application URI, say by editing, adding, or removing it can be performed from the Oracle Enterprise Manager Fusion Middleware Control console. This configuration page is different for each human workflow component. Access this by navigating to a specific composite and selecting the human task service component under the **Components** table. Click on the **Administration** tab and then on the **Add URI** button to create an accessible endpoint for the task by providing the **Host Name**, **HTTP Port**, or **HTTPS Port** values for the URI.

The primary reasons why this information (depicted in *Figure 7.34*) needs to be configured at the task level are as follows:

- When the SOA managed server in the infrastructure is SSL enabled, you must manually enable SSL by changing the workflow task to use the correct protocol and port number. To enable the use of the SSL (HTTPS) URL, ensure that the **HTTP Port** setting is left blank.

- If there is a clustered setup with multiple managed servers servicing incoming requests, then **Host Name** and **HTTP Port** will have to be substituted with the frontend host and port of the cluster or the load balancer address, if there is one configured. If there is more than one independent managed server, click on **Add URI** to enter details for as many of them as you wish to.

The following screenshot shows the URI being updated:

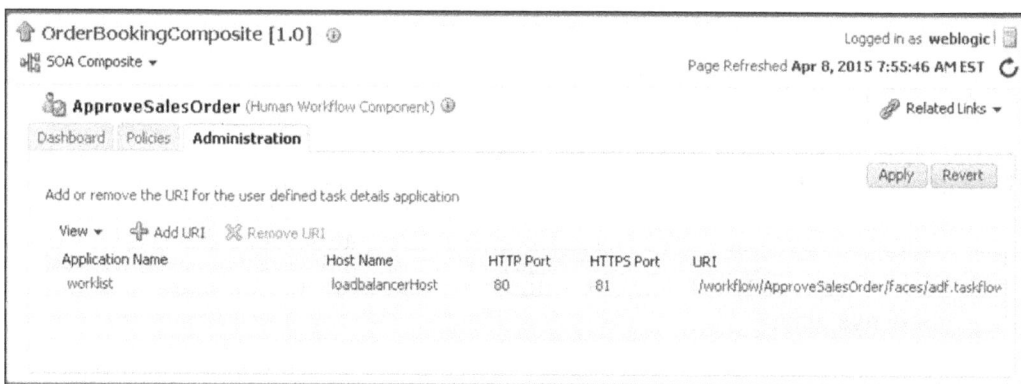

Figure 7.34: Configuring Human Task Workflow Component URI

Seeding organizational users and groups

When human task flow components are created at design time, they are simply mapped to logical or application roles. Upon deployment to the human workflow service engine, you need to assign real human users to participate and act on workflow tasks. Participants can act on tasks during runtime from the worklist application, such as to approve/reject a sales order, delegate approvals, provide feedback on a help desk request, and so on. To engage real users, it is necessary to integrate a directory service to maintain your organization's users and groups, like an LDAP server with the infrastructure running your composites.

By default, the underlying Oracle WebLogic Server identity service uses an embedded LDAP server as the default authentication provider. *Figure 7.35* shows the visual steps to change your default authentication provider in an existing security realm with an existing LDAP based directory server:

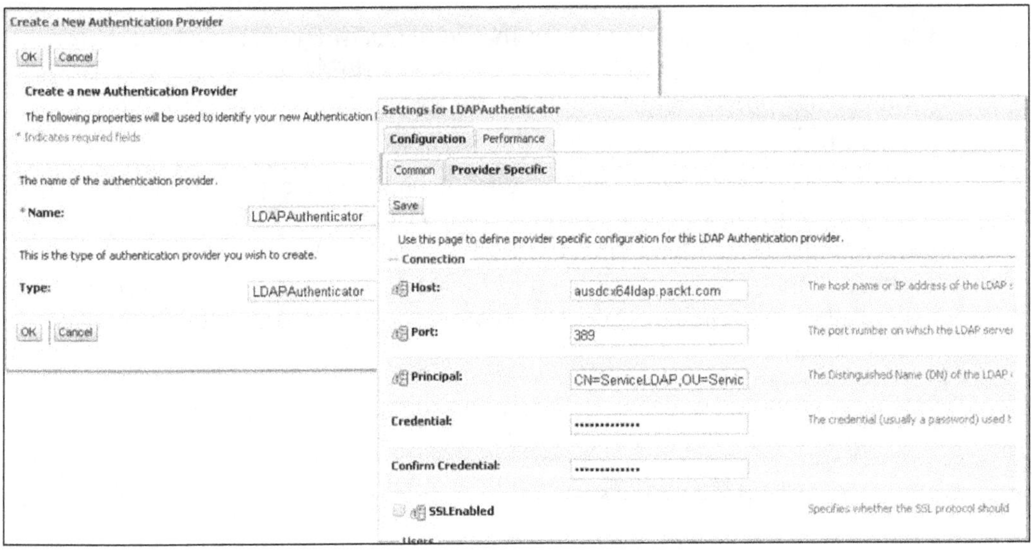

Figure 7.35: Registering an LDAP server as Authentication Provider in WebLogic Server

The sequence of steps to create a new LDAP authentication provider is as follows:

1. Log in to the Oracle WebLogic Server Administration Console.

2. Click on **Security Realms** under the **Your Application's Security Settings** pane.

3. Click on the name of a realm in the list (**myrealm** is the default realm).

4. Navigate to **Providers | Authentication** and click on the **New** button.

5. When the **Create a New Authentication Provider** page appears, type a name for the provider (for example, **LDAP**), and select **LDAPAuthenticator** on the **Type** dropdown.

6. Clicking on **OK** will create the authentication provider skeleton without the actual configuration. Additional configuration properties are required to point it to an actual active directory server.

7. Click on the authentication provider that was just created.

8. From the **Control Flag** drop-down list, choose **SUFFICIENT** (do the same for all other authenticators too), and click on **Save**. This flag instructs the WebLogic Server to accept authentication from this authenticator and not invoke additional authenticators. If the authentication fails, the server will attempt to authenticate a user using the next authenticator in the hierarchy list.

9. Next, go to the **Provider Specific** tab to specify connection parameters of the authenticator server. The following table provides a brief explanation of some of the properties.

10. Enter the provider-specific information about the authentication provider, check the **Use Retrieved User Name as Principal** checkbox, and click on **Save**.

Here are the properties to connect to an LDAP server:

Provider-specific property	Remarks
Host	The hostname or IP address of the authenticator (for example, `ausdcx64ldap.packt.com`).
Port	The port number on which the authenticator server is running. The default is `389`.
Principal	The **Distinguished Name** (**DN**) of the authentication server user that WebLogic Server should use when connecting to it. An example principal is as follows: `CN=ServiceLDAP,OU=Service Accounts,DC=packt,DC=com`
Credential	The credential property is usually a password used to connect to the authenticator server.
User Base DN	The base **Distinguished Name** (**DN**) of the tree in the LDAP directory that contains users (for example, `DC=packt,DC=com`).
Group Base DN	The base Distinguished Name (DN) of the tree in the LDAP directory that contains groups.
Use Retrieved User Name as Principal	Specifies whether to use the user name retrieved from the LDAP server as the principal in the subject.

Provider-specific property	Remarks
User Name Attribute	The attribute of an LDAP user object class that specifies the name of the user (for example, UID, CN, MAIL, and so on) (for example, `sAMAccountName`).

These properties are sufficient to connect to an LDAP server. Use the default setting for the rest of the fields if in case these values are not known.

1. Click on **Security Realms | Providers | Authentication** to return to the list of authentication providers and click **Reorder** to move the new provider to top.

2. After reordering, **Default Authenticator** should appear at the bottom of the list. This action enables the system to handle logins such as `weblogic` that are not typically in an LDAP directory but must still be authenticated to start the server.

3. Once these changes are saved and the changes are activated, a restart of both the admin and all managed servers is required.

After the restart, under the **Users and Groups** tab in **Security Realms**, all of the organization's users and groups set up in Active Directory are listed alphabetically, as shown in the following screenshot:

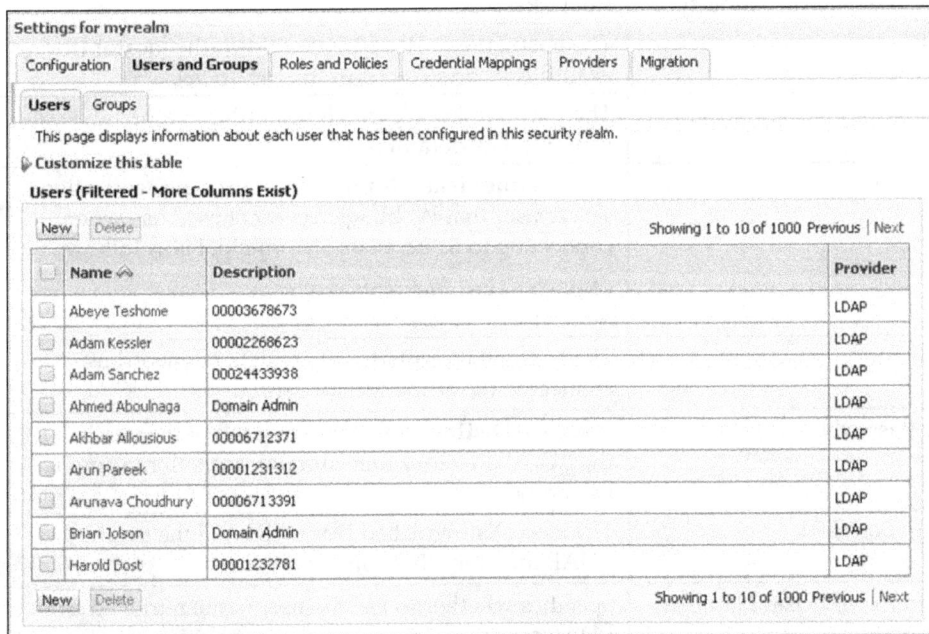

Figure 7.36: Registering an LDAP server as the Authentication Provider in WebLogic Server

By default, only usernames in human tasks are case agnostic (case insensitive). This behavior is controlled by the value of the caseSensitive property in System MBeans Browser for users, which is set to false by default. Group names in human tasks must be identical to what is seeded in the user directory. However, if you also want group names in human tasks to be case agnostic, you must set the caseSensitiveGroups property to false. To enable case-agnostic behavior for group names in human tasks, follow these steps:

1. Log in to Oracle Enterprise Manager Fusion Middleware Control.

2. Right-click on **soa-infra** and navigate to **Administration | System MBean Browser**.

3. Expand **Application Defined MBeans | oracle.as.soainfra.config | [server_name] | WorkflowIdentityConfig | human-workflow | WorkflowIdentityConfig.PropertyType | caseSensitiveGroups**.

4. Click on the **Operations** tab.

5. Click on the **setValue** property.

6. Enter a value of false in the form field, and click on **Invoke**.

Mapping users and groups to application roles

Every deployed component or module (both custom and out of the box) in Oracle SOA Suite 12*c* inherits a security model where users or groups available from an organization have to be mapped to appropriate application roles. For example, you might want to give certain users in the organization the right to access and edit human task configurations from the SOA Composer at runtime, or in case of a deployed BPM project, map users to swimlane roles. Mapping users and groups to application roles is a regular administrative activity for large scale SOA and BPM implementations in an organization. The following steps along with *Figure 7.37* outline a mechanism to achieve this:

1. Log in to Oracle Enterprise Manager Fusion Middleware Control.

2. Under the navigator, select **WebLogic Domain | [Domain_Name] | Weblogic Domain | Security | Application Roles**.

3. To search for a specific role, select the radio button beside **Select Application Stripe to Search**.

4. The dropdown is now enabled. Select **OracleBPMProcessRolesApp** and press the ⓘ icon. All default application roles for this application stripe are listed.

5. Alternatively, enter an existing and known role name in the search text box to retrieve matching roles in the stripe.

6. From the retrieved tabular list of available roles, click on any role (in this example, **OrderBookingComposite.SalesAgent**) under the **Role Name** column. This enables an option to add available users or groups to the selected role.

7. Click on the **Add** button, where a wildcard-based search can be performed to retrieve a list of matching users from the configured directory providers.

8. Select a user from the list **Searched Principals** and click on the **OK** button to add them to the role.

The same steps can be used to associate groups in organizations or other available Application Roles to the selected role. Take a look at the following screenshot:

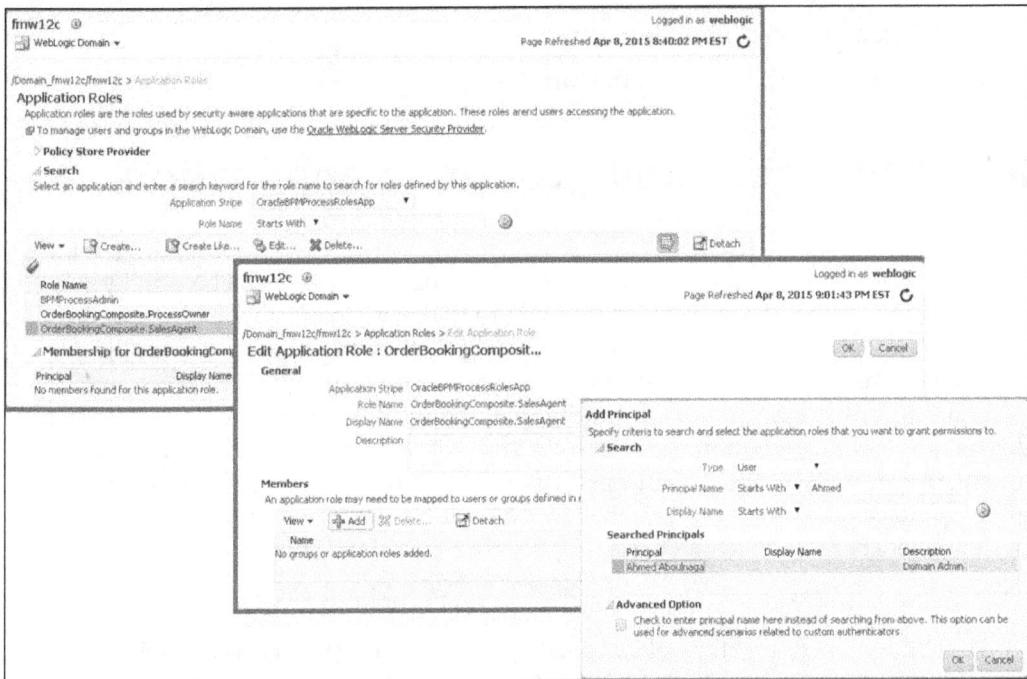

Figure 7.37: Mapping organizational users to Application Roles

Configuring multiple authentication providers for human workflow

When working with human workflow based composites, customers frequently have an external identity store that acts as a directory, holding the application end users and related enterprise groups. In many cases, they may also want to keep WebLogic's embedded LDAP server for administration accounts. Many large organizations also tend to have multiple user directories based on geographies, but the human workflow solution may require all users and groups to be brought together. If multiple authentication providers are configured, authentication occurs through all of them, according to the control flags set. **Java Portlet Specification (JPS)** however provides authorization in order of the hierarchical list of providers. An additional LDAP authentication provider can be configured for the worklist application but **Oracle Platform Security Services (OPSS)** by default doesn't support multiple authenticators. To overcome this challenge, Oracle SOA Suite 12*c* bundles a library named LibOVD, providing virtualization capabilities over multiple LDAP authentication providers.

To configure support for multiple authentication providers, a prerequisite is to have the Control Flag for all the providers set to SUFFICIENT. This can be set by accessing the property from the WebLogic Server Administration Console by navigating to **Security Realms** | **myrealm** | **Providers** | **Authentication** | **[Provider]** | **Common**.

Once this property change is implemented, support for multiple authentication providers can be configured through any one of the following options:

Option 1: A configuration change through Enterprise Manager Fusion Middleware Control:

1. Log in to Oracle Enterprise Manager Fusion Middleware Control.

2. Navigate to **WebLogic Domain** | **[Domain Name]** | **Security** | **Security Provider Configuration** | **Identity Store Provider** and click on the **Configure** button.

3. Add a new property named virtualize and set its value to true, as shown in Figure 7.38.

4. Click **OK** to save the changes.

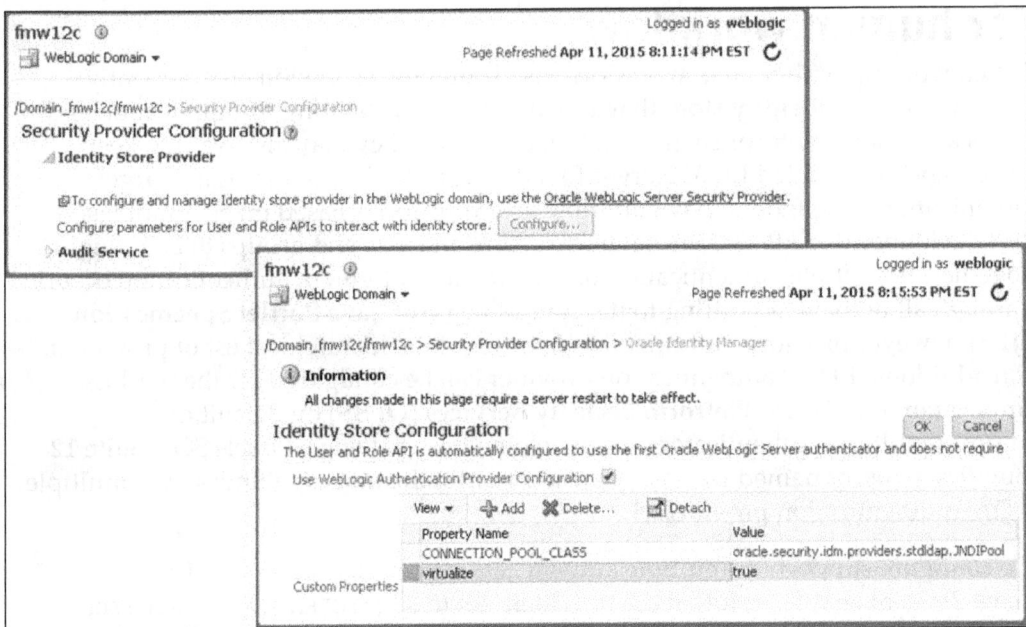

Figure 7.38: Adding support for multiple authentication providers for Human Workflow Components

Option 2: Modifying the `jps-config.xml` file:

1. Change selection to the `$DOMAIN_HOME/config/fmwconfig` directory and take a backup of the `jps-config.xml` file.

2. Next, edit the file and modify the service instance `idstore.ldap.provider` to add the virtualization flag.

Let's have a look the following configuration snippet:

```
<serviceInstance provider='idstore.ldap.provider' name= 'idstore.
ldap'>
    <property value= 'oracle.security.jps.wls.internal.idstore.
WlsLdapIdStoreConfigProvider' name="idstore.config.provider"/>
    <property value='oracle.security.idm.providers.stdldap.JNDIPool'
name='CONNECTION_POOL_CLASS'/>
    <property value='true' name='virtualize'/>
</serviceInstance>
```

Both these options require a domain level restart.

Migrating human workflow data from test to production

Process participants working on tasks assigned to them in the worklist or the workspace application may not find the default inbox view very helpful. For instance, they may need to view additional columns required to prioritize tasks or view process indicators in the inbox. These additional columns may be added from the default available column list, or users may use a mapped attributes (flex fields) to store and display important values from the task payload. Mapped attributes in human workflow store and query custom attributes that typically come from the task payload values.

However, the problems it poses for you as an administrator, in the long run, is migrating worklist customizations across different environments. Assume that a bunch of participants create custom views and vacation rules and add mapped attributes in the test environment, which are then necessary to promote to staging and production environments. Oracle SOA Suite 12*c* provides a Human Workflow User Config Data Migrator that is available as a utility script wrapped with Ant.

The Data Migrator provides administrators the following operations:

- **Export**: This operation extracts all the human workflow user-configurable data from the source SOA server and saves it to an XML file.

- **Import**: This operation recreates all human workflow custom configurations and imports data in the target SOA server by reading them from a source XML file.

The Data Migrator utility relies on two key files:

- The `migration.properties`: This contains all required input properties in terms of key-value pairs for migration operations. It also determines what type of user configuration is to be imported or exported.

- The `ant-worklist-t2p.xml`: This is an Ant build file containing the default Ant target, `runHwfMigrator`, responsible for exporting customizations from one environment and importing them to another depending upon the operation.

Figure 7.39 shows a custom view configured by the `weblogic` user in the worklist application for task approvals. A **Priority Approvals** view is configured to accommodate and show the **orderDiscount** field (mapped attribute) on the worklist screen. The following section will describe how to set up and execute the Data Migrator wizard to extract these customizations in an XML file and then import them into another server. Observe the following screenshot:

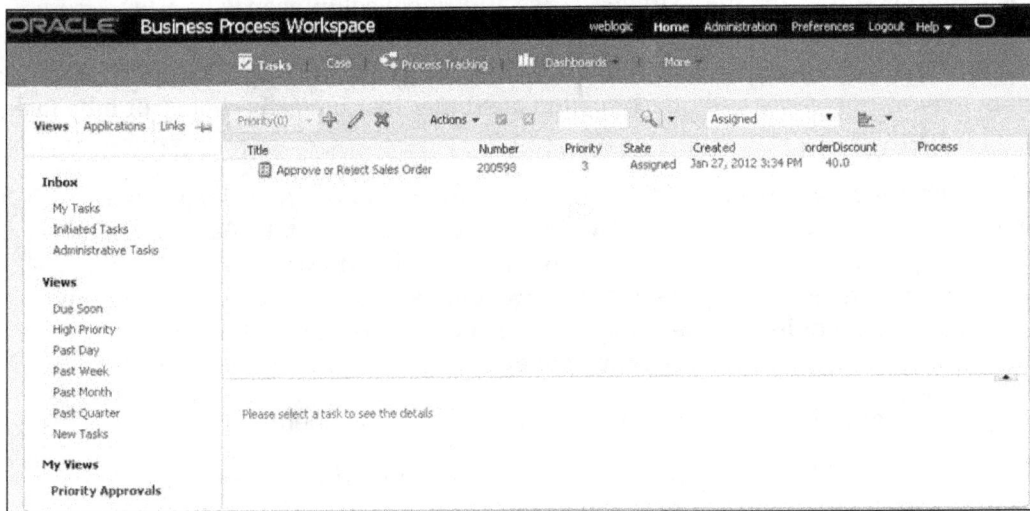

Figure 7.39: Custom views and mapped attributes in the BPM Worklist Application

To move human workflow data from test to production environments, perform the following steps:

1. Ensure that the PATH environment variable contains JAVA_HOME (the location of the complaint JDK path) and ANT_HOME.

   ```
   export JAVA_HOME=/u01/app/oracle/middleware/jdk1.7.0_15
   export ANT_HOME=$MW_HOME/oracle_common/modules/org.apache.
   ant_1.9.2
   export PATH=$PATH:$JAVA_HOME/bin:$ANT_HOME/bin
   ```

2. Now, change the prompt to $MW_HOME/soa/bin.

3. Create a `migration.properties` file in the `bin` directory to export user metadata for the worklist application (for example, group rules, views, mapped attribute mappings, and vacation rules) from the test environment. See here one such example of a `migration.properties` that contains properties to export custom worklist views. The connection and file location properties highlighted in the following snippet need to be replaced with values corresponding to your environment:

```
# Connection Properties
soa.hostname = localhost
soa.rmi.port = 8001
soa.admin.user = weblogic
soa.admin.password = welcome1
realm = jazn.com

# Migration File Location
migration.file = /tmp/worklist_data/export_all_migration.xml
map.file = /tmp/export_all_map_mapper.xml

# hwfMigrator Properties
operationType = EXPORT
objectType = VIEW
name = ALL
user = weblogic
group =
grantPermission = true
migrateAttributeLabel = true
override = true
skip = true
migrateToActiveVersion = true
```

4. The directory has an Ant build file containing the `runHwfMigrator` default target. Execute the Ant command by passing `ant-t2p-worklist.xml` as the file argument to export user configuration data.

```
ant -f ant-t2p-worklist.xml -Dbea.home=$MW_HOME -Dsoa.home=$MW_
HOME/soa
```

5. If all properties are correctly specified, you will get a successful build output and two files will be created in `/tmp/worklist_date`.

6. *Figure 7.40* shows how to verify that the export was successful by locating the migration and map file in the directory specified in the `migration.properties` file. The `export_all_migration.xml` file contains exported data for the Priority Approval View along with its view columns.

The following table explains each of the properties in detail:

Property	Definition
migration.file	This specifies the directory location where task definition mapping data is exported to or imported from.
map.file	This specifies the directory location where user configuration data is exported to or imported from.
operationType	Flag this to specify whether to export data from the server or import into it.
objectType	This property specifies the type of custom object to migrate. Possible values are either VIEW, RULE, and TASK_PAYLOAD_FLEX_FIELD_MAPPING.
Name	This specifies the object name if you specified VIEW or TASK_PAYLOAD_FLEX_FIELD_MAPPING values for the objectType properties. You can specify an individual viewName or taskDefinitionId. Specify ALL to identify all objects of this type.
User	This specifies the username for VIEW or RULE objectType properties. If a user is not specified for a VIEW, it implies STANDARD_VIEW.
Group	This specifies the group for only RULE objectType property to identify the group name. Leave it blank if the username property is specified.
grantPermission	A true flag migrates view definitions and grants whereas a false value migrates only view definitions. Applicable only for the VIEW objectType property.
migrateAttributeLabel	A true value migrates only attribute labels whereas the false flag doesn't migrate attribute labels.
Override	While using the IMPORT operationType this property species whether to override the data on the target SOA server if the flag is set to true.
Skip	If an error happens while migrating a true value of this flag specifies that errors are skipped and the migration utility continues processing. If set to false, the migration is halted if an error occurs.
migrateToActiveVersion	A true value maps task definition IDs to the active version in the target SOA server instance.

Let's have a look at the following screenshot:

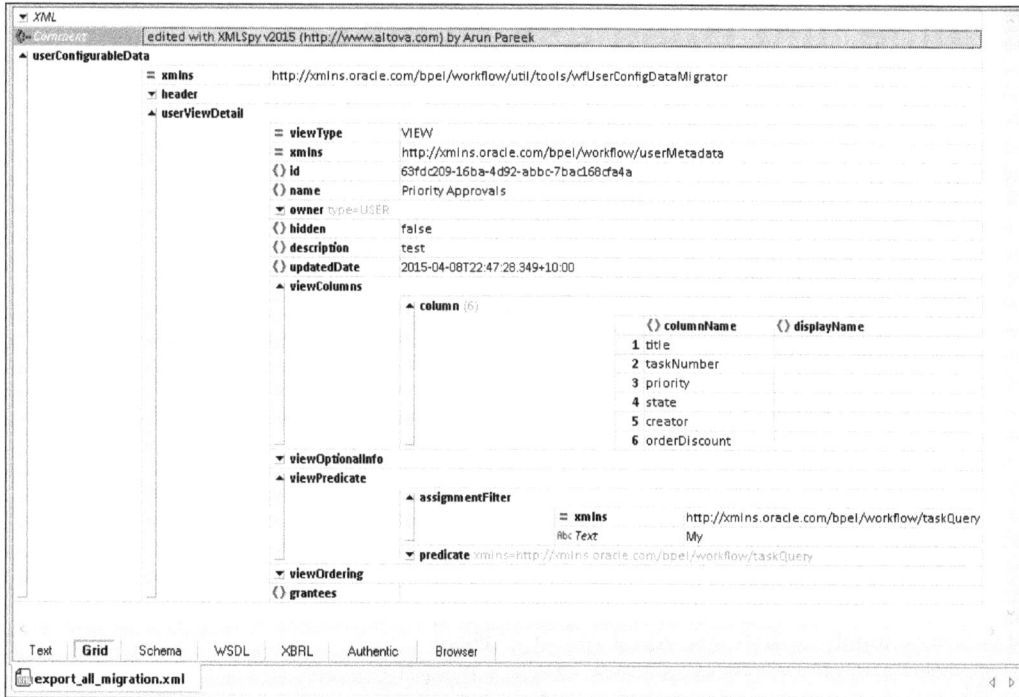

Figure 7.40: Output mapping and migration files from Worklist T2P Utility

However, keep the following things in mind while using the migration utility:

* Only one type of data (objectType) can be exported or imported at a time.
* Each particular user or group's data must be exported or imported in separate operations.
* Attribute labels must be exported or imported before mapped attribute mappings.
* Human workflow artifacts, such as task-mapped attribute mappings, rules, views, and approval groups, are defined based on namespace. The worklist data migration utility migrates human workflow artifacts based on namespace. Therefore, it is not possible to migrate human workflow artifacts based on a partition.

Administering and configuring Event Engine and Business Events

The **Event Delivery Network (EDN)** in Oracle SOA Suite 12*c* provides a declarative way to generate and consume business events that are managed by the event engine. When a business event is published, other service components or database agents can subscribe to it. The EDN-based event engine in Oracle SOA Suite 12*c* is a typical publisher-subscriber model that has two different implementations:

- **AQJMS (Advanced Queuing)** uses underlying database AQs as a backend store and depends on event delivery queue tables and stored procedures to manage events. The EDN AQs can be found under **[PREFIX]_SOAINFRA** schema with the EDN suffix.

- **WLJMS (WebLogic)** implementation uses backbone JMS queues. EDN-based event messages are published to and subscribed from EDNQueue (jms/fabric/EDNQueue) or EDNTopic (jms/fabric/EDNTopic) under **Services | JMS Modules | SOAJMSModule** in the WebLogic Server Administration Console.

There is no definite answer to preferentially using one mode over the other. However, switching between database AQJMS and WLJMS-based EDN is quite simple. By default, Oracle SOA Suite 12*c* uses the WLJMS mode for EDN. This can be verified and changed by accessing the **EDNConfig** MBean (refer to *Figure 7.41*) under **soa-infra | SOA Infrastructure | Administration | System MBean Properties | oracle.as.soainfra.config | Server: soa_server1 | EDNConfig**. The JMSType property holds the configuration for the EDN messaging type. By default, it is set to WLJMS, meaning that the infrastructure uses Java Messaging Services for handling events. To change the messaging framework to database queues for EDN, change the property value to AQJMS and initiate a server restart for the change to take effect.

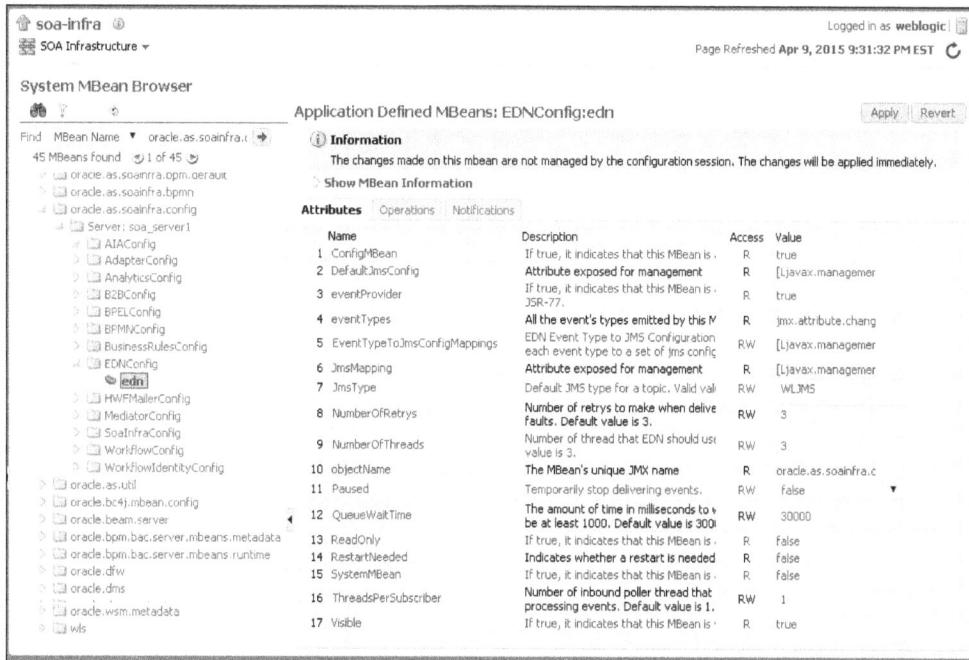

Figure 7.41: Viewing and modifying EDN messaging mode

Administering and testing Business Events

Oracle Enterprise Manager Fusion Middleware Control provides an ability to view, configure, test, and manage business events used by various service components across multiple composites. The EDN framework can be administered from the **SOA Infrastructure | Business Events** dashboard:

- The **Business Events** dashboard provides the ability to search for a specific business event by specifying a full or partial event name and clicking the **Search** icon.

- Click on **Show Event Definition** to see the schema used to build an event definition.

- *Figure 7.42* shows various events that are published and subscribed to, along with their total Subscriptions and Failed Deliveries count. The **Business Events** dashboard also allows testing the EDN framework as a standalone application by selecting a particular event, clicking on the **Test** button, and invoking the framework with a sample payload based on the event type in the pop-up window.

- A **The Event published successfully** message would confirm that an event message is published to the messaging framework used by the EDN channel.

Unit testing a business event is shown in the following screenshot:

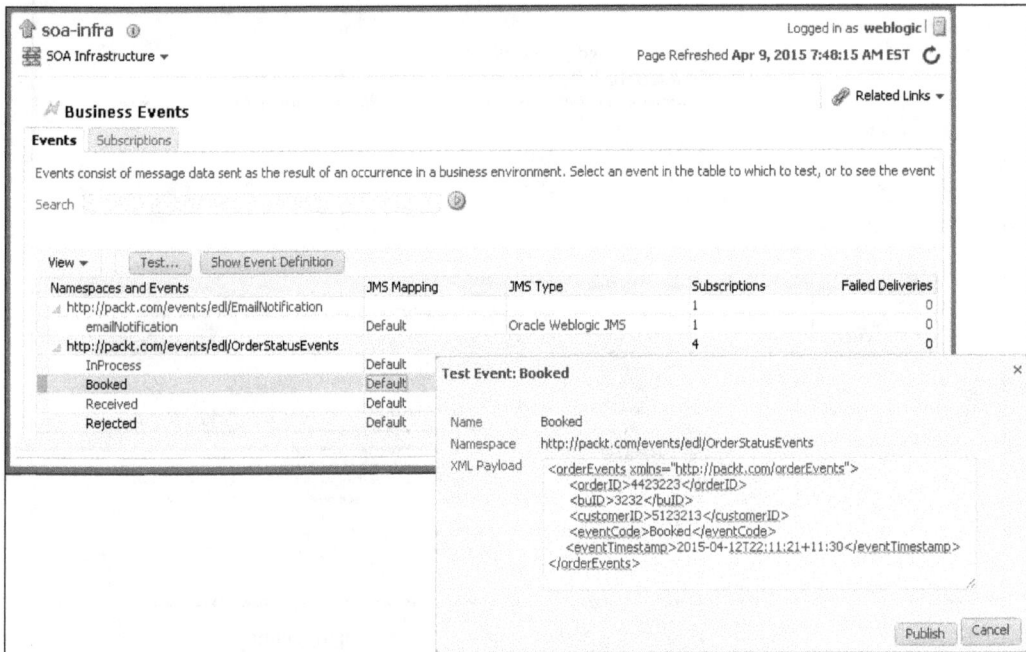

Figure 7.42: Managing and unit testing Business Events

The **Subscriptions** tab in the dashboard is used to view service component subscriptions that are created during design time.

> If a SOA composite application includes a business event subscription and different revisions of the composite are deployed, event subscriptions from all revisions of the composite are active and receive messages. To receive an event with the latest revision of the composite only, it is recommended that previous revisions of the composite be retired or undeployed.

Faulted and undelivered business events can be viewed and actioned (recovery or abortion) from the **Error Hospital** tab in the SOA Infrastructure or the partition dashboard.

Although the EDN framework is designed to be a black box to the administrator, there are mechanisms that you can use to view event payloads for troubleshooting purposes. If the messaging mode is set to WLJMS, pause consumption from EDNQueue or EDNTopic to see what payload is being sent to the event engine. Follow these steps to pause a Java Messaging Service on the WebLogic Server:

1. Log in to the Oracle WebLogic Server Administration Console.

2. Click on **JMS Modules** under the **Messaging** panel.

3. Click on **SOAJMSModule**.

4. Click on **EDNQueue**.

5. Click on the **Control** tab.

6. Select **SOAJMSModule!EDNQueue** under **Destinations**, click on the **Consumption** button, and press **Pause**.

7. Next time an event is published, you can view its details by going to the **Monitoring** tab, selecting **SOAJMSModule!EDNQueue**, and clicking on the **Show Messages** button.

When the messaging mode is configured to AQJMS, event messages are intermittently stored in the EDN_EVENT_QUEUE AQ table. To pause consumption on this AQ, connect to the [PREFIX]_SOAINFRA schema and execute the following query. The query will let the queue receive messages but will not transmit them to subscribers.

```
BEGIN
    SYS.DBMS_AQADM.START_QUEUE (
        QUEUE_NAME => 'DEV_SOAINFRA.EDN_EVENT_QUEUE',
        ENQUEUE    => TRUE,
        DEQUEUE    => FALSE
    );
END;
```

If an event is raised now, it will be available in EDN_EVENT_QUEUE_TABLE and can be queried from the USER_DATA column using the following query. The query filters the business event payload for a particular composite instance. To access all the event messages, remove the WHERE clause from the query.

```
SELECT XMLTYPE.EXTRACT(XMLTYPE(T.USER_DATA.EVENT), '/EDN_BUSINESS_
EVENT/PAYLOAD/*/*/*[LOCAL-NAME()="EVENTDATA"]', NULL).GETSTRINGVAL()
EVENT_MESSAGE FROM DEV_SOAINFRA.EDN_EVENT_QUEUE_TABLE T WHERE
XMLTYPE.EXTRACT(XMLTYPE(T.USER_DATA.EVENT), '/*/*/*/*/*[LOCAL-
NAME()="COMPOSITEINSTANCEID"]/TEXT()', NULL).GETSTRINGVAL() =
'990004';
```

Maintain extreme caution when pausing consumption on these queues for debugging purposes and ensure that consumption is resumed after the troubleshooting is complete.

Administering domain values maps and cross-references

Domain Value Maps (DVMs) are simply mapping objects. They are used in composites to map data that may be stored in one application in one format, to that of the target application in another format. For example, the contents of a CountryCodes.dvm file can be as follows:

```xml
<?xml version = '1.0'?>
<dvm name="CountryCodes" xmlns="http://xmlns.oracle.com/dvm">
  <description>DVM description</description>
  <columns>
    <column name="CountryCode"/>
    <column name="CountryName"/>
  </columns>
  <rows>
    <row>
      <cell>US</cell>
      <cell>United States</cell>
    </row>
    <row>
      <cell>UK</cell>
      <cell>United Kingdom</cell>
    </row>
    <row>
      <cell>ZA</cell>
      <cell>South Africa</cell>
    </row>
  </rows>
</dvm>
```

In this example, country code may be stored as US in one application and United States in another, and by using transformation functions within SOA composites, developers can look up and map values as needed.

Although database tables can be used as a substitute for DVMs, DVMs are static in nature and are optimized for speed and performance. DVMs are typically created by developers at design time, or they can be created manually and the .dvm files can be imported directly into the MDS via Ant.

Cross references are slightly different in that they are used to dynamically map values from one application to another. For example, you may have two applications, each maintaining its own customer table wherein customer-specific information such as customer ID, customer name, customer address, and other customer metadata is stored. However, each application may have a different format for the unique identifier called customer ID. For example, SAP may create customer IDs in a format different from Oracle E-Business Suite, as shown in the following table:

SAP	EBS
SAP_001	EBS_1001
SAP_002	EBS_1002

Thus, Cross references are used to map these dynamic customer IDs across applications. Cross References, or XREFs, consist of two parts:

- **Metadata** created as .xref files and stored in the MDS.
- **Data** consisting of actual values stored in the XREF_DATA table in the database.

Similar to DVMs, Cross references can be created by the developer at design time, or they can be created manually and the .xref files can be imported directly into the MDS via Ant. The good news is that, from an administrative standpoint, aside from using Ant to import .dvm and .xref files to the MDS, there is not much to do. In general, it is valuable to understand each.

Administering DVMs

In an earlier section in this chapter, we explained how SOA Composer can be used to manage runtime configuration changes for human workflow tasks. The web-based SOA Composer console can additionally be used to modify deployed domain value maps at runtime. This eliminates the need to use Ant to reimport DVMs if there is a need for dynamic changes. Access to the SOA Composer console is controlled by associating users and groups to the SOADesigner role under the soa-infra application stripe.

The expected administrative tasks related to DVMs include:

- Using Ant to import DVMs into the MDS.
- Using SOA Composer to add or edit values in a DVM at runtime.

Perform the following steps to modify DVM values at runtime:

1. Log in to SOA Composer at `http://<soahost>:<soaport>/soa/composer`.

2. Click on **Create Session** to initiate a change window.

3. By default, the SOA Composer organizes resources by **Deployment View** (that is, by the deployed composites that they are packaged into).

4. Change this to **Types View** by clicking on the ⌄ icon.

5. Expand **Domain Value Maps** to click on the DVM that needs to be edited.

6. Click on one of the add (✛), edit (✎), or delete (✖) icons as shown in *Figure 7.43* to modify a DVM row.

7. After the change is done, click on the **Save** button.

8. For the runtime change to come into effect, click on **Publish**.

The following screenshot displays an example DVM in the SOA Composer:

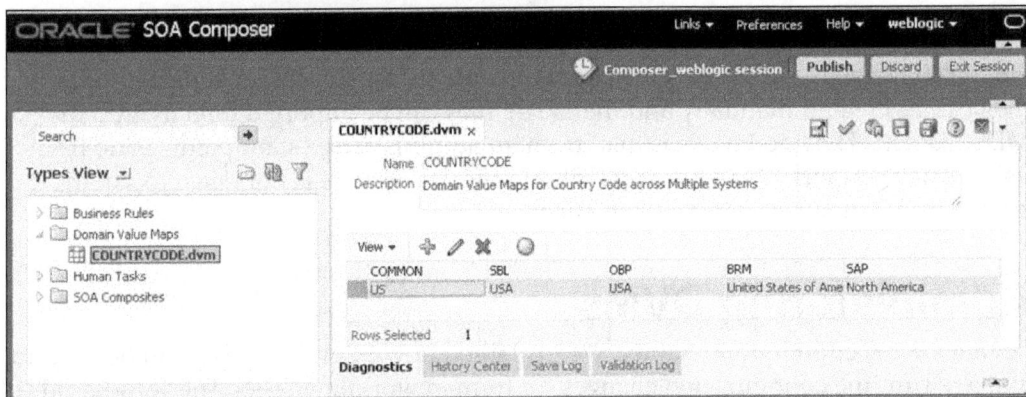

Figure 7.43: Modifying DVM values at runtime via the SOA Composer

Administering XREFs

The expected administrative tasks related to XREFs include:

- Using Ant to import XREF metadata into the MDS.

- Monitoring the growth of the `XREF_DATA` table.

- Monitoring the performance of composites that use XREF lookups. If performance is poor, consider creating custom XREF database tables.

> Be careful when manually promoting XREF data from one environment to another. Dynamic data and/or IDs may not be identical across applications in different environments, thus rendering the migrated XREF data invalid.

More information as on how to create custom XREF tables can be found here:

```
https://docs.oracle.com/middleware/1213/soasuite/develop-soa/cross-
references-designing.htm#SOASE1793.
```

Configuring infrastructure resources for developers

Developers are a demanding bunch, always wanting access! We describe in this final section of the chapter how to create read-only accounts that developers can use to log in to the various consoles as well have read-only access to the MDS. It is always recommended not to share the `weblogic` password with developers.

In this section, we also describe how to configure custom XPath functions.

The `Monitors` group provides read-only access to Oracle Fusion Middleware Enterprise Manager Control, while the `Deployers` group grants the ability to deploy applications to the SOA server.

Providing role-based access to the SOA Infrastructure

From time to time, administrators of Oracle SOA Suite 12*c* infrastructure are required to provide limited and role based access to developers and extended team members. For instance, administrators may be tasked with providing a group of users and developers access to view service status and health, composite instances, and audit trails. In other cases, the requirement may be to grant operators access to manage composite lifecycles. Fortunately, Enterprise Manager provides functionality to provide different levels of access to different users and groups access without allowing them to change any infrastructure settings. The following steps detail how administrators can provide role-based access to the SOA infrastructure:

1. Log in to WebLogic Server Administration Console.

2. The ideal way to manage access here is to create WebLogic groups, manage their membership by associating actual LDAP-based users and groups, and finally grant permissions to them.

3. Navigate to **Your Application's Security Settings | Security Realms | myrealm | Users and Groups | Groups** and create a two new groups: **SOAAuditViewer** and **SOAOperator**.

4. Click on one of these groups and then go to the **Membership** tab. This allows other groups (organizational) to be added to this logical group.

5. Alternatively, individual users can have their membership modified to be associated with these groups.

6. Next, log in to Oracle Enterprise Manager Fusion Middleware Control and navigate to **Weblogic Domain | [domain_name] | Weblogic Domain | Security | Application Roles**.

7. Select **soa-infra** from under the **Application Stripe** dropdown and click on the search button to search for existing application roles.

8. The following table provides a list of predefined application roles in the Oracle Fusion Middleware Infrastructure and their associated permissions.

Role	Permission
SOAAdmin	This has full access, including the ability to modify security settings.
SOAOperator	This has access to deploy/undeploy, start/stop, and activate/retire composites.
SOAMonitor	This has read-only access to Oracle EM FMW Console.
SOAAuditViewer	This has access to view instance and audit trails.
SOAAuditAdmin	This has access to modify audit levels.

Refer to the earlier section *Mapping Users and Groups to Application Roles* in this chapter for guidance on how to associate WebLogic users and groups to Fusion Middleware application roles.

Creating read-only MDS database accounts

Developers will require a database account to access the MDS during their development as it is necessary for them to create a database connection in JDeveloper 12c to the [PREFIX]_MDS schema in order to access MDS artifacts. Shared objects that are maintained in the MDS, such as DVMs, schemas, and WSDLs, need to be accessible to the developer during the development cycle. The last thing administrators want is to share the [PREFIX]_MDS schema password.

Follow these instructions to create a generic MDS_MDS_READONLY database account that can be shared with developers. The following instructions assume that the schema name for the MDS is DEV_MDS:

1. Log in to the database with a user account with SYSDBA privileges:

   ```
   SQLPLUS "/ AS SYSDBA"
   ```

2. Create the database user DEV_MDS_READONLY and grant access:

   ```
   CREATE USER DEV_MDS_READONLY IDENTIFIED BY WELCOME1;
   GRANT RESOURCE, CONNECT TO DEV_MDS_READONLY;
   ```

3. Execute the following commands to grant select access to the product tables to the DEV_MDS_READONLY user:

   ```
   GRANT SELECT ON DEV_MDS.MDS_PARTITIONS TO DEV_MDS_READONLY;
   GRANT SELECT ON DEV_MDS.MDS_LABELS TO DEV_MDS_READONLY;
   GRANT SELECT ON DEV_MDS.MDS_TXN_LOCKS TO DEV_MDS_READONLY;
   GRANT SELECT ON DEV_MDS.MDS_TRANSACTIONS TO DEV_MDS_READONLY;
   GRANT SELECT ON DEV_MDS.MDS_DEPL_LINEAGES TO DEV_MDS_READONLY;
   GRANT SELECT ON DEV_MDS.MDS_PATHS TO DEV_MDS_READONLY;
   GRANT SELECT ON DEV_MDS.MDS_STREAMED_DOCS TO DEV_MDS_READONLY;
   GRANT SELECT ON DEV_MDS.MDS_NAMESPACES TO DEV_MDS_READONLY;
   GRANT SELECT ON DEV_MDS.MDS_COMPONENTS TO DEV_MDS_READONLY;
   GRANT SELECT ON DEV_MDS.MDS_ATTRIBUTES TO DEV_MDS_READONLY;
   GRANT SELECT ON DEV_MDS.MDS_DEPENDENCIES TO DEV_MDS_READONLY;
   GRANT SELECT ON DEV_MDS.MDS_PURGE_PATHS TO DEV_MDS_READONLY;
   GRANT SELECT ON DEV_MDS.MDS_LARGE_ATTRIBUTES TO DEV_MDS_READONLY;
   GRANT SELECT ON DEV_MDS.MDS_SANDBOXES TO DEV_MDS_READONLY;
   ```

4. Create the appropriate synonyms for the database tables:

   ```
   CREATE SYNONYM DEV_MDS_READONLY.MDS_PARTITIONS FOR DEV_MDS.MDS_
   PARTITIONS;
   CREATE SYNONYM DEV_MDS_READONLY.MDS_LABELS FOR DEV_MDS.MDS_LABELS;
   CREATE SYNONYM DEV_MDS_READONLY.MDS_TXN_LOCKS FOR DEV_MDS.MDS_TXN_
   LOCKS;
   CREATE SYNONYM DEV_MDS_READONLY.MDS_TRANSACTIONS FOR DEV_MDS.MDS_
   TRANSACTIONS;
   CREATE SYNONYM DEV_MDS_READONLY.MDS_DEPL_LINEAGES FOR DEV_MDS.MDS_
   DEPL_LINEAGES;
   CREATE SYNONYM DEV_MDS_READONLY.MDS_PATHS FOR DEV_MDS.MDS_PATHS;
   CREATE SYNONYM DEV_MDS_READONLY.MDS_STREAMED_DOCS FOR DEV_MDS.MDS_
   STREAMED_DOCS;
   CREATE SYNONYM DEV_MDS_READONLY.MDS_NAMESPACES FOR DEV_MDS.MDS_
   NAMESPACES;
   CREATE SYNONYM DEV_MDS_READONLY.MDS_COMPONENTS FOR DEV_MDS.MDS_
   COMPONENTS;
   ```

```
CREATE SYNONYM DEV_MDS_READONLY.MDS_ATTRIBUTES FOR DEV_MDS.MDS_
ATTRIBUTES;
CREATE SYNONYM DEV_MDS_READONLY.MDS_DEPENDENCIES FOR DEV_MDS.MDS_
DEPENDENCIES;
CREATE SYNONYM DEV_MDS_READONLY.MDS_PURGE_PATHS FOR DEV_MDS.MDS_
PURGE_PATHS;
CREATE SYNONYM DEV_MDS_READONLY.MDS_LARGE_ATTRIBUTES FOR DEV_MDS.
MDS_LARGE_ATTRIBUTES;
CREATE SYNONYM DEV_MDS_READONLY.MDS_SANDBOXES FOR DEV_MDS.MDS_
SANDBOXES;
```

5. Create the appropriate synonyms for the database packages:

```
CREATE SYNONYM DEV_MDS_READONLY.MDS_INTERNAL_COMMON FOR DEV_MDS.
MDS_INTERNAL_COMMON;
CREATE SYNONYM DEV_MDS_READONLY.MDS_INTERNAL_SHREDDED FOR DEV_MDS.
MDS_INTERNAL_SHREDDED;
CREATE SYNONYM DEV_MDS_READONLY.MDS_INTERNAL_UTILS FOR DEV_MDS.
MDS_INTERNAL_UTILS;
```

6. Grant execute permissions to the packages:

```
GRANT EXECUTE ON DEV_MDS.MDS_INTERNAL_COMMON TO DEV_MDS_READONLY;
GRANT EXECUTE ON DEV_MDS.MDS_INTERNAL_SHREDDED TO DEV_MDS_
READONLY;
GRANT EXECUTE ON DEV_MDS.MDS_INTERNAL_UTILS TO DEV_MDS_READONLY;
```

Note that the same permission setting can be created for the [PREFIX]_SOAINFRA schema.

Setting up custom XPath

Developers tend to use a multitude of custom function libraries as they develop their SOA composites. These functions are mostly used within transformation files (that is, XSL and XQuery maps) or assignment activities. These functions can be used at design time in the composite editor by importing the library as User Defined Extension Jar files.

At runtime, however, administrators have to ensure that these libraries are appropriately placed to be part of the server runtime. Although describing how to create custom XPath functions is out of scope for this book, their deployment is not.

To deploy a custom XPath function to the Oracle SOA Suite 12*c* infrastructure, follow these steps:

1. Get a copy of the JAR file with the custom XPath functions (for example, `customXPathFunctions.jar`).

2. Copy the file to the location where all external function libraries are to be copied (that is, `$MW_HOME/soa/soa/modules/oracle.soa.ext_11.1.1`).

3. Restart the SOA managed server.

Now, any composite deployed to the server and requiring the use of these custom XPath functions will have access to them at runtime.

Summary

This was quite a long chapter, and a lot of diverse topics were presented! The goal was to provide you with different subject areas that you can reference any time on an as-needed basis. Oracle Fusion Middleware Enterprise Manager Control provides end-to-end monitoring and administration, and navigating it can be overwhelming at first. We revisited some of the approaches to navigating the numerous configuration screens. Of the several areas surrounding administration and configuration, we covered:

- Configuration of reference and service bindings of JCA adapters, and described the `Global Retry Count` property and why you should update it.

- Manual and automatic recovery of BPEL component faults.

- All Mediator Service Engine properties.

- The UMS architecture along with details on how to configure an e-mail messaging driver and notifications.

- Administering and configuring the Human Workflow Engine.

- Mapping LDAP users and groups to application roles.

- The Human Workflow User Config Data Migrator and how it helps in migrating human workflow data across environments.

- Event Engine and Business Events configuration, standalone testing, and administration.

- Mechanisms to start up and shut down the infrastructure using scripts.

- The administration of DVMs and XREFs.

- Specific configuration usually required by developers, such as read-only access and configuring custom XPath functions on the server.

Managing the Database

8

The single area causing most complaints with users of Oracle SOA Suite 11*g* is the issue of database growth. The importance of purging completed instances was initially not stressed in the previous 11*g* release, and this has led to numerous production stability issues for many customers. The purge scripts were adequate at best, and it took numerous patch sets to get them right. Fortunately, Oracle SOA Suite 12*c* has come with drastic improvements in the purging process, alleviating the number one cause of headaches for the production administrator.

The latter part of this chapter discusses less frequently used functionality surrounding partitions and version history, albeit the functionality that every SOA Suite administrator should be familiar with. Thus, we will cover the following areas related to database management in this chapter:

- Managing the dehydration store
- Managing metadata repository partitions
- Purging the metadata version history

Managing the dehydration store

Until now, you have been learning about common administrative tasks involving the MDS repository. The MDS repository maintains a small database footprint as it is simply used to store application metadata and runtime configurations changes. Another important schema that would require more frequent monitoring and close administration is the [PREFIX]_SOAINFRA database schema, which stores instance and transactional data that is executed in the infrastructure. This database schema is also referred to as the **dehydration store**. Oracle SOA Suite 12*c* leverages the dehydration store to maintain long-running processes and their current state information while these processes are executing over a period of time. Storing the process in a database preserves it and prevents any loss of state or reliability in case of a system shutdown or a network problem.

Configurations affecting the dehydration store

It is important to understand how the nature of deployed composites affects what is saved in the dehydration store. Business processes, in general, can be categorized either as transient (short lived, request-response-style synchronous processes) or durable (long-running asynchronous processes). Transient processes do not incur any intermediate dehydration during the process execution, and if there are unhandled faults or system downtime during the process execution, the instances of a transient process do not leave a trace in the system. Also, instances of transient processes cannot be saved in-flight, whether they are completed normally or abnormally. On the other hand, there are durable processes, which have one or more activities running in the background during the execution when their instances are dehydrated in the database. For example, in a BPEL component, a few activities that cause this intermittent dehydration are Receive, Pick, Wait, Reply, and CheckPoint.

> The term "dehydration" refers to the action of committing process state information to the database.

Instance data being saved to the dehydration store database depends on several factors such as the design of the process, nature of synchronicity, audit and logging levels, persistence policies, whether the instance is being optimized to be executed in the memory, and others. Practically, there are infinite combinations through which the amount of data being saved to the database can be controlled. It is vital to know about the typical configurations that can be set either at the individual process level or at the domain level and what their impact is on the dehydration store.

These configuration properties can be applied at the domain level, enabling you to set a global configuration for all composites deployed to the domain. You can also override these configuration properties at the individual component level. If a setting at the domain level conflicts with the same setting at the component level, the component-level setting takes priority. Component-level properties can be set at design time.

The following table shows the various properties that control data persistence in the dehydration store and their respective descriptions:

Property	Configuration level	Description
`completionPersistLevel`	Domain and component (BPEL only)	This property controls the type and amount of instance data being saved after its completion. When process instances get completed, the Oracle SOA Suite 12*c* engine, by default, saves the final state (for example, the variable values) of the instance. If these values are not required to be saved after completion, this property can be set to save only the instance metadata (the completion state, start and end dates, and so on). This property is used only when the `inMemoryOptimization` performance property is set to `true` and can have the following values: • `all` (default): The engine saves the complete instance, including the final variable values, work item data, and audit data. • `instanceHeader`: Only the instance metadata is saved.

Property	Configuration level	Description
completionPersistPolicy	Domain and component (BPEL only)	This property controls whether to persist instances and when to persist instances. If an instance is not saved, its flow trail does not appear in Fusion Middleware Control. This property is only used when inMemoryOptimization is set to true. This parameter strongly impacts the amount of data stored in the database and can also impact the throughput. It can be set to either of these values: • on (default): In this, completed instances are saved normally. • deferred: Here, completed instances are saved with a different thread and in another transaction. If the server fails, some instances may not be saved. • faulted: Here, only faulted instances are saved. • off: In this, no instances (and their data) are saved.
inMemoryOptimization	Component (BPEL only)	This works hand in hand with completionPersistLevel and completionPersistPolicy. This property can be set for transient processes. If inMemoryOptimization is set to true, the completionPersistLevel option is set to all and the completionPersistPolicy is set to faulted. The process will run in the memory without saving anything to the dehydration database unless the instance faults during when all instance data is saved.

Property	Configuration level	Description
deliveryPersistPolicy	Component (BPEL only)	This property enables and disables database persistence of messages entering the Oracle SOA Suite 12*c* engine. By default, incoming requests are saved in intermediate delivery service database tables, which are later acquired by worker threads and delivered to the targeted processes. In a case where performance is preferred over reliability, persisting the incoming messages in the database can be skipped. This property persists delivery messages and is applicable to durable processes.
largeDocumentThreshold	Domain	This property sets the large XML document persistence threshold. This is the maximum size (in kilobytes) of a variable before it is stored in a separate location from the rest of the instance scope data. This property is applicable to both durable and transient processes. Large XML documents impact the performance of the entire Oracle SOA Suite 12*c* engine if they are constantly read in and written out whenever processing on an instance must be performed.
auditDetailThreshold	Domain	This property sets the maximum size (in kilobytes) of an audit trail detail's string before it is stored separately from the audit trail. If the size of a detail is larger than the value specified for this property, it is placed in the AUDIT_DETAILS table. Otherwise, it is placed in the AUDIT_TRAIL table.
auditLevel	Domain and component	This property sets the audit trail logging level. This process is applicable to both durable and transient processes.

> For all asynchronous processes, `inMemoryOptimization` should be set to `False`. If it is set to `True`, you will need to set `completionPersistPolicy` to `Off` in order to avoid the dangling references in the database tables.

Database objects of the SOA dehydration store

The next important area to understand is the structure of the underlying dehydration store database. It is somewhat difficult to comprehend the relationship between the various tables required by the Oracle SOA Suite 12*c* dehydration store, as the tables have no foreign key constraints to police referential integrity (this is intentionally designed this way for performance reasons). Without these constraints, the relationship between the master and detail tables needs to be protected to avoid dangling references in the detail tables. Hence, the utmost care should be taken when executing any kind of manual instruction to the database. It is with experience that an administrator gains insight about the different tables and ways to perform common administration tasks such as purging, partitioning, and reclaiming disk space. Improper purging or ignorantly using a wrong mix of configuration parameters will eventually lead to orphaned instances that will make managing the database difficult. A good starting point is to use the out-of-the-box packages that are provided by Oracle to perform the purging and partitioning activities. It is essential to have an overall understanding of the key tables that make up majority of the dehydration store. A few of them are described in the following table, along with the type of instance-related data they store:

Table	Description
ATTACHMENT	Attachments of a process instance are persisted as variables in this table.
ATTACHMENT_REF	An attachment can be referenced by multiple process instances. The references to an attachment are saved in the ATTACHMENT_REF table.
AUDIT_DETAILS	Activities inside a process such as an assign activity logs variables as audit details by default in this table. This behavior is controlled through the `auditLevel` configuration property in place. The `auditDetailThreshold` configuration property is used by this table. If the size of a detail is larger than the value specified for this property, it is placed in this table. Otherwise, it is placed in the AUDIT_TRAIL table.

Table	Description
AUDIT_TRAIL	This stores the audit trail for instances. The audit trail viewed in the Fusion Middleware Control console is created from an XML document. As an instance is processed, each activity writes events to the audit trail as XML. This contains a column named LOG, which is a Large Object RAW column. Each step in a process gets logged into the LOG column in XML zipped form.
CUBE_INSTANCE	This stores the BPEL process instance metadata such as the instance creation date, current state, title, process identifier, and so on. For each process instance, an entry gets created in this table. The table also contains the relationship between parent and child instances in the fields: cikey, parent_id, and root_id.
CUBE_SCOPE	This stores the scope data for an instance (that is, all variables declared in the process flow and some internal objects that help route logic throughout the flow).
DLV_MESSAGE	This stores callback messages when they are received. This table only stores the metadata for a message such as the current state, process identifier, and receive date.
DLV_SUBSCRIPTION	This stores delivery subscriptions for an instance. Whenever an instance expects a message from a partner (for example, the receive or onMessage activity), a subscription is written out for that specific receive activity.
DOCUMENT_CI_REF	This stores cube instance references to the data stored in the XML_DOCUMENT table.
INSTANCE_PAYLOAD	All asynchronous invocation messages are stored in this table before they are dispatched to the engine. This stores incoming invocation messages (messages that result in the creation of an instance). This table only stores the metadata for a message that invokes a composite instance.
WORK_ITEM	This table stores information related to activities created by an instance. All process activities in a flow will have a column in the WORK_ITEM table created for them. This WORK_ITEM column contains metadata for activities such as the current state, label, expiration date (used by wait activities), and so on. When the engine needs to be restarted and instances need to be recovered, pending flows are resumed by inspecting their unfinished work items.
XML_DOCUMENT	This stores all the large objects in the system (for example, instance_payload documents, dlv_message documents, and so on). This table stores the data as **binary large objects** (BLOBs). Separating the document storage from the metadata enables the metadata to change frequently without being impacted by the size of documents.

Measuring database growth

It is necessary to measure the size of the dehydration store at regular intervals to be able to check whether there is enough free space available. Database space can be measured in a variety of ways, the easiest being the execution of a set of queries to get the free size of the tablespace for a given schema. Apart from regular measurements, if you are planning to execute purging, these measurements should be taken before and after the purging to ensure that there is a visible difference indicating the effectiveness of the purge. To measure the free space in the SOA_INFRA tablespace, run the following SQL query:

```
-- Measuring free space in SOA_INFRA tablespace
SELECT * FROM (SELECT C.TABLESPACE_NAME, ROUND(A.BYTES/1048576,2) MB_
ALLOCATED,ROUND(B.BYTES/1048576,2)                                MB_
FREE,ROUND((A.BYTES-B.BYTES)/1048576,2) MB_USED, ROUND(B.BYTES/A.BYTES
* 100,2) TOT_PCT_FREE, ROUND((A.BYTES-B.BYTES)/A.BYTES,2) * 100  TOT_
PCT_USED FROM (SELECT TABLESPACE_NAME, SUM(A.BYTES) BYTES FROM SYS.
DBA_DATA_FILES A GROUP BY TABLESPACE_NAME) A, (SELECT A.TABLESPACE_NAME,
NVL(SUM(B.BYTES),0) BYTES FROM SYS.DBA_DATA_FILES A, SYS.DBA_FREE_
SPACE B WHERE A.TABLESPACE_NAME = B.TABLESPACE_NAME (+) AND A.FILE_ID
= B.FILE_ID (+) GROUP BY A.TABLESPACE_NAME) B, SYS.DBA_TABLESPACES C
WHERE A.TABLESPACE_NAME = B.TABLESPACE_NAME(+) AND A.TABLESPACE_NAME
= C.TABLESPACE_NAME) WHERE TOT_PCT_USED >=0 AND TABLESPACE_NAME='DEV_
SOAINFRA' ORDER BY TABLESPACE_NAME;
```

The following screenshot shows an output of the free space measurement script that provides the percentage and free space in MB in the [PREFIX]_SOAINFRA schema:

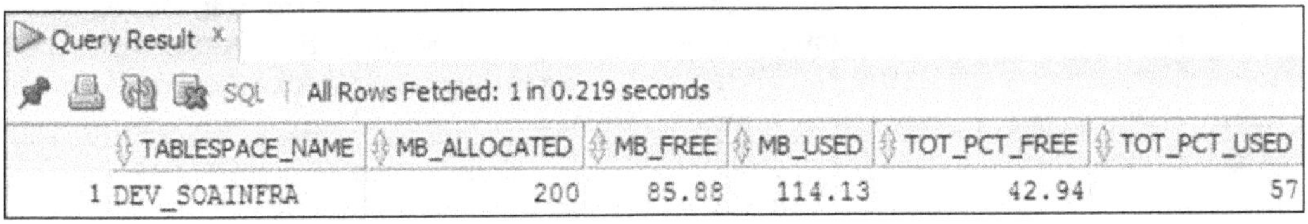

	TABLESPACE_NAME	MB_ALLOCATED	MB_FREE	MB_USED	TOT_PCT_FREE	TOT_PCT_USED
1	DEV_SOAINFRA	200	85.88	114.13	42.94	57

Query Result × — SQL | All Rows Fetched: 1 in 0.219 seconds

Figure 8.1: Measuring free space in the SOAINFRA database schema

Purging strategies

To manage database growth as a result of a high volume of instance processing and transactions, there must be a strategy in place that can delete historical data that is no longer required from a disk and reclaim its space. It is also impossible to have a generic strategy that can be applied to all types of infrastructure, as there is no one-size-fits-all solution to this. In this book, however, you get an insight into all the available mechanisms depending on the database profile, process requirements, and other factors. We recommend that regardless of which purging strategy you choose, you need to follow it up with proper testing against a production dataset. It is also advisable to engage a skilled DBA to review the dehydration store data management mechanism. In any case, the purging strategy cannot be left as an afterthought and needs to become a part of the performance exercise, and thorough testing is recommended to complete this cycle. If an ineffective purging strategy is implemented, the Oracle SOA Suite 12*c* tables may grow considerably to very large sizes, thereby negatively affecting the overall system performance. The larger the size of the tables, the harder it becomes to delete rows and reclaim space. Hence, it is important to schedule maintenance to frequently purge data.

Figure 8.4 displays a graph that shows the database usage based on the number of instances and their message size. The figure is indicative of a small process with a few dehydration points. Depending upon the size and nature of your database, you may be required to schedule more frequent maintenance.

There are three main purging strategies you can consider, which are as follows:

- A purge script, of which two options are available:
    - ° A script that is executed automatically from Fusion Middleware Control
    - ° A script that is executed manually from SQL*Plus
- A purge script with database table partitioning
- Partitioning all tables

The purge script should be scheduled to run automatically, say once a day, and purge data that is older than 7, 14, or 30 days, depending on how active your environment is and how much historical instance data you wish to maintain. By purging daily, you reduce the overall database overhead by regularly deleting small amounts of records instead of large numbers once a week.

The need to maintain audit and instance information for a long period of time is a mistake many organizations make. Oracle SOA Suite is not designed to maintain data-at-rest, thus the need to store this instance data for a long period of time should not be necessary. Once a transaction is successfully completed, it already has reached reaches its target destination.

> Oracle SOA Suite is not designed to maintain data-at-rest, thus the need to maintain audit and instance information for a long period of time is not only unnecessary, but bad for performance.

Automatically, scheduled purge scripts are completely suitable for the majority of environments, and this is the focus of this section.

However, there are some environments that may need to store this audit and instance information for a much longer period of time (for example, longer than 2 weeks) for regulatory or compliance purposes. In this case, partitioning the database tables may be required. It is generally more complex to set up and also requires additional ongoing database maintenance efforts. This chapter does not dive into the approaches regarding table partitioning, since the majority of users rarely require this, but it is detailed in *Chapter 13* of the *Oracle Fusion Middleware Administering Oracle SOA Suite and Oracle Business Process Management Suite 12c (12.1.3)* document.

Understanding what is purged

The purge scripts supplied with Oracle SOA Suite 12*c* delete instances that are essentially completed, whether successfully or unsuccessfully, and in specific instances with the following states:

- Completed successfully
- Faulted
- Terminated by a user
- Aborted
- Unknown (where instance tracking is disabled)

It is not possible to purge the following:

- Running instances (in-flight transactions)
- Recoverable instances (at either the BPEL process service engine or SOA composite application levels, or instances in the recovery-required state)
- Oracle B2B-related tables (Oracle B2B has its own set of purge scripts)

Setting up automatic purging

Fortunately, setting up automatic purging in Oracle SOA Suite 12*c* is exceptionally easy and needs to be done only once, as per the following instructions:

1. Log in to Oracle Enterprise Manager Fusion Middleware Control at `http://adminhost:7001/em`.

2. On the navigator, expand **SOA** and right-click on **soa-infra**.

3. Navigate to **SOA Administration | Auto Purge**.

4. Select one of the two following predefined **Auto Purge Jobs** from the drop-down menu:

    ° **delete_instances_auto_job1**: This runs from Monday to Friday at midnight (this job is enabled by default).

    ° **delete_instances_auto_job2**: This runs on Saturday and Sunday.

5. Check the **Enabled** checkbox to enable the selected job if it is not already enabled.

6. Modify the **Job Schedule**. By default, it runs daily at midnight. Examples of other calendaring expressions you can use are defined in the following table:

Job schedule	Calendaring expression
Run every day at midnight	`FREQ=DAILY; BYHOUR=00;`
Run every weekday at midnight	`FREQ=DAILY;` `BYDAY=MON,TUE,WED,THU,FRI; BYHOUR=00;`
Run every weekend at midnight and 5:00am	`FREQ=DAILY; BYDAY=SAT,SUN;` `BYHOUR=00,05;`

Run every weekday at 30 minutes past midnight	`FREQ=DAILY;`
	`BYDAY=MON,TUE,WED,THU,FRI; BYHOUR=00;`
	`BYMINUTE=30;`

Run every weekend at 30 minutes past midnight and 5:00am	`FREQ=DAILY; BYDAY=SAT,SUN;` `BYHOUR=00,05; BYMINUTE=30;`
Run every Friday at midnight	`FREQ=DAILY; BYDAY=FRI; BYHOUR=0;`

7. Select the purge type, **Single** or **Parallel**. Select **Parallel** if you have a multi-CPU database server and are scheduling the purge during off hours.

8. Enter the number of days you wish to retain data in the **Retain Data** field. The default is 7.

Keep the Maximum Flows to Purge, and Batch Size and Degrees of Parallel at their default settings initially.

> You cannot add auto purge jobs. You must select one of the two predefined jobs.

That's it! Setting up the purge process is quite simple, and the most you will need to consider is the schedule (we recommend daily), how many days you wish to retain data (we recommend 7 days), and whether single or parallel purge types should be used (we recommend single if the purge is scheduled to run daily).

Understanding parallel purging

The looped purge script is good enough to purge historical data of instances from the dehydration store for small database profiles or SOA Suite 12*c* environments that do not have a significant number of transactions to process. There is, however, a performance implication of using these scripts if purging is to occur during business hours, as there is CPU and I/O impact on the database servers. To overcome this limitation, either purging can be scheduled to run at regular intervals at the end of business hours or you can use the multithreaded script to spawn multiple jobs and shorten the time required to purge. A parallel-threaded purge is functionally the same as a single-threaded purge with the advantage that it distributes the workload across multiple jobs to fully utilize host resources and optimizes the amount of data that can be deleted. The parallel purge script uses a `dbms_scheduler` package to spawn multiple purge jobs, with each job working on a subset of data. This procedure is designed to purge large dehydration stores housed on high-end database nodes with multiple CPUs and fast good I/O subsystems. It is recommended that this procedure is executed during non-peak times, as it acquires a lot of resources and may be contending with normal online operations. To determine the optimal number of jobs in order to spawn, you we will require constant on-site testing and tuning. As a rule of thumb, the number of jobs should not exceed the number of CPUs on the node by more than 1. For example, on a database box with 4 CPUs, the degree of parallelism can be set to a value of 1 to 4 to match the number of CPUs.

> The performance of the parallel purge relies primarily on factors such as CPU and I/O, and deleting very large tables is challenging, as parsing large amounts of data can jeopardize the elapsed time of the entire purge script. It is also recommended that you drop indexes before the expected large purges to speed up the process and then recreate the them indexes afterwards.

Monitoring the status of purging

When connected to the database as the `[PREFIX]_SOAINFRA` user, you can run some simple SQL statements to view the status of the purge process.

This SQL statement displays detailed information about the executed jobs, such as the status, start and end times, run duration, and total CPU used, wherein the job name is specified in the `WHERE` clause, either `DELETE_INSTANCES_AUTO_JOB1` or `DELETE_INSTANCES_AUTO_JOB2`:

```
SELECT   log_date, status, req_start_date,
         actual_start_date, run_duration, cpu_used
FROM     user_scheduler_job_run_details
WHERE    job_name = 'DELETE_INSTANCES_AUTO_JOB1'
ORDER BY log_date DESC;
```

An example of the query output is shown in the following figure:

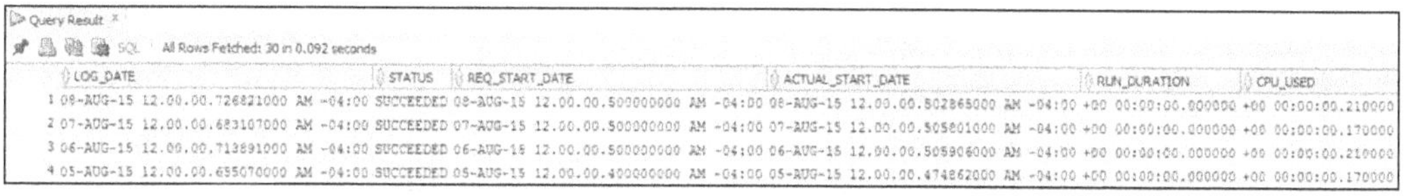

Query Result

All Rows Fetched: 30 in 0.092 seconds

	LOG_DATE	STATUS	REQ_START_DATE	ACTUAL_START_DATE	RUN_DURATION	CPU_USED
1	08-AUG-15 12.00.00.726821000 AM -04:00	SUCCEEDED	08-AUG-15 12.00.00.500000000 AM -04:00	08-AUG-15 12.00.00.502865000 AM -04:00	+00 00:00:00.000000	+00 00:00:00.210000
2	07-AUG-15 12.00.00.683107000 AM -04:00	SUCCEEDED	07-AUG-15 12.00.00.500000000 AM -04:00	07-AUG-15 12.00.00.505801000 AM -04:00	+00 00:00:00.000000	+00 00:00:00.170000
3	06-AUG-15 12.00.00.713891000 AM -04:00	SUCCEEDED	06-AUG-15 12.00.00.500000000 AM -04:00	06-AUG-15 12.00.00.505906000 AM -04:00	+00 00:00:00.000000	+00 00:00:00.210000
4	05-AUG-15 12.00.00.655070000 AM -04:00	SUCCEEDED	05-AUG-15 12.00.00.400000000 AM -04:00	05-AUG-15 12.00.00.474862000 AM -04:00	+00 00:00:00.000000	+00 00:00:00.170000

Figure 8.2: Obtaining the detailed status of the executed purge jobs from the database

This SQL statement displays information about the running job such as the time elapsed and CPU used:

```
SELECT session_id, running_instance, elapsed_time, cpu_used
FROM   user_scheduler_running_jobs
WHERE  job_name = 'DELETE_INSTANCES_AUTO_JOB1';
```

If no records are returned, this is an indication that there are no jobs currently running.

The following SQL statement displays the job schedule of the predefined jobs:

```
SELECT schedule_name, start_date, repeat_interval
FROM   user_scheduler_schedules
WHERE  schedule_name = 'DELETE_INSTANCES_AUTO_SCH1'
OR     schedule_name = 'DELETE_INSTANCES_AUTO_SCH2';
```

An example of the output of this query is shown in the following figure:

Query Result ×

SQL | All Rows Fetched: 2 in 0.09 seconds

	SCHEDULE_NAME	START_DATE	REPEAT_INTERVAL
1	DELETE_INSTANCES_AUTO_SCH1	20-JUL-15 12.57.32.096460000 PM -04:00	freq=daily; byhour=0; byminute=0; bysecond=0
2	DELETE_INSTANCES_AUTO_SCH2	20-JUL-15 12.57.32.099676000 PM -04:00	freq=daily; byhour=0; byminute=0; bysecond=0

Figure 8.3: Displaying the purge job schedule from the database

These various SQL queries can come in handy when we want to quickly monitor the status of the purge jobs.

Reclaiming disk and segment space

After purging old and unused data in the dehydration store, as an administrator, you will sometimes be surprised that the freed space is not visible on the disk. Reclaiming the disk and segment space is not included in the purging script, as this is a database maintenance task. Seen at a very high level, the space occupied by data in an Oracle database is spread over tablespaces, which themselves are spread over data files. Data files have a given size determined during tablespace creation. It is recommended that you allocate a small size to the data files initially and configure them to autoextend when additional space is required. However, these data files do not shrink automatically if data contained in them is deleted. After executing the purge scripts, a certain amount of space will be freed up from the `SOAINFRA` tablespace. The freed space is, however, not visible on the disk because the size of the data files belonging to that tablespace is not decreased. You can execute the script discussed earlier to measure the free size in the tablespaces to get a rough indication of the amount of free space made available within the database by the purge operations. You can reclaim the disk space from the database by using a few common techniques that are highlighted here:

- Deallocate unused space
- Enable database row movement
- Rebuild indexes and coalesces
- Shrink and compact segment space

The following queries are used for these techniques:

```
ALTER TABLE <TABLE_NAME> DEALLOCATE UNUSED;
ALTER TABLE <TABLE_NAME> ENABLE ROW MOVEMENT;
ALTER TABLE <TABLE_NAME> SHRINK SPACE COMPACT;
ALTER TABLE <TABLE_NAME> SHRINK SPACE;
ALTER TABLE <TABLE_NAME> DISABLE ROW MOVEMENT;
```

It is recommended that you leverage the skills of a competent Oracle DBA that probably already has procedures in place to address this.

Reducing audit levels

Another way to control database growth is to reduce the audit level for composites by controlling the amount of instance data being written to the dehydration store. We strongly recommend that all production environments should have the audit level set to Production. Depending upon the business requirement, each composite and/or component can override the default with its own audit level as needed. Changing the audit level from development to production results in significantly less interaction with the database and greatly enhances performance. You can further improve performance by turning off auditing, although this should be used in rare circumstances or for individual composites.

Setting the level of auditing tells SOA Infrastructure how much information you want logged to assist in the monitoring and troubleshooting of instances. For example, if the audit level is completely off, the administrator will have no visibility into any composite instance. No instance data is logged and it is impossible to tell anything at this point (although instances are actually created and requests are serviced just fine). On the other hand, if the audit level is set to development, not only is the instance data logged, but the payload at every operation is logged, giving the administrator complete visibility into the step-by-step execution of every instance!

Although setting the audit level to development may appear tempting, it has both performance and storage implications. Audit data is stored in the database, and if you have a large number of transactions, the database growth can be huge. One large customer of Oracle SOA Suite 12*c* has audit data that grows by nearly 10 gigabytes per day, faster than they are able to purge it! The following figure shows that as the payload size increases, the resulting database storage needs to drastically increase for development versus production audit levels. For example, for a sampling of **500** messages with an average message size of **400 Kb**, successful transactions result in **90 MB** of storage space needed for development audit levels versus **31 MB** for production. For faulted transactions, it's even worse; **488 MB** is needed if the development audit level is set versus **190 MB** for production:

Sampling for 500 Message Invocations (0% Faults)		
	AUDIT Level	
Message Size (KB)	▲ Development (MB)	▲ Production (MB)
100	40	22
200	65	27
400	90	31
800	170	31
1500	350	35

Sampling for 500 Message Invocations (100% Faulted and Recovered)		
	AUDIT Level	
Message Size (KB)	▲ Development (MB)	▲ Production (MB)
100	314	134
200	359	169
400	488	190
800	612	220
1500	916	460

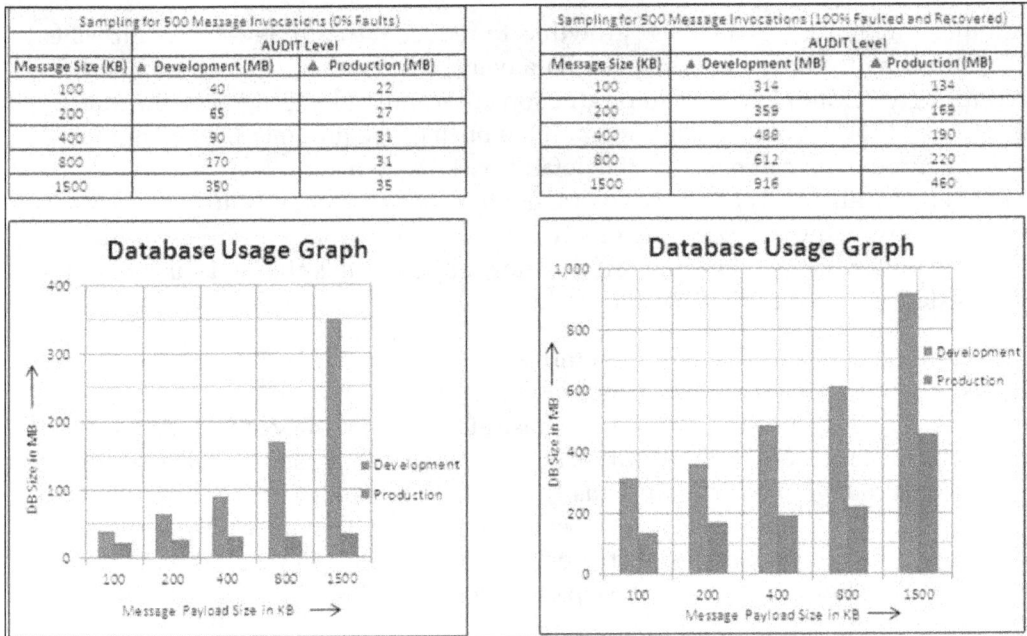

Figure 8.4: Database storage growth of development versus production audit levels

Not only this, but the performance implications are severe. Enabling the development audit level at SOA Infrastructure can result in a 40 percent average decline in the composite instance performance!

Understanding audit levels

Although audit levels can be configured in various areas, as we shall describe shortly, they mostly (but not in every case) fall under one of these four levels:

- **Off**: Here, absolutely no composite instance or payload information is collected. Although this is the best in terms of performance, it severely limits the visibility as no information is logged, rendering it an option that is not recommended in most cases. Instances are created, but nothing is logged to the database or displayed on the console.

- **Development**: Here, both the composite instance and payload information are collected. Though this option provides the most detail, it is the worst performing of all the audit levels. It is recommended that you set this in development environments for debugging purposes, but not in production environments except for transactions that specifically require that degree of auditing.

- **Production**: Here, although composite instance information is collected, most payload details are not. This is the typical setting for production environments and provides the best balance between performance and visibility. If payload details need to be captured, it is best to consider setting the audit level to development only for specific composites, components, or services, as we shall describe later.

- **Inherit**: Here, audit levels are inherited from the next level (we will describe this shortly).

To view the instance details, click on the composite on the navigator on the left-hand side of the page, click on the **Flow Instances** tab, and then click on the instance ID. A pop-up window will reveal the details of this instance, including the audit trails. The following screenshots show the differences between the development and production audit levels:

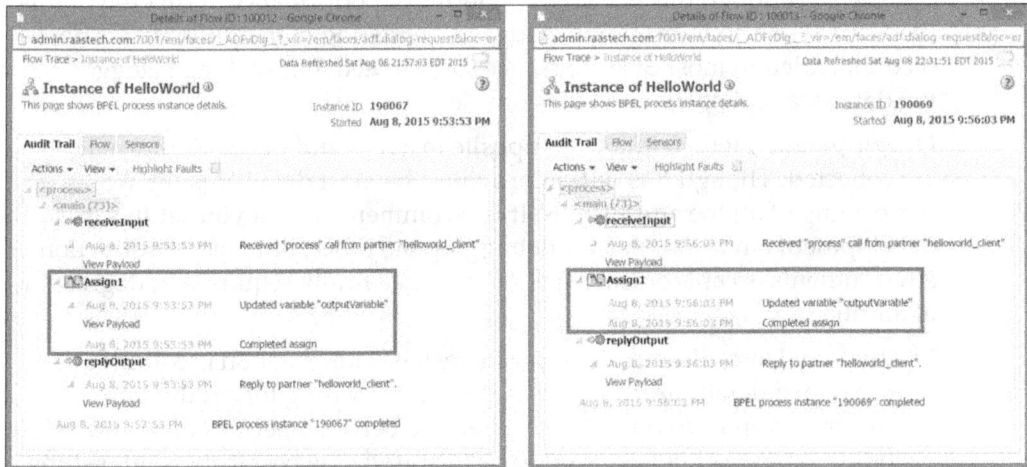

Figure 8.5: The differences between development and production audit levels

Audit levels set to development capture payloads throughout most activities, such as **Assign** and **Transform**. By clicking on the **View Payload** link in the **Assign** activity, the payload will be displayed. As you can see, the development audit level is advantageous in that it allows you to see the changes made to the message across every activity or routing rule, but as stated earlier, there are both storage and performance implications as a result. On the other hand, the production audit level on the right-hand side of the page does not store the XML payloads in all intermediary activities.

The order of precedence for audit level settings

Before describing the order of precedence for audit-level settings and what they are exactly, let's recap the specific terminology first:

- **Component**: Examples The examples of components include a BPEL process, Mediator service, or BPMN process. Within JDeveloper, these components are the building blocks for composite applications.

- **Composite**: A composite consists of zero or more components. For example, a single composite can include a BPEL component and two Mediator components. Composite applications are packaged into a single JAR file that is deployed to SOA Infrastructure.

- **Service engine**: Service engines are the actual engines that execute the code. There are three main service engines: the BPEL Service Engine, Mediator Service Engine, and BPMN Service Engine. As their names imply, the BPEL Service Engine executes BPEL code; the Mediator Service Engine executes Mediator code; and the BPMN Service Engine executes BPMN code.

- **SOA Infrastructure**: SOA Infrastructure is the underlying infrastructure, which is comprised of the preceding service engines, and to which the composite applications are deployed.

Why have we described these terms? Because audit levels can be manipulated across each of these. It is possible to set the audit level at the component level, composite level, or even the service engine level. However, if the audit level is set at the composite level as development and at the SOA Infrastructure level as production to development at the composite level and production at the SOA Infrastructure level, which one takes precedence?

At a high level, the order of precedence is as follows:

Component > Composite > Service Engine > SOA Infrastructure

At a high level, the order of precedence is SOA Infrastructure

What this means is that, for example, if the audit level is set to development at the composite level and production at the SOA Infrastructure level, the setting at the composite level overrides that of SOA Infrastructure. If the composite audit level is set to inherit, it will inherit the settings from the applicable service engine. If the service engine is also set to inherit, it will inherit the settings from SOA Infrastructure. As a general rule, we recommend you to set all audit-level settings to inherit and control them at the SOA Infrastructure level. Then, as the need for different levels of auditing arises, start manipulating the service engine, composite, and component audit levels as needed.

Unfortunately, the rules of what takes precedence become rather complicated as you start changing each of them. Even if auditing at the service engine level is enabled and if the composite audit level is set to **off**, there is no audit trail generated for this composite and all service engines used within. However, the component inherits the service engine settings. When the audit level of a composite is set to inherit, the audit level of SOA Infrastructure is used.

Modifying audit levels

We have previously mentioned that audit levels can be set at the component, composite, service engine, and SOA Infrastructure levels. Here, we describe how to set each of these.

Modifying component audit levels

Component-level auditing can be manipulated for BPEL and BPMN components, but not Mediator components. This is generally done at design time by the developer.

For example, developers can modify BPEL component-level auditing by inserting the `bpel.config.auditLevel` property within their component reference in the `composite.xml` file of their project, as shown here:

```
<component name="HelloWorld">
  <implementation.bpel src="HelloWorld.bpel" />
  <property name="bpel.config.auditLevel">Off</property>
</component>
```

Modifying composite audit levels

Audit levels can be changed during runtime at the composite level. To do so, perform the following steps:

1. On the navigator, expand **SOA** then click on **soa-infra**.

2. Expand the partition (for example, `default`) and click on the composite name (for example, `HelloWorld`).

3. Click on the **Settings** button.

4. Click on the **Composite Audit Level** menu item.

5. Choose between one of the four audit levels:

   ° Inherit

   ° Off

   ° Production

   ° Development

Modifying service engine audit levels

The BPEL Service Engine, BPMN Service Engine, and Mediator Service Engine have a fifth audit level: minimal. The minimal audit level collects instance information, but not payload details in the flow audit trails.

To set the audit level for the BPEL Service Engine, perform the following steps:

1. On the navigator, expand **SOA** and and then right-click on **soa-infra**.

2. Navigate to **SOA Administration | BPEL Properties**.

3. Set the **Audit Level** field.

4. Click on the **Apply** tab.

To set the audit level for the BPMN Service Engine, take these steps:

1. On the navigator, expand **SOA** and then right-click on **soa-infra**.

2. Navigate to **SOA Administration | BPMN Properties**.

3. Set the **Audit Level** field.

4. Click on the **Apply** tab.

To set the audit level for the Mediator Service Engine, go through the following steps:

1. On the navigator, expand **SOA** and then right-click on **soa-infra**.

2. Navigate to **SOA Administration | Mediator Properties**.

3. Set the **Audit Level** field.

4. Click on the **Apply** tab.

Modifying SOA Infrastructure audit levels

The SOA Infrastructure audit level can be configured by performing the following steps:

1. On the navigator, expand **SOA** and then right-click on **soa-infra**.

2. Navigate to **SOA Administration | Common Properties**.

3. Set the **Audit Level** field.

4. Click on the **Apply** tab.

Managing metadata repository partitions

In an MDS repository, each application (Oracle SOA Suite, Oracle Web Services Manager, and so on) is deployed to its own partition so that they can be logically separated. Not to be confused with partitions, as described in *Chapter 4, Managing Services*, a metadata repository partition is an independent logical directory within a physical MDS repository that is used to manage the metadata of these different Oracle Fusion Middleware components and applications.

When Oracle SOA Suite 12*c* is installed, a default repository called **mds-soa** with a default partition called **soa-infra** is already created, as shown in the following screenshot. So, as long as the product is installed and satisfies your needs, you may never need to create additional partitions.

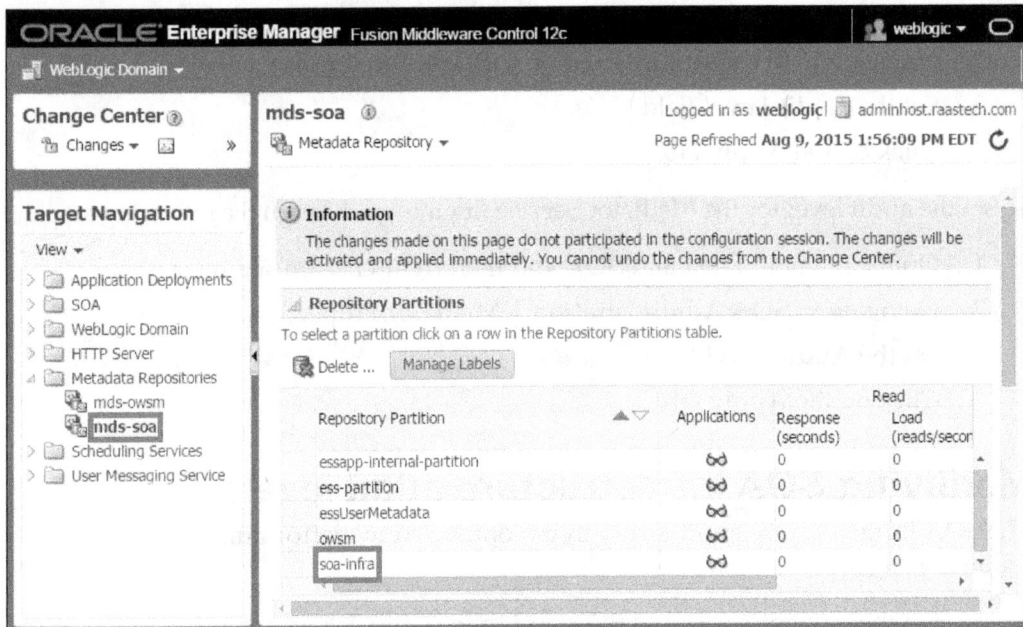

Figure 8.6: The default partition mds-soa is created with every Oracle SOA Suite 12*c* installation

However, partition management is more than simply creating a new, empty partition for fresh use. You can also clone, delete, import, and export metadata from a partition. It is possible to leverage either the Fusion Middleware Control console or WLST for all partition management activities. To view the existing metadata repository partitions, simply log in to Fusion Middleware Control, navigate to **Metadata Repositories**, and then click on one of the repositories or execute the **listPartitions** MBean operation.

Creating a new partition

Partitions in a metadata repository can be created by accessing the MDS domain runtime MBean object and invoking the `createMetadataPartition` operation from Oracle Enterprise Manager Fusion Middleware Control. Follow the sequence of steps highlighted here in order to browse to **MDSDomainRuntime** MBean and then invoke specific operations that it exposes:

1. On the navigator, expand **WebLogic Domain** and then right-click on your SOA domain (for example, `soa_domain`).

2. Then, click on **System MBean Browser**.

3. Navigate to **Application Defined MBeans | oracle.mds.lcm | Domain: [Domain_Name] | MDSDomainRuntime | MDSDomainRuntime** and click on the **Operations** tab.

4. Click on the **createMetadataPartition** operation and in the parameter list, enter a valid name on an existing MDS repository and a suitable partition name to be able to create a new partition.

Alternatively, you can also create a new partition using the `createMetadataPartition` command from the WLST command line. It is important to note that a partition name must be unique within a repository. The following script creates a partition named `soa-custom` in the `mds-soa` repository:

```
createMetadataPartition(repository='mds-soa', partition='soa-custom')
```

Yet another way to create partitions is by invoking the `createPartiton` target in the `ant-sca-mgmt.xml` Ant script available in the `$MW_HOME/Oracle_SOA1/bin` directory of your SOA Suite 12*c* installation:

```
ant -f $MW_HOME/Oracle_SOA1/bin/ant-sca-mgmt.xml createPartition
-Dhost=<soahost> -Dport=<soaport> -Duser=<username> -Dpassword=<password>
-Dpartition=<partition_name>
```

The same Ant file can also be executed with other targets that take care of various partition management tasks such as `deletePartiton`, `startCompositesInPartition`, `stopCompositesInPartition`, `activateCompositesInPartition`, and `retireCompositesInPartition`. These targets can be executed with the same set of arguments used in the previous script.

Cloning a partition

Another efficient way to create a new partition is to clone an existing partition from a source repository to a different repository. Cloning a partition is advantageous, as it preserves the metadata version history, including all customizations made to the deployed composites. However, cloning a partition is permitted only if the source and target repositories are both based on a database with the same type and version. Here again, **MDSDomainRuntime** MBean contains an operation to clone a partition. The `cloneMetadataPartition` operation can be invoked by passing a list of input parameters that specify `fromRepository`, `fromPartition`, `toRepository`, and `toPartition`. The arguments required for the function are self-explanatory and should be replaced with actual values specific to your environment. Have a look at the following steps that outline the details of how to clone a partition dynamically at runtime:

1. On the navigator, expand **WebLogic Domain** and then right-click on your SOA domain (for example, `soa_domain`).

2. Then, click on **System MBean Browser**.

3. Navigate to **Application Defined MBeans | oracle.mds.lcm | Domain: [Domain_Name] | MDSDomainRuntime | MDSDomainRuntime** and click on the **Operations** tab.

4. Click on the **cloneMetadataPartiton** operation.

5. In the parameter list, enter suitable values to clone an existing partition from an existing source repository to a target one (for example, `mds-soa` for the repository and `soa-infra` for the partition).

6. Ensure that the partition name is unique for the new target repository. If the **toPartition** property is left blank, the name of the source partition is used for the target partition.

7. Click on **Invoke,** as depicted in *Figure 8.7*, to clone a partition.

8. Optionally, you can verify that the partition has been created by clicking on the repository in the navigation pane. The partition is listed in the **Partitions** table on the **Metadata Repository** home page.

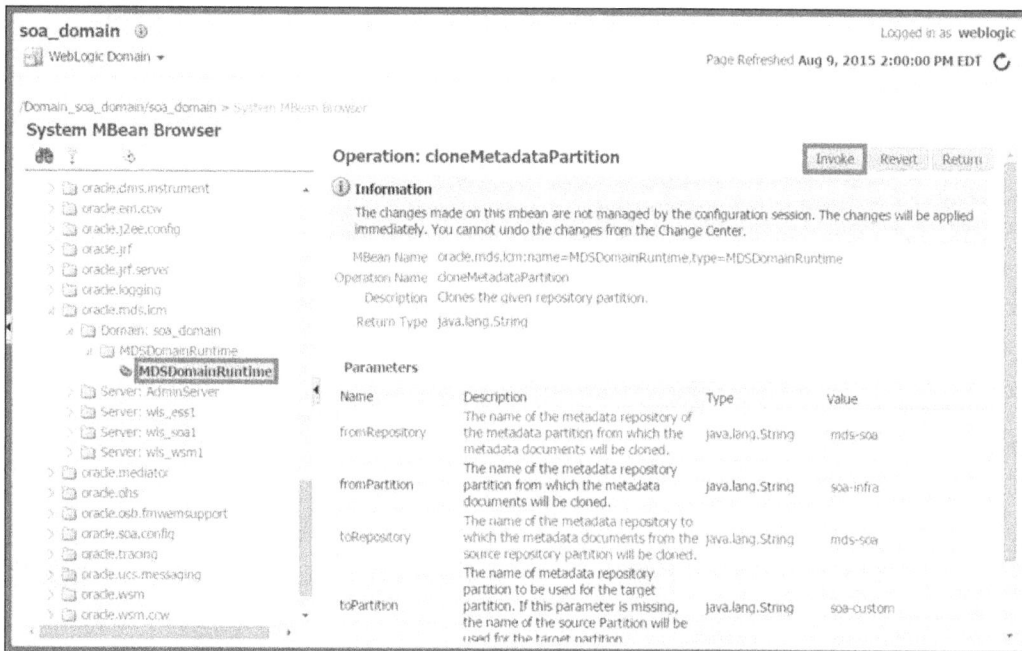

Figure 8.7: Cloning an MDS partition from the MDSDomainRuntime MBean

It is often difficult to navigate through Metadata MBeans, which are accessible from Fusion Middleware Control, particularly if the same configurations need to be duplicated across multiple environments. To maintain consistency, an easy and reusable method is to invoke a WLST command and enter the following metadata partition cloning command provided to clone the soa-infra partition in the mds-soa repository to another partition in the same repository:

```
cloneMetadataPartition(fromRepository='mds-soa', fromPartition='soa-
infra', toRepository='mds-soa', toPartition='soa-custom')
```

As seen in the following screenshot, you will find the newly created **soa-custom** partition:

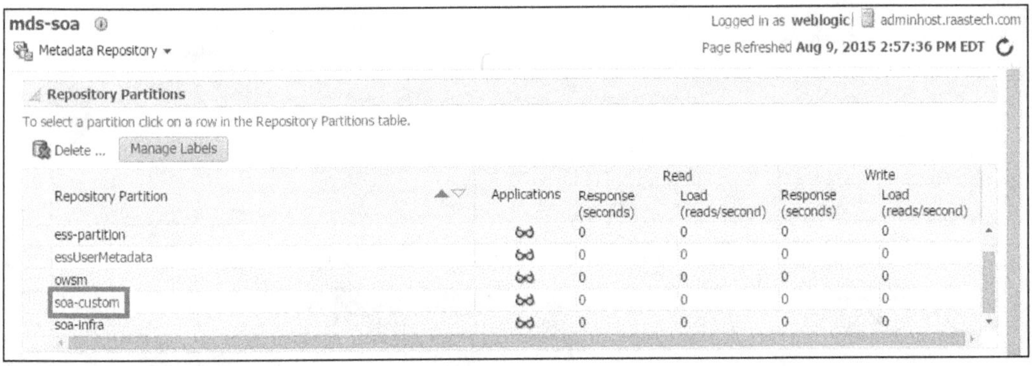

Figure 8.8: Cloning a partition from soa-infra to soa-custom

Exporting and importing composites from/to a partition

Moving composite(s) from one environment to another is an activity that will constantly engage your work as the platform administrator. As an example, you may want to move composites from a development system to a test system and then to a production system. The most effective and convenient approach is to transfer the entire metadata repository and/or the partition. Transferring the metadata gives you an option to not only move composite applications targeted to it but also customizations that are made and tested at runtime. In order to transfer metadata from one partition to another, you will need to first export it from a partition on the source environment and then import it into a partition on the target environment. Depending on your preference, you can either use a graphical interface via Fusion Middleware Control or a scripted approach via WLST. It is our recommendation that you use scripts as much as possible, as they are efficient, save time, and only require small customizations. The following steps specify the way to export all composites from a partition from the **MDS Configuration** dashboard, as shown in *Figure 8.10*:

1. You can either export an individual composite or the whole MDS depending on your requirements. To export the entire partition, on the navigator, expand **SOA** and then right-click on **soa-infra**.

2. Navigate to **Administration | MDS Configuration**.

3. The **MDS Configuration** dashboard page shows the properties, such as the repository name, type, and partition being used by the infrastructure to be exported.

4. Enter the filesystem location to save the archived MDS file, click on the **Export** button, and enter the fully qualified path to the export file, as shown here:

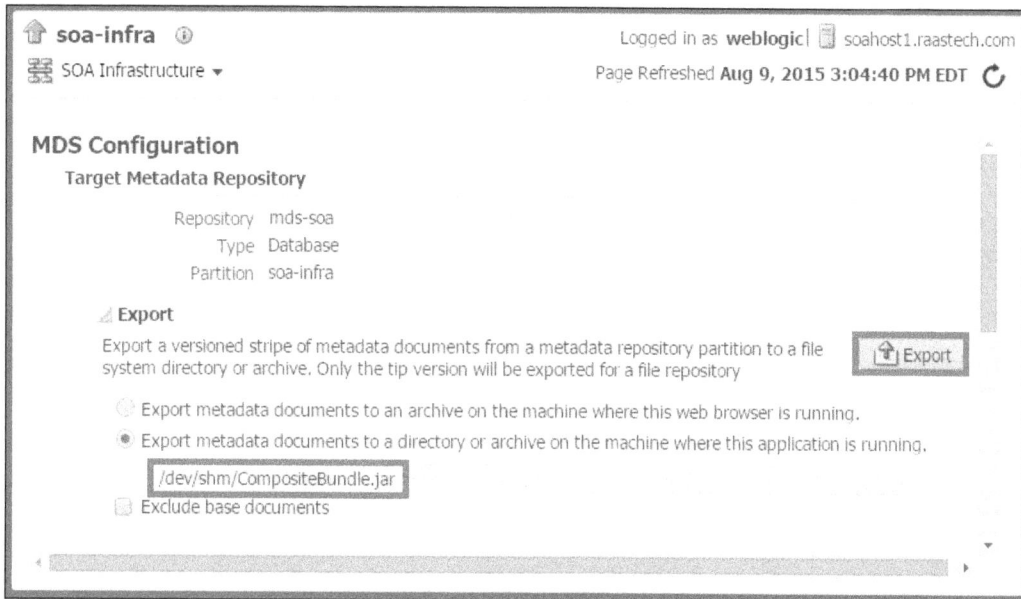

Figure 8.9: Exporting composites from an MDS partition

5. If the **Exclude base documents** option is checked, only the customizations made to the composite are exported and not the base documents.

6. Once the MDS archive is exported to the server filesystem, you may transfer/copy it to the target filesystem (if it is on a different machine altogether).

7. Navigate to the MDS Configuration page on the target server and under the **Import** panel, either enter the location manually where the archive is copied or use the **Browse** button to go to the directory.

8. Click on the **Import** button to import all the archived composites and their customizations on the partition of the target server.

> It is important that the export directory specified exists either on the machine where the SOA server is running or where the browser is running, depending on the export option selected. The browser does not prompt you to browse for a filesystem path. If the location does not exist in the filesystem, a directory is created. However, when the name ends with .jar or .zip, an archive is created. If a directory name is specified, then the metadata archive is written to a subdirectory of the directory specified with the name of the partition that was exported as the name of the subdirectory.

In order to similarly export items from within an MDS repository and import them to another server using the WLST command line, follow the steps listed here:

1. Execute the `wslt.sh` file to administer an MDS repository on the source server instance from the `$ORACLE_HOME/common/bin` directory:

```
cd $ORACLE_HOME/common/bin
```

```
./wlst.sh
```

2. Connect to the server instance from the offline prompt and enter the `exportMetadata()` command to extract all composites and metadata deployed to a partition in a temporary folder:

```
wls:/offline>connect('<username>', '<password>',
'<host>:<adminport>')
```

```
wls:/DomainName/serverConfig>exportMetadata(application='s
oa-infra', server='<soa_managed_server>', toLocation='<export_
folder>', docs='/**')
```

```
wls:/DomainName/serverConfig>exit()
```

If you are unsure about the composite name, you can obtain it from the composite dashboard from Fusion Middleware Control. The server name has to be the server to which the MDS repository is targeted. The `/**` wildcard filter indicates that all documents from the root folder will need to be extracted out. However, you can even specify a path filter to traverse the MDS path internally to export any desired file or folder. The following WLST command illustrates how to export all the .xml files from the `/soa/configuration/default` directory under the MDS root:

```
exportMetadata(application='soa-infra', server='soa_server1',
toLocation='export_folder',docs='/soa/configuration/default/*.xml')
```

3. Next, copy the export folder containing the extracted archive to the machine where the target server is running.

4. Open a new WLST command line prompt from the middleware installation on the destination machine.

5. Execute the `importMetadata()` command to import the exported metadata archive into the target server:

```
wls:/DomainName/serverConfig>importMetadata(application='soa-
infra', server='<soa_managed_server>', fromLocation='import_
folder', docs='/**')
```

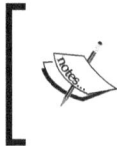

> The value of the `fromLocation` parameter must be on the same system that is running WLST or on a mapped network drive or directory mount. Direct network references such as `\\sharedFolder\repositories\` cannot be used though.

Purging the metadata version history

As the metadata repository is usually maintained in a database, it would be necessary to purge unnecessary and archaic customizations made to composites that are no longer applicable. Purging is only required for database-based MDS repositories, as file-based repositories do not maintain composite version histories. Purging the metadata version history from a partition deletes all unlabeled documents from it, leaving only the tip version (the latest version) even if it is unlabeled. Purging the metadata version history on a regular basis is a necessary maintenance activity to control database size or when its performance starts to degrade. Purging an MDS repository is performance intensive and hence should either be attempted in a maintenance window or when the system is not busy. To use Fusion Middleware Control in order to purge the metadata version history, take the following steps:

1. You can purge the version history of unlabeled documents from a partition that is older than a selected time period. On the navigator, expand **SOA** and then right-click on **soa-infra**.

2. Navigate to **Administration | MDS Configuration**.

3. The **MDS Configuration** dashboard page is displayed.

4. In the **Purge all unlabeled past versions that are older than** field, enter a number and select the unit of time.

5. Click on **Purge**.

6. A progress box is displayed. When the operation completes, a completion box similar to *Figure 8.10* is displayed.

7. Click on the **Close** tab.

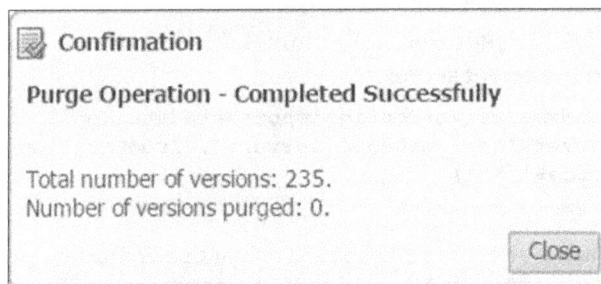

Figure 8.10. Confirmation of a successful metadata version purge

It is also possible to purge the metadata version history using the purgeMetadata() command in WLST. You can specify the documents to be purged using the olderThan parameter, specifying the number of seconds. The following example purges all documents that are older than 100 seconds:

```
purgeMetadata(application='soa-infra', server='soa_server1', olderThan=100)
```

Summary

The MDS is a repository used by Oracle SOA Suite 12c to store the metadata of composites and their customizations that are deployed to the service infrastructure. The dehydration store, on the other hand, maintains instance-related information. Both are generally stored in the same physical database. As an Oracle SOA Suite 12c administrator, you will likely be required to manage both of these database-based repositories.

This chapter covered numerous administrative activities as they pertain to the dehydration store, namely:

- Understanding configurations that affect the dehydration store
- Understanding the underlying database objects that comprise the dehydration store
- Explaining how to measure database growth
- Describing the available purging strategies and what is purged
- Setting up automatic purging through Fusion Middleware Control
- Explaining parallel purging
- Using SQL to monitor the status of purging

- Using DBA commands to reclaim disk and segment space on the database
- Explaining audit levels and the order of precedence for audit-level settings
- Modifying audit levels

Additionally, this chapter covered numerous administrative activities surrounding MDS management, which include:

- Creating and cloning metadata repository partitions
- Purging the metadata version history

Troubleshooting the Oracle SOA Suite 12*c* Infrastructure

In a perfect world, all code would work one hundred percent of the time, servers would not fail, and connections would never timeout. However in the real world, we are not so fortunate. Sometimes, you may come across an issue, it may be trivial in nature because either you have experienced the issue before or the problem's source is self-evident. When digging through issues, it's always good to have a number of tools under your belt.

Taking the time to analyse the situation and starting with the simplest possible solution is usually the first place to start. There's nothing worse than overlooking the simple answer only to find out later that it's the ultimate solution to the problem. In many cases, the root causes of issues are clear, for example when a composite fails to insert a record into a database with an `ORA-12541` error, which is quite straightforward, as the error indicates the database listener is unreachable. The solution could be to simply startup the listener.

However, there are cases where some types of errors require a greater level of effort to resolve. For example, when the SOA managed server crashes frequently or on a given occasion, this is obviously not normal behavior. Is it because the JVM ran out of memory? Even if it is confirmed that an `OutOfMemoryError` exception is found in the logs, why did this happen?

> The four core problem areas an Oracle SOA Suite 12c administrator will often troubleshoot revolve around infrastructure, code deployment, performance, and instances.

There is no step-by-step guide that walks you through exactly what to do in every scenario, as the types of errors you will encounter are endless. However, we will address the four core troubleshooting areas to provide a guideline on what you should consider for your troubleshooting strategies. These are infrastructure, code deployment, performance, and instance errors.

In this chapter, we focus more on introducing a troubleshooting methodology, which, when coupled with the foundational knowledge you learned in the previous chapters, will better equip you with the ability to solve most problems.

We begin this chapter with describing the art of troubleshooting followed by various troubleshooting areas that include the following:

- Troubleshooting infrastructure problems
- Troubleshooting performance issues
- Troubleshooting instances
- Troubleshooting deployment issues

The art of troubleshooting – where do you start?

Troubleshooting is part art, part science. Without a proper understanding of Oracle SOA Suite 12c, it becomes very difficult to know which tools, features, and capabilities are available to help you in your troubleshooting efforts. Furthermore, it helps to understand certain fundamentals on how both the infrastructure and transactions behave.

Fortunately, the previous chapters covered numerous areas to prepare you for this:

- *Chapter 2*, *Navigating Enterprise Manager Fusion Middleware Control 12c*, introduced the various consoles, and more importantly, Oracle Enterprise Manager Fusion Middleware Control, the Oracle Service Bus Console, and the Oracle WebLogic Server Administration Console. These are the core consoles for all the administration, configuration, and monitoring that you need to perform.

- *Chapter 6*, *Monitoring Oracle SOA Suite 12c*, described various areas of monitoring. You should now know how to monitor the Oracle WebLogic Server and the JVM, leverage SQL queries to obtain instance specific information, use the DMS Spy Servlet to get various runtime values, and have a thorough understanding of the various server log files.

- *Chapter 7, Configuration and Administration*, talked about further configuration and administration of the infrastructure—everything from JCA-binding properties, to fault management, configuring timeouts, and overriding adapter properties.

With this, you are now armed with the tools and knowledge to troubleshoot any number of issues. Before troubleshooting any issue, you must at least have a starting point for which you can ask yourself the following questions:

- Is this an infrastructure issue?
- Is this a performance issue?
- Is this an issue specific to a single SOA or OSB instance?
- Is this a deployment issue?

Based on the type of problem, you can somewhat narrow down the troubleshooting activity. The goal in this chapter is not to walk through all possible errors and their resolutions. You will encounter many examples of errors throughout this chapter, each and every one of them requiring further investigation. It is not often the case that you will stumble upon an error and immediately identify its resolution. Therefore, some of the other approaches you should consider utilizing are as follows:

- Perform web searches for your error
- Search within the My Oracle Support and the Oracle Technology Network forums
- Review the multiple log files (for example, `wls_soa1.out`, `wls_soa1.log`, and `wls_soa1-diagnostic.log`)
- Increase logging
- Engage Oracle support

Troubleshooting infrastructure problems

Infrastructure issues can be related to these problems: starting up the server, the server being unavailable or unresponsive, or transactions failing. It might even be due to errors in backbone resources that your infrastructure is dependent upon. These are all examples of infrastructure problems, and in most of these cases, the logs will guide you to the root of your issue. However, in other cases, the log information may not be sufficient, at which you may have to consider increasing the logger levels to obtain more information.

Extending logging

Chapter 6, *Monitoring Oracle SOA Suite 12c*, included a section titled *Identifying and viewing log file entries*, wherein we described how to configure logger levels. For example, you can easily increase a logger from NOTIFICATION:1 (INFO) to TRACE:32 (FINEST) to dump more information into the logs. Regardless of the type of problem (including composite issues), increasing the logger level temporarily may help you obtain more information.

The following screenshot shows top-level logger names and default log levels:

Logger Name	Oracle Diagnostic Logging Level (Java Level)	
▷ oracle.integration	NOTIFICATION:1 (INFO) [Inherited from parent]	⬍
▷ **oracle.osb**	NOTIFICATION:1 (INFO) [Inherited from parent]	⬍
oracle.sdp	NOTIFICATION:1 (INFO) [Inherited from parent]	⬍
oracle.sdpinternal	NOTIFICATION:1 (INFO) [Inherited from parent]	⬍
▷ oracle.soa	NOTIFICATION:1 (INFO) [Inherited from parent]	⬍
▷ oracle.sysman	WARNING:1 (WARNING)	⬍
▷ oracle.wsm	NOTIFICATION:1 (INFO) [Inherited from parent]	⬍

Figure 9.1: The top-level logger names and default log levels

Logger levels can provide more information on pretty much everything. The top-level logger names are shown in *Figure 9.1*. For example, some of the loggers that can be modified include: DVMs (oracle.soa.dvm), the BPEL engine (oracle.soa.bpel.engine.*), Mediator filters (oracle.soa.mediator.filter), human workflow (oracle.soa.services.workflow.*), Enterprise Manager Console (oracle.sysman), Oracle Web Services Manager (oracle.wsm.*), and Oracle Service Bus (oracle.osb.*). There are too many loggers to mention and there is no comprehensive list that describes each one. However, many are self-descriptive and often Oracle Support can guide you to what you may need to increase during your troubleshooting efforts. The logs themselves can point you to a logger. Observe the logger highlighted in the following code snippet:

```
<Aug 5, 2014 12:00:02 AM EDT> <Error> <oracle.soa.bpel.engine.
dispatch> <BEA-000000> <failed to handle message
javax.ejb.EJBException: EJB Exception: : java.lang.StackOverflowError
```

Here, the `oracle.soa.bpel.engine.dispatch` logger threw a `StackOverflowError` exception. Increasing this specific logger may (or may not) yield additional useful information.

An important thing to keep in mind is that loggers contain hierarchies. Exercise caution when setting root-level loggers to `FINE`, `FINER`, or `FINEST`. Consider the case from the preceding code, where you have encountered an EJB exception in the BPEL engine. If the root logger (that is, `oracle.soa.bpel.engine`) is set to `FINEST`, all the descendants that inherit from it will have the same logging level. As a result, a large amount of unused log entries are produced, which might actually make troubleshooting the issue much more difficult. Therefore, if possible, you should set only the corresponding child logger (`oracle.soa.bpel.engine.dispatch`) to a lower level without enabling the root logger.

Using logs

You will likely notice a lot of errors in the `wls_soa1.out` log file. The key is to be able to differentiate between infrastructure errors and composite instance errors. In most cases, it is obvious, though some cases may require further troubleshooting. Here, we describe nine examples of various errors.

An infrastructure error – StackOverflowError

`StackOverflowError` is usually an indication of an infrastructure error, as the error does not appear tied to any specific composite. Based on the `oracle.soa.bpel. engine.dispatch` logger, it is thrown by the BPEL dispatch engine, as shown in the following example:

```
<Aug 5, 2015 12:00:02 AM EDT> <Error> <oracle.soa.bpel.engine.
dispatch> <BEA-000000> <failed to handle message
javax.ejb.EJBException: EJB Exception: : java.lang.StackOverflowError
```

For an error like this, when you have little or no information even after you throttle all your loggers to full, it is wise to search My Oracle Support (`https://support. oracle.com`) or engage Oracle Support.

A composite instance error – SOAPFaultException

Here, the Mediator Service Engine (as shown by the `oracle.soa.mediator.serviceEngine` logger) appears to have thrown `SOAPFaultException`, which in itself is not very useful. However, the details of the error are quite clear. This is a business exception thrown by an external service or resource. Though there is no information here to tie it back to a specific composite or instance, the same error, in more detail, can be found in the `wls_soa1.log` file, which will provide the specific information. Rest assured, this exception will also appear in the composite instance fault on the console. Refer to the following log entry:

```
<Aug 6, 2015 10:10:33 AM EDT> <Error> <oracle.soa.mediator.
serviceEngine> <BEA-000000> <Got an exception: oracle.fabric.common.
FabricInvocationException: javax.xml.ws.soap.SOAPFaultException:
CreateOrder failed with Message: Cannot insert the value NULL into
column 'OrderID', table '@Orders'; column does not allow nulls. INSERT
fails.
```

The error is obvious; a table column does not allow `NULL` and therefore insertion is rejected by the database.

An infrastructure error – DeploymentException

Some infrastructure exceptions are related to the backend components that are unavailable or configured improperly. Some of them may be categorized by a warning instead of an error, but this is still a problem. Refer to the error in the following log entry that appears to be related to a WebLogic JMS Server. In this case, the JMS Server named `CustomJMSServer` was referencing the persistent file store `CustomFileStore` that did not exist:

```
<Aug 25, 2015 7:30:41 PM EST> <Warning> <Management> <BEA-141197> <The
deployment of CustomJMSServer failed.
weblogic.management.DeploymentException: Internalrror activating the
JMS Server CustomJMSServer: weblogic.management.DeploymentException:
The persistent store "CustomFileStore" does not exist
```

Such exceptions can be resolved by making sure that the required backbone infrastructure is present. This specific issue is resolved by creating the required file store and restarting the targeted managed servers.

A composite instance error – FabricInvocationException

`FabricInvocationException` is thrown by the Mediator Service Engine. The `Unable to access the following endpoint` error is somewhat misleading, as it could be related to any number of exceptions:

```
<Aug 29, 2015 11:45:06 AM EST> <Error> <oracle.soa.mediator.
serviceEngine> <BEA-000000> <Got an exception: oracle.fabric.common.
FabricInvocationException: Unable to access the following endpoint(s):
http://payment-processing-server-dev:7777/proc/servlet/createCustomer
```

By reviewing the nested exception later on (not shown here), you will find that this particular error was due to a timeout of the external service. Though technically this is not a coding error since it is something that occurred only at runtime, it is not a SOA infrastructure error either, as it is related to an external service on which we have no control. From a development standpoint, the developer should be able to handle these cases by enabling some type of retry and/or error logging. You can also enable more detailed logging for these issues by enabling debugging while starting the server as follows:

```
-Djavax.net.debug=all
```

> You can also consider increasing the timeout for external services should these errors happen frequently. Refer to *Chapter 7, Configuration and Administration*, to see how you can do this.

An infrastructure error – Unable to allocate additional threads

This `Unable to allocate additional threads` error appears to be quite serious, but it really is not. However, this is an infrastructure-related issue and should be remedied.

Let's refer to the following log snippet:

```
<Sep 30, 2015 11:30:04 PM EDT> <Warning> <oracle.integration.platform.
instance.store.async> <BEA-000000> <Unable to allocate additional
threads, as all the threads [10] are in use. Threads distribution :
Fabric Instance Activity = 1,Fabric-Instance-Manager = 9,>
```

This error is apparently due to a failed transaction that continues to retry. The Oracle WebLogic Server is unable to process more messages in parallel and has run out of threads that would eventually clear themselves. It is possible to increase the number of threads if this becomes a persistent problem.

An infrastructure or composite instance error – MDSException

The following exception is due to the fact that at runtime, the XSD was not available:

```
java.io.IOException: oracle.mds.exception.MDSException: MDS-00054: The
file to be loaded oramds:/apps/Fault/Common/XSD/SalesOrderHeader.xsd
does not exist.
```

This actually could either be a coding error or an infrastructure error. Therefore, further investigation is required. If the **soa-mds** data source is unavailable, this error would be attributed to an infrastructure problem. If the data source is available though, then it is likely due to the code referring to a resource that does not exist in the MDS.

An OSB instance error – BEA-380000

The following exception is returned in the `wls_osb1.log` file. From the looks of it, a particular OSB business service is responsible for this error:

```
####<Aug 16, 2015 10:57:11 AM EDT> <Info> <OSB Kernel> <soahost1>
<wls_osb1> <[ACTIVE] ExecuteThread: '1' for queue: 'weblogic.
kernel.Default (self-tuning)'> <<anonymous>> <> <c3674305f67d3622:-
7bff816b:136a9bbdd80:-8000-0000000000008a10> <1334588231098> <BEA-
398102> <
 [OSB Tracing] Exiting route node with fault:
<con:fault xmlns:con="http://www.bea.com/wli/sb/context">
  <con:errorCode>BEA-380000</con:errorCode>
  <con:reason>Request Entity Too Large</con:reason>
  <con:location>
    <con:node>CustomerBusSvc</con:node>
    <con:path>response-pipeline</con:path>
  </con:location>
</con:fault>>
```

Since this error appears to be specific to a single OSB service, a few online searches reveal the root cause of the `Request Entity Too Large` error, which is that authentication cannot be handled automatically in chunked mode, and this particular service was using authentication. A simple request to the developer to disable the **Use Chunked Streaming Mode** setting can remedy this, or the administrator can make this change dynamically at runtime.

An infrastructure error – BeanInstantiationException

By now, you must know that the engine that is responsible for executing composite instances in your infrastructure is **soa-infra**, which in itself is a J2EE application. The soa-infra application, in some cases, may fail to load in all the managed servers across a cluster and is partially available due to the following exception:

```
Instantiation of bean failed; nested exception is org.
springframework.beans.BeanInstantiationException: Could not
instantiate bean class [oracle.integration.platform.blocks.cluster.
CoherenceClusterInterfaceImpl]: Constructor threw exception; nested
exception is com.tangosol.net.RequestTimeoutException: Timeout during
service start: ServiceInfo(Id=0, Name=Cluster, Type=Cluster
```

The preceding issue is due to the fact that the coherence multicast channel in use by the domain in a clustered mode is overloaded. The coherence cluster address for the domains is set to a unique multicast address and port in the setDomainEnv.sh file. To confirm whether the multicast channel in use is not overloaded, use a simple multicast test by following the steps in the code:

```
source setAntEnv.sh
export CLASSPATH=${ORACLE_HOME}/wlserver/server/lib/weblogic.jar
java utils.MulticastTest -N [managedServerName] -A [multicastHost] -P
[multicastPort] -T 10 -S
```

The issue can be resolved by untargeting the soa-infra application from all servers in the cluster, bouncing back all managed servers, and retargeting it back to the cluster. This is an infrastructure problem.

An infrastructure error – unable to extend lob segment

Not all errors are directly due to issues within your SOA Infrastructure. All running and completed instances in Oracle SOA Suite 12*c* are saved in a backend data store. Lack of space in the database may prevent the composite instances to complete their processing. For instance, you are most likely to see the following exception if your database runs out of disk space:

```
oracle.toplink.exceptions.DatabaseException
Internal Exception: java.sql.BatchUpdateException: ORA-01691: unable
to extend lob segment DEV_SOAINFRA.SYS_LOB$$ by 128 in tablespace DEV_
SOAINFRA
```

These messages typically indicate space issues in the database that will likely require you to add more data files or more space to the existing data files. Additionally, completed instances can be purged and disk space can be reclaimed. This is discussed in *Chapter 8, Managing the Database*. Another useful guide to dealing with databases can be found in *Managing Database Growth of the Oracle® Fusion Middleware Administering Oracle SOA Suite and Oracle Business Process Management Suite*, which can be found at `https://docs.oracle.com/middleware/1213/soasuite/ administer/soa-database-growth-manage.htm#SOAAG97257`.

We have covered several types of exceptions that can be encountered to give you an idea of the types of errors that you might expect. It is impossible to provide a comprehensive list of errors, and our intent is to show you why we have classified some errors as infrastructure errors and others as instance errors. Most of the time, the type of error is obvious, but other times, it is not. Differentiating between both helps you narrow your troubleshooting efforts to a particular area.

Using thread dumps

The following figure shows a warning on AdminServer. Warnings do not necessarily mean that the managed server is unresponsive, but is an indication for us to look into the root cause(s) of the warning.

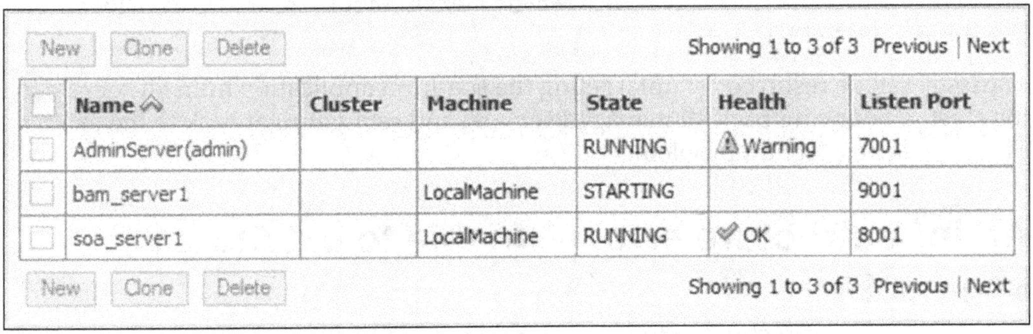

	Name ⌃	Cluster	Machine	State	Health	Listen Port
	AdminServer(admin)			RUNNING	⚠ Warning	7001
	bam_server1		LocalMachine	STARTING		9001
	soa_server1		LocalMachine	RUNNING	✅ OK	8001

New   Clone   Delete   Showing 1 to 3 of 3   Previous | Next

New   Clone   Delete   Showing 1 to 3 of 3   Previous | Next

Figure 9.2: A managed server warning in the Oracle WebLogic Server Administration Console

Without understanding that the health of a managed server in a **Warning** state is usually related to stuck threads, you won't know that you need to click on **AdminServer** and navigate to **Monitoring | Threads** to get more information.

The following screenshot illustrates how to monitor the threads of a managed server:

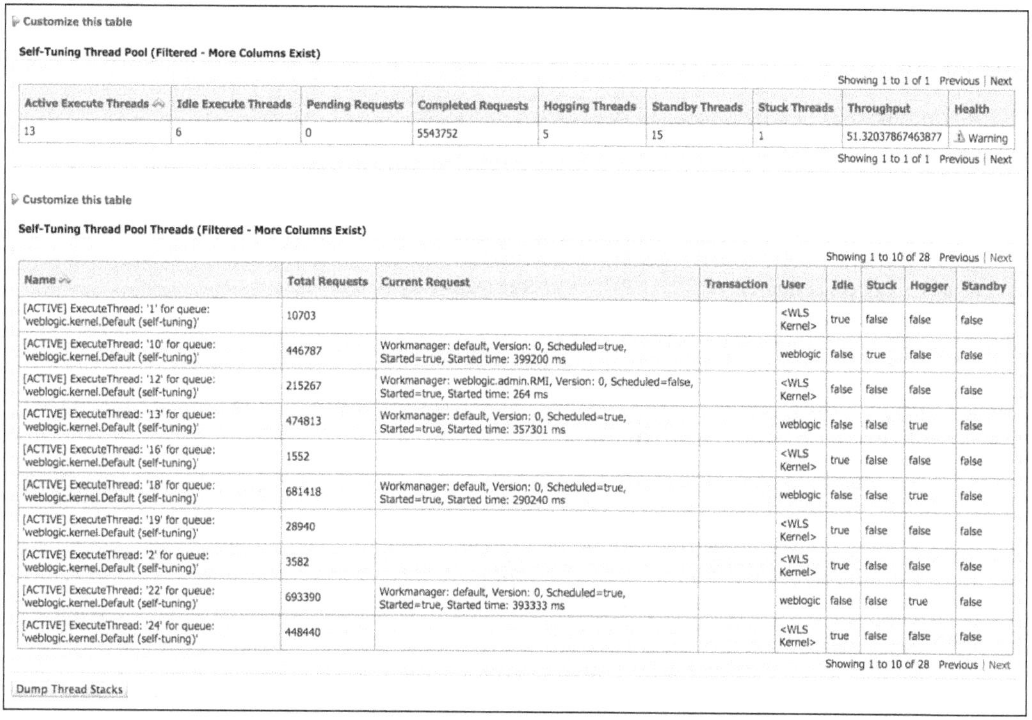

Customize this table

Self-Tuning Thread Pool (Filtered - More Columns Exist)

Showing 1 to 1 of 1 Previous | Next

Active Execute Threads	Idle Execute Threads	Pending Requests	Completed Requests	Hogging Threads	Standby Threads	Stuck Threads	Throughput	Health
13	6	0	5543752	5	15	1	51.32037867463877	Warning

Showing 1 to 1 of 1 Previous | Next

Customize this table

Self-Tuning Thread Pool Threads (Filtered - More Columns Exist)

Showing 1 to 10 of 28 Previous | Next

Name	Total Requests	Current Request	Transaction	User	Idle	Stuck	Hogger	Standby
[ACTIVE] ExecuteThread: '1' for queue: 'weblogic.kernel.Default (self-tuning)'	10703			<WLS Kernel>	true	false	false	false
[ACTIVE] ExecuteThread: '10' for queue: 'weblogic.kernel.Default (self-tuning)'	446787	Workmanager: default, Version: 0, Scheduled=true, Started=true, Started time: 399200 ms		weblogic	false	true	false	false
[ACTIVE] ExecuteThread: '12' for queue: 'weblogic.kernel.Default (self-tuning)'	215267	Workmanager: weblogic.admin.RMI, Version: 0, Scheduled=false, Started=true, Started time: 264 ms		<WLS Kernel>	false	false	false	false
[ACTIVE] ExecuteThread: '13' for queue: 'weblogic.kernel.Default (self-tuning)'	474813	Workmanager: default, Version: 0, Scheduled=true, Started=true, Started time: 357301 ms		weblogic	false	false	true	false
[ACTIVE] ExecuteThread: '16' for queue: 'weblogic.kernel.Default (self-tuning)'	1552			<WLS Kernel>	true	false	false	false
[ACTIVE] ExecuteThread: '18' for queue: 'weblogic.kernel.Default (self-tuning)'	681418	Workmanager: default, Version: 0, Scheduled=true, Started=true, Started time: 290240 ms		weblogic	false	false	true	false
[ACTIVE] ExecuteThread: '19' for queue: 'weblogic.kernel.Default (self-tuning)'	28940			<WLS Kernel>	true	false	false	false
[ACTIVE] ExecuteThread: '2' for queue: 'weblogic.kernel.Default (self-tuning)'	3582			<WLS Kernel>	true	false	false	false
[ACTIVE] ExecuteThread: '22' for queue: 'weblogic.kernel.Default (self-tuning)'	693390	Workmanager: default, Version: 0, Scheduled=true, Started=true, Started time: 393333 ms		weblogic	false	false	true	false
[ACTIVE] ExecuteThread: '24' for queue: 'weblogic.kernel.Default (self-tuning)'	448440			<WLS Kernel>	true	false	false	false

Showing 1 to 10 of 28 Previous | Next

Dump Thread Stacks

Figure 9.3: Monitoring the threads of a managed server

Under **Self-Tuning Thread Pool** in *Figure 9.3*, we see a warning, which is likely due to the **Hogging Thread Count** being greater than 0. In the **Self-Tuning Thread Pool Threads** table immediately under it, we are able to see the stuck thread, indicated by `[STUCK] ExecuteThread: '0' for queue: 'weblogic.kernel.Default (self-tuning)'`. All we can ascertain from this error is that **ExecuteThread '0'** is the stuck thread, yet this is still not enough information.

Looking at the `${DOMAIN_HOME}/servers/AdminServer/logs/AdminServer.log` file, we can see the stuck thread, which apparently had kept on working for over 10 minutes:

```
####<Mar 23, 2015 6:03:49 PM EST> <Error> <WebLogicServer> <soahost1>
<AdminServer> <[ACTIVE] ExecuteThread: '8' for queue: 'weblogic.
kernel.Default (self-tuning)'> <<WLS Kernel>> <> <cb680017c6a0acfe:-
606797c4:134357968da:-8000-0000000000001062> <1324681429443> <BEA-
000337> <[STUCK] ExecuteThread: '0' for queue: 'weblogic.kernel.
Default (self-tuning)' has been busy for "658" seconds working on the
request "weblogic.kernel.WorkManagerWrapper$1@2a8605ce", which is more
than the configured time (StuckThreadMaxTime) of "600" seconds.
```

It turns out that we had just tried to unsuccessfully start the BAM managed server 10 minutes earlier. By observing `${DOMAIN_HOME}/servers/wls_bam1/logs/wls_bam1.log`, we find that the same **ExecuteThread '0'** thread is unable to register MBean due to an `java.lang.OutOfMemoryError` exception:

```
####<Mar 23, 2015 5:53:36 PM EST> <Error> <JMX> <soahost1> <bam_
server1> <[ACTIVE]
ExecuteThread: '0' for queue: 'weblogic.kernel.Default (self-tuning)'>
<<WLS Kernel>> <> <> <1324680816405> <BEA-149500> <An exception
occurred while registering the MBean com.bea:Name=AdminServer,
Type=WebServiceRequestBufferingQueue,
WebServiceBuffering=AdminServer,Server=AdminServer,
WebService=AdminServer.
java.lang.OutOfMemoryError: PermGen space
```

Fortunately, looking back at the `AdminServer.log` file a few hours later, we see that **ExecuteThread '0'** has become **unstuck**:

```
####<Mar 23, 2015 10:42:42 PM EST> <Info> <WebLogicServer> <soahost1>
<AdminServer> <[STUCK] ExecuteThread: '0' for queue: 'weblogic.kernel.
Default (self-tuning)'> <<WLS Kernel>> <> <cb680017c6a0acfe:-606797c4
:134357968da:-8000-0000000000001070> <1324698162702> <BEA-000339>
<[STUCK] ExecuteThread: '0' for queue: 'weblogic.kernel.Default (self-
tuning)' has become "unstuck".>
```

In this example, we navigated to multiple areas, starting from the stuck thread, to get to the root cause of the warning on the health state of **AdminServer.** To recap, we performed the following:

- We found AdminServer to be in a **Warning** state, which is usually due to a stuck thread
- We confirmed that there was indeed a stuck **ExecuteThread** thread, as shown on both the Oracle WebLogic Administration Console and the `AdminServer.log` file
- By reviewing the `wls_soa1.log` and `wls_bam1.log` files, we found startup errors in the BAM server log
- The BAM server was unable to register an AdminServer MBean due to a `java.lang.OutOfMemoryError` exception that was thrown
- Eventually, the stuck thread was able to self-tune and unstuck itself

No action was needed in this scenario, but by inspecting the log files, we identified the root cause. Also, keep in mind that stuck threads can happen during regular executions of various applications and aren't inherently bad, but they do have the potential to locate inefficiencies.

Troubleshooting performance issues

Troubleshooting performance issues is a rather vast and complicated area, which we will only be able to touch upon lightly. In general, performance becomes a concern when a transaction is unable to be executed within a reasonable or expected time or when the system is unable to process expected volumes. Sometimes, this may be specific to a single transaction; other times, it may be something that affects every composite instance running on the server.

Server-wide performance issues

When server-wide performance problems occur, they impact most or all of the transactions currently being executed on your infrastructure. For example, if the dehydration store database is down, this will definitely have an impact on all the running instances.

Consider asking yourself a few questions to determine whether there is an overarching infrastructure problem:

- Is logging in to Oracle Enterprise Manager Fusion Middleware Control extremely slow?

- Are all composite instances getting completed in an unusually long period of time?

- Are the logs or your dehydration database growing unusually quickly?

- Are you seeing an exceptionally high number of errors in the logs?

These are usually indications that there may be a server-wide performance problem. Performance issues impacting the entire server are usually related to either one or a few specific issues. In this case, take a look at the following:

- **Check available disk space**: Lack of available disk space is known to have an adverse effect on an instance execution. Sometimes, this is due to excessive logging that fills up the disk or logs not being rotated.

  The following code is an example of how to view the available disk space. Here, the /u01 mount point on which our software is installed has 10.8 GB available, so space is not an issue:

```
oracle@soahost1:/home/oracle> df -m
Filesystem  1M-blocks   Used Available Use% Mounted on
/dev/sda6         730    387       306  56% /
/dev/sda7         244     35       197  15% /home
/dev/sda5         996    804       141  86% /var
/dev/sda3        1984     38      1844   2% /tmp
/dev/sda2        4841   3514      1077  77% /usr
```

```
/dev/sda1            99      12       83   13%  /boot
/dev/sdb          20159    8267    10869   44%  /u01
tmpfs              3992       0     3992    0%  /dev/shm
soadb.packt.com:/u01/share
                   40318          37175     1095  98%
```

- **Check CPU, memory, and I/O utilization**: Some processes can hog the CPU, be it a backup job, bug in AdminServer, unauthorized code deployments, or your monitoring tool agent. For example, some intelligent monitoring agents, such as the Oracle Enterprise Manager Cloud Control Agent, perform constant queries against the database to retrieve metrics and statistics, which may result in undue burden on your environment. Also, ensure that there is sufficient memory available and that SWAP space (Unix) or virtual memory (Windows) is not actively being used.

  By reviewing the output of the vmstat Linux command in the following example, we see that SWAP utilization is 0 MB (good!), the amount of free memory is 87 MB (keep an eye on it!), the number of bytes in and bytes out at this point in time (to measure I/O) is 6 and 49, respectively (not bad!), and the CPU is 94 percent idle (no problem here!):

```
oracle@soahost1:/home/oracle> vmstat -S m
procs -----------memory---------- ---swap-- -----io---- --system--
-----cpu------
 r  b   swpd   free  buff  cache   si   so   bi   bo   in   cs
us sy id wa st
 0  0   1095     87   153    454    0    0    6   49   26   34
 4  1 94  2  0
```

- **Check operating system resources and logs**: For example, in Linux, the /var/log/messages log reveals critical events at the operating system level. This log file can reveal errors that may have a direct impact on the stability, behavior, and/or performance of SOA Infrastructure. In the following example, it appears that we have exceeded certain ulimit resources:

```
root@soahost1:/root> cat /var/log/messages
Aug 31 20:53:22 uslx286 sshd[22480]: fatal: setresuid 10000:
Resource temporarily unavailable
```

  The lsof command in Linux can list the number of open files. Too many may exhaust operating system resources:

```
root@soahost1:/root> lsof | wc -l
6064
```

The `ps` command in Linux can list the number of running processes. Ultimately, too many may also exhaust operating system resources:

```
root@soahost1:/root> ps -A | wc -l
297
```

- **Check JVM available memory and frequency of full garbage collection**: Not enough available heap may result in excessive garbage collection, or depending on the garbage collection algorithm being used, increased pause time may occur, which could also result in higher CPU utilization. We recommend you review the *Oracle Fusion Middleware Performance and Tuning for Oracle WebLogic Server 12c Release 1* documentation at `http://docs.oracle.com/cd/E24329_01/web.1211/e24390/wls_tuning.htm#PERFM173` for details regarding additional JVM tuning.

- **Check connection pools**: When connection pools are exhausted, this may lead to transactional failures. However, the errors are apparent in both the logs and in the Flow Trace of the composite instances.

- **Check database performance**: Often under heavy load, a larger number of writes to the database are experienced, which have a direct impact on database server I/O. Tools such as Oracle Enterprise Manager Database Control or Oracle Enterprise Manager Cloud Control can provide insight into the performance of the database. Other times, data growth can also contribute to slow console performance. Oracle Database tuning is a huge topic in itself, but running a few queries, such as the one shown here, can be useful to determine whether your database has adequate free space to process instance requests:

```
SELECT a.tablespace_name,
       b.autoextensible,
       b.increment_by,
       SUM(a.bytes)/1024/1024 free_space_mb,
       SUM(a.blocks) free_blocks,
       SUM(b.bytes)/1024/1024 allocated_space_mb
FROM sys.dba_free_space a,
     sys.dba_data_files b
WHERE a.tablespace_name = b.tablespace_name
AND a.tablespace_name ='DEV_SOAINFRA'
GROUP BY a.tablespace_name,
         b.autoextensible,
         b.increment_by;
```

The output of this query in *Figure 9.4* shows that the **AUTOEXTENSIBLE** column of **SOAINFRA** data space is **TRUE** (good!) and the amount of free space is ~25 MB (worrisome) of a total allocated space of 500 MB:

TABLESPACE	AUTOEXTENSIBLE	INCREMENT_BY	FREE_SPACE_MB	FREE_BLOCKS	ALLOCATED_SPACE_MB
DEV_SOAINFRA YES		6400	25.6875	3288	500

Figure 9.4: Database schema free and allocated space query

Hardware may not be able to keep up with all the transactions, but by monitoring the various hardware, operating system, and infrastructure metrics, over time you should be able to determine whether you have maxed out your current hardware capacity or not.

Is your environment always slow or does it only demonstrate poor performance under heavy loads? Monitoring the performance of your environment is not a one-time activity. You should have monitoring tools in place to help you pinpoint unusual or high utilization and compare them to average usage times. In *Chapter 6, Monitoring Oracle SOA Suite 12c*, we proposed using Oracle Enterprise Manager Cloud Control, which provides end-to-end monitoring and alerting (and even some administration) capabilities for both your SOA Infrastructure and operating system. By adding the SOA Management Pack, you would also be able to get composite-specific information of all your environments through a single console.

SOA composite instance performance

When we refer to composite instance performance, we mean to say that a particular SOA composite is behaving poorly. In these cases, performance issues are often isolated to one (or a few) composites, but not all. For example, this could be due to the response time from external systems, a badly designed process, due to a suddenly poor performing database, or a queue that the SOA composite is using to read/write data.

Consider a scenario where your composite begins processing an instance by consuming messages from a JMS queue. During peak load, if sufficient threads are not available to the polling adapter, the overall performance of the composite is degraded. There may be no problem with your infrastructure and it may be capable of handling extra load by allocating more threads. The easiest way to overcome this bottleneck is to increase the value of the `adapter.jms.receive.threads` property that controls the number of threads from its default value of 1. This is a binding property that can be set in an individual composite:

```
<property name="adapter.jms.receive.threads" type="xs:string"
many="false">4</property>
```

> Starting with Oracle SOA Suite 12*c*, Mediator instance metadata is no longer stored in the database, but payloads are, depending on the audit level.

We cannot address all scenarios that may cause a specific composite to behave poorly, as they are unlimited. However, we can provide the means and direction to identify poorly behaving composites and help retrieve the specific composite instance ID of the offending instance so that we may navigate to its details and find out more about what's going on.

Average, minimum, and maximum duration of BPEL/BPMN components

The queries in this section will help you get an idea of the performance of runtime components. The majority of the commands performed provide an easy-to-read format and may initially look complex. However, the queries themselves are relatively basic.

This first query, when run against the [PREFIX]_SOAINFRA schema, returns the name of the BPEL or BPMN component, the partition it is deployed to, its state, as well as average, minimum, and maximum execution time along with the total count. The following query is filtered to retrieve statistics for the last 24 hours via the SYSDATE-1 clause. If preferred, you can further limit the query to a specific composite (COMPOSITE_NAME LIKE '%<composite_name>%') or component (COMPONENT_NAME LIKE '%<component_name>%'):

```
--------------------------------------------------
-- BPEL/BPMN AVG/MIN/MAX                         --
--------------------------------------------------
SELECT domain_name,
       component_name,
       DECODE(state,'5','COMPLETE','9','STALE','10','FAULTED') AS
state,
       TO_CHAR(AVG((TO_NUMBER(SUBSTR(TO_CHAR(modify_date - creation_
date),12,2)) * 60 * 60) + (TO_NUMBER(SUBSTR(TO_CHAR(modify_date -
creation_date), 15, 2)) * 60) + TO_NUMBER(SUBSTR(TO_CHAR(modify_date
- creation_date), 18, 4))), '999990.000') AS avg,
       TO_CHAR(MIN((TO_NUMBER(SUBSTR(TO_CHAR(modify_date - creation_
date),12,2)) * 60 * 60) + (TO_NUMBER(SUBSTR(TO_CHAR(modify_date -
creation_date), 15, 2)) * 60) + TO_NUMBER(SUBSTR(TO_CHAR(modify_date
- creation_date), 18, 4))), '999990.000') AS min,
       TO_CHAR(MAX((TO_NUMBER(SUBSTR(TO_CHAR(modify_date - creation_
date),12,2)) * 60 * 60) + (TO_NUMBER(SUBSTR(TO_CHAR(modify_date -
creation_date), 15, 2)) * 60) + TO_NUMBER(SUBSTR(TO_CHAR(modify_date
- creation_date), 18, 4))), '999990.000') AS max,
```

```
          COUNT(1) AS count
FROM      cube_instance
WHERE     creation_date >= SYSDATE - 1
--AND       component_name LIKE '%%'
--AND       composite_name LIKE '%%'
GROUP BY domain_name,
          component_name,
          state
ORDER BY component_name,
          state;
```

The output of the preceding query is shown in *Figure 9.5*. Here, we can see that the `ChangeAddress` BPEL component had `112` executions within the last 24 hours with an average execution time of `0.279` seconds and a maximum execution time of `7.3` seconds:

DOMAIN_NAME	COMPONENT_NAME	STATE	AVG	MIN	MAX	COUNT
default	ChangeAccount	Complete	0.144	0.000	1.300	36
default	ChangeAddress	Complete	0.279	0.100	7.300	112
default	DeleteAccount	Complete	0.547	0.100	2.200	62
default	DeleteAddress	Complete	0.620	0.300	0.900	5
default	UpdateAccount	Complete	0.486	0.100	1.400	85
default	UpdateAddress	Complete	0.550	0.300	0.800	2

Figure 9.5: Output of the SQL query returning aggregated statistics of the
BPEL/BPMN component performance

> Poor execution times of BPEL, BPMN, and Mediator components
> may not be due to the slowness of the infrastructure or code,
> but could be due to poor response time from the invocation of
> external services or resources.

This query comes in very handy as it is simple to use and quickly retrieves good, aggregated information of your overall component instance performance.

The duration of a single BPEL/BPMN component instance

In other cases, the performance may be isolated to a single transaction, which could be related to one or more composite and/or component. Regardless, you will have to start somewhere and have a general idea of the composite that is reportedly responding poorly.

This following SQL query lists all BPEL and BPMN instances within the last 24 hours (refer to SYSDATE - 1 in the WHERE clause) that have been completed in over 10 seconds (refer to 10 in the WHERE clause):

```
--------------------------------------------------
-- BPEL/BPMN COMPONENT INSTANCE DURATION TIMES  --
--------------------------------------------------
SELECT cmpst_id,
       TO_CHAR(creation_date, 'YYYY-MM-DD HH24:MI') AS creation_date,
       component_name,
       componenttype,
       DECODE(state, '5', 'COMPLETE', '9', 'STALE', '10', 'FAULTED')
AS state,
       TO_CHAR((TO_NUMBER(SUBSTR(TO_CHAR(modify_date - creation_
date), 12, 2)) * 60 * 60) + (TO_NUMBER(SUBSTR(TO_CHAR(modify_date -
creation_date), 15, 2)) * 60) + TO_NUMBER(SUBSTR(TO_CHAR(modify_date
- creation_date), 18, 4)),'999990.000') AS duration
FROM   cube_instance
WHERE  TO_CHAR(creation_date, 'YYYY-MM-DD HH24:MI') >= TO_CHAR(SYSDATE
- 1,'YYYY-MM-DD HH24:MI')
AND    (TO_NUMBER(SUBSTR(TO_CHAR(modify_date - creation_date), 12, 2))
* 60 * 60) + (TO_NUMBER(SUBSTR(TO_CHAR(modify_date - creation_date),
15, 2)) * 60) + TO_NUMBER(SUBSTR(TO_CHAR(modify_date - creation_date),
18, 4)) > 10
--AND    component_name LIKE '%%'
--AND    composite_name LIKE '%%'
ORDER BY component_name,
         creation_date;
```

You can further limit the query to a specific composite or component as needed.

Figure 9.6 shows the output of this query. Now, we can see that we have 7 instances that have taken longer than 10 seconds, and one in particular took 26.7 seconds. The good thing is that the query outputs the composite instance ID! Now we can log in to the console and navigate to the Flow Trace of that particular instance to find out exactly what activity took so long:

CMPST_ID	CREATION_DATE	COMPONENT_NAME	COMPONENTTYPE	STATE	DURATION
85436814	2012-02-03 19:02	SimpleApprovalBPEL	bpel	Faulted	14.100
85436815	2012-02-03 19:02	SimpleApprovalBPEL	bpel	Faulted	14.100
85497427	2012-02-03 22:07	SimpleApprovalBPEL	bpel	Faulted	14.100
85497428	2012-02-03 22:07	SimpleApprovalBPEL	bpel	Faulted	14.000
85498409	2012-02-03 22:12	SimpleApprovalBPEL	bpel	Faulted	14.200
85498410	2012-02-03 22:12	SimpleApprovalBPEL	bpel	Faulted	14.000
85506489	2012-02-03 22:09	SimpleApprovalBPEL	bpel	Complete	26.700

Figure 9.6: Output of the SQL query returning individual BPEL/BPMN component instance performance

Troubleshooting SOA composite instances

This section is not about troubleshooting SOA composite instance failures, but rather about troubleshooting composite instances in general. Just because a composite is not reported as failed does not mean it does not warrant investigation. For example, it is entirely possible that when dealing with asynchronous services, there might be synchronization issues between concurrent threads that are trying to access a schema and the thread locking mechanism being unable to avoid deadlocks. This would leave the transaction in a pending state and not faulted. This behavior may require further investigation.

Chapter 6, Monitoring Oracle SOA Suite 12c, described in detail how to administer and manage faults. Faulted instances, in a way, are easier to deal with than non-faulted instances, as at least you have an error to begin with. Refer to this chapter to understand how to recover faults manually, automatically, and in bulk.

In the section titled *Identifying and viewing log file entries* in *Chapter 6, Monitoring Oracle SOA Suite 12c*, we described how to search through logs for a particular ECID and how to enable Selective Tracing. This will help you trace the lifecycle of an ECID from beginning to end. You may have to increase logger levels if you would like more logging specific to a certain behavior (for example, if you only need to increase logging for adapter invocations).

How do you obtain the ECID anyway? There are a few approaches that can help.

If you are troubleshooting a particular instance in the console, the ECID is one of the columns in **Search Results** under **Flow Instances**, as shown in the following figure:

Initiating ECID	Flow ID	Initiating Composite	Flow State
1063e612-47f5-4e9c-b9b1-7897053a07a7-...	10017	BPELWeather ...	✅ Completed
1063e612-47f5-4e9c-b9b1-7897053a07a7-...	10016	BPELWeather ...	✅ Completed
1063e612-47f5-4e9c-b9b1-7897053a07a7-...	10015	BPELWeather ...	✅ Completed

Figure 9.7: The initiating ECID is shown in the search results

Another approach is by obtaining the payload from any of the applications within the integration. For example, if the payload is still in an **Oracle Advanced Queue (AQ)**, it is possible to perform some SQL queries to retrieve the payload. The ECID is included in the `<instra:tracking.ecid>` header element of the payload, as highlighted in the following code:

```
<env:Envelope xmlns:env="http://schemas.xmlsoap.org/soap/envelope/"
xmlns:wsa="http://www.w3.org/2005/08/addressing">
  <env:Header>
    <wsa:MessageID>urn:5e0df372-0197-11e5-98b2-000c29547ca1</
wsa:MessageID>
    <wsa:ReplyTo>
      <wsa:Address>http://www.w3.org/2005/08/addressing/anonymous</
wsa:Address>
      <wsa:ReferenceParameters>
        <instra:tracking.ecid xmlns:instra="http://xmlns.oracle.com/
sca/tracking/1.0">1063e612-47f5-4e9c-b9b1-7897053a07a7-00009ccb</
instra:tracking.ecid>
        <instra:tracking.FlowEventId xmlns:instra="http://xmlns.
oracle.com/sca/tracking/1.0">10019</instra:tracking.FlowEventId>
        <instra:tracking.FlowId xmlns:instra="http://xmlns.oracle.com/
sca/tracking/1.0">10004</instra:tracking.FlowId>
        <instra:tracking.CorrelationFlowId xmlns:instra="http://xmlns.
oracle.com/sca/tracking/1.0">0000Kq2n3mE6ATMS6MGNsy1LMrKi000006</
instra:tracking.CorrelationFlowId>
      </wsa:ReferenceParameters>
    </wsa:ReplyTo>
    <wsa:FaultTo>
      <wsa:Address>http://www.w3.org/2005/08/addressing/anonymous</
wsa:Address>
    </wsa:FaultTo>
  </env:Header>
```

```
    <env:Body>
        .
        .
        .

    </env:Body>
</env:Envelope>
```

Now that you have the ECID, you can use it to search the logs.

We now move to an example where, perhaps, no action would be necessary on the part of the administrator. For example, the console reported a failure of a specific instance. On navigating to the faulted instance in the console, we see in *Figure 9.8* how the instance appears to have retried:

Instance	Type	Usage	State	Time
Customer_ep	Web Service	Service	Completed	Feb 2, 2015 4:05:00 PM
Customer	Mediator Component		Completed	Feb 2, 2015 4:05:27 PM
ValidateCustomer	Web Service(Local Invocation	Referen	Completed	Feb 2, 2015 4:05:02 PM
ValidateCustomer_ep	Web Service(Local Invocation	Service	Faulted	Feb 2, 2015 4:05:02 PM
ValidateCustomer	Mediator Component		Faulted	Feb 2, 2015 4:05:22 PM
CreateCustomerReference	Web Service(Local Invocation	Referen	Completed	Feb 2, 2015 4:05:02 PM
CreateCustomer1_ep	Web Service(Local Invocation	Service	Faulted	Feb 2, 2015 4:05:02 PM
CreateCustomer1	Mediator Component		Faulted	Feb 2, 2015 4:05:22 PM
CreateCustomer2	Mediator Component		Faulted	Feb 2, 2015 4:05:22 PM
CustomerWebService	Web Service	Referen	Faulted	Feb 2, 2015 4:05:02 PM
ValidateCustomer	Web Service(Local Invocation	Referen	Completed	Feb 2, 2015 4:05:27 PM
ValidateCustomer_ep	Web Service(Local Invocation	Service	Completed	Feb 2, 2015 4:05:27 PM
ValidateCustomer	Mediator Component		Completed	Feb 2, 2015 4:05:27 PM
CreateCustomerReference	Web Service(Local Invocation	Referen	Completed	Feb 2, 2015 4:05:27 PM
CreateCustomer1_ep	Web Service(Local Invocation	Service	Completed	Feb 2, 2015 4:05:27 PM
CreateCustomer1	Mediator Component		Completed	Feb 2, 2015 4:05:27 PM
CreateCustomer2	Mediator Component		Completed	Feb 2, 2015 4:05:27 PM
CustomerWebService	Web Service	Referen	Completed	Feb 2, 2015 4:05:27 PM

Figure 9.8: The Flow Trace showing a retried composite executing successfully the second time

By clicking on `CreateCustomer2` to drill down options in that component's flow, we get an output similar to the one shown in *Figure 9.9*. We can see here that there was an invocation to an external service which apparently took 20 seconds (compare 4:05:02 to 4:05:22). It turns out that we have a 20 second timeout configured on this reference. Excellent! This is the behavior we prefer. However, referring to *Figure 9.8*, we see that the instance was retried. This turns out to be a function of the fault policy attached to this particular composite. The composite has retried and the subsequent invocation went through just fine. Note that the retried instances are actually new instances. The reason why we see both the original transaction and the retried one in the same flow trace is because the same ECID is maintained between instance retries.

The following screenshot shows the Mediator component instance Flow Trace showing a timeout to an external service invocation:

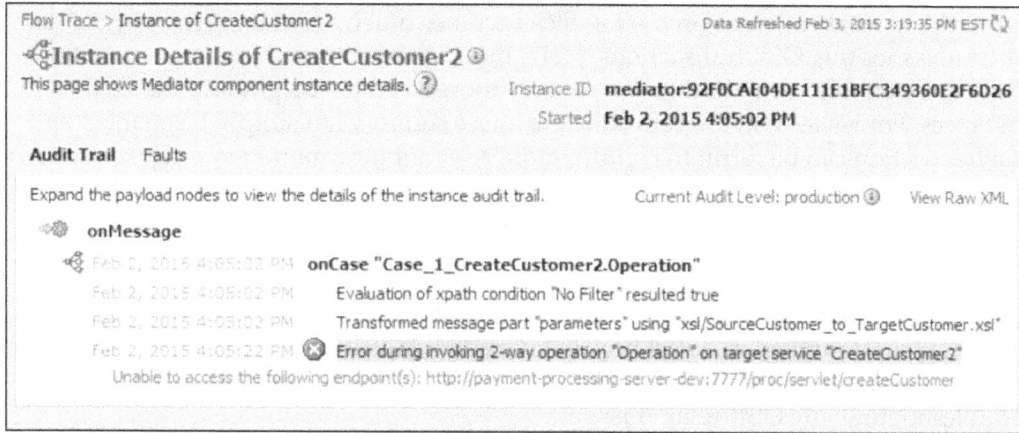

Figure 9.9: The Mediator component instance Flow Trace showing a timeout to an external service

In this example, aside from trying to find out why the external service timed out the first time, there may not be much to do at this point.

Troubleshooting generic SOA composite instance errors

More often than not, it is likely that you will encounter a generic `ORABPEL-05002` error in your infrastructure. The error may be thrown for a host of common issues such as transaction errors, adapter errors, coding, configuration, and even transformation errors. The `ORABPEL-05002` message is a wrapper-type generic error message and is always associated with an embedded error message, which causes the actual issue. It is therefore necessary to investigate an `ORABPEL-05002` error in your log files and its entire trail to find out additional information within it. In case there is no additional message logged, set the BPEL engine loggers to `FINEST`, as discussed earlier. This will narrow down the subsystem or component causing the actual issue. Observe the error in the following code snippet where an `ORA-01432` error, which occurs due to an invalid database insert, is wrapped inside the `ORABPEL-05002` message:

```
Failed to handle dispatch message ... Exception ORABPEL-05002
Error while attempting to process the message "com.collaxa.cube.
engine.dispatch.message.invoke.InvokeInstanceMessage"; the reported
exception is: Exception not handled by the Collaxa Cube system. An
unhandled exception has been thrown in the Collaxa Cube system;
exception reported is "java.sql.SQLDataException: ORA-01438: value
larger than specified precision allowed for this column
```

Troubleshooting OSB instances

Unlike SOA composite instances, given that console-based troubleshooting of OSB is relatively weak, reliance on the log files becomes much more important in the case of troubleshooting OSB transactions. Here, message tracing and logging are features that can be enabled and disabled to provide more runtime insight into the OSB instances. For issues that are reproducible, these settings can simply be enabled and the transaction can be rerun to capture more relevant information in order to assist in the troubleshooting process. In cases that are not reproducible, if these settings were not enabled beforehand, you may have little information to fall back on to assist in troubleshooting. Thus, the challenge is finding an acceptable medium.

Chapter 6, Monitoring Oracle SOA Suite 12c, included a section titled *Monitoring OSB instances* that described in detail how to take advantage of multiple operational settings to increase different types of logging. They provide valuable insight into troubleshooting any OSB-related issues.

Using selective tracing

When trying to troubleshoot a particularly difficult problem, there is a often need to increase logging. However, as a side effect of running logs with verbose logging, it can be very time consuming to filter through all of the messages in the log. Many of the messages may be unrelated to the process, which can further increase the amount of time it takes to find the source of the issue. Thankfully, there is a capability within WebLogic Server that allows us to get a better idea of what's happening when there is an issue in SOA or OSB without needing to completely overload the log files with unnecessary information.

To access Selective Tracing, expand the `WebLogic Domain` folder when you log in to Fusion Middleware Control and right-click on the target domain. A menu will pop up, as shown in the following figure, where you need to navigate to **Logs | Selective Tracing**:

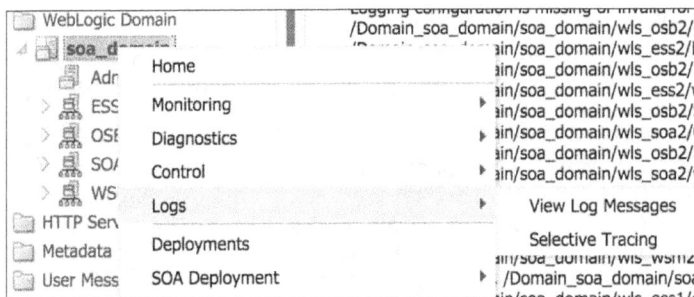

Figure 9.10: The domain menu showing the path to Selective Tracing

Once the selective tracing page has loaded, you will be presented with a form asking for **Application Name**, **Level**, **Duration**, **Trace ID**, and **Description**. It also provides the ability to add fields. In order to trace a composite, there are only a couple of modifications needed. First, set **Duration** to whichever length is necessary for tracing purposes. If possible, make the tracing duration minimal because if you do so, there are less logs to dredge through and it will have less of an impact on performance. This may be exceptionally critical when dealing with a production system. Next, adjust the **Level** used to the desired setting; once again, this setting will vastly affect the amount of logs collected during the tracing. Any other settings can be adjusted as desired; however, one last field must be set to effectively trace a single composite.

To specify a particular composite, click on **Add Fields** and check the box next to **Composite Name**. Click on the **Add** button. Type the name of the composite into the **Composite Name** field, as demonstrated in *Figure 9.11*. The name should not consist of a revision, so if there is a **HelloWorld [1.0]** window deployed, then only the title **HelloWorld** should be typed in the field. Finally, click on **Start Tracing** to begin the selective trace.

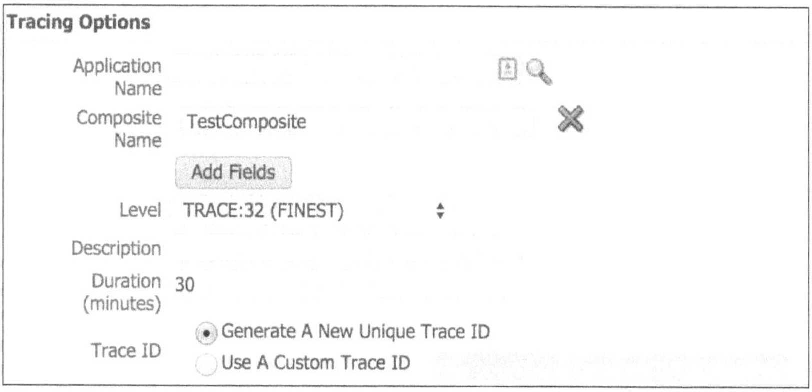

Figure 9.11: The Tracing Options menu

To view the information on the current trace, click on **Active Traces and Tracing History**. This will provide you with a list of the active and historical traces. This will allow you to disable active traces if relevant information has already been gathered. By clicking on the **Trace ID** for any given trace, the log messages pertaining only to the trace will be visible.

While this example has only referenced SOA Suite, this can be used for any application on a domain and can be filtered by any of the fields available.

Troubleshooting SOA deployment issues

It is important to understand that deploying SOA composites does in fact take server resources. If you deploy tens or hundreds of composites to the server, you will see a direct impact on the size of the JVM heap (that is, the available heap will continue to go down as more and more composites are deployed within a short period of time). We therefore recommend you to not deploy during expected heavy or peak times.

Chapter 5, Deploying Code, describes how to use Ant to deploy composite projects, but here we take a closer look at the entire deployment process.

Knowing where to look

Let's observe the output of the Ant deployment of the HelloWorld composite in the following code. As you can see, the deployment failed due to a java.lang. OutOfMemoryError: PermGen space error:

```
deploy:
    [input] skipping input as property serverURL has already been set.
    [input] skipping input as property sarLocation has already been
set.
    [deployComposite] setting user/password..., user=weblogic
    [deployComposite] Processing sar=/u01/svn/HelloWorld/deploy/sca_
HelloWorld_rev1.0.jar
    [deployComposite] Adding sar file - /u01/svn/HelloWorld/deploy/
sca_HelloWorld_rev1.0.jar
[deployComposite] INFO: Creating HTTP connection to host:soahost1,
port:8001
    [echo]
    [echo] ERROR IN TRYCATCH BLOCK:
    [echo] /u01/scripts/build.soa.xml:112: The following error
occurred while executing this line:
    [echo] /u01/scripts/build.soa.xml:138: The following error
occurred while executing this line:
    [echo] /u01/share/oracle/middleware/products/fmw1213/soa/bin/ant-
sca-deploy.xml:188: java.lang.OutOfMemoryError: PermGen space
```

Here, it appears that the SOA server has somehow run out of memory. This is not the case. In fact, this OutOfMemoryError exception is on the machine that executes the Ant command, not the SOA server itself. This could be confusing, couldn't it?

It is thus important to understand a few points regarding Ant deployments:

- Deploying SOA composites is really a two-phase process: the compilation of code followed by the deployment itself.

- The compilation of the composite takes place on the machine that executes Ant, not necessarily the SOA server.

- The compilation process will validate external references. For example, if there is a schema imported in to the composite that resides on some external web server, it is validated at compilation time. If, for example, that web server is down during the compilation, the compilation will fail.

- Although deployment failures are usually a result of some issue on the SOA server, this is not always the case.

The earlier error was thrown by the `ant-sca-deploy.xml` script, and therefore, we can assume that the error occurred in the local Ant runtime. The solution in this case is simple: increase the `PermSize` and `MaxPermSize` values in the `ANT_OPTS` environment variable prior to running Ant. To do so in Linux is simple:

```
export ANT_OPTS="-Xmx1536M -Xms1536M  -XX:NewSize=800M
-XX:+UseConcMarkSweepGC -XX:SurvivorRatio=12 -XX:MaxNewSize=800M
-XX:+UseParNewGC"
```

Compilation issues

The compilation of a composite takes place via the `package` target in the `ant-sca-package.xml` build script. This target calls several other targets to complete the compilation process.

It first calls the `clean` target, which removes any existing SAR files:

```
clean:
     [echo] deleting /u01/svn/HelloWorld/SOA/deploy/sca_HelloWorld_
rev1.0.jar
```

It then creates the deploy subdirectory via the `init` target if it does not exist:

```
init:
     [mkdir] Created dir: /u01/svn/HelloWorld/SOA/deploy
```

The `compile-source` target is invoked:

```
compile-source:
     [echo] oracle.home = /u01/app/oracle/middleware/Oracle_SOA1/bin/..
```

The `scac-validate` target is subsequently called, which sets certain environment variables:

```
scac-validate:
     [echo] Running scac-validate in /u01/svn/HelloWorld/SOA/
composite.xml
     [echo] oracle.home = /u01/app/oracle/middleware/Oracle_SOA1/
bin/..
```

Finally, the `scac` target is called, which performs the actual compilation itself:

```
scac:
     [scac] Validating composite "/u01/svn/HelloWorld/SOA/composite.
xml"
     [scac] error: location {/ns:composite/ns:import[@location='file:/
u01/svn/HelloWorld/SOA/WSDLs/HelloWorld.wsdl']}: Load of wsdl
"HelloWorldWebService.wsdl with Message part element undefined
in wsdl [file:/u01/svn/HelloWorld/SOA/WSDLs/HelloWorld.wsdl] part
name = parameters type = {http://soahost1/SOA/HelloWorldWebService}
GetHelloWorldResponse" failed
     [scac] error: location {/ns:composite/ns:import[@location='file:/
u01/svn/HelloWorld/SOA/WSDLs/HelloWorldWebService.wsdl']}: Load of
wsdl "HelloWorldWebService.wsdl with Message part element undefined
in wsdl [file:/u01/svn/HelloWorld/SOA/WSDLs/HelloWorldWebService.
wsdl] part name = parameters  type = {http://soahost1/SOA/
HelloWorldWebService}GetHelloWorldResponse" failed
     [echo]
     [echo] ERROR IN TRYCATCH BLOCK:
     [echo] /u01/app/oracle/middleware/Oracle_SOA1/bin/ant-sca-
package.xml:46: The following error occurred while executing this
line:
     [echo] /u01/app/oracle/middleware/Oracle_SOA1/bin/ant-sca-
compile.xml:269: Java returned: 1 Check log file : /tmp/out.err for
errors
```

A lot of times when compiling composites, the error returned on the prompt is not descriptive enough. Additional information can be found in the automatically created `out.err` file. This is located in `/tmp/out.err` on operating systems based on Linux/Unix and `C:\Users\[user]\AppData\Local\Temp\out.err` on Windows. If the error on the standard output is not clear, we always recommend to review the `out.err` file for additional information.

Most compilation errors are actually due to coding issues. In the preceding example, one of the schemas in the project was to import a nonexistent schema. `HelloWorldWebService.wsdl` had the following import statement:

```
<xs:import schemaLocation="http://externalserver/schema.xsd"
namespace="http://soahost1/SOA/HelloWorldWebService"/>
```

Trying to access `http://externalserver/schema.xsd` returned a `HTTP Error 503. The service is unavailable` error. Because this imported schema was not available and could not be validated at compilation time, the compilation failed as expected.

Another common issue at compilation time is when you use the `oramds://` protocol to refer to external resources that are available in the metadata store. Here, you can see that the composite build failed when the `HelloWorld.xsd` that was being referenced from the MDS was not loaded during compilation:

```
oracle.fabric.common.wsdl.SchemaBuilder.loadEmbeddedSchemas
(SchemaBuilder.java:492) Caused by: java.io.IOException: oracle.mds.
exception.MDSException: MDS-00054: The file to be loaded oramds:/apps/
Common/HelloWorld.xsd does not exist.
```

It is important to understand that at compilation time, Ant would refer to an MDS location that is configured in `adf-config.xml`. This file contains information to connect either a file-based or database-based MDS, and it is available in one of the following two locations:

- Under the `[Composite_Home]\SCA-INF\classes\META-INF` project folder where the MDS configuration is specific to a particular composite

- In the `[Application_Home]\.adf\META-INF\adf-config.xml` file under the application folder

An example of the database-based `adf-config.xml` is shown in the following code. This configuration file essentially tells your composite where your MDS is located, so that `oramds://` lookups know where to look. As you can see, the highlighted text refers to the MDS database instance:

```xml
<?xml version="1.0" encoding="windows-1252" ?>
<adf-config xmlns="http://xmlns.oracle.com/adf/config"
xmlns:adf="http://xmlns.oracle.com/adf/config/properties">
  <adf:adf-properties-child xmlns="http://xmlns.oracle.com/adf/config/
properties">
    <adf-property name="adfAppUID" value="TemporaryMDS-2296"/>
  </adf:adf-properties-child>
  <adf-mds-config xmlns="http://xmlns.oracle.com/adf/mds/config">
    <mds-config xmlns="http://xmlns.oracle.com/mds/config">
      <persistence-config>
        <metadata-namespaces>
          <namespace metadata-store-usage="mstore-usage_1" path="/
apps"/>
        </metadata-namespaces>
        <metadata-store-usages>
          <metadata-store-usage id="mstore-usage_1">
```

```
                      <metadata-store class-name="oracle.mds.persistence.stores.
        db.DBMetadataStore">
                    <property value="DEV_MDS" name="jdbc-userid"/>
                    <property value="welcome1" name="jdbc-password"/>
                    <property value="jdbc:oracle:thin:@//dbhost:1521/orcl"
        name="jdbc-url"/>
                    <property value="soa-infra" name="partition-name"/>
                </metadata-store>
            </metadata-store-usage>
          </metadata-store-usages>
        </persistence-config>
      </mds-config>
    </adf-mds-config>
  </adf-config>
```

It is recommended that developers set the MDS configuration at the application folder level, since it is not deleted after compilation and applies globally to all composite projects in the application.

Common deployment issues

Deployment issues have their own set of challenges. In some cases, the error is quite obvious:

```
deploy:
    [input] skipping input as property serverURL has already been set.
    [input] skipping input as property sarLocation has already been
set.
[deployComposite] setting user/password..., user=welcome1
[deployComposite] Processing sar=/u01/svn/HelloWorld/deploy/sca_
HelloWorld_rev1.0.jar
[deployComposite] Adding sar file - /u01/svn/HelloWorld/deploy/sca_
HelloWorld_rev1.0.jar
[deployComposite] INFO: Creating HTTP connection to host:soahost1,
port:8001
[deployComposite] java.net.UnknownHostException: soahost1
```

In other cases, it is more difficult. Consider the common error in the following code that you may face during composite deployment:

```
<Error> <oracle.integration.platform> <SOA-20003> <Unable to register
service. oracle.fabric.common.FabricException: Error in getting XML
input stream:
 http://soahost1:8001/soa-infra/services/default/QueryOrder?WSDL:
Response: '503: Service Unavailable' for url:
```

This is a common deployment error that you are almost certain to encounter either when you are deploying a composite or when the composite is trying to register external references during server startup. However, you might find yourself in a predicament when the same error keeps on recurring, even when the reference service is available. What can you make of errors like these? First, let's understand what happens here. When you start a SOA server or deploy a composite, the engine tries to activate the composite by trying to register with all its endpoints (when lazy loading is not active). If unsuccessful, the composite is marked as inactive.

A target service being down can cause a composite to become inactive; the errors in this case can be prevented in the following two ways:

1. From Oracle Enterprise Manager Fusion Middleware Control, navigate to the composite dashboard and reactivate the composite. The composite will now once again try to establish a communication with all its endpoints and attempt to start gracefully. This is often the first attempt made by the administrator.

2. You can also altogether prevent the composite from going into a retired state in the first place by using abstract WSDLs of all the external services. When you use an abstract WSDL, the engine treats it as local and keeps the composite active. The concrete WSDL can be copied to a shared MDS location and in turn be referred from the abstract WSDL. This must be done at design time by the developer.

To briefly understand the difference between concrete and abstract WSDLs, click on the 🔧 icon on the composite dashboard of the referenced composite service. Refer to the following figure; this is the concrete WSDL:

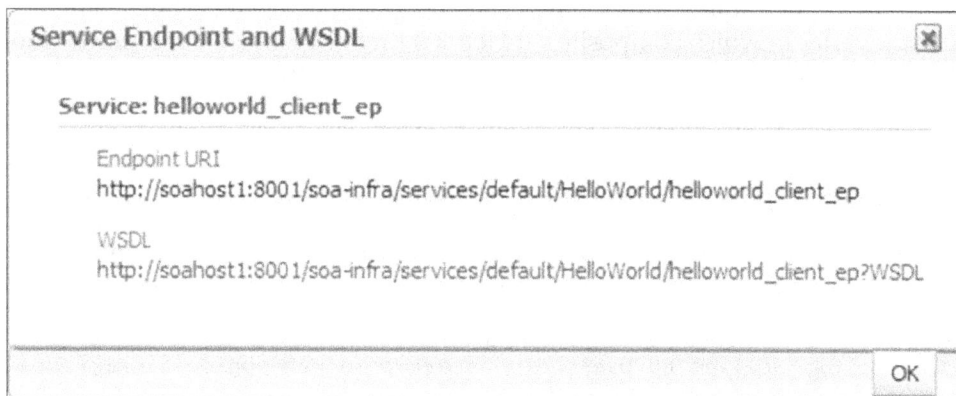

Service Endpoint and WSDL

Service: helloworld_client_ep

Endpoint URI
http://soahost1:8001/soa-infra/services/default/HelloWorld/helloworld_client_ep

WSDL
http://soahost1:8001/soa-infra/services/default/HelloWorld/helloworld_client_ep?WSDL

OK

Figure 9.12: The concrete WSDL as shown on the composite dashboard

If you click on the concrete WSDL, a new browser window opens, displaying its contents. In it, you can obtain the abstract WSDL, as shown in the following figure:

```
<?xml version="1.0" encoding="UTF-8"?>
<wsdl:definitions xmlns:soap="http://schemas.xmlsoap.org/wsdl/soap/" xmlns:wsdl="http://schemas.xmlsoap.org/wsdl/"
xmlns:client="http://xmlns.oracle.com/SOA11g/HelloWorld/HelloWorld"
xmlns:pink="http://schemas.xmlsoap.org/ws/2003/05/partner-link/"
targetNamespace="http://xmlns.oracle.com/SOA11g/HelloWorld/HelloWorld" name="HelloWorld">
  - <wsdl:documentation>
        <abstractWSDL>http://soahost1:8001/soa-infra/services/default/HelloWorld!1.0/HelloWorld.wsdl</abstractWSDL>
    </wsdl:documentation>
```

Figure 9.13: The abstract WSDL can be retrieved from the concrete WSDL

Figure 9.13 shows a version-specific abstract WSDL, which is:

```
http://soahost1:8001/soa-infra/services/default/HelloWorld!1.0/
HelloWorld.wsdl
```

The default version can be referenced as follows:

```
http://soahost1:8001/soa-infra/services/default/HelloWorld/
HelloWorld.wsdl
```

Here, it is the responsibility of the developer to make this change and ensure that references are made to abstract versus concrete WSDLs.

Consider another scenario where you have multiple composites deployed to your infrastructure and they refer to each other to achieve a business function. During server startup, if one composite A calls another composite B with a concrete WSDL file and composite A starts up before composite B, you will get the same error as shown earlier. This is because composite A is unable to load composite B's WSDL, which is not yet available. Unfortunately, it is not possible in Oracle SOA Suite 12c to control the order in which composites are loaded. In this case too, the same solutions that were discussed previously apply. The second approach is preferred, in order to save repetitive activation of composites every time.

Undeploying corrupt composites

In rare cases, the soa-infra application could cause the SOA managed server (for example, wls_soa1) to go into the ADMIN mode with a BEA-101216 error in the logs:

```
<Oct 4, 2015 12:45:23 PM EDT> <Error> <HTTP> <BEA-101216> <Servlet:
"FabricInit" failed to preload on startup in Web application: "/soa-
infra".
oracle.fabric.common.FabricException: Error in getting XML input
stream: oramds:/deployed-composites/HelloWorld_rev1.0/composite.xml:
oracle.mds.exception.MDSException: MDS-00054: The file to be loaded
oramds:/deployed-composites/HelloWorld_rev1.0/composite.xml does not
exist.
```

Here, the SOA Infrastructure is unable to start up due to a corrupt composite. The challenge is how to undeploy a SOA composite if the soa-infra application is not up and running. Fortunately, Oracle has provided a solution for this, which is detailed as follows:

1. Confirm that the SOA managed servers are down (they should be).

2. Refer to the Oracle Support document `ID 1380835.1` and download `ShareSoaInfraPartition.ear` (this EAR file works for both 11*g* and 12*c*).

3. Copy the `ShareSoaInfraPartition.ear` file to the `$MW_HOME/oracle_common/common/bin` folder.

4. Start a WLST session by running the following commands:

   ```
   cd $MW_HOME/oracle_common/common/bin
   ./wlst.sh
   connect()
   ```

5. Deploy the `ShareSoaInfraPartition` application:

   ```
   deploy('ShareSoaInfraPartition','ShareSoaInfraPartition.
   ear',upload='true')
   ```

6. Export a list of deployed composites to an XML file under the `/tmp` folder:

   ```
   exportMetadata(application='ShareSoaInfraPartition',server='Admi
   nServer',toLocation='/tmp',docs='/deployed-composites/deployed-
   composites.xml')
   ```

7. In a separate window, edit the exported XML file:

   ```
   vi /tmp/deployed-composites/deployed-composites.xml
   ```

8. Delete the five lines of the composite you want removed. For example, these following entries for the corrupt `HelloWorld` composite are deleted:

   ```
   <composite-series name="default/HelloWorld" default="default/
   HelloWorld!1.0">
   <composite-revision dn="default/HelloWorld!1.0" state="on"
   mode="active" location="dc/soa_9c645f3a-09eb-4878-bf05-
   178c62742955">
   <composite dn="default/HelloWorld!1.0*soa_9c645f3a-09eb-4878-
   bf05-178c62742955" compositeFileLabel="soa_cf_60902431-4473-408c-
   bc83-2ba9d7902903" scaEntityId="20001" deployedTime="2015-08-
   02T13:02:52.336-04:00"/>
   </composite-revision>
   </composite-series>
   ```

9. Back in the WLST prompt, run this final command to import the XML file into the server:

```
importMetadata(application='ShareSoaInfraPartition',server='Admin
Server',fromLocation='/tmp',docs='/deployed-composites/deployed-
composites.xml')
exit()
```

10. Start up the SOA managed server.

Troubleshooting OSB deployment issues

In *Chapter 5, Deploying Code*, we provided instructions on how to use a combination of WLST and Python scripts to deploy OSB projects through the command line, which is the preferred approach. Troubleshooting OSB deployment generally involves inspecting the output of this script.

At a high level, the behind-the-scenes OSB deployment process involves creating a session, uploading the JAR file, applying customizations (if specified), and then activating the session.

For a successful deployment, you will likely see a **deployment successful** message, as shown here:

```
Attempting to import : /home/oracle/code/HelloWorldOSB.jar on ALSB
Admin Server listening on : t3://soahost1:7001
Read file /home/oracle/code/HelloWorldOSB.jar
Created session SessionScript1432687858164
SessionMBean started session
Jar Uploaded
Deployment of : /home/oracle/code/HelloWorldOSB.jar successful
```

Additional information is provided in the diagnostic log file, which is generally located in the $DOMAIN_HOME/servers/wls_osb1/logs/wls_osb1-diagnostic.log file. The following are examples of entries logged into this log file:

```
[2015-05-26T20:58:04.544-04:00] [AdminServer] [NOTIFICATION] [OSB-
390100] [oracle.osb.configfwk] [tid: [ACTIVE].ExecuteThread: '27' for
queue: 'weblogic.kernel.Default (self-tuning)'] [userId: weblogic]
[ecid: 1063e612-47f5-4e9c-b9b1-7897053a07a7-0000d3fe,0] Session
SessionScript1432688274847 is being activated

[2015-05-26T20:58:11.026-04:00] [AdminServer] [NOTIFICATION] []
[oracle.osb.debug.uddi] [tid: [ACTIVE].ExecuteThread: '27' for queue:
'weblogic.kernel.Default (self-tuning)'] [userId: <WLS Kernel>] [ecid:
1063e612-47f5-4e9c-b9b1-7897053a07a7-0000d3fe,0] UDDIAutoImportHelper.
modifyAutoImportEntries - There are no services for which auto import
```

entries need to be modified

```
[2015-05-26T20:58:11.027-04:00] [AdminServer] [NOTIFICATION] [OSB-
394523] [oracle.osb.uddi.services.uddiconfiguration] [tid: pool-
19-thread-1] [userId: <anonymous>] [ecid: 1063e612-47f5-4e9c-
b9b1-7897053a07a7-00000004,0:16] [APP: Service Bus UDDI Manager]
AutoPublish: Auto Publish Task started
```

```
[2015-05-26T20:58:12.075-04:00] [AdminServer] [NOTIFICATION] [OSB-
390102] [oracle.osb.configfwk] [tid: [ACTIVE].ExecuteThread: '27' for
queue: 'weblogic.kernel.Default (self-tuning)'] [userId: weblogic]
[ecid: 1063e612-47f5-4e9c-b9b1-7897053a07a7-0000d3fe,0] Session
SessionScript1432668274847 was activated successfully
```

For a failed deployment, the output of errors is often provided directly on the screen. In this particular example, the deployment process was unable to locate the customization file called `customizeX.xml`:

```
Unexpected error: java.io.FileNotFoundException
Unexpected error:  java.io.FileNotFoundException
No stack trace available.
Problem invoking WLST - Traceback (innermost last):
  File "/home/oracle/code/osb_deploy_scripts/import.py", line 197, in
?
  File "/home/oracle/code/osb_deploy_scripts/import.py", line 108, in
importToALSBDomain
        at java.io.FileInputStream.open(Native Method)
        at java.io.FileInputStream.<init>(FileInputStream.java:146)
        at java.io.FileInputStream.<init>(FileInputStream.java:101)
        at sun.reflect.NativeConstructorAccessorImpl.
newInstance0(Native Method)
        at sun.reflect.NativeConstructorAccessorImpl.newInstance(Nativ
eConstructorAccessorImpl.java:57)
        at sun.reflect.DelegatingConstructorAccessorImpl.newInstance(D
elegatingConstructorAccessorImpl.java:45)
        at java.lang.reflect.Constructor.newInstance(Constructor.
java:526)
java.io.FileNotFoundException: java.io.FileNotFoundException:
customizeX.xml (No such file or directory)
```

Summary

Without an appropriate understanding of how the SOA Infrastructure and the underlying composites behave, it would be very difficult for us to know where to begin when troubleshooting a particular issue. Fortunately, the previous chapters covered a lot of ground in this regard and prepared you up to this point.

The approaches covered in this chapter are intended to provide you with more of a troubleshooting methodology instead of a typical approach of listing common errors and their resolutions. This includes:

- Understanding how and when to increase logger levels
- Understanding how to use logs and thread dumps to troubleshoot infrastructure problems
- Troubleshooting service wide infrastructure performance problems
- Leveraging SQL queries to obtain various composite durations to help identify composite instance performance bottlenecks
- Troubleshooting common instance issues
- Understanding the compilation and deployment process and how to address common problems

This chapter relied on the information you learned in the previous chapters, but hopefully, it introduced you to a different approach that will guide you in your troubleshooting efforts. There may be cases where you might have exhausted your knowledge and skills in troubleshooting particular errors, and you should remember that Oracle SOA Suite 12c is still a relatively new technology and it is not uncommon to run into bugs or product-related issues. Do not hesitate to contact Oracle Support for assistance.

10
Backup and Recovery

As an administrator, you have already recognized the importance of establishing well-defined backup and recovery procedures. It is easy to write at length on this topic alone, discussing various backup, restore, failover, migration, and disaster recovery strategies. Fortunately, we will focus on the most important areas in this chapter to simplify the process for you as best as we can. As long as you understand a few core concepts regarding the overall backup and recovery strategy for Oracle SOA Suite 12*c*, you can implement it in any number of ways.

Establishing a backup and restore strategy is important because it provides you the ability to restore your environment in the event of a critical infrastructure or hardware failure. For instance, if you experience a hard drive failure, the disks may have to be replaced and the software restored from backup. It also provides you the ability to restore your environment to a previously working snapshot in the event of a faulty patch, faulty code deployment, or faulty configuration. In some cases, these faulty updates are not undoable and thus a restore may be needed.

In this chapter, we will cover the following key areas:

- Understanding what needs to be backed up
- The recommended backup strategy
- Implementing the backup process
- Recovery strategies

There are really two types of backups you can perform — offline backups and online backups. **Offline backups** are taken when the entire environment is down. This is the preferred approach, as all tiers are backed up at the same point, ensuring that a full restore will be an exact point in the time snapshot. Unfortunately, it is usually difficult to find the downtime needed for a full offline backup, and **online backups** are more commonly implemented. They are taken while the system is running and require no downtime. Compared to offline backups, online backups are generally more involved in their initial setup, and certain additional factors need to be considered to ensure that a proper restore is performed.

The types of data that are typically backed up are as follows:

- Static files (for example, domain configuration files, software binaries, and patches)
- Runtime artifacts (for example, application deployments, instance data and metadata, messages in queuing systems, and transaction logs)

So when should you back up your static files? As long as they don't change; technically, a single valid backup is all that is required. Configuration changes or the application of patches tend to change the contents of these static files, hence prompting the need to create another backup. Runtime artifacts or dynamic data, such as continually updated instance data in the database, may need to be backed up regularly. There are cases where both online and offline backups may be valid for these types of data, and we will discuss them in more detail later on in this chapter.

In the unfortunate event that a recovery is needed, performing a complete restore can guarantee full restoration of your environment. However, this is time consuming and the appropriate downtime may not be afforded to do so. Thus, once you understand the different types of files that need to be backed up, you will know what needs to be restored. Installing a highly available infrastructure helps reduce the risk by ensuring the continued operation of your environment in the event of a software or hardware failure, simplifying the restoration process. This is discussed in detail in *Chapter 12, Clustering and High Availability*.

Understanding what needs to be backed up

Before describing how to back up your environment, it is important to understand what needs to be backed up first. We differentiate between static files, which are files that do not change frequently such as the software installation binaries, and dynamic data, otherwise referred to as runtime artifacts, which could include frequently updated data such as instance information and deployment metadata.

Static files

Static files and directories are those that do not change frequently. These files should be backed up when required, particularly when configuration changes, patching, or installations have been performed since the last backup. In most cases, static files can be backed up both online and offline.

Oracle system files

System files include the `oraInst.loc` and `beahomelist` files. These files point to the location of Oracle Inventory and WebLogic Server Home, respectively. This enables future patching or installations of other Oracle products to easily recognize where your software is installed, check for their existing versions, and update these inventories accordingly, if needed. In Oracle SOA Suite 12*c*, Oracle inventory resides in Oracle SOA Home by default.

The `beahomelist` file is typically located in the users' home directory and varies according to the operating system. The BEA Home list contains the location of your Oracle WebLogic Server installation (which is also installed under Oracle SOA Home).

The `oraInst.loc` configuration file contains the location of your Oracle inventory. Oracle inventory contains metadata of all the installed Oracle products on your server. It is updated when new Oracle products are installed on your server or the existing software is upgraded. An example of the contents of `oraInst.loc` is as follows:

```
inventory_loc=/u01/oracle/products/Oracle_SOA1/inventory
inst_group=oinstall
```

The locations of each of these files in a standard Linux installation are shown in the following table:

File	Description	Sample location
The BEA Home List	This points to the Oracle WebLogic Server installation directory and is typically created in the users' home directory.	`/home/oracle/bea/beahomelist`
Oracle Installation Location	This is a configuration file that points to the location of Oracle Inventory.	`/etc/oraInst.loc`
Oracle Inventory	The location is determined by `oraInst.loc`.	`/u01/oracle/products/Oracle_SOA1/inventory`

These files should be backed up after initial installation or after any patch update or upgrade. A standard filesystem backup is sufficient.

JDK

A JDK is typically installed outside of Oracle SOA Home. The location of your JDK can be shared between the servers in your cluster or it may be installed on each server separately.

Regardless of its location, your JDK should be backed up after new installations and/or a patch update or upgrade. Starting with Java 7, JRockit and Hotspot are merged into a single JVM to make a best breed of JVM. In the previous version of Java, you would have to select either the Sun JDK or JRockit JDK for installation—this is no longer the case with Java 7.

Here is an example of the location of a JDK installation outside your Oracle SOA Home:

```
/u01/oracle/products/jdk1.7.0_79
```

Oracle SOA Home

Oracle SOA Home contains numerous files, components, and shared components. This possibly includes the binaries and configuration files for Oracle WebLogic Server, Oracle SOA Suite, OSB, OEP, BPM Suite, BAM, and Oracle Common components.

For example, Oracle SOA Home, denoted as the `$ORACLE_HOME` environment variable, may be set to `/u01/oracle/products/Oracle_SOA1`. The backup commands later on in this chapter back up everything under `$ORACLE_HOME` and should be run after initial installation or after any patch update or upgrade. A standard filesystem backup is sufficient.

Runtime artifacts

The Oracle documentation refers to data that is dynamically updated and required for runtime operations as **runtime artifacts**. In essence, it is the data and/or configuration that is regularly accessed and/or updated during runtime. We will describe each of these areas in the later sections of this chapter.

Database

A database is configured during the installation to store the SOA Infrastructure (instance-specific data) and MDS (deployment metadata) data. Oracle SOA Suite 12*c*, or rather, Oracle Fusion Middleware 12*c* (12.1.3) is currently certified only on Oracle database versions 12.1.0.1+, 11.2.0.3+, and 11.1.0.7+. The Oracle database can be backed up via a tool such as Oracle **Recovery Manager** (**RMAN**).

The database maintains data related to in-flight instances, deployed SOA composites, and configuration, among other things. For example, if you deploy a composite today and perform a database restore for the day before, that deployed composite will not be available. Also note that some configurations, such as that of the Oracle BPEL Process Manager Engine, Oracle BPM Engine, Mediator, and Common Configuration, are stored in the database.

Configuration data is typically stored in the database, ensuring that each managed server in the cluster has a consistent view of this data.

The schemas that need to be backed up are listed in the following table. It is recommended to have nightly backups of the database for critical business applications:

Schema	Description
`<PREFIX>_ESS`	Enterprise Scheduler Service
`<PREFIX>_IAU` `<PREFIX>_IAU_VIEWER` `<PREFIX>_IAU_APPEND`	Audit Services
`<PREFIX>_MDS`	Metadata Services
`<PREFIX>_MFT`	Managed File Transfer
`<PREFIX>_ORABAM`	Business Activity Monitoring
`<PREFIX>_OPSS`	Oracle Platform Security Services
`<PREFIX>_SOAINFRA`	SOA Infrastructure
`<PREFIX>_STB`	Services Tools Bundle
`<PREFIX>_UMS`	User Messaging Service

JMS file stores

Persistent stores host information such as JMS queues and JMS topics, also referred to collectively as JMS destinations. Persistent stores can either be file-based or JDBC-enabled (that is, saved in the database). Most Oracle SOA Suite 12*c* clustered installations utilize file-based stores for performance purposes. File-based stores essentially provide persistence capabilities to Oracle WebLogic Server subsystems and services through the use of a built-in, high-performance storage solution.

Because these file-based persistent stores save JMS messages, durable subscriber information, and temporary messages sent to unavailable destinations using the Store-and-Forward features, it is not possible for us to take their consistent backups. Restoring these persistent stores may result in data inconsistency, even if they were backed up offline. These persistent stores often (and should) reside on redundant fault-tolerant storage that is accessible to all nodes of the Oracle SOA Suite 12*c* cluster. Alternatively, you may have already used JDBC-enabled stores for your JMS destinations so that they are maintained in, and thus backed up with, the database (meaning filesystem backups of these objects are not necessary).

> Backing up and restoring the JMS file-based persistent stores may result in data inconsistency. Instead, you can ensure the availability of the file store to all servers in your cluster.

The following table shows an example of the location of persistent stores required by Oracle SOA Suite 12*c* clusters. These stores are shared and accessible to all nodes of the clusters (in this example, a two-node cluster):

JMS file store name	Sample location	Shared
BPMJMSFileStore_auto_1	/share/soa_domain/soacluster/jms/BPMJMSFileStore_auto_1	Yes
BPMJMSFileStore_auto_2	/share/soa_domain/soacluster/jms/BPMJMSFileStore_auto_2	Yes
MFTJMSFileStore_auto_1	/share/soa_domain/soacluster/jms/MFTJMSFileStore_auto_1	Yes
MFTJMSFileStore_auto_2	/share/soa_domain/soacluster/jms/MFTJMSFileStore_auto_2	Yes
SOAJMSFileStore_auto_1	/soa_domain/soacluster/jms/SOAJMSFileStore_auto_1	Yes
SOAJMSFileStore_auto_2	/soa_domain/soacluster/jms/SOAJMSFileStore_auto_2	Yes
UMSJMSFileStore_auto_1	/share/soa_domain/soacluster/jms/UMSJMSFileStore_auto_1	Yes
UMSJMSFileStore_auto_2	/share/soa_domain/soacluster/jms/UMSJMSFileStore_auto_2	Yes

By virtue of the file stores being shared, they are accessible to all nodes in the cluster. The recommendation here is to implement one of the following backup strategies for JMS file-based persistent stores:

- Move the JMS modules to a JDBC-enabled persistent store. Database backups will ensure the consistency of the data in the event of a database restore, but restoring to older backups of the database may result in data inconsistency.

- Ensure that the file-based persistent stores reside in fully redundant shared storage accessible to all nodes of the cluster, and guarantee its availability. Backing up these stores is possible, but there are implications regarding message loss and message duplication should you choose to restore them.

Perhaps the only scenario where file stores can be backed up is in non-production environments, where data consistency is not critical. In this case, it is still recommended that you take an offline backup (that is, where all midtier nodes are shut down while the backup is performed). Restoring from this backup essentially performs a point-in-time recovery, where the file stores may contain older JMS messages that have already been consumed and processed. It may also result in lost messages. For example, this may include messages that may have been enqueued but not consumed before the backup. The only advantage of backing up your JMS file store is that it allows the administrator to always take a single, working, and consistent backup of the environment, but with the risk of data duplication and/or inconsistency as a result of restoring older file stores.

Transaction logs

Transaction logs store information about committed transactions that are coordinated by Oracle WebLogic Server that may not have been completed. The transaction logs, or **TLOGs**, provide Oracle WebLogic Server with a mechanism to recover from system crashes or network failures.

TLOGs can either be saved to WebLogic Server's **Default Store** or to a database via a JDBC store. TLOGs that are targeted to Default Store are file-based, and thus the backup behavior is similar to that of JMS file-based persistent stores. Oracle WebLogic Server 12*c*, however, allows transaction logs to be stored in a JDBC store, thus eliminating the need for filesystem backups. The following screenshot shows where to select the Transaction Log Store type:

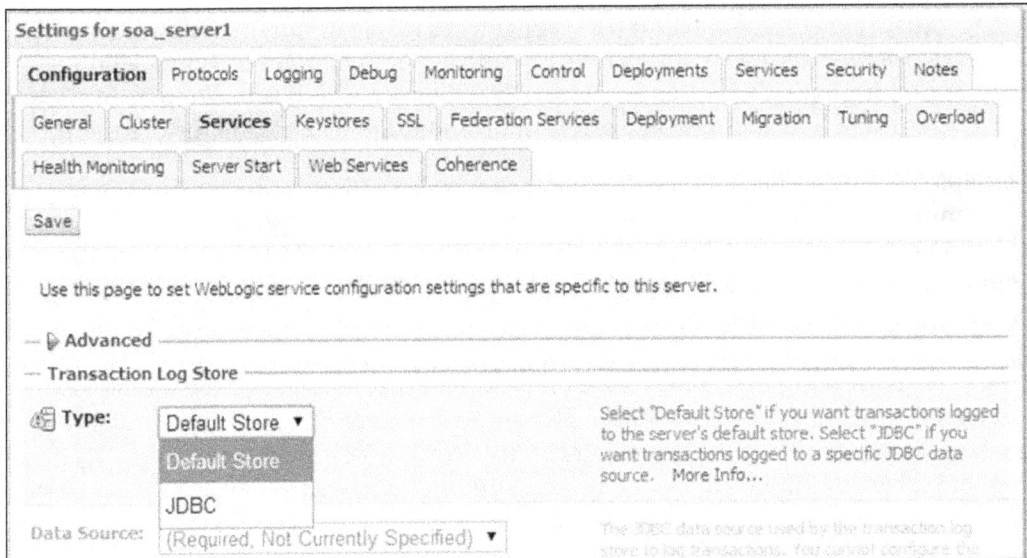

Figure 10.1: Selecting the Transaction Log Store type in the WebLogic Server Administration Console

In the event that the Default Store is selected, it is recommended to set it to a directory on highly available and shared storage. This is typically a requirement for multinode installations of Oracle SOA Suite 12*c* anyway. This can be configured by logging in to the Oracle WebLogic Server Administration Console, navigating to **Environment | Servers | soa_server1 | Configuration | Services**, and setting the value of **Directory**.

> Do not attempt to delete or restore TLOGs that are file-based. It may result in data inconsistency.

The recommendation, therefore, is to ensure that the transaction logs that are logged to Default Store reside in fully redundant shared storage that is accessible to all nodes of the cluster and guarantee its availability. Backing up the transaction logs is suggested, but there are implications regarding message loss and message duplication should you choose to restore them.

For transaction logs that are stored in the database, ensure that the appropriate database schema they are connected to is backed up regularly via RMAN.

The SOA domain

Typically, every Oracle SOA Suite 12*c* installation includes at least one domain extended with SOA extensions (for example, `soa_domain`), which hosts your administration and managed servers configuration. Though many of the files in your Domain Home are static in nature, several of them change periodically (for example, log files). By default, Domain Home is located under the Oracle SOA Suite installation directory (for example, `$ORACLE_HOME/user_projects/domains/soa_domain`), but it may reside elsewhere depending on what was specified during the domain creation. A typical SOA domain will fall within the 2 GB to 4 GB size range and will contain a multitude of file types that include the following:

- Startup scripts
- Libraries
- Domain configuration files
- Logs
- Deployed and extracted Java applications

The configuration files most relevant to your domain installation are listed in the following table. Backing up your domain is usually recommended if one or more of these files are updated:

Component	Configuration file location
Domain, JMS, BAM, B2B, Business rules, BPM, OWSM, and OPSS configuration	`$DOMAIN_HOME/config/*`
Oracle WebLogic Server Startup Scripts	`$DOMAIN_HOME/bin/*`
Oracle WebLogic Server Node Manager	`$DOMAIN_HOME/nodemanager/nodemanager.properties`
Oracle WebLogic Server	`$ORACLE_HOME/wlserver/common/bin/wlsifconfig.sh`
Oracle WebLogic Server	`$ORACLE_HOME/wlserver/common/bin/commEnv.sh`

In most cases, you do not need to back up managed server directories separately because `AdminServer` contains information about all the managed servers in its domain.

Managed servers do not require `AdminServer` to be up during normal operation. However, as an administrator, your view of the health and performance of the infrastructure may be restricted. Furthermore, it prevents you from making any changes to the domain's configuration if `AdminServer` is down.

A managed server maintains a local copy of the domain configuration. If you attempt to start a managed server while `AdminServer` is down, the managed server uses a local copy of the domain configuration and continues to periodically attempt to reconnect with `AdminServer`. Therefore, the managed server runs in what is called the **Managed Server Independence (MSI)** mode. When it connects successfully, the configuration state is synchronized.

It is, therefore, recommended that you take a full backup of your Domain Home periodically while your infrastructure, especially `AdminServer`, is offline. Technically, backing up Domain Home on the machine that runs `AdminServer` is sufficient, though it might make your life easier to back up the domain on the other servers in your cluster as well.

The recommended backup strategy

Generally speaking, your environment should be backed up on a regularly scheduled basis. These are standard operating procedures, and we will discuss them toward the end of this section. In addition to this, occasional one-off backups may be needed. By considering the proposed backup strategy outlined here, you should be protected for the majority of cases and will be able to perform effective recovery, if needed.

The following table is a summary of the actions described in this section, as well as when and what type of backup to perform:

Event	When	Backup schedule	Backup type
New installation	After installation	One-off	Offline
Upgrading	Before and/or after upgrading	One-off	Offline
Applying patches	Before and/or after patching	One-off	Offline
Configuration changes	Before and/or after changes	One-off	Offline
Architectural changes	Before and/or after changes	One-off	Offline
Code deployment	Only if needed	Never	Offline

After a new installation

Installing Oracle SOA Suite 12*c* involves creating a database; running the **Repository Creation Utility** (**RCU**) to create all the required database schemes; installing the binaries for Oracle WebLogic Server 12*c*, JDK, and Oracle SOA Suite 12*c*; followed by the creation of the SOA domain. In high-availability installations of two or more nodes, further configuration and setup is required.

It is, therefore, recommended that you perform a full offline backup of your environment after confirming the successful installation of your infrastructure. This includes taking a back up of the following:

- Oracle system files
- JDK
- Oracle SOA Home
- SOA domain
- Database (using a tool such as RMAN)

Before upgrading

Prior to upgrading from Oracle SOA Suite 12*c* (12.1.3) to a later patchset, you may decide on performing a back up of the environment for the purpose of rolling back in the event of an unforeseen upgrade problem.

In this case, it is recommended that you perform a full offline backup of the entire infrastructure, which includes:

- Oracle system files
- JDK
- Oracle SOA Home
- JMS file stores
- Transaction logs
- SOA domain
- Database (using a tool such as RMAN)

Before applying patches

The overwhelming majority of Oracle patches are downloaded from Oracle Support and come in the form of an **OPatch**. Many, but not all, of these patches provide some form of rollback mechanism. If the patch application is unsuccessful, it will not be installed. If the patch application is successful but does not resolve your particular problem, it can be rolled back (in other words, uninstalled).

These patches can be OPSS patches, JDK patches, OWSM patches, Oracle WebLogic Server patches, Oracle SOA Suite patches, Oracle BPM patches, OSB patches, BAM patches, or any type of patch related to one of the many underlying subcomponents. Even though most (but not all) patches can be rolled back, there are rare cases where patches can corrupt or produce undesirable results in your system. It is both our and Oracle's recommendation that you take a back up of your environment prior to applying a patch. However, by reviewing the readme of the patch and deciphering the type of change, it may not be necessary to perform a full backup, and a partial backup may only be needed.

If the patch is a JDK patch, simply perform an offline backup of the JDK.

If the patch is an Oracle SOA Suite 12*c* patch (including Oracle WebLogic Server), simply perform an offline backup of the following:

- Oracle SOA Home
- SOA domain
- Database (using a tool such as RMAN)

When in doubt, perform a full offline backup of the entire infrastructure, which includes backing up the following:

- Oracle system files
- JDK
- Oracle SOA Home
- JMS file stores
- Transaction logs
- SOA domain
- Database

Before configuration changes

There are many types of configuration changes that can be performed and an even more endless list of possible backup scenarios for each of the configuration changes. Some settings are stored in configuration files (for example, `config.xml`) and startup scripts (for example, `setSOADomainEnv.sh`), while other settings such as BPEL Process Manager configuration settings are stored in the database. When in doubt, perform a full offline backup prior to making any configuration change (though this may be excessive in most cases).

Configuration changes can usually be rolled back by simply undoing the configuration change itself, though there are rare scenarios where damaging repercussions can occur. For example, modifying the number of maximum connections in your connection pool typically involves zero risk. On the other hand, in certain scenarios where a second SOA server has never yet been started and conflicting JVM configuration is found across the cluster, irrecoverable startup issues may occur on that second SOA server.

We, therefore, recommend you to perform a back up, at minimum, of the following, prior to making configuration changes:

- SOA domain
- Database

Configuration changes that are committed to the database can usually be rolled back by undoing them or restoring the database itself. Configuration changes to any of the software installs (for example, files under `$ORACLE_HOME/soa`, `$JAVA_HOME`, and `$ORACLE_HOME/wlserver`) are usually undoable by simply restoring the configuration change to its original settings.

Before architectural changes

Examples of architectural changes include extending your domain to install additional products or converting your single-node installation to a cluster. Even though performing these activities should not be a problem, the administrator often has to deal with unforeseen setbacks. Some architectural changes are simple while others are more involved. Performing a full offline backup of the entire infrastructure is recommended in these cases:

- Oracle system files
- JDK
- Oracle SOA Home
- SOA domain

The database, JMS file stores, and transactions logs may not need to be backed up, as the impact on transactional data due to these changes is usually low.

After upgrade, patch, configuration, or architectural changes

After finishing an upgrade, applying one or more patches, or performing major configuration or architectural changes, you probably want to perform a full offline backup of your environment in order to maintain a snapshot of a working installation that you can recover in the future, if need be.

For that reason, performing a full offline backup of the entire infrastructure in the event of any of these actions is recommended. The components to be backed up are:

- Oracle system files
- JDK
- Oracle SOA Home
- JMS file stores
- Transaction logs
- SOA domain
- A database

Before or after a code deployment

It is often unnecessary to perform backups before or after a code deployment, unless major architectural changes or high-risk activities are involved. You should have a change control strategy defined for code deployments, wherein if a deployment fails or a code deployment is successful but needs to be rolled back, you have the ability to redeploy the prior version of the code. Code could include Java applications, SOA composites, DVMs, or even schemas and WSDLs.

Prior to a restore and to avoid any issues, it is recommended that you delete the contents under `$DOMAIN_HOME/servers/soa_server1/dc`, which contain the converted SOA source code downloaded from the database. All SOA composites and artifacts are stored in the MDS. In the event that no formal change control strategy is in place, reverting to a previous snapshot of the database will restore your SOA composites to their original version at the time of the database backup. Therefore, if you require it, you may perform a full database backup before or after SOA code is deployed to protect yourself.

Ongoing backups

As part of your operation, maintenance, and support activities, you will want to regularly schedule backups of your environment. Some backups may be nightly, while others may be weekly. If little to no changes take place in your midtiers, nightly delta filesystem backups of the Oracle SOA Home, JDK, and SOA domain may suffice (after a full offline backup is performed at least once). In this case, the only ongoing change that really does occur is the growth of log files.

As for the JMS file store and transaction logs, as mentioned earlier, these are not backed up. In the event of their irrecoverable failure, the best option will be to recreate them.

As a good practice, your databases should be backed up consistently. Daily and weekly full backups of databases are not uncommon, and the database administrator will need to be engaged in this activity.

> With the exception of logs, files within your SOA domain rarely change unless there is a code deployment or configuration change. If neither of these two activities are performed, delta filesystem backups are often sufficient.

As for ongoing backups, certain components such as the Oracle system files, JDK, and Oracle SOA Home do not require frequent backing up unless changes occur to them. Regardless of this, implementing some type of ongoing and regular backup is typically recommended. This table provides suggested guidelines for your backup schedule, but should be customized based on your needs and operational standards:

Component	Backup schedule	Backup type	Comments
Oracle system files	Monthly	Online	
JDK	Monthly	Online	
Oracle SOA Home	Monthly	Online	
JMS file stores	Never	-	Recreate if recovery is needed. Data loss or inconsistency may occur.
Transaction logs	Never	-	Recreate if recovery is needed.
SOA domain	Weekly	Online	Online backups are acceptable as long as no changes to the domain have been made.
Database	Daily	Online	

Implementing the backup process

Now that we have described the types of files to be backed up, the frequency of backup needed, and the locations of what needs to be backed up, you may use third-party tools or commands to perform your filesystem backups. The backup commands and instructions in this section are meant to serve as workable guidelines to cover all areas requiring backup and are general in nature. They assume a Linux-based operating system with `gtar` installed, but they may be substituted with alternative file manipulation commands as needed. We recommend that you dedicate a backup mount point with ample storage and timestamp each backup file with the date and time in the file name. Many backup solutions that can be leveraged to automate and simplify the administration of the entire backup process are available on the market.

Oracle system files

The Oracle system files are comprised of server specific files under the `/etc` system directory as well as `beahomelist`.

1. Set up your environment if it is not already set up using the following commands. This may vary depending on your installation:

    ```
    export BACKUP_DIR=/backup

    export TIME=`date "+%Y%m%d_%k%M"`
    ```

2. Execute the following commands to take a backup of the Oracle system files under `/etc` and `/home/oracle/bea`:

    ```
    gtar -czvf $BACKUP_DIR/etcora.${TIME}.tgz /etc/oraInst.loc /etc/
    oratab

    gtar -czvf $BACKUP_DIR/beahomelist.${TIME}.tgz /home/oracle/bea
    ```

JDK

Back up the JDK as per the following instructions and modify the directory locations accordingly:

1. Set up your environment if it is not already set up. This may vary depending on your installation:

    ```
    export BACKUP_DIR=/backup

    export JAVA_HOME=/u01/oracle/products/jdk1.7.0_55

    export TIME=`date "+%Y%m%d_%k%M"`
    ```

2. Execute the following command to take a backup of the JDK:

```
gtar -czvf $BACKUP_DIR/jdk.${TIME}.tgz $JAVA_HOME
```

Oracle SOA Home

Oracle SOA Home consists of several installed components such as WebLogic Server, SOA Suite, OSB, coherence, shared libraries and utilities, and more. Back up the JDK as per the following instructions:

1. Set up your environment if it is not already set up. This may vary depending on your installation:

```
export BACKUP_DIR=/backup
export ORACLE_HOME=/u01/oracle/products/Oracle_SOA1
export TIME=`date "+%Y%m%d_%k%M"`
```

2. Execute the following command to take a backup of the files:

```
gtar -czvf $BACKUP_DIR/oraclehome.${TIME}.tgz $ORACLE_HOME
```

Domain Home

The Domain Home is sometimes created under the $ORACLE_HOME/user_projects/ domains directory, but it is not a requirement and often is different in clustered installations. It is only necessary to take a back up of the domain on which AdminServer is running, but you may also opt to take a back up of the domain on all other nodes of the cluster for ease of restoration in future using the following instructions:

1. Set up your environment if it is not already set up. This may vary depending on your installation:

```
export BACKUP_DIR=/backup
export DOMAIN_NAME=soa_domain
export DOMAIN_HOME=/u01/oracle/products/Oracle_SOA1/user_projects/
domains/${DOMAIN_NAME}
export TIME=`date "+%Y%m%d_%k%M"`
```

2. Execute the following command to take a backup of the files:

```
gtar -czvf $BACKUP_DIR/domain.${TIME}.tgz $DOMAIN_HOME
```

Database

Contact your DBA and use a backup utility such as RMAN to perform nightly hot backups.

Another crude way to take a backup of your database is to use Oracle Data Pump utility commands, such as `expdp`, that can be used to export the database schemas and the `impdp` command that is used to import the dump file to the database. Because these are the low-level database methods, this approach is more suitable when performing an initial data migration to a fresh installation or the cloning of an environment that does not contain any business data yet.

Recovery strategies

The purpose of recovering your environment is to restore it due to a software failure (such as a faulty patch or misconfiguration), hardware failure (such as an internal hard disk failure), or due to a need to perform a point-in-time recovery (to undo configuration or architectural changes that have proven defective or problematic).

Multiple factors should be considered before recovering an environment. It depends on which component failed and what point in time you want to recover it. Additional factors, such as ensuring consistency among components, is equally important. Full restores of the entire midtier and database to the same point in time are perhaps the simplest and least risky of all approaches, but are time consuming in nature. Furthermore, when a simple faulty configuration change needs to be rolled back, do you really need to restore the entire environment or just restore that particular component?

The installation of an Oracle SOA Suite 12*c* environment relies on interdependent components that contain configuration information, applications (including Java, composite, and Service Bus), and data that must be kept in synchronization. As a consequence, both backing up and restoring an Oracle SOA Suite 12*c* installation requires more thought than merely unzipping the backup files.

By now, you have a good understanding of how Oracle SOA Suite 12*c* functions, which files and components it requires and relies on, and what area to perhaps recover in the event of a failure. You also understand the implications of restoring different components separately.

All components, with the exception of the database, are backed up using standard file system commands or tools. To recover your Oracle SOA Suite 12*c* environment, simply restore the file or files of the component that needs to be restored. For example, any combination of the following may need to be restored depending on the type of failure:

- **Domain**: This can be used, for example, in the event of a severe configuration failure of the domain in which it is unable to start.

- **Oracle SOA Home**: This can be used, for example, to restore the entire infrastructure (or subset of it) to a previous release after a patch has been applied.

- **JDK**: This can be used, for example, if you want to revert to a previous version of your JDK.

- **Oracle system files**: This can be used, for example, in the event of a bad software installation and you wish to restore the Oracle Inventory to its original state. Many Oracle patches include their own rollback mechanism. Refer to their README files for rollback instructions in order to avoid a lengthy restore process.

In almost all cases, your Oracle SOA Suite 12*c* environment must be offline to recover. Though this is possible, it is dangerous to try to recover Oracle SOA Suite, Oracle WebLogic Server, the JDK, or any other component while the infrastructure is running.

There are implications to recovering JMS data to a previous point in time. As discussed earlier, we generally do not recommend the backing up (or restoring) of the JMS file stores unless you have a full understanding of the implications of such an activity as it can result in duplicate or lost messages. In many cases, it is probably better to recreate the persistent stores in the event that they are accidentally deleted or are in need of recovery.

Since the transaction log is accessible to all nodes of your cluster, in the event of a server failure, the other machines should be able to process the transactions. Even in the unlikely event of a full environment crash, the Transaction Recovery Service gracefully handles transaction recovery once the servers are brought up.

Furthermore, we recommend that you clear the following temporary and state-based directories after a restore, but prior to starting the managed servers, as their contents are dynamically generated/loaded:

- `$DOMAIN_HOME/servers/*/cache/*`
- `$DOMAIN_HOME/servers/*/data/*`
- `$DOMAIN_HOME/servers/*/dc/*`
- `$DOMAIN_HOME/servers/*/tmp/*`

Summary

Backing up and restoring an environment should be relatively simple. After all, software is merely a bunch of files scattered across various filesystems. However, the two challenges that Oracle SOA Suite 12*c* administrators face when the need to restore arises are as follows:

- To identify what exactly needs to be recovered
- At what state or point in time you should recover them

In this chapter, we described all the various components that need to be backed up in an Oracle SOA Suite 12*c* environment, then followed up with detailing how to actually perform the backup. Specifically, we covered the following:

- The various static files in an Oracle SOA Suite 12*c* installation such as Oracle system files, the JDK, and the Oracle SOA Home
- Runtime artifacts that include the database and SOA domain
- The implications of backing up and restoring JMS file stores and transaction logs
- A backup strategy; focusing on what needs to be backed up after installations, upgrades, patches, and configuration changes; as well as a recommended regular backup schedule
- The backup commands for Linux-based installations
- Key recovery strategies and considerations

At this point, you should be fully capable of backing up your environment with a thorough enough understanding of when to restore individual components as needed.

11
Introducing Oracle Enterprise Scheduler

Concurrent or scheduled processes are programs that run in the background. Oracle **Enterprise Scheduler Service (ESS)** provides us the ability to manage the complete lifecycle of a scheduled process, including development, distribution, scheduling, and monitoring. ESS has been around since 2011, supporting applications such as Oracle Fusion Applications, and has finally been formally bundled with the 12*c* release of Oracle SOA Suite. It is now called **Oracle Enterprise Scheduler**, although the short name ESS still sticks.

Enterprise applications require the ability to respond to many real-time transactions requested by online users or web services. They also require the ability to offload larger transactions in order to run at a future time or automate the running of application maintenance work based on a defined schedule. ESS provides the ability to run different job types according to a preconfigured schedule, including Java, PL/SQL, binary scripts, web services, and EJBs distributed across the nodes in an Oracle WebLogic Server cluster. ESS runs these jobs securely with high availability and scalability and provides monitoring and management through Oracle Enterprise Manager Fusion Middleware Control.

In a nutshell, ESS does exactly what it is named after, the scheduling of jobs. These jobs can perform a variety of activities ranging from triggering web services, custom scripts, and packaged code to managing the activation and deactivation of composites and scheduling fault management. For instance, an ESS job can control inbound adapters, wherein polling services could be configured to consume messages on predefined schedules. Furthermore, notifications of faulted instances and subsequent recovery of these faults can also be scheduled through ESS jobs. ESS is not just an administrative module, but a first-class component of Oracle SOA Suite 12*c*, wherein jobs can also be called from within a BPEL process. Jobs and schedules can be defined from client applications, through a Java API, or through the Fusion Middleware Control user interface.

Additionally, ESS also exposes a web service through which (predefined) jobs can be scheduled. With ESS, jobs can be scheduled, dependencies between jobs can be declared, and services can be turned on and off according to a specific schedule.

This chapter, however, concentrates on introducing ESS to SOA Suite 12*c* administrators and covers core areas of administration, namely the following:

- Discovering the ESS Administration Console
- Understanding basic ESS terminology
- Defining jobs, schedules, job sets, incompatibilities, and dependencies in ESS
- Monitoring job requests
- Setting up an ESS purge policy
- Tuning and troubleshooting ESS
- Using ESS WLST commands

Discovering the ESS consoles

In order to explore the core administrative functions offered by ESS in Oracle SOA Suite 12c, the base domain needs to be extended with **ESS managed server** and **EM Plugin for ESS**. Note that the ESS components can be targeted to an existing managed server or a separate and dedicated ESS managed server. The EM plugin for ESS is, by default, targeted to the Administration Server. Once the domain is created and the server where the ESS extensions are targeted is started, scheduling components can be accessed from the Oracle Enterprise Manager Fusion Middleware Control console. The following screenshot displays the **scheduling services** components of ESS:

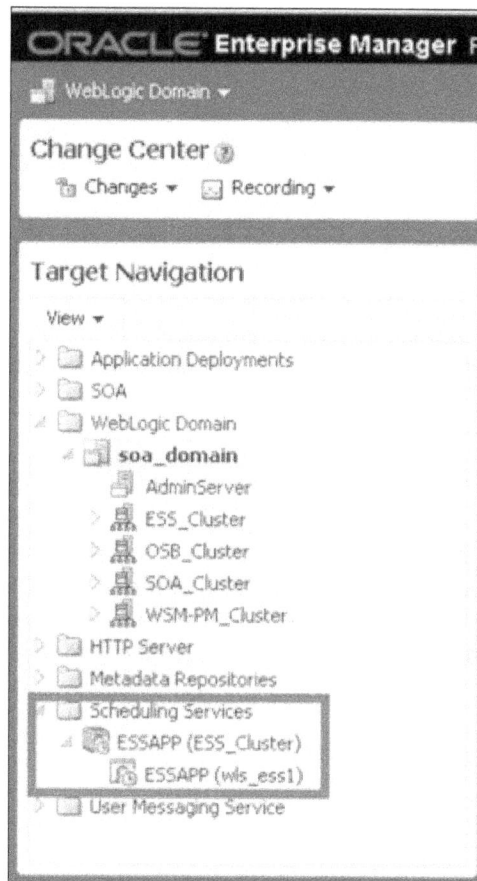

Figure 11.1: Screenshot of the Scheduling Services components with ESSAPP

Alternatively, at any point in time, administrators can use the ESS health check console at `http://<host>:<port>/ess` to submit an internal job that provides the current status of all ESS servers in the cluster, as shown in the following screenshot:

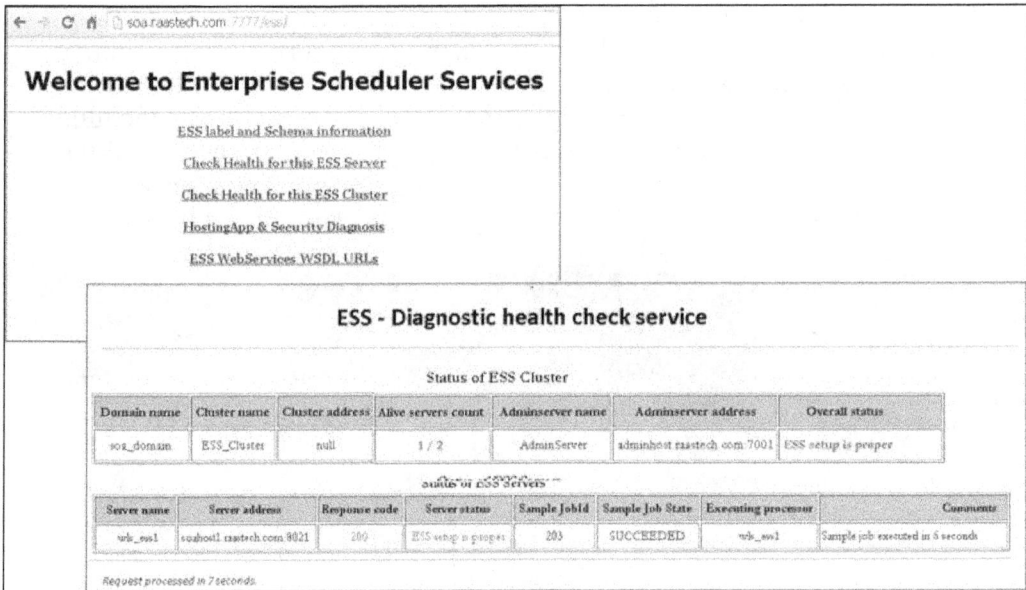

Figure 11.2: The ESS health check console and server status

Understanding ESS terminology

Familiarizing yourself with the terminology of a relatively new technology component is not only necessary in order to understand the remaining sections of this chapter, but essential to fulfill your responsibilities as an administrator. Let's begin by understanding a simple component diagram, as shown in the following figure, followed by a brief description of each of the components.

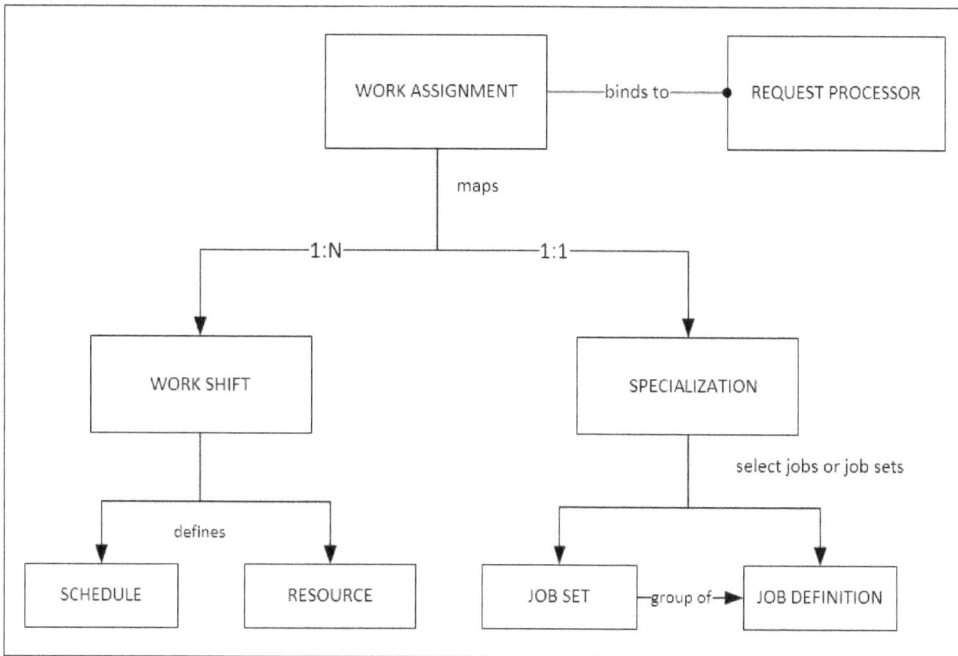

Figure 11.3: The component diagram of Enterprise Scheduling Services

Job type

A **job type** is a basic predefined type that indicates what a job would comprise, such as Java or EJB code, PL/SQL, a command line, or web service.

Job definition

A **job definition** is the metadata associated with a job, such as parameter values specific to the request being executed.

Job

A **job** is essentially the smallest unit of work executed by the Scheduler Service engine; it is defined by the associated **job type**.

Job request

A **job request** is simply the execution of a job definition on a schedule. Every request remains in a **WAITING** state in the ESS repository.

Job set

A **job set** is a collection of jobs that can either be configured to run concurrently or in a sequence.

Schedule

A **schedule** is a predefined time or recurrence for a period of time. Schedules are defined independent of **jobs** and are used to define when to execute a job request, work assignment, work shift, or purge policy. A **schedule** can be associated with one or many **job definitions** to describe when the jobs should be executed. A recurring schedule has a frequency that describes how the moments in time are distributed over time. A recurring schedule can have a start time and an end time to specify the period during which the recurrence should take place.

Work shift

A **work shift** defines resources such as threads and throttling that are to be allocated and the duration for which these resources will be available for job requests.

Specialization

A **specialization** defines the criteria to select job requests based on parameters such as the user, product, request category, job, or job set.

Work assignment

A **work assignment** maps a set of **work shifts** to jobs that are selected through a **specialization** criterion.

Request processor

A **work assignment** is bound to a **request processor** that provides threads to job requests.

Request dispatcher

A **request dispatcher** polls for job requests. For example, the request dispatcher polls the ESS repository for requests that are ready to run, setting their state to **READY**. The request dispatcher can be enabled or disabled, and the polling interval is configurable.

Purge policy

A **purge policy** defines when job requests should be deleted. This is primarily for the purpose of controlling the growth of data associated with each job request instance.

Incompatibility

The **incompatibility** definition specifies which jobs should not be running at the same time.

Starting and stopping ESS

The ESSAPP application module is deployed to the ESS managed server, allowing you to control the starting/stopping of job scheduling and processing. The application module also provides an interface to view and edit job definitions, search for job requests, set up purge polices, and so on. Oracle Enterprise Manager Fusion Middleware Control can be used to conveniently start/stop an ESS instance, as depicted in the following screenshot via the Start Up and Shut Down buttons:

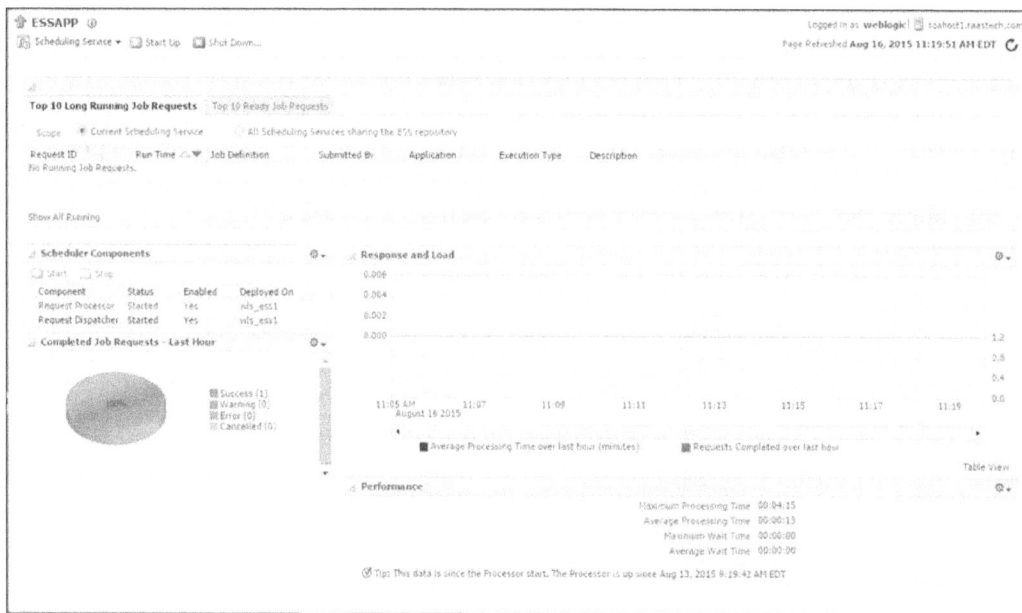

Figure 11.4: The Enterprise Scheduling Services dashboard

To start/stop an ESS instance in the ESSAPP application:

1. Log in to Oracle Enterprise Manager Fusion Middleware Control.

2. Navigate to **Scheduling Services | ESSAPP | [PREFIX]_ESS | Scheduling Service**, and then click on **Job Metadata | Incompatibilities**.

3. In the directory tree, expand **Scheduling Services** and click on **ESSAPP**.

4. The ESSAPP dashboard provides the **Start Up** and **Shut Down** options using green and red icons, respectively.

Scheduling jobs

Let's begin to understand the core concepts and usage of ESS functions through a series of real-life examples. For an Oracle SOA Suite 12*c* environment to be performant, the dehydration data store needs to be optimized by ensuring that it is cleaned up periodically. Thus, imagine that as an Oracle SOA Suite 12*c* administrator you want to create a schedule to perform a very important administration activity: purging completed instances.

Conceptualize the illustration depicted in the following figure. Here, we have a simple composite that invokes the **delete_instances_auto** procedure in the **SOA** package under the **soa_infra** schema. This package expects a set of parameters that determine the purging behavior, such as minimum and maximum date ranges for instances to be deleted, their states, and retention period, to name a few. The composite exposes a one-way service endpoint that accepts these purging parameters as arguments, which would allow the auto purge package to be executed as a service:

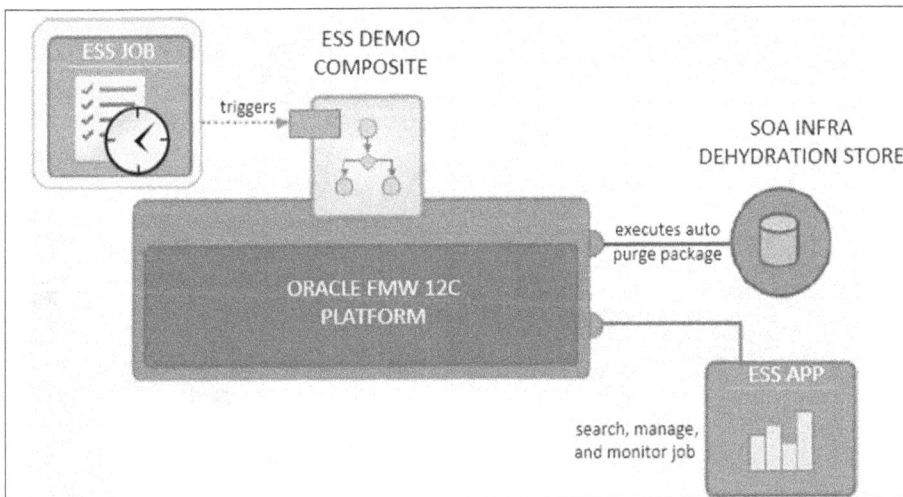

Figure 11.5: Job scheduling using Oracle Enterprise Service

However, instead of invoking the composite as a service, we can use ESS to create a schedule that periodically executes the purge. Scheduling jobs in ESS is based on three basic components:

- Job definitions
- Schedules
- Job requests

Creating Job Definitions

The following instructions will guide you through the steps required to create a **job definition** using the ESSAPP module through Oracle Enterprise Manager Fusion Middleware Control:

1. Log in to Oracle Enterprise Manager Fusion Middleware Control.

2. Navigate to **Scheduling Services | ESSAPP | ESSAPP | Scheduling Service Group** and then click on **Job Metadata | Job Definitions**.

3. If there are existing job definitions created on the server, they will be listed under the **Results** pane as shown:

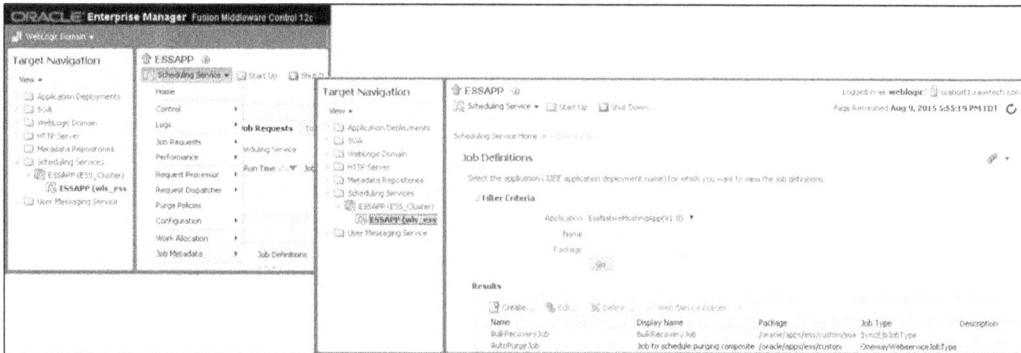

Figure 11.6: Creating Job Definitions in ESS

4. Click on the **Create** icon to create a new **Job Definition**.

5. A **Create Job Definition** dialog will prompt you to specify the metadata in order to create a new job definition. Currently, only the following **Job Types** are supported in Oracle SOA Suite 12*c*:

  ° **JavaJobType**

  ° **PlsqlJobType**

  ° **ProcessJobType**

      ◦   **SyncEjbJobType**

      ◦   **AsyncEjbJobType**

      ◦   **SyncWebserviceJobType**

      ◦   **AyncWebserviceJobType**

      ◦   **OnewayWebserviceJobType**

6. In order to create a new job definition, a unique name and display name have to be mandatorily entered. This is how the job definition will be listed in the ESS console. Optionally, you can also enter a brief description and place it into a self-defined package.

7. From the **Job Type** drop-down list, select **OnewayWebserviceJobType** (refer to *Figure 11.7*).

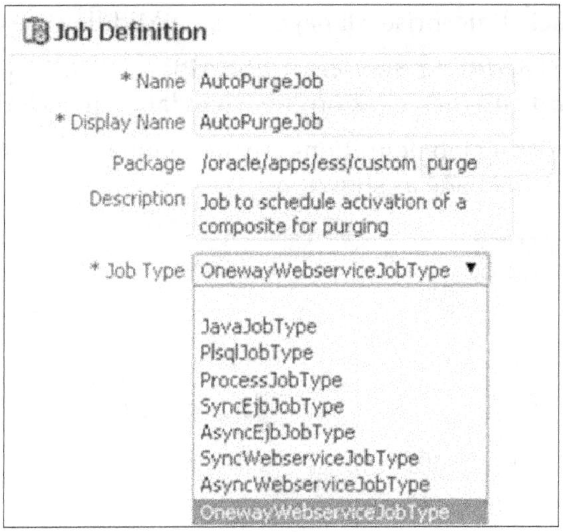

Figure 11.7: Selecting Job Types when creating a Job Definition

8. Enter the endpoint of the composite WSDL and select the **Web Service Type** as **SOA** from the drop-down menu.

9. Clicking on the **Go** button will allow the wizard to resolve the web service endpoint, provide a dynamic interface to select the operations defined in the web service, and enter an XML payload as shown in *Figure 11.8*.

10. Once these details have been entered, click on **OK** to save the job definition.

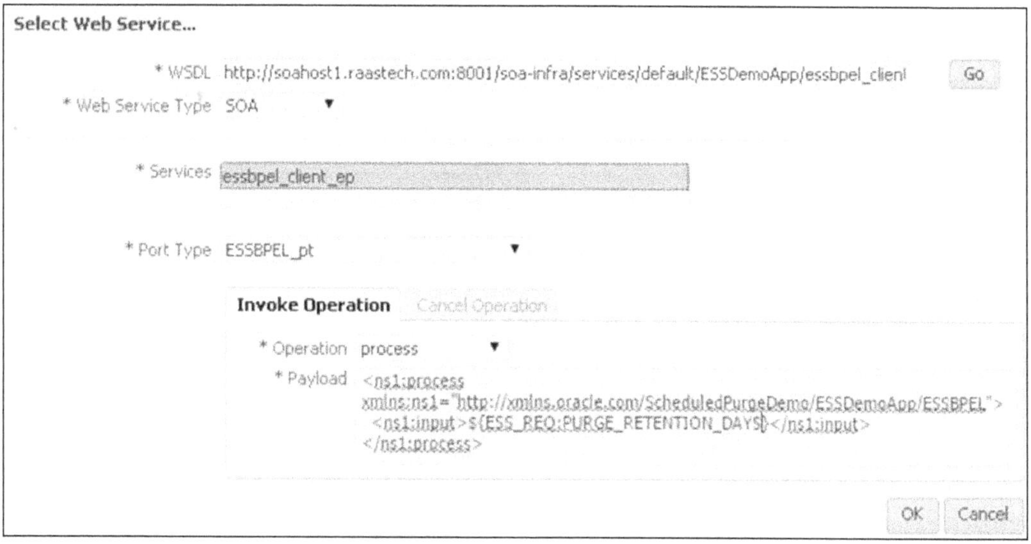

Figure 11.8: Invoking a one-way synchronous web service job in ESS

This newly created job definition will now appear under the **Results** tab of the **Job Definitions** dashboard and can be used to submit a scheduled job.

Parameterizing Job Definitions

A job definition is essentially a reusable component. It can potentially be used across multiple job requests, as you will learn in the Submitting Job Requests section later in this chapter.

Any input parameters in a job definition payload can be parameterized using the ESS_REQ token, which is used to access request arguments. In the previous example, let's assume that the one-way web service requires the number of days to retain composite instances to be passed as an integer. In the argument, this can be tokenized as ${ESS_REQ:PURGE_RETENTION_DAYS}.

The value for this token can either be stored statically in the job definition or passed dynamically when this job definition is referred. Edit the job definition and click on the ✛ icon in the **Application Defined Properties** panel. In the pop-up window, create a property with the same name as defined in the payload argument, PURGE_RETENTION_DAYS. Then, choose its **Type** as **Integer** and enter an **Initial Value** of **7**, as depicted in the following screenshot:

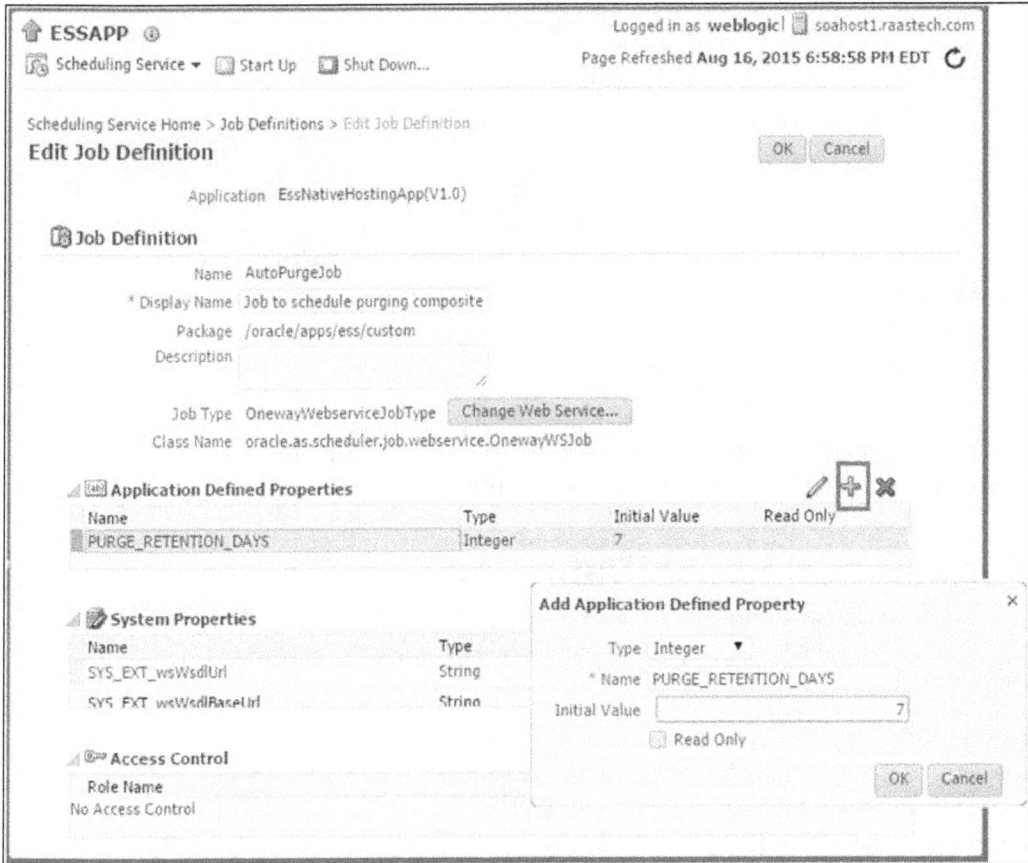

Figure 11.9: Configuring application-defined properties for a Job Request

Creating Schedules

The next step after creating a job definition is to define a job schedule. A **Schedule** describes when and how often a job is run. It allows you to define a precise point in time as well as intervals with predefined start/end points. A schedule can be associated with one or many **Job Definitions** to describe when those jobs should be executed.

To create a schedule, login to Oracle Enterprise Manager Fusion Middleware Control and select **Scheduling Services | ESSAPP**. Then, from the **Scheduling Service** drop-down list at the top of the page, select **Job Requests | Define Schedules**, as shown in the following screenshot:

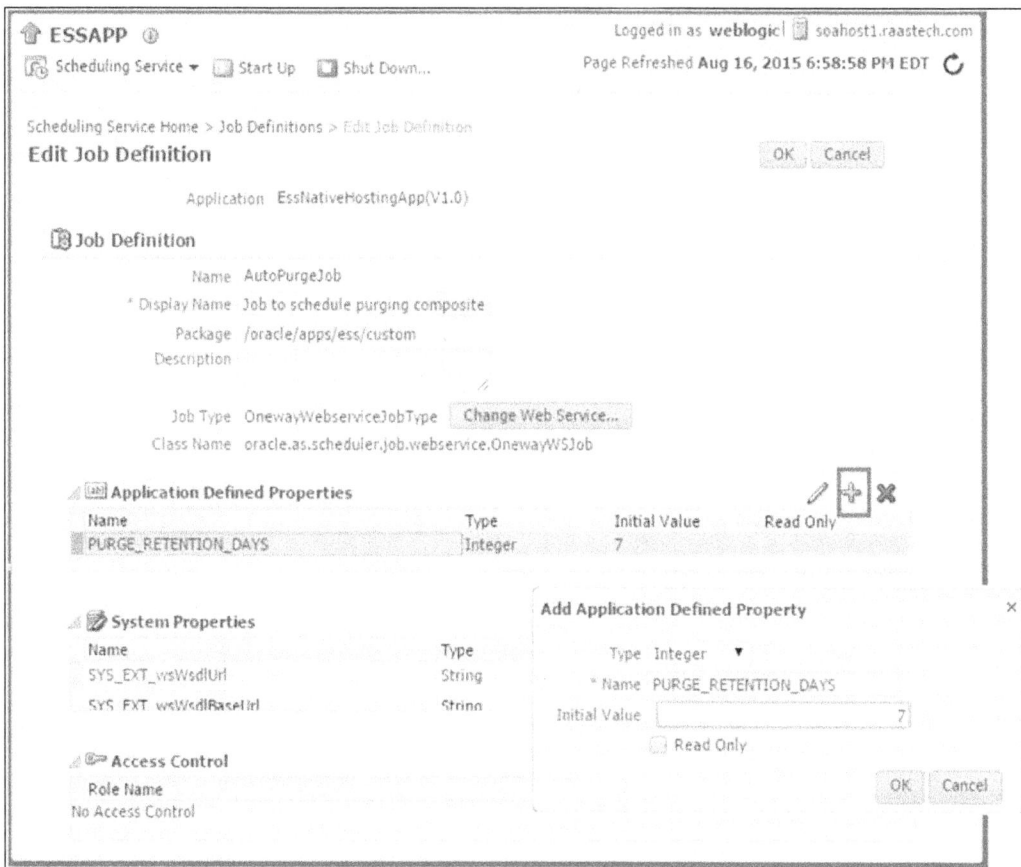

Figure 11.10: Defining a schedule in ESS

Click on the **Create** button on the landing page to create a new schedule. A
schedule can be created by specifying some metadata including a name, display
name, description, package name, start and end times, and most importantly, a
frequency, as depicted in *Figure 11.11*. A frequency determines how often a schedule
is executed; its periodicity can range from daily, hourly, monthly, and daily to just
once. The frequency can also be selected as **Custom**, wherein multiple start times
can be defined. Click on **OK** to save this schedule. A wide range of sophisticated
recurrence schedules can be created through either the Java API exposed by ESS
or through JDeveloper. These options cannot be set through the Oracle Enterprise
Manager Fusion Middleware Control console in the current version (12.1.3).

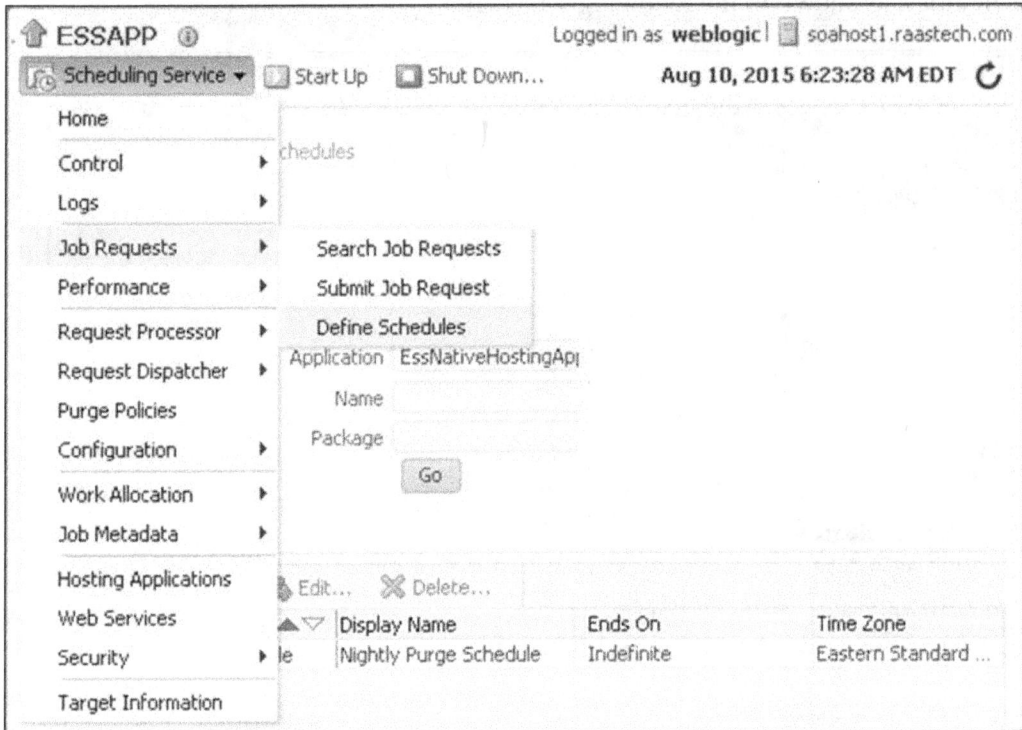

Figure 11.11: Creating a schedule

Once a schedule is created, click **OK** to save it.

With the introduction of ESS as a first-class component of Oracle SOA Suite 12*c*, schedules are widely used in a number of other features in the platform, a few of the more important ones being:

- Auto purge:
  - Oracle SOA Suite 12*c* implicitly uses ESS as a mechanism to set an auto purge job. This can be defined by navigating to **SOA | soa_infra | SOA Infrastructure | SOA Administration | Auto Purge** on Oracle Enterprise Manager Fusion Middleware Control. *Chapter 8, Managing the Database*, discusses this in more detail.

- Error notification rules:
  - Another feature introduced in 12*c* that uses schedules is the Error Notification Rules. Error notification rules can be configured to trigger alerts when specific fault criteria are met.

- Activating and deactivating Inbound Adapter Endpoints
- Bulk Fault Recover or Error Hospital

Submitting Job Requests

Once a Job Definition and a Job Schedule are defined, submitting a job request is straightforward. It can be done by navigating to **Scheduling Services | ESSAPP | Scheduling Service | Job Requests | Submit Job Request**, as shown:

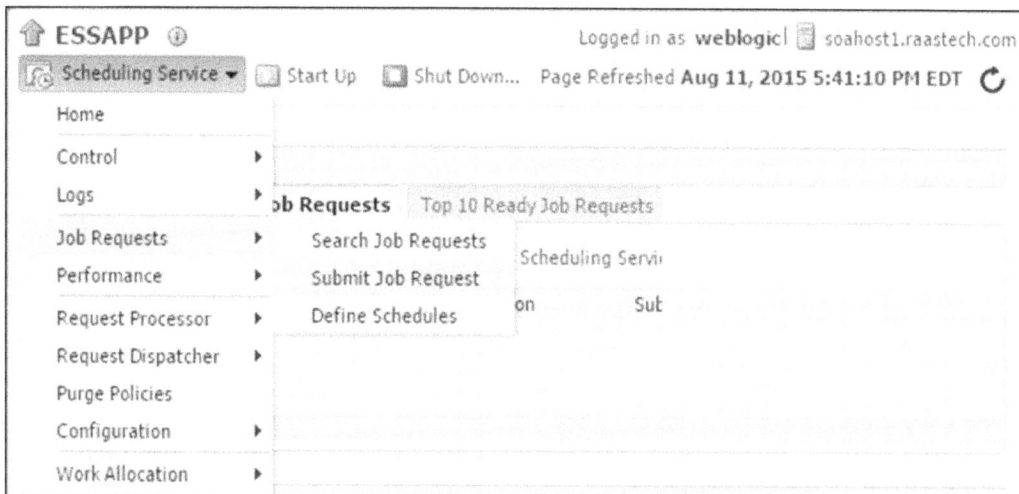

Figure 11.12: Navigating to the Submit Job Request page of ESS

In the next landing page, you can submit an ad hoc job by selecting a previously defined job definition and a schedule. Alternatively, a schedule can also be created from here and associated with the job request.

If a job definition was created with **Application Defined Properties** that were parameterized in the XML input, their values can be dynamically passed while submitting the Job Request. *Figure 11.13* shows an example of how to create a Job Request:

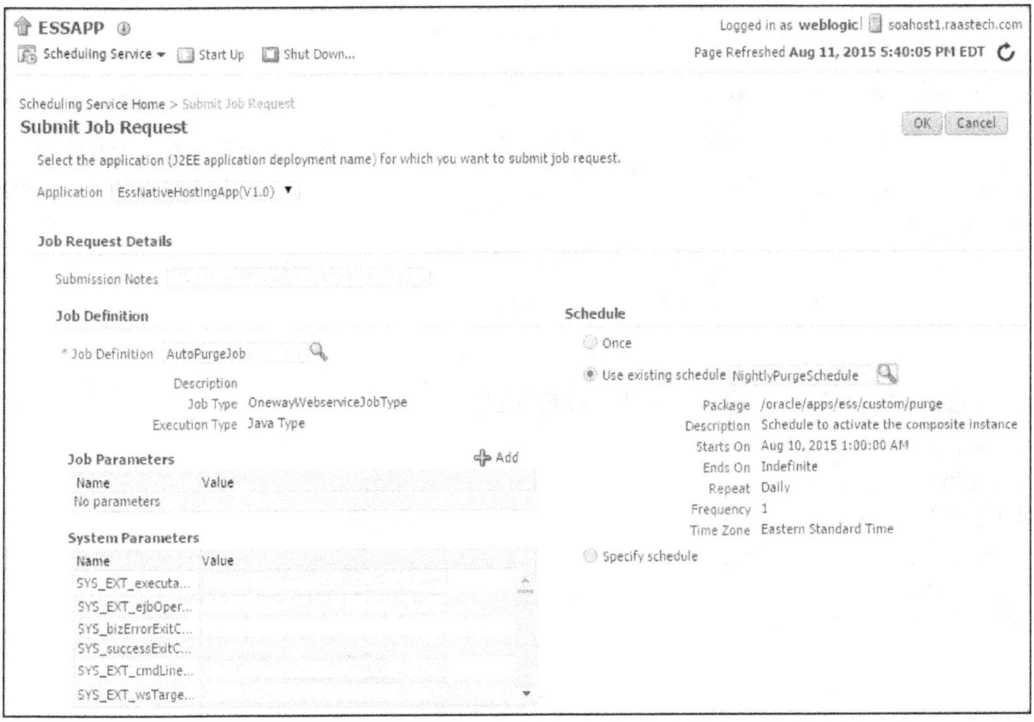

Figure 11.13: Example configuration form for an ESS Job Request

Monitoring Job Requests

Once job requests are submitted, the ESSAPP module deployed to Oracle Enterprise Manager Fusion Middleware Control provides the capability to perform simple and advanced searches on them. Navigate to **Scheduling Services | ESSAPP** and then, from the **Scheduling Service** drop-down menu, click on **Job Requests | Search Job Requests** to open the **Request Search** page. This dashboard provides the ability to search on a range of filters. Selecting the **All Scheduling Services sharing the ESS repository** radio button lets you look at all the current and past instances of job requests, as shown in *Figure 11.14*. For example, the following can be performed:

- You can conduct a simple search that returns a list of job request details, including the job request ID, the executing application, the job request status, and so on

- You can conduct an advanced search that returns the same information as the simple search, plus the date and time of execution, the runtime or wait time of the job request, the number of retries, and any error type that may have occurred during execution

Request ID △▽	Parent ID	Status	Scheduled Time	Processing Start Time	Run Time	Application	Job Definition	Submitted By
312	311	Wait	8/12/15 1:00:00 AM EDT			EssNativeHost...	AutoPurgeJob	weblogic
311	n/a	Wait	n/a	n/a	n/a	EssNativeHost...	AutoPurgeJob	weblogic
310	309	Wait	8/12/15 1:00:00 AM EDT			EssNativeHost...	AutoPurgeJob	weblogic
307	303	Error	8/10/15 7:17:12 PM EDT	8/11/15 4:26:45 PM	00:00:01.840	EssNativeHost...	AutoPurgeJob	weblogic
306	301	Succeeded	8/8/15 7:27:16 PM EDT	8/8/15 7:27:17 PM	00:00:00.386	EssNativeHost...	BulkRecoveryJob	weblogic
305	301	Succeeded	8/8/15 7:24:00 PM EDT	8/8/15 7:24:01 PM	00:03:14.624	EssNativeHost...	BulkRecoveryJob	weblogic
203	n/a	Succeeded	8/4/15 6:53:05 AM EDT	8/4/15 6:53:11 AM	00:00:00.116	ESSAPP	EssHealthcheckJo...	weblogic
1	n/a	Succeeded	6/27/15 10:23:00 PM EDT	6/27/15 10:23:12 F	00:00:01.287	ESSAPP	EssHealthcheckJo...	weblogic

Figure 11.14: Searching and monitoring completed and in-progress Job Requests

Clicking on a completed job **Request ID** will drill down to the details of the execution status. The **Execution Trail** status bar provides a bar chart to show the progress of the job request statuses over a timeline (refer to *Figure 11.15*). As the submitted job in this example invoked a one-way composite, its flow trace can also be viewed from this page by navigating to **Action | SOA Composite Flow trace**.

At the bottom of the Request Detail page is the **Log and Output** job output panel. Expand this panel to see the XML input of the web service response:

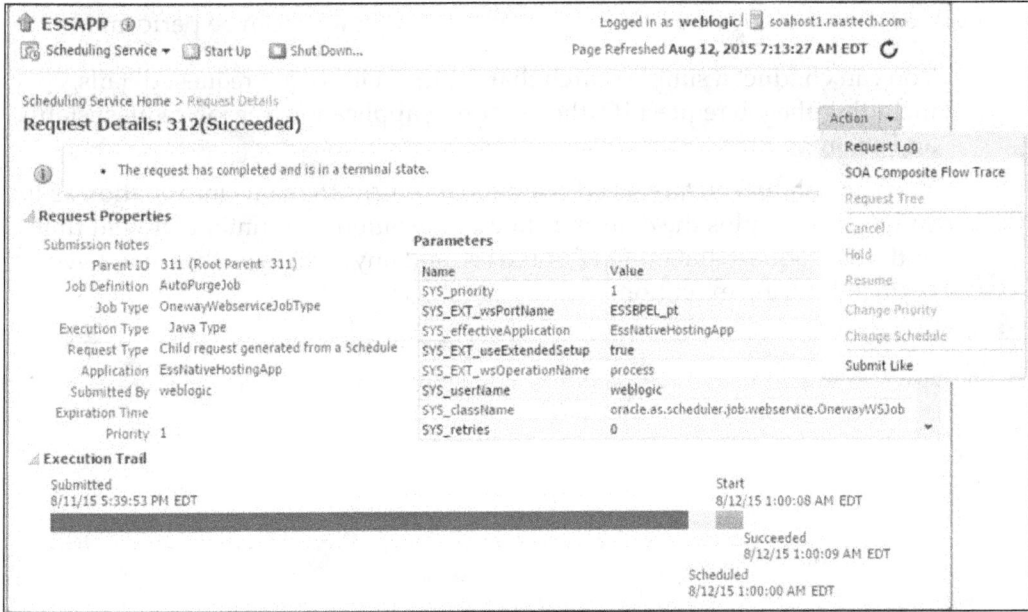

Figure 11.15: An Execution Trail of a completed Job Request

Altering Job Requests

It may often be necessary to alter a submitted job when it is in a **Wait** state, waiting to be executed at the defined schedule. The **Action** button, as shown in the previous screenshot, provides options via a drop-down menu to **Cancel**, **Hold**, and **Resume** a Job Request, along with changing its priority and schedule.

Incompatibility

An Oracle SOA Suite 12c platform is most likely shared by multiple tenants that may have deployed many composites, each of which may have different scheduling requirements. As an administrator managing this infrastructure, you may start to encounter race conditions between different ESS job requests, slow response times, and possibly data corruption when these requests run concurrently. For instance, you may accidently submit the same job request (based on the same job definition and schedule) twice, or submit different requests using the same schedule. This should be avoided, as it can potentially choke the platform of resources. Ideal scenarios to run job requests are as follows:

- Only a single instance of a job definition should run at particular time
- Some jobs should not be run during the execution of other jobs irrespective of their parameters
- Some jobs should not be run during the execution of other jobs when acting on the same object (that is, having the same value for a particular parameter)

In ESS, all of these requirements can be addressed using an **Incompatibility** definition.

Incompatibility defines which **Job** and **Job Set** definitions, referred to as entities, are incompatible with other entities in the system and should not be allowed to run together. Incompatibility can be defined for a given resource or globally. A resource is identified by a property name available in the entities being marked for incompatibility. Such a resource can be referred to by the same or a different property name.

At runtime, the system will check whether the given entities access the same resource (identified as the values of the properties defined in the incompatibility definition) and prevent them from running concurrently.

In the scenarios discussed previously, the first requirement is addressed using the **Self Incompatible** option. The second and third requirements can be met using the **Global** and **Domain** type incompatibility definitions.

To create an **Incompatibility** definition, follow the given steps, using *Figure 11.16* as a reference:

1. Log in to Oracle Enterprise Manager Fusion Middleware Control.
2. Navigate to **Scheduling Services | ESSAPP | ESSAPP | Scheduling Service Group** and click on **Job Metadata | Incompatibilities**.
3. Click on the **Create** button.

4. Enter the **Name**, **Display Name**, and optionally **Package** and **Description** for the new incompatibility, and set its type in the **Type** field to **Global**.

5. Under the **Entities** panel, click on the ⊹ icon and perform a default search.

6. This will display all the job definitions created on the server. Choose **AutoPurgeJob** that was created as part of this example.

7. Click on **OK** to save the **Incompatibility** definition.

8. Now, go back to the **Incompatibility** dashboard and edit the newly created **AutoPurgeSelfIncompatibility** option by selecting it.

9. Click on the 🐷 icon under the **Entities** panel. This will open a popup, allowing you to check the **Self Incompatible** flag.

10. Click on **OK** to save it. Refer following screenshot:

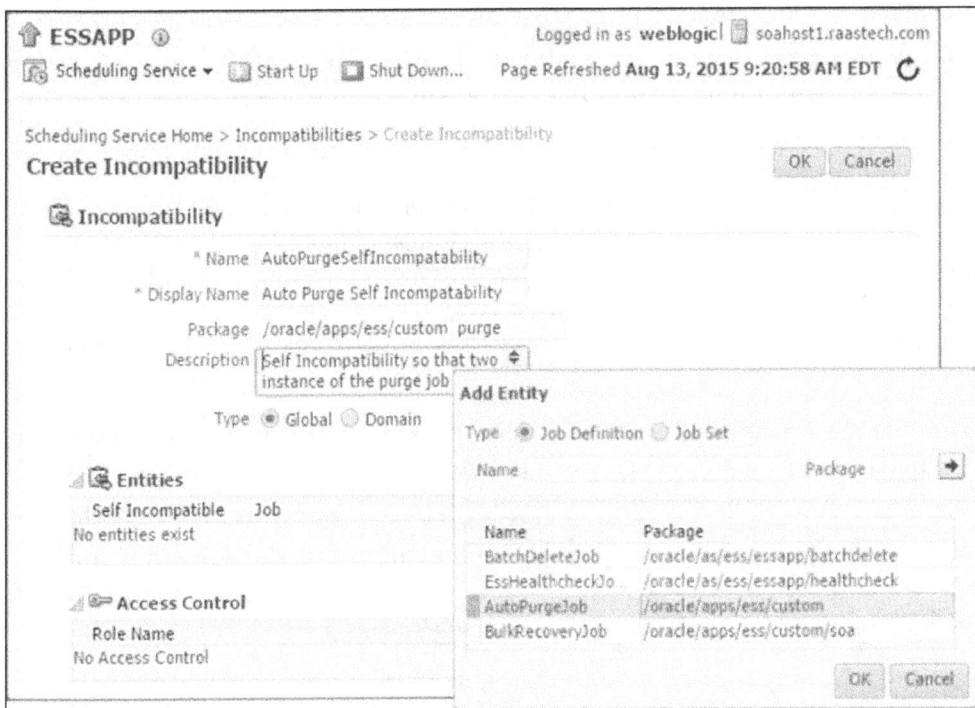

Figure 11.16: Creating an incompatibility in ESS

This **Incompatibility** definition will direct the Oracle SOA Suite 12*c* platform to only run one instance of this job at any given time. You may also have a similar requirement where, when an **AutoPurgeJob** is run, any other submitted Job Request should not run. An incompatibility for this scenario can also be created by adding these two job definitions under the **Entities** panel. The **Self Incompatible** flag should not be set in this case.

Defining Job Sets

Another powerful feature of ESS in Oracle SOA Suite 12*c* is the ability to create collections of job definitions that can be grouped together to run as a single unit called a job set. Each job definition or job set included within a job set is referred to as a **Job Set Step**.

A job set is defined as either a serial job set or a parallel job set. At runtime, ESS runs parallel Job Set Steps concurrently. In a serial job set, the steps are run one after another in a specific sequence. Using a serial job set, ESS also supports conditional branching between steps based on the execution status of a previous step.

Furthermore, a job set may be nested, which means that it may contain a collection of job definitions or one or more child job sets.

A job set can be defined by navigating to **Scheduling Services | ESSAPP | ESSAPP | Scheduling Service Group | Job Metadata | Job Sets** in Oracle Enterprise Manager Fusion Middleware Control.

Creating a dependency between Job Requests

While an **Incompatibility** definition prevents two jobs from running at the same time, a dependency can be created to execute multiple jobs in a custom sequence. For instance, let's assume that as an administrator, you want to set up a nightly error notification rule to send out an e-mail about faulted instances. However, before executing this job, you want the fault bulk recovery to be completed. This scenario can be implemented by creating a Job Set with two dependent steps in a serial configuration, as follows:

1. On the **Job Sets** landing page, click on **Create** to define a new job set.

2. Enter the mandatory metadata information about the job set, such as its **Name, Display Name, Description**, and **Package**.

3. Under the **Job Sets** panel, click on the ⊕ icon to include the first step in the job set.

4. An **Add Step** pop-up window appear, allowing you to select an existing job. *Figure 11.17* shows how **BulkRecoveryJob** has been added as a step with **Step ID** as **performErrorHospital**.

5. If a job requires any parameters to be passed, use **Application Defined Properties** and map it to the parameters.

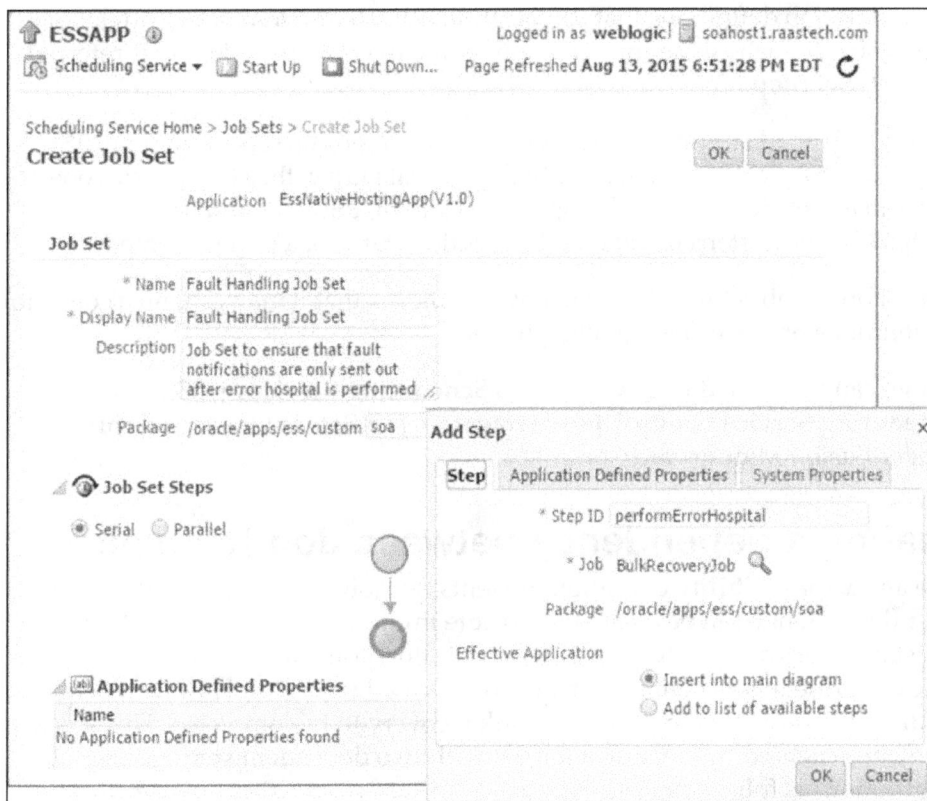

Figure 11.17: Creating a Job Set with dependent steps

6. In a similar way, add another step by selecting the job created for **Error Notification Rule**.

7. Check the **Serial** radio button to direct the ESS engine that these jobs should run one after another.

8. A job set definition always allows you to specify jobs that need to be executed in case the main steps (Job Definitions) error out or go into a warning state. *Figure 11.18* shows a fully defined Job Set with a serial pipeline of two Job Definitions.

9. The ✔ icon indicates that the sequence will execute the next step when the current step is successfully executed. Additional steps can be configured on error and warning conditions as indicated by the icons ⊗ and ⚠, respectively.

⬆ **ESSAPP** ⓘ   Logged in as **weblogic** | 🗒 soahost1.raastech.com

🔧 Scheduling Service ▾   🖥 Start Up   🖥 Shut Down...   Page Refreshed **Aug 15, 2015 7:47:31 AM EDT** ↻

Scheduling Service Home > Purge Policies > Set up Purge Policy

Set up Purge Policy   OK   Cancel

Description   Purge Completed Auto Purge Jobs

Request Criteria for Purge

Application	All ▾	Execution Type	All ▾
Product		Submitted By	
Job Definition	AutoPurgeJob 🔍		

Retention Criteria for Purge

☑ Specifying a retention period for Success, Error, Warning and Cancelled states will override the default retention period specified

		Retention period - Success (in days)	7
* Default retention period (in days)	7	Retention period - Error (in days)	7
		Retention period - Warning (in days)	7
		Retention period - Cancelled (in days)	7

Schedule

○ Once

◉ Use existing schedule NightlyPurgeSchedule 🔍

Package	/oracle/as/ess/essapp/custom
Description	Schedule to execute nightly purging of Jobs
Starts On	Aug 15, 2015 11:44:58 PM
Ends On	Indefinite
Repeat	Daily
Frequency	1
Time Zone	Eastern Standard Time

◢ **Advanced**

Maximum requests to be processed   100

Figure 11.18: A serial Job Set showing a linear dependency in ESS

In addition to the use case explained here, there may be other scenarios where certain types of job need to run in parallel. This can be done by creating a job set pipeline and setting the step execution mode to **Parallel**.

Setting up a Purge Policy

All the metadata of ESS job components discussed so far are stored in the [PREFIX]_ESS schema in the database. Once a job has finished its execution, its metadata-related and execution-related audit trail remains in the database. Over a period of time, it will be necessary for you as an administrator to purge the completed job requests. Completed job requests can be purged either through the Oracle Enterprise Manager Fusion Middleware Control console from the ESS module or by directly executing a purge package in the database.

> Executing ESS purging through Oracle Enterprise Manager Fusion Middleware Control marks the jobs as purged, but they are not physically removed from the underlying database tables.

Purging from Fusion Middleware Control

The ESS module deployed to Oracle Enterprise Manager Fusion Middleware Control provides a flexible way to purge completed jobs. You can purge requests by job type, job definition, product, and application, or for jobs submitted by a specific user. A purge policy configuration also allows you to set up retention parameters, and can be scheduled to run at defined intervals. Follow the given steps to schedule a purge policy:

1. Log in to Oracle Enterprise Manager Fusion Middleware Control.

2. Navigate to **Scheduling Services | ESSAPP | ESSAPP | Scheduling Service Group** and click on **Purge Policies**.

3. Click on the **Set up New** icon to create a new purge policy. *Figure 11.19* shows a user-defined purge policy to delete any completed **AutoPurgeJobs** created earlier.

In this example, any job data that is completed and past 7 days is purged, but it is restricted to a maximum of 100 jobs in one instance of the purge execution. Completed jobs exceeding the first 100 jobs will not be deleted, even though they are older than the retention period.

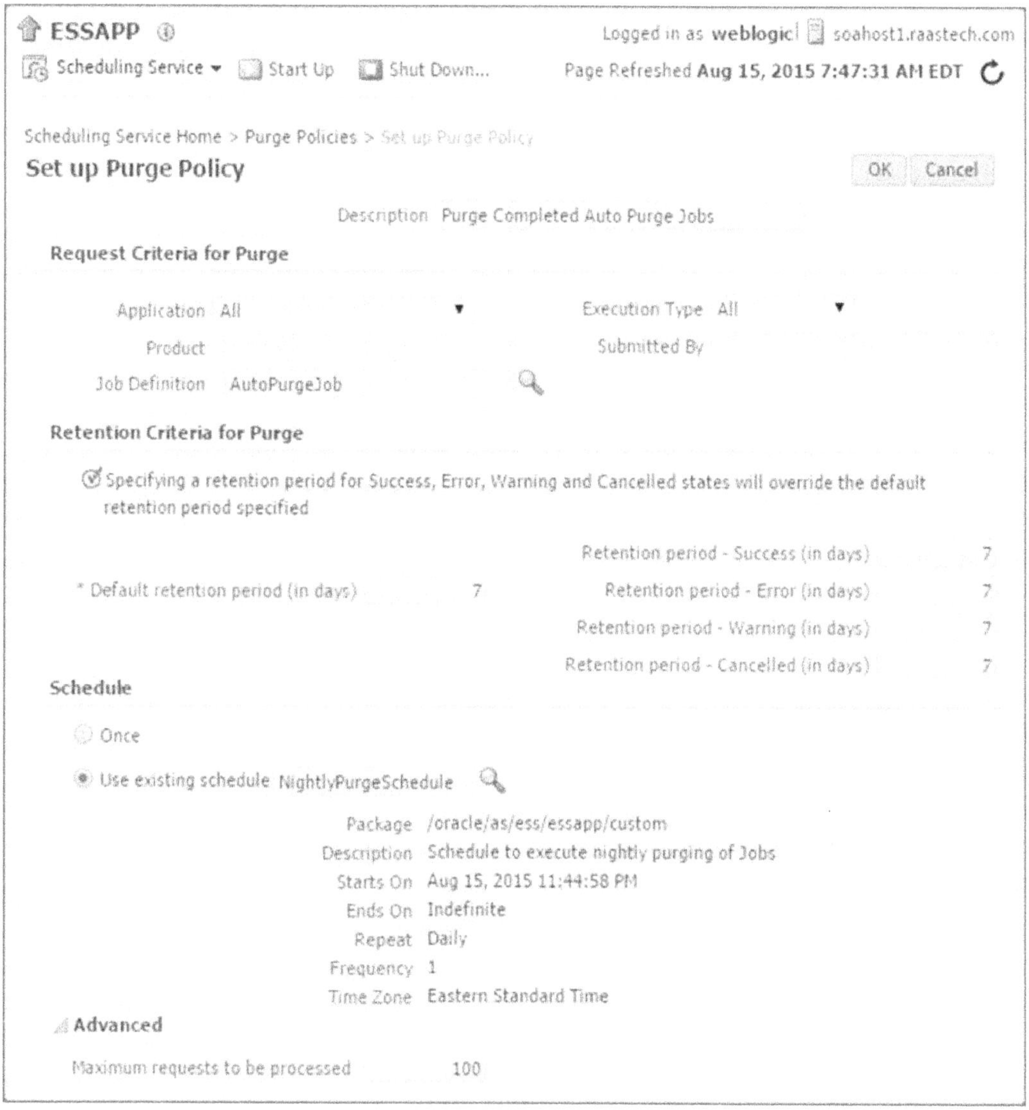

Figure 11.19: Creating a Purge Policy for completed Job Requests

Purging through the database

In the previous example, a purge policy executed through Oracle Enterprise Manager Fusion Middleware Control may create the impression that this instance data beyond the retention period is deleted from the database, but this is not the case. The data is still persisted in the backend tables. The purged jobs simply will no longer show up in the job history dashboard using the **Search Job Requests** report. This purging is logical as the rows corresponding to the purged job in the [PREFIX]_ESS schema continue to exist. The purge policy updates the deleted column in the REQUEST_HISTORY table without physically deleting them.

Over time, the tablespace continues to grow with records that are completed but not removed. To completely delete the job's history, the ESSPURGE.PURGE_REQUESTS procedure needs to be executed. This procedure will physically remove all the instance data for jobs that have completed and have been marked as logically deleted. The procedure is executed as follows:

```
EXECUTE esspurge.purge_requests(<older_than_days>, <max_count>, <max_runtime> );
```

Tuning and troubleshooting ESS

Troubleshooting the ESS components is an important administrative function that you would additionally be expected to perform. There are multiple ways to troubleshoot ESS issues, such as changing log levels, setting up tracing, viewing database logs, and so on. This section covers some common problems you may encounter with ESS components and how to effectively manage them. For instance, if a job remains in the **WAIT** or **RUNNING** state when it was scheduled to run in the past, there may be a number of reasons for this. The first step is to perform a sanity check of the infrastructure and ensure that all the components are in an active state:

- Ensure that the ESS cluster and the managed servers are up and running.
- Check whether the ESS application module is in a started state.
- Make sure that the Request Dispatcher and the Request Processor processes are up and running. They can be checked by navigating to **Scheduling Services | ESSAPP | ESSAPP | Scheduling Service Group** and then clicking on each of their links, respectively.

- Check the **Thread Count** allocation (maximum number of threads used to process job requests) under the **Advanced Configuration** option in the **Request Processor** dashboard to ensure that an adequate number is set based on the number of jobs running in the environment.

- Sometimes, a job may run for a long time and would be seen consuming a large number of CPU cycles and memory. Check the free heap sizes of the ESS managed server and the database nodes to check whether there is sufficient free memory available.

The Oracle Diagnostic Log files can also reveal important information regarding the state of the ESS application for troubleshooting purposes. The default log level can be changed to **FINEST** to ensure that ESS request logs are saved to the server log file. ESS inherits the logging level and log handlers configured for the parent logger, typically the Oracle logger or the root logger. To change the log level of the server diagnostic file for the ESS components, perform the following steps:

1. Log in to Oracle Enterprise Manager Fusion Middleware Control.

2. Navigate to **ESS_Cluster | [ess_server]**.

3. Click on the **WebLogic Server** menu and select **Logs**, and then select **Log Configuration**.

4. In the **Log Configuration** pane, expand **Root Logger**.

5. The scheduler loggers can be accessed by further expanding **oracle | oracle. as | oracle.as.scheduler[*]**, as shown in *Figure 11.20*.

6. Depending on which component you want to troubleshoot, set its corresponding log level to **Trace:32 (FINEST)** and then click on **Apply**.

7. Run a diagnostic test, and the diagnostic logs will be written under the `<DOMAIN_HOME>/servers/<SERVER_HOME>/logs/<ess_server>` directory.

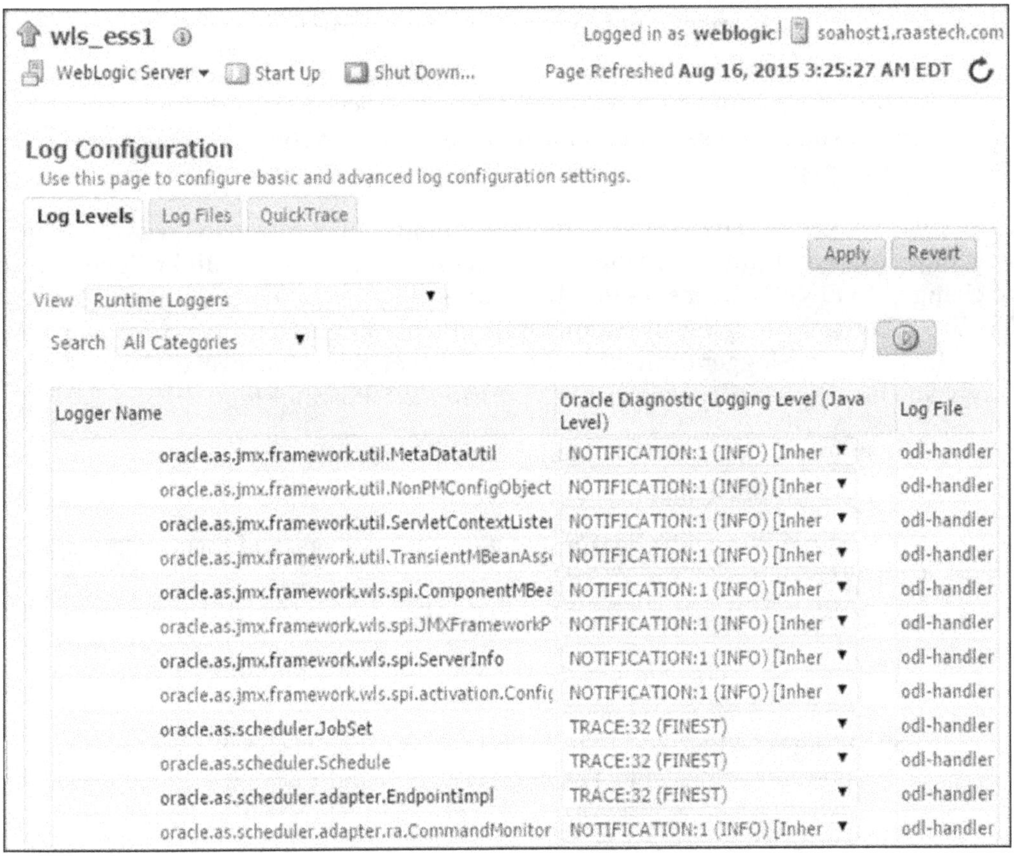

Figure 11.20: Configuring the log levels for the ESS loggers

Another mechanism to quickly check for a problem with an ESS Job Request is to directly query the REQUEST_HISTORY table in the [PREFIX]_ESS schema. The following query will list the current state of any request based on its request ID, along with any error or warning during its execution:

```
SELECT requestid, name, username, submitter, listener, state, error_
warning_message, error_warning_detail, definition, logworkdirectory,
outputworkdirectory

FROM [PREFIX]_ESS.REQUEST_HISTORY

WHERE requested = ?
```

Tuning ESS for optimal performance

Performance and scalability of an Oracle SOA Suite 12*c* platform, which is extended with ESS, is affected by a number of factors, such as a concurrent job execution, shared databases, availability of CPU resources, and overloading of the platform, to name a few. As such, it is inevitable that you may have to apply a few optimizations and tweaks and tune the environment for better performance.

As a bare minimum, administrators can configure a job incompatibility not only to prevent two incompatible jobs from running, but also to prevent both intensive jobs from heavily loading the same resource. In order to maintain good performance, you can define an incompatibility for such jobs so that they never run at the same time. In addition to this, a number of other parameters and settings can be altered to enhance the health of the platform, some of which are summarized in the following sections.

Tuning the Request Dispatcher

The request dispatcher manages requests that are awaiting their scheduled execution. The request processor handles job requests once they have been executed. The request dispatcher has a configurable parameter called `Maximum Poll Interval` that specifies the maximum frequency, in seconds, at which a check is performed to dispatch job requests. The default value of this parameter is `15` seconds. Consider increasing the value of this parameter to either `60` seconds or `3,600` seconds (1 hour), depending upon the types of jobs scheduled.

Tuning the Request Processor

The request processor manages those job requests for which the scheduled execution time has arrived and that are ready to execute. The request processor leverages the `Maximum Processor Threads` property that specifies the maximum number of threads used to process job requests. This represents the total number of worker threads that might run concurrently for all active work assignments for the ESS server. By default, this parameter is set to `25`. If there is potential for a large number of jobs to run concurrently on the server, consider increasing this value so that the count of these jobs is less than the configured threads.

Tuning the ESS data source

The connection pool size for the ESS JDBC data source should be based on the request processor tuning values configured for the `Maximum Processor Threads` and `Starvation Threshold` parameters. The recommended pool size should be the number of maximum processor threads plus 20.

Tuning dead database connections

Oracle ESS spawned jobs connect to the database using SQL*Net. If the spawned jobs are cancelled, ESS kills these processes at the operating system level. It is possible, however, that the database connections used by these processes will still exist in the database. To reduce dead connections in the database, update the SQLNET.EXPIRE_TIME setting to a desired value.

Using ESS WLST commands

So far in this chapter, you have seen how the ESS module deployed on the ESS managed server allows the creation of scheduling components from within Oracle Enterprise Manager Fusion Middleware Control. However, many administrators prefer to automate these activities so that repetitive steps can be scripted to save time and ensure consistency across environments. ESS provides an exhaustive list of custom WLST scripts for all the administrative functions that you have learned in this chapter.

The scripts shown in the following section will recreate the components covered in the earlier part of this chapter, such as Job Definitions, Schedules, Job Submissions, and Purge Policies.

Setting an environment variable and classpath

The WLST shell script wlst.sh is located in the $ORACLE_HOME/soa/common/bin folder, where $ORACLE_HOME is the environment variable set that points to the SOA Suite 12*c* installation directory.

The ESS WLST commands are only available when the base script classpath is modified in such a way that it can add a few JAR files. Modify the setWlstEnv.sh file as highlighted in the following code:

```
CLASSPATH="${CLASSPATH}:${ORACLE_HOME}/oracle_common/modules/
jmxframework.jar:${ORACLE_HOME}/wlserver/server/lib/weblogic.
jar:${ORACLE_HOME}/oracle_common/ess/lib/ess-admin.jar"
```

Connecting to WLST offline

Once the required JAR files have been added to the classpath, connect to the WebLogic administration server to execute the rest of the WLST scripts that we discussed earlier:

```
./$ORACLE_HOME/soa/common/bin/wlst.sh
connect('weblogic', 'welcome1', 't3://adminhost:7001')
```

The `enableESSPrint()` and `help('OracleScheduler')` commands can be issued to enable the print output and get usage information for the ESS native commands, respectively.

Managing Job Definitions using WLST

The ESS WLST function to manage job definitions can be used to either create, update, or delete a job definition. The syntax of the function is as follows:

```
manageSchedulerJobDefn(operation,appName,[jobName],[jobType],
[desc],[props])
```

The parameters of this function are self-explanatory. Do you recollect the Auto Purge job that was created through the ESS web module in the console? The same job can be created using the following WLST code:

```
#
# Create a Job Definition that invokes a Web Service
#
manageSchedulerJobDefn('CREATE','EssNativeHostingApp',jobName='WL
ST_PURGE',jobType='OnewayWebserviceJobType',desc='WLST Auto Purge
Job', props={'SYS_EXT_wsWsdlUrl':'/soa-infra/services/default/
ESSDemoApp/essbpel_client_ep?WSDL','SYS_EXT_wsServiceName':'essbpel_
client_ep','SYS_EXT_wsPortName':'ESSBPEL_pt','SYS_EXT_
wsOperationName':'process', 'SYS_EXT_wsWsdlBaseUrl':'http://
soahost1.raastech.com:8001','SYS_EXT_invokeMessage':'<ns1:process
xmlns:ns1="http://xmlns.oracle.com/ScheduledPurgeDemo/ESSDemoApp/
ESSBPEL"> <ns1:input>A</ns1:input> </ns1:process>','SYS_
externalJobType':'SOA'})
```

Note that the script can accept any number of properties that are used to completely configure a job definition. Additionally, the following scripts can be used to update or delete the job definition:

```
#
# Update a Job Definition
#
manageSchedulerJobDefn('UPDATE','EssNativeHostingApp',jobName='WLST_
PURGE',desc='Updating description of WLST Auto Purge Job')


#
# Delete a Job Definition
#
manageSchedulerJobDefn('DELETE','EssNativeHostingApp',jobName='WLST_
PURGE')
```

All existing job definitions can be turned into queries by passing SHOW as a value for the operation parameter in the script:

```
manageSchedulerJobDefn('SHOW','EssNativeHostingApp')
```

> A default package named /oracle/apps/ess/custom/ is to prepended to the name of any ESS component created from these WLST scripts.

Managing schedules using WLST

The queryWorkSchedules() command prints out all the currently defined schedules on the WLST console. Other commands to manage a schedule have the following syntax:

```
manageSchedulerSchedule(operation,appName,[schName],[schDesc],[beg
in_time],[frequency],[interval],[count],[end_time],[month],[week],[da
y],[date])
```

As you can see from the syntax, the command accepts an Operation parameter that can have a value of either CREATE, UPDATE, or DELETE. The schName parameter is used to specify the name of the schedule definition. A number of other parameters can be used to comprehensively define a time-based schedule, such as a frequency, an interval, a start time, end time, and count, to name a few. The following commands are an example of how to create a schedule as well as how to update and delete a schedule, using the preceding syntax:

```
#
# Create an ESS Schedule that runs every day for 30 days at 1:00 A.M
midnight from the point of creation.
#
manageSchedulerSchedule('CREATE','EssNativeHostingApp',schName=
'soa/WLST_NightlyPurgeSchedule',schDesc='Schedule created for a
Nightly Purge Job',frequency='DAY',interval=1,count=30, begin_
time='01:00:00:10:08:15')


#
# Update an ESS Schedule to modify the schedule start time.
#
manageSchedulerSchedule('UPDATE','EssNativeHostingApp',schName='soa/
WLST_NightlyPurgeSchedule',schDesc=' Updating the Schedule created for
a Nightly Purge job', begin_time='03:00:00:10:00:00')
```

```
#
# Delete a schedule
#
manageSchedulerSchedule('DELETE','EssNativeHostingApp',schName='soa/
WLST_NightlyPurgeSchedule')
```

Managing Job Requests using WLST

ESS also provides an extensive set of WLST functions to manage the lifecycle of job requests. A simple `querySchedulerRequests()` command displays a list of existing job requests configured on the ESS server along with their metadata. Job requests can also be queried based on their state by simply providing an overloaded state parameter to the same function, namely `querySchedulerRequests(state="RUNNING")`.

The syntax of the WLST method to submit a Job Request in ESS is provided in the following code:

```
submitSchedulerRequest(appName,[jobName],[schMeth],[note],[schName],[R
schName],[schDesc],[o_time],[begin_time],[frequency],[freqNum],[count]
,[end_time],[month],[week],[day],[date],[reqParams])
```

A job request command can be issued by simply passing a job definition name along with a schedule. While a job definition must be predefined, the schedule can be defined in an ad hoc manner using this command. If the job definition input is parameterized using application-defined properties, then they can be passed using the `reqParams` argument in the function. The following example demonstrates how a Job Request for a pre-existing job `AutoPurgeJob` can be submitted in various ways:

```
#
# Submit a request for immediate job execution (one-time only)
#
submitSchedulerRequest('EssNativeHostingApp','AutoPurgeJob')


#
# Submit a job request using a predefined schedule
#
submitSchedulerRequest('EssNativeHostingApp',jobName='AutoPurgeJob',sc
hName='NightlyPurgeSchedule')
```

A few other WLST functions that are useful to manage a lifecycle of a Job Request, along with their descriptions, is provided here in case you need them:

```
#
# Cancel a currently running job request based on its Id
#
```

```
manageSchedulerRequest(<jobId>, "CANCEL")

#
# Recover a failed job request based on its Id
#
manageSchedulerRequest(<jobId>, "RECOVER")

#
# View the request log for a job request based on its Id
#
getSchedulerRequestContent(<jobId>, "LOG")

#
# Get all the output of a job request
#
getSchedulerRequestContent(<jobId>, "OUTPUT")
```

Purging Job Requests using WLST

In addition to using Oracle Enterprise Manager Fusion Middleware Control to delete completed ESS job requests, ESS also provides scripts that an administrator can use to define a set of delete criteria and thus submit a batch delete request. The delete criteria for the batch job is specified in the form of application request parameters:

```
batchDeleteSchedulerRequests([desc],[schId],[start],[end],[params])
```

The simplest way to purge completed instances is to execute the ESS WLST batch delete `batchDeleteSchedulerRequests()` function that is executed once to delete all the purgeable job requests without any other parameters. You can also choose to run the delete job using an existing schedule:

```
#
# Submit batch delete job request using the schedule /oracle/as/ess/
essapp/custom/NightlyPurgeSchedule:
#
batchDeleteSchedulerRequests(desc='Batch Purge using Nightly Schedule'
,schId='NightlyPurgeSchedule')
```

Summary

Oracle Enterprise Scheduler has been finally inducted in Oracle SOA Suite 12*c* without any additional licensing costs. It is an incredibly powerful addition that provides a completely metadata-driven approach to create scheduling components.

In this chapter, we introduced various components within Oracle ESS and discussed their capabilities using some real-life scenarios. On a whole, this chapter broadly covered the following topics:

- Introduction to Oracle ESS, its administration consoles, and terminology
- Creation of Job Definitions, Schedules, and Job Requests
- Submission and monitoring of Job Requests, including viewing their log and audit trails
- Creating Incompatibilities to run jobs that are mutually exclusive of one another
- Creating Job Sets that execute jobs in serial (Job Dependencies) and parallel
- Understanding how to purge and delete completed job requests using both Oracle Enterprise Manager Fusion Middleware Control and database packages
- Tuning and troubleshooting ESS components to recover stuck jobs within the ESS infrastructure
- Using various ESS WLST commands

12
Clustering and High Availability

High availability (**HA**) refers to the ability to maintain operational integrity when a server failure occurs. This can be achieved by installing two or more Oracle SOA Suite 12*c* nodes in a cluster to protect against failure. Server failures could be software induced, such as a JVM crashing due to it being out of memory, or due to hardware failure, such as a local disk going bad. Installing an Oracle SOA Suite 12*c* cluster requires additional setup and configuration that are different from that of a single-node installation.

In this chapter, we describe how to set up a two-node Oracle SOA Suite 12*c* cluster in an active-active mode, wherein if a server fails, the other will continue processing transactions, ensuring a relatively high degree of availability. This type of architecture provides a high degree of **failover**, wherein most asynchronous transactions are failed over on the active node in the cluster, with little loss of transactional data.

There are many ways in which you can set up a highly available SOA Infrastructure, such as vertical and/or horizontal scaling over physical machines, hardware partitioning using virtualization, and cloud computing. The *Oracle Fusion Middleware Enterprise Deployment Guide for Oracle SOA Suite 12c (12.1.3)*, informally referred to as the **Enterprise Deployment Topology** (**EDG**), provides a detailed example of how to install a highly available production-quality environment. This guide is comprehensive and complete, discussing all aspects of enterprise deployment. With 290 pages, the Oracle documentation is extremely detailed (and somewhat complicated) for the non-experienced administrator, requiring a deep understanding of Oracle WebLogic Server clustering and failover concepts.

This chapter describes many more scaled down and simplified instructions, and despite the limitations of our architecture (which will be described later), is completely acceptable for most mid-sized to large production environments. The intent of this chapter is to provide instructions that are easy to execute and entirely repeatable, while remaining light on concepts and explanation.

Architecture

There are many types of architectures that can be implemented in an enterprise deployment topology, and this chapter focuses on one of the simpler ones. With reduced complexity comes certain disadvantages.

Software versions

The resulting installation as documented in this chapter, is based on the following 64-bit software products:

- Supported Linux versions:
    - ° Oracle Linux 5 Update 6+
    - ° Oracle Linux 6 Update 1+
    - ° Red Hat Enterprise Linux 5 Update 6+
    - ° Red Hat Enterprise Linux 6 Update 1+
- Oracle JDK 7 (1.7.0_55-b13)
- Oracle Web Tier 12*c* (12.1.3)
- Oracle WebLogic Server 12*c* (12.1.3.0.0)
- Oracle SOA Suite 12*c* (12.1.3.0.0)

An architectural diagram

Figure 12.1 depicts the architecture of our two-node Oracle SOA Suite 12*c* cluster. It relies on two physical servers called SOAHOST1 and SOAHOST2 (also aliased as WEBHOST1 and WEBHOST2). A single domain, **soa_domain**, is created in this architecture. The managed servers are clustered as depicted in the following figure. Oracle HTTP Server, installed on each of the separate physical hosts, listens on port 7777 and routes console requests to the Admin Server, and transactional requests to the SOA and OSB managed servers. Each node of the cluster requires access to a shared filesystem and shared database.

Oracle Web Services Manager (WSM) is installed on a separate managed server and must be started up prior to bringing up SOA and OSB. ESS is also installed on its own independent managed servers.

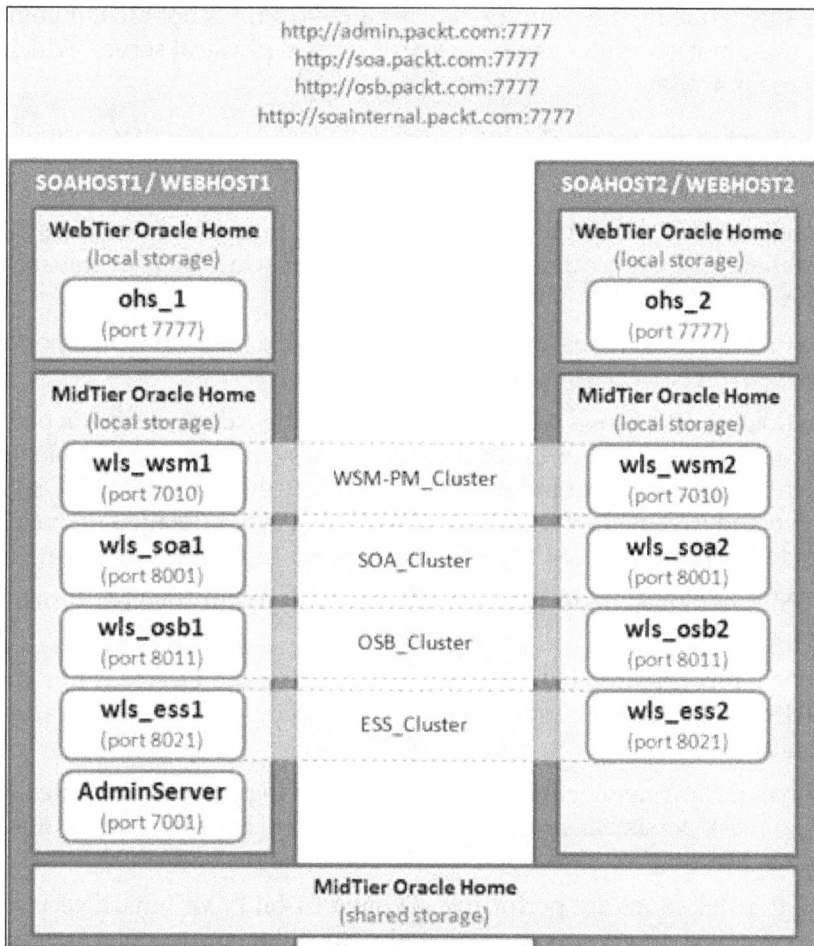

Figure 12.1: Architecture of the two-node cluster

Multiple load-balanced URLs should be set up and defined on an external hardware load balancer, such as F5 BIG-IP. No secure communication, such as SSL, is defined in this architecture, as it assumes that the installation is exclusively used internally. This can be reconfigured later if needed. The EDG located at `http://docs.oracle.com/cd/E12839_01/core.1111/e12036/toc.htm` details this.

Architectural considerations

Certain design considerations are made in the architecture outlined in this chapter. Failover of certain components may not be possible, all for the purpose of considerably reducing the complexity. This architecture is not ideal if your environment cannot guarantee the recovery of a failed physical server, which is rarely the case nowadays.

Thus, the following are the considerations that deviate from the EDG with reference to our architecture:

- Oracle BAM is not installed, primarily for the purpose of avoiding the installation of a reporting tool on the same hardware as your transactional SOA infrastructure.

- No firewall restrictions are assumed. For more details on which ports must be open in your network, refer to the EDG.

- No floating IP address will be utilized; thus, the Admin Server is tied exclusively to SOAHOST1 for the sole purpose of reducing complexity in the network setup and failover. In the unlikely event that SOAHOST1 is down and irrecoverable, additional work that is not detailed in this chapter is needed to reconfigure SOAHOST2 in order to bring up the Admin Server.

- WSM is deployed on its own managed servers to improve performance and availability.

- No SSL is configured between the load balancer and **Oracle HTTP Server (OHS)**, OHS and WebLogic Server, and WebLogic Server and Oracle Database.

- A shared filesystem is utilized for transaction logs, deployment descriptors (plan files), persistent stores, as well as software binaries that include the Oracle JRockit JDK, Oracle WebLogic Server, and Oracle SOA Suite.

- 64-bit installations are performed. Though 64-bit JVMs have a very slight performance disadvantage compared with 32-bit equivalents, memory space is hypothetically unlimited.

- Oracle Web Tier is utilized to allow the WebLogic Server cluster membership to be reconfigured. This is used to easily add and remove servers without changing the load balancing configuration.

- A total of five Node Managers will be running: one for the Admin Server, one for each of the managed server's domain directory, and one for each of the OHS instances.

- Unicast, versus multicast, is leveraged for communication between the members of the cluster, as it does not require cross-network configuration and reduces potential network errors that can occur from multicast address conflicts.

- WebTier and MidTier are installed on the same physical server.

- There is no utilization of virtual hosts and virtual IP addresses, and the WebLogic whole server migration is not set up. Thus, the automatic restart of a server instance on a separate physical machine is not available. Furthermore, messages in JMS destinations bound to the failed managed server are not picked up by any of the active servers of the cluster.

- Contrary to the instructions in the EDG, a dedicated, centralized LDAP-compliant authentication provider is not utilized.

Understanding the variables and terms

Certain terms and variables described in this chapter require familiarization prior to the installation. Refer to the following table for a set of explanations:

Term	Explanation
MidTier	A single domain is created to host the software installation, residing on the Oracle Home that is split between the local and shared storage. This installation of WebLogic Server, WSM, SOA Suite, OSB, and ESS is referred to as MidTier.
WebTier	The term WebTier and OHS are used interchangeably. This is a separate independent installation on the same physical box, but under a separate Oracle Home than the MidTier. Both MidTier and WebTier require different environment variables.
SOAHOST1	Considering this is a two-node cluster, any reference to SOAHOST1 should be executed on the first node of the cluster, and any reference to SOAHOST2 should be executed on the second node of the cluster.
WEBHOST1	Both WebTier and MidTier reside on the same physical server, so any references to WEBHOST1 and SOAHOST1 technically refer to the same physical server. However, during installation and configuration, there are some notable differences.
$ORACLE_HOME	Any variables that appear in this form should be typed as is.
[ORACLE_HOME]	If you encounter a variable name surrounded by square brackets, the actual value must be substituted. Note that the value of the variable may differ depending on whether you are executing a MidTier or WebTier instruction. Simply type either source envMidTier.sh or source envWebTier.sh followed by echo $ORACLE_HOME to retrieve the value of the variable.

Downloading the software

All the software required for the installation is available from three separate sites, and an Oracle account (which can be created for free) is needed to download them. Copy the software to the `/u01/share/install_software` shared directory.

Downloading Oracle Fusion Middleware 12*c*

The Oracle software is available on the Oracle Software Delivery Cloud website. Follow the given steps to download it:

1. Navigate to https://edelivery.oracle.com/osdc/faces/Home.jspx

2. Login using your Oracle account.

3. Accept the Oracle Trial License Agreement and Export Restrictions.

4. In the Product Field Type: Oracle WebLogic Server, Enterprise Edition

5. Click on the Platform dropdown

6. Check box next to: Linux x86-64 and click Select

7. Repeat Steps this time with the following Product:

    ° Oracle SOA Suite For Oracle Middleware

8. Click Continue

9. Uncheck the box next to Available Release

10. Expand Oracle Weblogic Server Enterprise Edition

11. Check the box next to Oracle Fusion Middleware 12c (12.1.3.0.0), 1 file

12. Collapse Oracle Weblogic Server Enterprise Edition

13. Expand Oracle SOA Suite For Oracle Middleware

14. Check the box next to:

    ° Oracle BPEL Process Manager (12.1.3.0.0), 2 files

    ° Oracle Service Bus (12.1.3.0.0), 1 file

15. Click Continue

16. Read the Terms which are presented, check the box to agree to them, and click Continue

17. Click on and download each of these three files:

    ° Oracle Fusion Middleware 12c (12.1.3.0.0) Infrastructure (Size: 1.5G, Filename: V44416-01.zip)

    ° Oracle Fusion Middleware 12c (12.1.3.0.0) SOA Suite and Business Process Management (Size: 1.3G, Filename: V44420-01.zip)

    ° Oracle Fusion Middleware 12c (12.1.3.0.0) Service Bus (Size: 344M, Filename: V44423-01.zip)

Downloading Oracle Java

Follow the next steps to download the certified version of Java:

1. Navigate to `http://www.oracle.com/technetwork/java/javase/downloads/java-archive-downloads-javase7-521261.html`.

2. Accept the license agreement.

3. Download the **jdk-7u55-linux-x64.tar.gz** file (size: 132 MB).

Downloading Oracle Web Tier 12*c*

Follow the given steps to download Oracle Web Tier 12*c*, which includes OHS:

1. Navigate to `http://www.oracle.com/technetwork/middleware/webtier/downloads/index-jsp-156711.html`.

2. Accept the license agreement.

3. Under **Oracle WebTier 12c** and under **Oracle HTTP Server 12.1.3**, select **Linux 64-bit**.

4. Download the **fmw_12.1.3.0.0_ohs_linux64_Disk1_1of1.zip** file (size 514 M).

Installation prerequisites

The steps highlighted in this section must be completed prior to the installation.

Ensuring hardware requirements

The hardware requirements given here are recommendations based on the EDG and should be treated as general guidelines and not strict requirements, as hardware sizing can vary drastically as it is based on numerous factors. The following table assumes an installation of Web Tier, SOA Suite, OSB, ESS, and WSM on a single server:

Component	Requirement (per host)
Memory/RAM	24 GB
File descriptors	15,000
Operating system processes	1,000
SWAP	1 GB
/tmp	1.5 GB
Disk space (shared storage)	5 GB
Disk space (local storage)	15 GB (includes software installation files)

Setting up the load balancer .

Contact the network team to set up the following load balancer URLs that are needed for the installation. Modify the names according to your naming requirements:

Load Balancer Host/Ports	Target Servers/Ports	Description
soa.packt.com:7777	soahost1.packt.com:7777 soahost2.packt.com:7777	SOA services are accessed through here.
osb.packt.com:7777	soahost1.packt.com:7777 soahost2.packt.com:7777	OSB services are accessed through here.
soainternal.packt.com:7777	soahost1.packt.com:7777 soahost2.packt.com:7777	For internally optimized composites and service access. This is not to be shared publicly.
admin.packt.com:7777	soahost1.packt.com:7777 soahost2.packt.com:7777	Used for the various admin console access.

Setting up the hostname

There are two physical servers in our architecture, but five separate hostnames that are to be set up. They can be set up in DNS as follows:

Hostname	Physical server
soahost1.packt.com	Node 1
webhost1.packt.com	
adminhost.packt.com	
soahost2.packt.com	Node 2
webhost2.packt.com	

Alternatively, they can be set up manually in your /etc/hosts path on both nodes. For example:

```
192.168.0.20 soahost1.packt.com webhost1.packt.com adminhost.
packt.com
192.168.0.21 soahost2.packt.com webhost2.packt.com
```

Preparing the filesystem

Create the local and shared mount points as defined in the following table. These mount points will be accessible by the **oracle** Unix user on both nodes of the cluster. Additionally, two locally stored mount points are needed to host the MidTier and WebTier installations:

Directory	Storage type	Unix environment variable
/u01/share/install_software	Shared	SOFTWARE_DIR
/u01/share/oracle/middleware	Shared	SHARED_DRIVE_APP
/u01/oracle/middleware	Local	LOCAL_DRIVE_APP
/u01/oracle/webtier	Local	LOCAL_DRIVE_OHS

A profile script is defined in the subsequent section, which sets various environment variables to each of these directories.

Configuring the operating system

This section describes various Linux operating system tasks.

Verifying the temp and SWAP space

Ensure that /tmp has at least 1.5 GB of available disk space and that SWAP is configured with at least 1 GB of memory.

Creating operating system accounts

These instructions assume that the entire software stack will be installed by the operating system user **oracle** that has a primary group of **oinstall**.

As **root**, run the following commands to create the operating system account:

```
groupadd oinstall
groupadd dba
useradd nobody
useradd -c "Oracle Software Owner" -g oinstall -G dba oracle
passwd oracle
```

Configuring operating system prerequisites

Certain recommended Linux operating system prerequisites are needed before installing Oracle SOA Suite 12*c* and creating the domain. The steps here are specific to the 64-bit versions of Oracle Linux or Red Hat Linux Enterprise Server. All instructions here must be run as the **root** user.

Execute these instructions on both SOAHOST1 and SOAHOST2:

1. As **root**, update the following in /etc/sysctl.conf on both the servers:

    ```
    kernel.sem = 256 32000 100 142
    kernel.shmmax = 4294967295
    ```

2. Run the following command:

    ```
    /sbin/sysctl -p
    ```

3. Add the following at the end of /etc/security/limits.conf:

    ```
    oracle   soft    nofile   4096
    oracle   hard    nofile   65536
    oracle   soft    nproc    2047
    oracle   hard    nproc    16384
    ```

4. Add the following at the end of /etc/profile:

```
if [ $USER = "oracle" ]; then
  if [ $SHELL = "/bin/ksh" ]; then
    ulimit -Su 16383
    ulimit -Hu 16383
    ulimit -Sn 63535
    ulimit -Hn 63535
  else
    ulimit -Hn 63535 -Sn 63535 -Hu 16383 -Su 16383
  fi
fi
```

5. Ensure that the latest versions of the following **Red Hat Package Manager packages (RPMs)** are installed. Note that versions of these RPMs may vary depending on the specific release of your operating system:

   ○ binutils-2.17.50.0.6-20.el5

   ○ compat-libstdc++-33-3.2.3-61-x86_64

   ○ compat-libstdc++-33-3.2.3-61-i386

   ○ elfutils-libelf-0.137

   ○ elfutils-libelf-devel-0.137

   ○ gcc-4.1.2

   ○ gcc-c++-4.1.2

   ○ glibc-2.5-81-x86_64

   ○ glibc-2.5-81-i686

   ○ glibc-common-2.5-81

   ○ glibc-devel-2.5-81-x86_64

   ○ glibc-devel-2.5-81-i386

   ○ libaio-0.3.106-x86_64

   ○ libaio-0.3.106-i386

   ○ libaio-devel-0.3.106

   ○ libgcc-4.1.2-x86_64

   ○ libgcc-4.1.2-i386

   ○ libstdc++-4.1.2-x86_64

   ○ libstdc++-4.1.2-i386

- ◦ libstdc++-devel-4.1.2
- ◦ make-3.81
- ◦ sysstat-7.0.0

6. Reboot the servers.

Creating custom environment scripts

The following environment scripts allow you to easily switch between the MidTier and WebTier environments by setting up their respective shell environment variables. Execute these instructions on both SOAHOST1 and SOAHOST2:

1. Login as the oracle user.

2. Create a new MidTier profile script:

   ```
   vi /home/oracle/envMidTier.sh
   ```

3. Insert the following in to the file. Modify the hostnames as needed:

   ```
   #----------
   # Oracle SOA Suite 12c: MidTier environment variables
   #----------


   #----------
   # Top-level directories
   #----------
   export SHARED_DRIVE_APP=/u01/share/oracle/middleware
   export LOCAL_DRIVE_APP=/u01/oracle/middleware
   export SOFTWARE_DIR=/u01/share/install_software


   #----------
   # Environment variables
   #----------
   if [ "$HOSTNAME" == "soahost1.packt.com" ] || [ "$HOSTNAME" ==
   "soahost1" ]; then
     export OHS_INSTANCE=ohs_1
   fi
   if [ "$HOSTNAME" == "soahost2.packt.com" ] || [ "$HOSTNAME" ==
   "soahost2" ]; then
     export OHS_INSTANCE=ohs_2
   ```

```
fi
```

```
export ORACLE_HOME=$SHARED_DRIVE_APP/products/fmw1213
```

```
export ORACLE_COMMON_HOME=$SHARED_DRIVE_APP/products/fmw1213/
oracle_common
```

```
export WL_HOME=$SHARED_DRIVE_APP/products/fmw1213/wlserver
```

```
export SOA_DIR=$SHARED_DRIVE_APP/products/fmw1213/soa
```

```
export OSB_DIR=$SHARED_DRIVE_APP/products/fmw1213/osb
```

```
export EM_DIR=$SHARED_DRIVE_APP/products/fmw1213/em
```

```
export JAVA_HOME=$SHARED_DRIVE_APP/products/jdk1.7.0_55
```

```
export ASERVER_HOME=$SHARED_DRIVE_APP/config/domains/soa_domain
```

```
export MSERVER_HOME=$LOCAL_DRIVE_APP/config/domains/soa_domain
```

```
export APPLICATION_HOME=$SHARED_DRIVE_APP/config/applications/
soa_domain
```

```
export DEPLOY_PLAN_HOME=$SHARED_DRIVE_APP/config/dp
```

```
export OHS_ADMIN_CONFIG_DIR=$SHARED_DRIVE_APP/config/domains/soa_
domain/config/fmwconfig/components/OHS/$OHS_INSTANCE
```

```
export LC_ALL=en_US.UTF-8
```

```
export LANG=en_US.UTF-8
```

```
export PATH=~:$JAVA_HOME/bin:/usr/bin:/bin:/usr/local/bin:/usr/
sbin:.
```

4. Create a WebTier profile script:

```
vi /home/oracle/envWebTier.sh
```

Insert the following in the file. Modify the hostnames as needed:

```
#----------
# Oracle SOA Suite 12c: WebTier environment variables
#----------


#----------
# Top-level directories
#----------
export LOCAL_DRIVE_OHS=/u01/oracle/webtier
export SOFTWARE_DIR=/u01/share/install_software


#----------
# Environment variables
#----------
```

```
if [ "$HOSTNAME" == "soahost1.packt.com" ] || [ "$HOSTNAME" ==
"soahost1" ]; then

  export OHS_INSTANCE=ohs_1

fi

if [ "$HOSTNAME" == "soahost2.packt.com" ] || [ "$HOSTNAME" ==
"soahost2" ]; then

  export OHS_INSTANCE=ohs_2

fi

export ORACLE_HOME=$LOCAL_DRIVE_OHS/products/fmw1213

export ORACLE_COMMON_HOME=$LOCAL_DRIVE_OHS/products/fmw1213/
oracle_common

export WL_HOME=$LOCAL_DRIVE_OHS/products/fmw1213/wlserver

export OHS_DIR=$LOCAL_DRIVE_OHS/products/fmw1213/ohs

export EM_DIR=$LOCAL_DRIVE_OHS/products/fmwnnnn/em

export MSERVER_HOME=$LOCAL_DRIVE_OHS/config/domains/soa_domain

export APPLICATION_HOME=$LOCAL_DRIVE_OHS/config/applications/soa_
domain

export JAVA_HOME=$LOCAL_DRIVE_OHS/products/jdk1.7.0_55

export OHS_WEBHOST_CONFIG_DIR=$LOCAL_DRIVE_OHS/config/domains/soa_
domain/config/fmwconfig/components/OHS/instances/$OHS_INSTANCE

export LC_ALL=en_US.UTF-8

export LANG=en_US.UTF-8

export PATH=~:$JAVA_HOME/bin:/usr/bin:/bin:/usr/local/bin:/usr/
sbin:.
```

5. Update the permissions:

```
chmod 700 /home/oracle/env*Tier.sh
```

Unzipping the software

Unzip the software which we have downloaded to the shared storage to prepare for the installations:

1. On SOAHOST1, unzip the software to prepare for the installation:

```
cd $SOFTWARE_DIR

unzip V44416-01.zip

unzip V44420-01.zip

unzip V44423-01.zip

unzip fmw_12.1.3.0.0_ohs_linux64_Disk1_1of1.zip
```

Installing Java and Infrastructure

Oracle Java is installed and downloaded on both the shared storage (for the MidTier installation) and the local storage (for the WebTier installation).

Installing Java and Infrastructure on MidTier

Both Java and Oracle Infrastructure will be installed on shared storage, which is accessible by both the nodes of nodes of the MidTier. The same applies to the installation of the initial Oracle Infrastructure as well:

1. On SOAHOST1, extract Java and then start the Oracle Infrastructure installer on the shared storage:

   ```
   source envMidTier.sh

   mkdir -p $JAVA_HOME

   cd $JAVA_HOME/..

   tar -xzvf $SOFTWARE_DIR/jdk-7u55-linux-x64.tar.gz

   java -d64 -jar $SOFTWARE_DIR/fmw_12.1.3.0.0_infrastructure.jar
   ```

2. In the **Inventory Directory** field, enter /u01/share/oracle/oraInventory and then click on **OK**.

3. Click on **Next**.

4. In the **Oracle Home** field, enter the value for **[ORACLE_HOME]** (for example, /u01/share/oracle/middleware/products/fmw1213) and then click on **Next**.

5. Click on Next.

6. Click on Next.

7. Uncheck **I wish to receive security updates via My Oracle Support**, click on **Next**, and then click on **Yes**.

8. Click on **Install**.

9. Click on **Finish** once the installation is done.

Installing Java and Infrastructure on WebTier

Java and the Oracle Infrastructure will be installed on local storage for the two WebTier servers. The following steps will help you do this:

1. On SOAHOST1, extract Java and then start the Oracle Infrastructure installer:

    ```
    source envWebTier.sh
    mkdir -p $JAVA_HOME
    cd $JAVA_HOME/..
    tar -xzvf $SOFTWARE_DIR/jdk-7u55-linux-x64.tar.gz
    java -d64 -jar $SOFTWARE_DIR/fmw_12.1.3.0.0_infrastructure.jar
    ```

2. In the **Inventory Directory** field, enter `/u01/oracle/webtier/oraInventory` and then click on **OK**.

3. Click on **Next**.

4. In the **Oracle Home** field, enter the value for **[ORACLE_HOME]** (for example, `/u01/oracle/webtier/products/fmw1213`) and then click on **Next**.

5. Click on Next.

6. Click on Next.

7. Uncheck **I wish to receive security updates via My Oracle Support**, click on **Next**, and then click on **Yes**.

8. Click on **Install**.

9. Click on **Finish** once the installation is done.

10. Repeat steps 1 to 9 on SOAHOST2.

Running the Repository Creation Utility

The **Repository Creation Utility (RCU)** is used to create the relevant database schemas. Go through the following steps to run the RCU:

1. On SOAHOST1, start the RCU installer:

    ```
    source envMidTier.sh
    cd $ORACLE_HOME/oracle_common/bin
    ./rcu
    ```

2. Click on **Next**.

3. Select **Create Repository**, choose **System Load and Product Load**, and click on **Next**.

4. Enter your database information as shown in *Figure 12.2*, and click on **Next**:

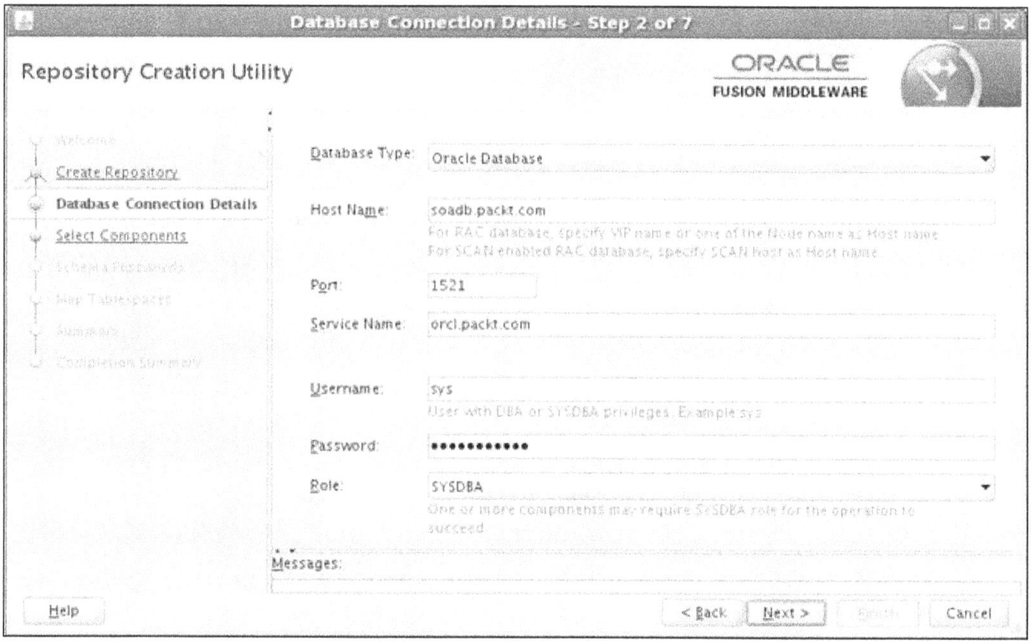

Figure 12.2: Entering database connection details in the Repository Creation Utility

5. Click on **OK** to confirm the validation of the global prerequisites.

6. In the **Create new prefix** field, enter a prefix such as DEV.

7. Click on the checkbox **AS Common Schemas** and then click on **Next**.

8. Click on **OK** to confirm the validation of the component prerequisites.

9. In the password fields, enter a password (for example, welcome1) and then click on **Next**.

10. Click on Next.

11. If prompted to create tablespaces, click on **OK**.

12. Click on **OK** to confirm the validation of tablespaces.

13. Click on **Create**.

14. Click on **Close** once the RCU is complete.

Creating a new domain

A WebLogic domain will be created on the shared storage. Follow the given steps to create a new domain:

1. On SOAHOST1, start WebLogic Server Configuration Wizard to create the WebLogic domain:

    ```
    source envMidTier.sh
    $ORACLE_HOME/oracle_common/common/bin/config.sh
    ```

2. Click on **Create a new domain**, and in the **Domain Location** field, enter the value of **[ASERVER_HOME]** (for example `/u01/share/oracle/middleware/config/domains/soa_domain`) and then click on **Next**.

3. Select **Oracle Enterprise Manager – 12.1.3.0 [em]** and **Oracle WSM Policy Manager – 12.1.3.0 [oracle_common]**, and then click on **Next**.

4. In the **Application location** field, enter the value for **[APPLICATION_ HOME]** (for example, `/u01/share/oracle/middleware/config/applications/soa_domain`) and then click on **Next**.

5. Enter the password for the WebLogic user (for example, `welcome1`) and then click on **Next**.

6. In the **Domain Mode** option, select **Production** and click on **Next**.

7. Select **RCU Data** and enter your database information. Keep the **Schema Owner** field as DEV_STB (or whatever prefix you chose earlier).

8. Click on **Get RCU Configuration** when done and then click on **Next**.

9. Click on Next.

10. Check all connections and then click on **Test Selected Connections**.

11. Click on **Next**.

12. Check **Administration Server, Node Manager, Managed Servers, Clusters and Coherence**, and **JMS File Store**, and then click on **Next**.

13. In the **Listen Address** field, enter the load balancer URL value `admin.packt. com` and then click on **Next**.

14. Under **Node Manager Credentials**, for **Username** enter `weblogic`, but for **Password**, enter a password different from the one we used in the step 5 (for example, `welcome2`).

15. Click on **Next**.

16. Click on **Add** twice, then, enter the server names `wls_wsm1` and `wls_wsm2`, with the hostnames `soahost1.packt.com` and `soahost2.packt.com`, both listening on port `7010`. Select **JRF-MAN-SVR**, **WSM-CACHE-SVR**, and **WSMPN-MAN-SVR** for both records, as shown in the following figure.

17. Click on **Next**.

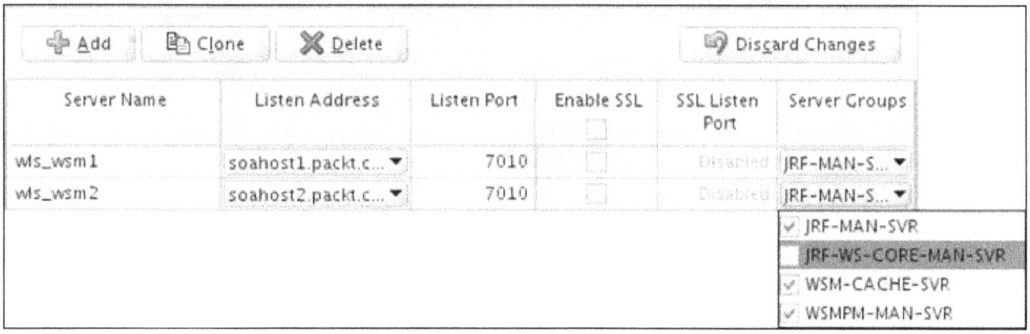

	Server Name	Listen Address	Listen Port	Enable SSL	SSL Listen Port	Server Groups
				☐		
	wls_wsm1	soahost1.packt.c... ▼	7010	☐	Disabled	JRF-MAN-S... ▼
	wls_wsm2	soahost2.packt.c... ▼	7010	☐	Disabled	JRF-MAN-S... ▼

(Add, Clone, Delete, Discard Changes buttons)

Server Groups dropdown:
- ✓ JRF-MAN-SVR
- JRF-WS-CORE-MAN-SVR
- ✓ WSM-CACHE-SVR
- ✓ WSMPM-MAN-SVR

Figure 12.3: Advanced managed server configuration

18. Click on **Add**, and in the **Cluster Name** field enter `WSM-PM_Cluster`, then click on **Next**.

19. Add both **wls_wsm1** and **wls_wsm2** servers to the cluster **WSM-PM_Cluster** and then click on **Next**.

20. In the **Unicast Listen Port** field, enter port `9991` and click on **Next**.

21. Click on the **Unix Machine** tab.

22. Click on **Add** three times, and then enter the names `soahost1`, `soahost2`, and `adminhost` with the hostnames of your servers `soahost1.packt.com`, `soahost2.packt.com`, and `adminhost.packt.com`, as shown in the following figure.

23. Click on **Next**.

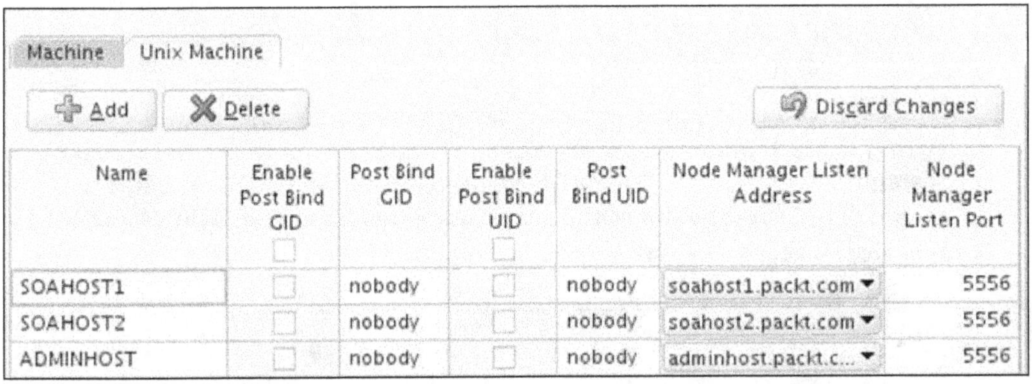

Name	Enable Post Bind GID ☐	Post Bind GID	Enable Post Bind UID ☐	Post Bind UID	Node Manager Listen Address	Node Manager Listen Port
SOAHOST1	☐	nobody	☐	nobody	soahost1.packt.com ▼	5556
SOAHOST2	☐	nobody	☐	nobody	soahost2.packt.com ▼	5556
ADMINHOST	☐	nobody	☐	nobody	adminhost.packt.c... ▼	5556

Figure 12.4: Advanced machine configuration

24. Assign **AdminServer** to the **adminhost** machine.

25. Assign **wls_wsm1** to the **soahost1** machine.

26. Assign **wls_wsm2** to the **soahost2** machine.

27. Click on **Next**.

28. In the **Directory** field, enter the value for **[ASERVER_HOME]/WSM_PM_Cluster** (for example, `/u01/share/oracle/middleware/config/domains/soa_domain/WSM-PM_Cluster`).

29. Click on **Next**.

30. Click on **Create**.

31. Click on **Next** and then **Finish**.

Starting Node Manager in the Admin Server domain home

Node Manager is started up in the Admin Server domain directory on port `5556`.

On SOAHOST1, start Node Manager in the Admin Server domain:

```
cd $ASERVER_HOME/bin
nohup ./startNodeManager.sh > nm.out&
```

Creating the boot.properties file

Create the `boot.properties` file so that you are not prompted for the WebLogic username and password every time the Admin Server and managed servers are started up. Furthermore, this is also required to allow Node Manager to start up the managed server. Follow the next steps to create the `boot.properties` file:

1. On SOAHOST1, create the `boot.properties` file:

   ```
   source envMidTier.sh
   mkdir -p $ASERVER_HOME/servers/AdminServer/security
   cd $ASERVER_HOME/servers/AdminServer/security
   echo "username=weblogic" > boot.properties
   echo "password=welcome1" >> boot.properties
   ```

2. Copy `boot.properties` to the rest of the managed server directories:

   ```
   mkdir -p $MSERVER_HOME/servers/wls_wsm1/security
   mkdir -p $MSERVER_HOME/servers/wls_soa1/security
   mkdir -p $MSERVER_HOME/servers/wls_osb1/security
   mkdir -p $MSERVER_HOME/servers/wls_ess1/security
   cp boot.properties $MSERVER_HOME/servers/wls_wsm1/security
   cp boot.properties $MSERVER_HOME/servers/wls_soa1/security
   cp boot.properties $MSERVER_HOME/servers/wls_osb1/security
   cp boot.properties $MSERVER_HOME/servers/wls_ess1/security
   ```

3. On SOAHOST2, copy `boot.properties` to the rest of the managed server directories:

   ```
   source envMidTier.sh
   cd $ASERVER_HOME/servers/AdminServer/security
   mkdir -p $MSERVER_HOME/servers/wls_wsm2/security
   mkdir -p $MSERVER_HOME/servers/wls_soa2/security
   mkdir -p $MSERVER_HOME/servers/wls_osb2/security
   mkdir -p $MSERVER_HOME/servers/wls_ess2/security
   cp boot.properties $MSERVER_HOME/servers/wls_wsm2/security
   cp boot.properties $MSERVER_HOME/servers/wls_soa2/security
   cp boot.properties $MSERVER_HOME/servers/wls_osb2/security
   cp boot.properties $MSERVER_HOME/servers/wls_ess2/security
   ```

Starting the Admin Server

To start up the Admin Server, perform the following steps:

1. On SOAHOST1, type the following commands:

   ```
   cd $ASERVER_HOME/servers/AdminServer/logs

   nohup $ASERVER_HOME/bin/startWebLogic.sh > AdminServer.out &
   ```

2. Verify that the following consoles are accessible:

   ```
   http://admin.packt.com:7001/console

   http://admin.packt.com:7001/em
   ```

Creating a domain directory for managed servers on MidTier

Copy the newly created domain to the local storage for both MidTier nodes:

1. On SOAHOST1, pack the domain from the shared storage and unpack it to the MidTier local storage:

   ```
   source envMidTier.sh

   cd $ORACLE_COMMON_HOME/common/bin


   ./pack.sh -managed=true -domain=${ASERVER_HOME}
   -template=soadomaintemplate.jar -template_name=soa_domain_template


   ./unpack.sh -domain=${MSERVER_HOME} -overwrite_domain=true
   -template=soadomaintemplate.jar -log_priority=DEBUG -log=/tmp/
   unpack.log -app_dir=$
   ```

2. On SOAHOST2, unpack the domain to the MidTier local storage:

   ```
   source envMidTier.sh

   cd $ORACLE_COMMON_HOME/common/bin


   ./unpack.sh -domain=${MSERVER_HOME} -overwrite_domain=true
   -template=soadomaintemplate.jar -log_priority=DEBUG -log=/tmp/
   unpack.log -app_dir=${APPLICATION_HOME}
   ```

Starting Node Manager in the MidTier domain directory

Start up Node Manager in the SOAHOST1 and SOAHOST2 domain directories using port `5557`. To do so, follow the given steps:

1. On SOAHOST1, edit the Node Manager property file:

    ```
    vi $MSERVER_HOME/nodemanager/nodemanager.properties
    ```

2. Edit these values:

    ```
    OLD:    ListenAddress=adminhost.packt.com
    NEW:    ListenAddress=soahost1.packt.com
    OLD:    ListenPort=5556
    NEW:    ListenPort=5557
    ```

3. Start up Node Manager:

    ```
    cd $MSERVER_HOME/bin
    nohup ./startNodeManager.sh > nm.out&
    ```

4. Repeat steps 1 to 3 on SOAHOST2.

Modifying the Node Manager ports for MidTier

Via the WebLogic Server Administration Console, modify the Node Manager port `5557` to provide the ability to start up the MidTier managed servers from the console. To do so, go through the following steps:

1. Navigate to `http://admin.packt.com:7001/console`.
2. Log in as the **weblogic** user.
3. Navigate to **soa_domain | Environment | Machines | SOAHOST1 | Configuration | Node Manager**.
4. Change **Listen Port** to `5557`.
5. Repeat steps 3 and 4 for SOAHOST2.
6. Save and activate the changes.

Modifying the te directories to absolute paths

The `upload` and `stage` directories for the WLS_WSM1 and WLS_WSM2 managed servers should be updated to use absolute paths. You can update them using the following steps:

1. Navigate to `http://admin.packt.com:7001/console`.

2. Log in as the **weblogic** user.

3. Navigate to **soa_domain | Environment | Servers | wls_wsm1 | Configuration | Deployment**.

4. Set **Staging Directory Name** to **[MSERVER_HOME]/servers/wls_wsm1/ stage** (for example, /u01/oracle/middleware/config/domains/soa_ domain/servers/wls_wsm1/stage).

5. Set **Upload Directory Name** to **[ASERVER_HOME]/servers/AdminServer/ upload** (for example, /u01/share/oracle/middleware/config/domains/ soa_domain/servers/AdminServer/upload).

6. Save and activate the changes.

7. Repeat steps 3 to 6 for wls_wsm2, but using the stage directory folder of wls_wsm2 instead.

Starting the WSM managed servers

Start up the WSM Managed Servers and verify that they are installed and running correctly. To do so, follow the given steps:

1. On SOAHOST1, type following commands:

   ```
   source envMidTier.sh
   mkdir -p $MSERVER_HOME/servers/wls_wsm1/logs
   cd $MSERVER_HOME/servers/wls_wsm1/logs


   nohup $MSERVER_HOME/bin/startManagedWebLogic.sh wls_wsm1 http://
   admin.packt.com:7001 > wls_wsm1.out &
   ```

2. On SOAHOST2, type following commands:

   ```
   source envMidTier.sh
   mkdir -p $MSERVER_HOME/servers/wls_wsm2/logs
   cd $MSERVER_HOME/servers/wls_wsm2/logs


   nohup $MSERVER_HOME/bin/startManagedWebLogic.sh wls_wsm2 http://
   admin.packt.com:7001 > wls_wsm2.out &
   ```

3. Verify that WSM is up and running on both hosts by navigating to these links and clicking on **Validate Policy Manager**:

```
http://soahost1.packt.com:7010/wsm-pm/
```

```
http://soahost2.packt.com:7010/wsm-pm/
```

Configuring WebTier

OHS is installed on the local storage of both the WebTier servers and on shared storage for MidTier.

Installing OHS on MidTier

To install OHS on a shared storage for MidTier, perform the following steps:

1. On SOAHOST1, start the OHS installer:

   ```
   source envMidTier.sh
   ```

   ```
   $SOFTWARE_DIR/fmw_12.1.3.0.0_ohs_linux64.bin
   ```

2. In the **Inventory Directory** field, enter `/u01/share/oracle/oraInventory` and then click on **OK**.

3. Click on **Next**.

4. In the **Oracle Home** field, enter the value for **[ORACLE_HOME]** (for example, `/u01/share/oracle/middleware/products/fmw1213`).

5. Click on **Next**.

6. Select **Collocated HTTP Server (Managed through WebLogic server)** and then click on **Next**.

7. Click on **Next**.

8. Click on **Install**.

9. Click on **Finish**.

Installing OHS on WebTier

To install OHS on local storage for both WebTier hosts, follow the given steps:

1. On WEBHOST1, start the OHS installer:

   ```
   source envWebTier.sh
   ```

   ```
   $SOFTWARE_DIR/fmw_12.1.3.0.0_ohs_linux64.bin
   ```

2. In the **Inventory Directory** field, enter `/u01/oracle/webtier/oraInventory` and then click on **OK**.

3. Click on **Next**.

4. In the **Oracle Home** field, enter the value for **[ORACLE_HOME]** (for example, `/u01/oracle/webtier/products/fmw1213`).

5. Click on **Next**.

6. Select **Collocated HTTP Server (Managed through WebLogic server)** and then click on **Next**.

7. Click on **Next**.

8. Click on **Install**.

9. Click on **Finish**.

10. Repeat steps 1 to 9 on WEBHOST2.

Extending domain with OHS

Extend the initial enterprise deployment domain to include the required OHS instances. Go through the following steps in order to do this:

1. On SOAHOST1, stop the Admin Server:

   ```
   source envMidTier.sh
   $ASERVER_HOME/bin/stopWebLogic.sh
   ```

2. Start the WebLogic Server Configuration Wizard:

   ```
   cd $ORACLE_COMMON_HOME/common/bin
   ./config.sh
   ```

3. Click on **Update an existing domain**.

4. In the **Domain Location** field, enter the value for **[ASERVER_HOME]** (for example, `/u01/share/oracle/middleware/config/domains/soa_domain`).

5. Click on **Next**.

6. Check **Oracle HTTP Server (Collocated) – 12.1.3.0 [ohs]** and then click on **Next**.

7. Click on Next.

8. Click on Next.

9. Check **System Components** and then click on **Next**.

10. Click on **Add** twice and then enter `ohs_1` and `ohs_2` under **System Component**.

11. Click on **Next**.

12. For **Admin Host**, enter `adminhost.packt.com`.

13. For **Admin Port**, enter `7001`.

14. For **Listen Address**, enter `webhost1.packt.com`.

15. In the drop-down list, select **ohs_2**.

16. For **Admin Host**, enter `adminhost.packt.com`.

17. For **Admin Port**, enter `7001`.

18. For **Listen Address**, enter `webhost2.packt.com`.

19. Click on **Next**.

20. Click on **Unix Machine** and then click on **Add** twice.

21. Under **Name**, enter `webhost1` and `webhost2` for each of the two new entries.

22. Under **Node Manager Listen Address**, enter `webhost1.packt.com` and `webhost2.packt.com` for each of the two new entries.

23. Under **Node Manager Listen Port**, enter `5558` for each of the two new entries.

24. Click on **Next**.

25. Assign **ohs_1** to the **webhost1** machine.

26. Assign **ohs_2** to the **webhost2** machine.

27. Click on **Next**.

28. Click on **Update**.

29. Click on **Next**.

30. Click on **Finish**.

Propagating the extended domain to WebTier

Pack the domain and unpack it on the local storage of WebTier using the following steps:

1. On SOAHOST1, pack and unpack the domain:

   ```
   source envMidTier.sh

   cd $ORACLE_COMMON_HOME/common/bin


   ./pack.sh -managed=true -domain=${ASERVER_HOME} -template=soadomai
   ntemplateExtOHS.jar -template_name=soadomaintemplateExtOHS


   source envWebTier.sh


   ./unpack.sh -domain=${MSERVER_HOME} -template=soadomaintemplateExt
   OHS.jar -app_dir=${APPLICATION_HOME} -overwrite_domain=true
   ```

2. On SOAHOST2, pack and unpack the domain:

```
source envMidTier.sh
cd $ORACLE_COMMON_HOME/common/bin
source envWebTier.sh


./unpack.sh -domain=${MSERVER_HOME} -template=soadomaintemplateExt
OHS.jar -app_dir=${APPLICATION_HOME} -overwrite_domain=true
```

Updating the OPSS JPS configuration on WebTier

Update the configuration on WebTier using the following steps:

1. On WEBHOST1, edit the `jps-config-jse.xml` file:

```
source envWebTier.sh
vi $MSERVER_HOME/config/fmwconfig/jps-config-jse.xml
```

2. Replace this value and then save the file:

```
OLD:    <jpsContexts default="default">

NEW:    <jpsContexts default="bootstrap_credstore_context">
```

3. Repeat steps 1 and 2 for WEBHOST2.

Starting the Admin Server

To start the Admin Server on SOAHOST1, execute the following commands:

```
cd $ASERVER_HOME/servers/AdminServer/logs
nohup $ASERVER_HOME/bin/startWebLogic.sh > AdminServer.out &
```

Starting Node Manager on WebTier on port 5558

To start Node Manager on WebTier, use the following steps:

1. On WEBHOST1, start up Node Manager on WebTier:

```
source envWebTier.sh
cd $MSERVER_HOME/bin
nohup ./startNodeManager.sh > nm.out&
```

2. Repeat step 1 on WEBHOST2.

Configuring OHS

To configure OHS, perform the following steps:

1. On SOAHOST1, edit the `admin.conf` file:

   ```
   source envMidTier.sh

   vi $OHS_ADMIN_CONFIG_DIR/admin.conf
   ```

2. Replace these values and then save the file:

   ```
   OLD:    Listen adminhost.packt.com:7001

   NEW:    Listen webhost1.packt.com:7778

   OLD:    <VirtualHost adminhost.packt.com:7001>

   NEW:    <VirtualHost webhost1.packt.com:80>
   ```

3. Edit the `httpd.conf` file:

   ```
   vi $OHS_ADMIN_CONFIG_DIR/httpd.conf
   ```

4. Replace this value and then save the file:

   ```
   OLD:    #NameVirtualHost *:80

   NEW:    NameVirtualHost webhost1.packt.com:7777
   ```

5. Create this new file:

   ```
   vi $OHS_ADMIN_CONFIG_DIR/moduleconf/custom_vh.conf
   ```

6. Add the following to include all the routings for all the consoles:

   ```
   <VirtualHost webhost1.packt.com:7777>

     ServerName admin.packt.com:7777

     ServerAdmin noreply@packt.com

     RewriteEngine On

     RewriteOptions inherit

     # Admin Server and EM

     <Location /console>

       SetHandler weblogic-handler

       WebLogicHost adminhost.packt.com

       WeblogicPort 7001

     </Location>

     <Location /consolehelp>

       SetHandler weblogic-handler

       WebLogicHost adminhost.packt.com

       WeblogicPort 7001
   ```

```
      </Location>
      <Location /em>
        SetHandler weblogic-handler
        WebLogicHost adminhost.packt.com
        WeblogicPort 7001
      </Location>
      <Location /sbconsole>
        SetHandler weblogic-handler
        WebLogicHost adminhost.packt.com
        WeblogicPort 7001
      </Location>
      <Location /servicebus>
        SetHandler weblogic-handler
        WebLogicHost adminhost.packt.com
        WeblogicPort 7001
      </Location>
      <Location /lwpfconsole >
        SetHandler weblogic-handler
        WebLogicHost adminhost.packt.com
        WeblogicPort 7001
      </Location>
    </VirtualHost>
    <VirtualHost soahost1.packt.com:7777>
      ServerName soainternal.packt.com:7777
      ServerAdmin noreply@packt.com
      RewriteEngine On
      RewriteOptions inherit
    </VirtualHost>
```

7. Repeat steps 1 to 6 on SOAHOST2, replacing all occurrences of **webhost1** with **webhost2**.

8. On SOAHOST1, stop and start the Admin Server to propagate the changes to WebTier:

```
source envMidTier.sh

$ASERVER_HOME/bin/stopWebLogic.sh

cd $ASERVER_HOME/servers/AdminServer/logs

nohup $ASERVER_HOME/bin/startWebLogic.sh > AdminServer.out &
```

9. Log in to `http://admin.packt.com:7001/em`.

10. Expand **HTTP Server**.

11. Click on **ohs_1** then **Start Up**.

12. Click on **ohs_2** then **Start Up**.

   Ensure that the frontend load balancers are now configured correctly:

```
http://admin.packt.com:7777/console

http://soainternal.packt.com:7777/index.html

http://soainternal.packt.com:7777/wsm-pm
```

Installing Oracle SOA Suite

Oracle SOA Suite is installed on a shared storage. Follow the next steps to install Oracle SOA Suite:

1. On SOAHOST1, start the SOA installer:

```
source envMidTier.sh

$JAVA_HOME/bin/java -d64 -jar $SOFTWARE_DIR/fmw_12.1.3.0.0_soa.jar
```

2. In the **Inventory Directory** field, enter `/u01/share/oracle/oraInventory` and then click on **OK**.

3. Click on **Next**.

4. In the **Oracle Home** field, enter the value for **[ORACLE_HOME]** (for example, `/u01/share/oracle/middleware/products/fmw1213`) and then click on **Next**.

5. Select **SOA Suite** and then click on **Next**.

6. Click on **Next**.

7. Click on **Install**.

8. Click on **Finish** once the installation is done.

Creating Oracle SOA Suite database schemas

To create the SOA database schemas, use the following steps:

1. On SOAHOST1, start the RCU:

   ```
   source envMidTier.sh
   cd $ORACLE_HOME/oracle_common/bin
   ./rcu
   ```

2. Click on **Next**.

3. Select **Create Repository** and choose **System Load and Product Load**, and then click on **Next**.

4. Enter your database information as shown in *Figure 12.2*, and click on **Next**.

5. Click on **OK** to confirm the validation of the global prerequisites.

6. Select **Select existing prefix** and then choose **DEV**.

7. Click on the **SOA Suite** checkbox and then click on **Next**.

8. Click on **OK** to confirm the validation of the component prerequisites.

9. In the password fields, enter a password (for example., `welcome1`) and then click on **Next**.

10. Change the value from **SMALL** to **LARGE** and then click on **Next**.

11. Click on Next.

12. If prompted to create tablespaces, click on **OK**.

13. Click on **OK** to confirm the validation and creation of the tablespaces.

14. Click on **Create**.

15. Click on **Close** once the RCU is complete.

Configuring SOA schemas for transaction recovery

Follow these steps to configure SOA schemas for transaction recovery:

1. On the database server, start SQL*Plus as the `sysdba`:

   ```
   sqlplus "/ as sysdba"
   ```

2. On the SQL*Plus prompt, run the following commands:

   ```
   GRANT select ON sys.dba_pending_transactions TO DEV_soainfra;
   GRANT force any transaction TO DEV_soainfra;
   ```

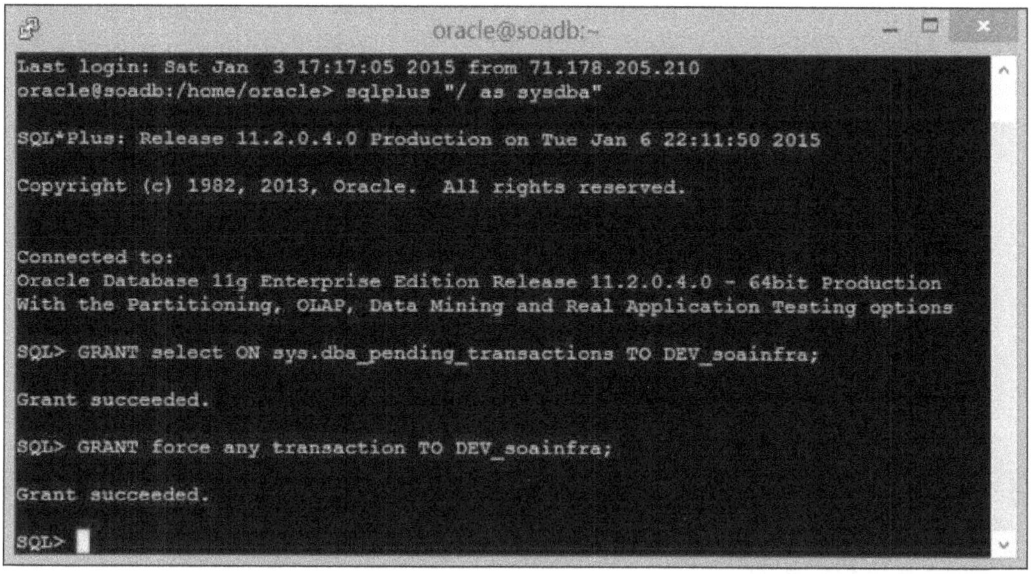

Figure 12.5. Executing SQL commands from the SOA database host

Extending the domain with Oracle SOA Suite

To extend the domain with Oracle SOA suite, follow these steps:

1. On SOAHOST1, stop the Admin Server:

   ```
   source envMidTier.sh
   $ASERVER_HOME/bin/stopWebLogic.sh
   ```

2. Start the WebLogic Server Configuration Wizard:

   ```
   cd $ORACLE_HOME/oracle_common/common/bin
   ./config.sh
   ```

3. Click on **Update an existing domain**.

4. In the **Domain Location** field, enter **[ASERVER_HOME]** (for example, /u01/share/oracle/middleware/config/domains/soa_domain).

5. Click on **Next**.

6. Check **Oracle SOA Suite – 12.1.3.0 [soa]** and then click on **Next**.

7. Click on **Get RCU Configuration**.

8. Click on Next.

9. Click on Next.

10. Click on **Next**.

11. Check **Managed Servers, Clusters and Coherence**, and **JMS File Store**, and then click on **Next**.

12. Rename **soa_server1** as `wls_soa1`.

13. Change **Listen Address** to **soahost1.packt.com**.

14. Change port **7003** to `8001`.

15. Under **Server Groups**, select only **SOA-MGD-SVRS-ONLY**.

16. Click on **Add** and then enter `wls_soa2`, `soahost2.packt.com`, and `8001`; then select only **SOA-MGD-SVRS-ONLY**.

17. Click on **Next**.

18. Click on **Add**.

19. For **Cluster Name**, enter `SOA_Cluster`.

20. For **Frontend Host**, enter `soa.packt.com`.

21. For **Frontend HTTP Port**, enter `7777`.

22. For **Frontend HTTPS Port**, enter `4443`.

23. Click on **Next**.

24. Assign **wls_soa1** and **wls_soa2** to **SOA_Cluster** and then click on **Next**.

25. Click on Next.

26. Click on Next.

27. Assign **wls_soa1** to the **soahost1** machine.

28. Assign **wls_soa2** to the **soahost2** machine.

29. Click on **Next**.

30. Assign the **[ASERVER_HOME]/SOA_Cluster/jms** directory (for example, `/u01/share/oracle/middleware/config/domains/soa_domain/SOA_Cluster/jms`) for each of the SOA persistence store directories except for mds-owsm.

31. Click on **Next**.

32. Click on **Update**.

33. Click on **Next**.

34. Click on **Finish**.

Configuring the default persistence store for transaction recovery

Follow the next steps to configure the default persistence store for transaction recovery:

1. On SOAHOST1, start the Admin Server:

   ```
   source envMidTier.sh

   cd $ASERVER_HOME/servers/AdminServer/logs

   nohup $ASERVER_HOME/bin/startWebLogic.sh > AdminServer.out &
   ```

2. Navigate to `http://admin.packt.com:7001/console`.

3. Log in as the **weblogic** user.

4. Navigate to **soa_domain** | **Environment** | **servers** | **wls_soa1** | **Configuration** | **Services**.

5. In the **Directory** field, enter `[ASERVER_HOME]/SOA_Cluster/tlogs` (for example, /u01/share/oracle/middleware/config/domains/soa_domain/SOA_Cluster/tlogs).

6. Repeat steps 3 and 4 for **wls_soa2**.

7. Shut down the **wls_wsm1** and **wls_wsm2** managed servers.

8. Save and activate the changes.

9. Start up the **wls_wsm1** and **wls_wsm2** managed servers.

Propagating the domain to the domain directories and machines

Use the following steps to propagate the domain to the domain directories and machines:

1. On SOAHOST1, pack and unpack the domain:

   ```
   source envMidTier.sh

   cd $ORACLE_COMMON_HOME/common/bin


   ./pack.sh -managed=true -domain=${ASERVER_HOME} -template=soadomai
   ntemplateExtSOA.jar -template_name=soadomaintemplateExtSOA


   ./unpack.sh -domain=${MSERVER_HOME} -overwrite_domain=true -templa
   te=soadomaintemplateExtSOA.jar -app_dir=${APPLICATION_HOME}
   ```

2. On SOAHOST2, unpack the domain:

```
source envMidTier.sh
cd $ORACLE_COMMON_HOME/common/bin

./unpack.sh -domain=${MSERVER_HOME} -overwrite_domain=true -templa
te=soadomaintemplateExtSOA.jar -app_dir=${APPLICATION_HOME}
```

3. On SOAHOST1, start the SOA managed server:

```
source envMidTier.sh
cd $MSERVER_HOME/servers/wls_soa1/logs

nohup $MSERVER_HOME/bin/startManagedWebLogic.sh wls_soa1 http://
admin.packt.com:7001 > wls_soa1.out &
```

4. On SOAHOST2, start the SOA managed server:

```
source envMidTier.sh
cd $MSERVER_HOME/servers/wls_soa2/logs

nohup $MSERVER_HOME/bin/startManagedWebLogic.sh wls_soa2 http://
admin.packt.com:7001 > wls_soa2.out &
```

Configuring Oracle HTTP Server for Oracle SOA Suite

Follow these steps to configure Oracle HTTP ${MSERVER_HOME}:

1. On SOAHOST1, edit the soa_vh.conf file:

```
source envMidTier.sh
vi $OHS_ADMIN_CONFIG_DIR/moduleconf/soa_vh.conf
```

2. Add the OHS routing rules for SOA, OSB, WSM, and ESS:

```
<VirtualHost webhost1.packt.com:7777>
   ServerName soa.packt.com:7777
   ServerAdmin noreply@packt.com
   RewriteEngine On
```

```
RewriteOptions inherit
# SOA Infra
<Location /soa-infra>
  SetHandler weblogic-handler
  WebLogicCluster soahost1.packt.com:8001,soahost2.packt.
com:8001
  WLProxySSL ON
  WLProxySSLPassThrough ON
</Location>
# SOA inspection.wsil
<Location /inspection.wsil>
  SetHandler weblogic-handler
  WebLogicCluster soahost1.packt.com:8001,soahost2.packt.
com:8001
  WLProxySSL ON
  WLProxySSLPassThrough ON
</Location>
# Worklist
<Location /integration>
  SetHandler weblogic-handler
  WebLogicCluster soahost1.packt.com:8001,soahost2.packt.
com:8001
  WLProxySSL ON
  WLProxySSLPassThrough ON
</Location>
# UMS prefs
<Location /sdpmessaging/userprefs-ui>
  SetHandler weblogic-handler
  WebLogicCluster soahost1.packt.com:8001,soahost2.packt.
com:8001
  WLProxySSL ON
  WLProxySSLPassThrough ON
</Location>
# Default to-do taskflow
<Location /DefaultToDoTaskFlow>
  SetHandler weblogic-handler
```

```
      WebLogicCluster soahost1.packt.com:8001,soahost2.packt.
com:8001

      WLProxySSL ON

      WLProxySSLPassThrough ON

   </Location>

   # Workflow

   <Location /workflow>

      SetHandler weblogic-handler

      WebLogicCluster soahost1.packt.com:8001,soahost2.packt.
com:8001

      WLProxySSL ON

      WLProxySSLPassThrough ON

   </Location>

   #Required if attachments are added for workflow tasks

   <Location /ADFAttachmentHelper>

      SetHandler weblogic-handler

      WebLogicCluster soahost1.packt.com:8001,soahost2.packt.
com:8001

      WLProxySSL ON

      WLProxySSLPassThrough ON

   </Location>

   # SOA composer application

   <Location /soa/composer>

      SetHandler weblogic-handler

      WebLogicCluster soahost1.packt.com:8001,soahost2.packt.
com:8001

      WLProxySSL ON

      WLProxySSLPassThrough ON

   </Location>

   <Location /frevvo>

      SetHandler weblogic-handler

      WebLogicCluster soahost1.packt.com:8001,soahost2.packt.
com:8001

      WLProxySSL ON

      WLProxySSLPassThrough ON

   </Location>
```

```
<Location /ess>

  SetHandler weblogic-handler

  WebLogicCluster soahost1.packt.com:8021,soahost2.packt.
com:8021

  WLProxySSL ON

  WLProxySSLPassThrough ON

</Location>

<Location /EssHealthCheck>

  SetHandler weblogic-handler

  WebLogicCluster soahost1.packt.com:8021,soahost2.packt.
com:8021

  WLProxySSL ON

  WLProxySSLPassThrough ON

</Location>

</VirtualHost>

<VirtualHost webhost1.packt.com:7777>

  ServerName soainternal.packt.com:7777

  ServerAdmin noreply@packt.com

  RewriteEngine On

  RewriteOptions inherit

  # WSM-PM

  <Location /wsm-pm>

    SetHandler weblogic-handler

    WebLogicCluster soahost1.packt.com:7010,soahost2.packt.
com:7010

  </Location>

</VirtualHost>
```

3. Repeat steps 1 and 2 on SOAHOST2, replacing all occurrences of **webhost1** with **webhost2**.

4. On SOAHOST1, stop and start the Admin Server to propagate the changes to WebTier:

```
source envMidTier.sh

$ASERVER_HOME/bin/stopWebLogic.sh

cd $ASERVER_HOME/servers/AdminServer/logs

nohup $ASERVER_HOME/bin/startWebLogic.sh > AdminServer.out &
```

5. Log in to `http://admin.packt.com:7001/em`.

6. Expand **HTTP Server**.

7. Click on **ohs_1**, then click on **Shut Down** then **Start Up**.

8. Click on **ohs_2**, then click on **Shut Down** and **Start Up**.

9. Validate that the following URLs are accessible:

    `http://soahost1.packt.com:8001/soa-infra`

    `http://soahost2.packt.com:8001/soa-infra`

    `http://soa.packt.com:7777/soa-infra`

    `http://soa.packt.com:7777/integration/worklistapp`

    `http://soa.packt.com:7777/sdpmessaging/userprefs-ui`

    `http://soa.packt.com:7777/soa/composer`

    `http://soa.packt.com:7777/integration/services/IdentityService/identity?WSDL`

Configuring the WebLogic proxy plug-in

Follow these steps to configure the WebLogic proxy plug-in:

1. Navigate to `http://admin.packt.com:7001/console`.

2. Log in as the **weblogic** user.

3. Navigate to **soa_domain** | **Environment** | **Clusters** | **SOA_Cluster** | **Configuration** | **General** | **Advanced**.

4. For **WebLogic Plug-In Enabled**, set the value to **yes**.

5. Save and activate the changes.

6. Restart the **wls_soa1** and **wls_soa2** managed servers.

Configuring the Oracle File Adapter for Oracle SOA Suite

To configure the Oracle File Adapter, follow these steps:

1. On SOAHOST1, run the following commands to create the shared deploy plan directory:

    ```
    source envMidTier.sh
    mkdir -p $DEPLOY_PLAN_HOME/soaedg_domain
    ```

2. Navigate to `http://admin.packt.com:7001/console`.

3. Log in as the **weblogic** user.

4. Navigate to **Deployments | FileAdapter | Configuration | Outbound Connection Pools**.

5. Expand **javax.resource.cci.ConnectionFactory**.

6. Click on **eis/HAFileAdapter**.

7. For the **controlDir** property, enter the value `[ASERVER_HOME]/SOA_Cluster/ fadapter` (for example, /u01/share/oracle/middleware/config/domains/ soa_domain/SOA_Cluster/fadapter).

8. Click on **Save**.

9. On the **Save Deployment Plan Assistant** page, enter the Path `[DEPLOY_PLAN_ HOME]/soaedg_domain/FileAdapterPlan.xml` (for example, /u01/share/ oracle/middleware/config/dp/soaedg_domain/FileAdapterPlan.xml).

10. Click on **OK**.

11. Save and activate the changes.

Configuring the Oracle FTP Adapter for Oracle SOA Suite

To configure the Oracle FTP Adapter, follow these steps:

1. On the WebLogic Server Administration Console, click on **Deployments**.

2. Navigate to **Deployments | FtpAdapter | Configuration | Outbound Connection Pools**.

3. Expand **javax.resource.cci.ConnectionFactory**.

4. Click on **eis/Ftp/HaFtpAdapter**.

5. For the **controlDir** property, enter the value `[ASERVER_HOME]/SOA_Cluster/ fadapter` (for example, /u01/share/oracle/middleware/config/domains/ soa_domain/SOA_Cluster/fadapter).

6. Click on **Save**.

7. On the **Save Deployment Plan** page, enter the Path `[DEPLOY_PLAN_HOME]/ soaedg_domain/FtpAdapterPlan.xml` (for example, /u01/share/oracle/ middleware/config/dp/soaedg_domain/FtpAdapterPlan.xml).

8. Click on **OK**.

9. Save and activate the changes.

Configuring the Oracle JMS Adapter for Oracle SOA Suite

Follow these steps to configure the Oracle JMS Adapter:

1. On the WebLogic Server Administration Console, click on **Deployments**.

2. Navigate to **Deployments | JmsAdapter | Configuration | Outbound Connection Pools**.

3. Expand **oracle.tip.adapter.jms.IJmsConnectionFactory**.

4. Click on **eis/wls/Queue**.

5. In the **FactoryProperties** property, enter: `java.naming.factory.`
    `initial=weblogic.jndi.WLInitialContextFactory;java.naming.`
    `provider.url=t3://soahost1.packt.com:8001,soahost2.packt.`
    `com:8001;java.naming.security.principal=weblogic;java.naming.`
    `security.credentials=welcome1`

6. Click on **Save**.

7. On the **Save Deployment Plan** page, enter the Path `[DEPLOY_PLAN_HOME]/`
    `soaedg_domain/JmsAdapterPlan.xml` (for example, /u01/share/oracle/
    middleware/config/dp/soaedg_domain/JmsAdapterPlan.xml).

8. Click on **OK**.

9. Save and activate the changes.

10. Navigate to **Deployments | JmsAdapter | Configuration | Outbound Connection Pools**.

11. Expand **oracle.tip.adapter.jms.IJmsConnectionFactory**.

12. Click on **eis/wls/Topic**.

13. In the **FactoryProperties** property, enter: `java.naming.factory.`
    `initial=weblogic.jndi.WLInitialContextFactory;java.naming.`
    `provider.url=t3://soahost1.packt.com:8001,soahost2.packt.`
    `com:8001;java.naming.security.principal=weblogic;java.naming.`
    `security.credentials=welcome1`

14. Click on **Save**.

15. Click on **Deployments**.

16. Check the checkbox beside **JmsAdapter**.

17. Click on **Update**.

18. Click on **Finish**.

19. Activate the changes.

20. Restart the **wls_soa1** and **wls_soa2** managed servers.

Installing Oracle Service Bus

Oracle Service Bus is installed on shared storage. To install Oracle Service Bus, follow these steps:

1. On SOAHOST1, start the OSB installer:

   ```
   source envMidTier.sh

   $JAVA_HOME/bin/java -d64 -jar $SOFTWARE_DIR/fmw_12.1.3.0.0_osb.jar
   ```

2. In the **Inventory Directory** field, enter /u01/share/oracle/oraInventory and then click on **OK**.

3. Click on **Next**.

4. In the **Oracle Home** field, enter the value for **[ORACLE_HOME]** (for example, /u01/share/oracle/middleware/products/fmw1213) and then click on **Next**.

5. Select **Service Bus** and click on **Next**.

6. Click on **Next**.

7. Click on **Install**.

8. Click on **Finish** once the installation is done.

Extending the domain to include Oracle Service Bus

On Oracle Service Bus, in order to extend the domain, follow these steps:

1. On SOAHOST1, stop the Admin Server:

   ```
   source envMidTier.sh

   $ASERVER_HOME/bin/stopWebLogic.sh
   ```

2. Start the WebLogic Server Configuration Wizard:

   ```
   cd $ORACLE_HOME/oracle_common/common/bin

   ./config.sh
   ```

3. Click on **Update an existing domain**.

4. In the **Domain Location** field, enter the value for **[ASERVER_HOME]** (for example, /u01/share/oracle/middleware/config/domains/soa_domain).

5. Click on **Next**.

6. Check **Oracle Service Bus - 12.1.3.0 [osb]** and then click on **Next**.

7. Click on **Get RCU Configuration**.

8. Click on Next.

9. Click on Next.

10. Click on **Next**.

11. Check **Managed Servers, Clusters and Coherence**, and **JMS File Store** and then click on **Next**.

12. Rename **osb_server1** as **wls_osb1**.

13. Change **Listen Address** to **soahost1.packt.com**.

14. Change port **7003** to `8011`.

15. Under **Server Groups**, select only **OSB-MGD-SVRS-ONLY**.

16. Click on **Add** and then enter `wls_soa2`, `soahost2.packt.com`, `8011`, and then select only **OSB-MGD-SVRS-ONLY**.

17. Click on **Next**.

18. Click on **Add**.

19. For **Cluster Name**, enter `OSB_Cluster`.

20. For **Frontend Host**, enter `osb.packt.com`.

21. For **Frontend HTTP Port**, enter `7777`.

22. For **Frontend HTTPS Port**, enter `4443`.

23. Click on **Next**.

24. Assign **wls_osb1** and **wls_osb2** to **OSB_Cluster** and then click on **Next**.

25. Click on Next.

26. Click on Next.

27. Assign **wls_osb1** to the **soahost1** machine.

28. Assign **wls_osb2** to the **4443** machine.

29. Click on **Next**.

30. Assign the **[ASERVER_HOME]/OSB_Cluster/jms** directory (for example, `/u01/share/oracle/middleware/config/domains/soa_domain/OSB_Cluster/jms`) for the WsseFileStore and FileStore.

31. Click on **Next** all WsseFileStores and FileStores.

32. Click on **Update**.

33. Click on **Next**.

34. Click on **Finish**.

Configuring the default persistence store for transaction recovery

Follow these steps to configure the default persistence store:

1. On SOAHOST1, start the Admin Server:

   ```
   source envMidTier.sh

   cd $ASERVER_HOME/servers/AdminServer/logs

   nohup $ASERVER_HOME/bin/startWebLogic.sh > AdminServer.out &
   ```

2. Navigate to `http://admin.packt.com:7001/console`.

3. Log in as the **weblogic** user.

4. Navigate to **soa_domain | Environment | servers | wls_osb1 | Configuration | Services**.

5. In the **Directory** field, enter `[ASERVER_HOME]/OSB_Cluster/tlogs` (for example, /u01/share/oracle/middleware/config/domains/soa_domain/OSB_Cluster/tlogs).

6. Click on **Save**.

7. Repeat steps 4 to 6 for **wls_osb2**.

8. Shut down the **wls_wsm1** and **wls_wsm2** managed servers.

9. Shutdown the **wls_soa1** and **wls_soa2** managed servers.

10. Activate the changes.

11. Start up the **wls_wsm1** and **wls_wsm2** managed servers.

12. Start up the **wls_soa1** and **wls_soa2** managed servers.

Propagating the domain to the domain directories and machines

Use these steps to propagate the domain to domain directories and machines:

1. On SOAHOST1, pack and unpack the domain:

   ```
   source envMidTier.sh

   cd $ORACLE_COMMON_HOME/common/bin


   ./pack.sh -managed=true -domain=${ASERVER_HOME} -template=soadomai
   ntemplateExtOSB.jar -template_name=soadomaintemplateExtOSB


   ./unpack.sh -domain=${MSERVER_HOME} -overwrite_domain=true -templa
   te=soadomaintemplateExtOSB.jar -app_dir=${APPLICATION_HOME}
   ```

2. On SOAHOST2, unpack the domain:

```
source envMidTier.sh
cd $ORACLE_COMMON_HOME/common/bin

./unpack.sh -domain=[MSERVER_HOME] -overwrite_domain=true -templat
e=soadomaintemplateExtOSB.jar -app_dir=${APPLICATION_HOME}
```

3. On SOAHOST1, start the OSB managed server:

```
source envMidTier.sh
cd $MSERVER_HOME/servers/wls_osb1/logs

nohup $MSERVER_HOME/bin/startManagedWebLogic.sh wls_osb1 http://
admin.packt.com:7001 > wls_osb1.out &
```

4. On SOAHOST2, start the OSB managed server:

```
source envMidTier.sh
cd $MSERVER_HOME/servers/wls_osb2/logs

nohup $MSERVER_HOME/bin/startManagedWebLogic.sh wls_osb2 http://
admin.packt.com:7001 -Dweblogic.management.username=weblogic >
wls_osb2.out &
```

5. Validate that the following URLs are accessible:

```
http://osb.packt.com:7777/
http://osb.packt.com:7777/sbinspection.wsil
```

Configuring the WebLogic proxy plug-in

Follow next steps to configure the WebLogic proxy plug-in:

1. Navigate to `http://admin.packt.com:7001/console`.
2. Log in as the **weblogic** user.
3. Navigate to **soa_domain** | **Environment** | **Clusters** | **OSB_Cluster** | **Configuration** | **General** | **Advanced**.
4. For **WebLogic Plug-In Enabled**, set the value to **yes**.
5. Save and activate the changes.
6. Restart the **wls_osb1** and **wls_osb2** managed servers.

Installing Oracle Enterprise Scheduler

Oracle Enterprise Scheduler is installed on shared storage.

Extending the domain to include Oracle Enterprise Scheduler

Follow these steps to extend the domain:

1. On SOAHOST1, stop the Admin Server:

   ```
   source envMidTier.sh
   $ASERVER_HOME/bin/stopWebLogic.sh
   ```

2. Start the WebLogic Server Configuration Wizard:

   ```
   cd $ORACLE_HOME/oracle_common/common/bin
   ./config.sh
   ```

3. Click on **Update an existing domain**.

4. In the **Domain Location** field, enter **[ASERVER_HOME]** (for example, `/u01/share/oracle/middleware/config/domains/soa_domain`).

5. Click on **Next**.

6. Check **Oracle Enterprise Scheduler Service Basic - 12.1.3.0 [oracle_common]** and **Oracle Enterprise Manager Plugin for ESS - 12.1.3.0 [em]**, and then click on **Next**.

7. Click on **Get RCU Configuration**.

8. Click on **Next**.

9. Click on **Next**.

10. Click on **Next**.

11. Check **Managed Servers, Clusters and Coherence** and then click on **Next**.

12. Rename **ess_server1** as `wls_ess1`.

13. Change **Listen Address** to **soahost1.packt.com**.

14. Change port **7003** to `8021`.

15. Under **Server Groups**, select only **ESS-MGD-SVRS**.

16. Click on **Add** and then enter **wls_ess2, soahost2.packt.com**, and **8021**, and then select only **ESS-MGD-SVRS**.

17. Click on **Next**.

18. Click on **Add**.

19. For **Cluster Name**, enter `ESS_Cluster`.

20. For **Frontend Host**, enter `soa.packt.com`.

21. For **Frontend HTTP Port**, enter `7777`.

22. For **Frontend HTTPS Port**, enter `4443`.

23. Click on **Next**.

24. Assign **wls_ess1** and **wls_ess2** to **ESS_Cluster** and then click on **Next**.

25. Click on **Next**.

26. Click on **Next**.

27. Assign **wls_ess1** to the **soahost1** machine.

28. Assign **wls_ess2** to the **soahost2** machine.

29. Click on **Next**.

30. Click on **Update**.

31. Click on **Next**.

32. Click on **Finish**.

Configuring the default persistence store for transaction recovery

Follow these steps to configure the default persistence store:

1. On SOAHOST1, start the Admin Server:

   ```
   source envMidTier.sh
   cd $ASERVER_HOME/servers/AdminServer/logs
   nohup $ASERVER_HOME/bin/startWebLogic.sh > AdminServer.out &
   ```

2. Navigate to `http://admin.packt.com:7001/console`.

3. Log in as the **weblogic** user.

4. Navigate to **soa_domain** | **Environment** | **servers** | **wls_ess1** | **Configuration** | **Services**.

5. In the **Directory** field, enter `[ASERVER_HOME]/ESS_Cluster/tlogs` (for example, /u01/share/oracle/middleware/config/domains/soa_domain/ESS_Cluster/tlogs).

6. Click on **Save**.

7. Repeat steps 4 to 6 for **wls_ess2**.

8. Shut down the **wls_wsm1** and **wls_wsm2** managed servers.

9. Activate the changes.

10. Start up the **wls_wsm1** and **wls_wsm2** managed servers.

Propagating the domain to the domain directories and machines

Follow these steps to propagate the domain to the domain directories and machines:

1. On SOAHOST1, pack and unpack the domain:

   ```
   source envMidTier.sh

   cd $ORACLE_COMMON_HOME/common/bin


   ./pack.sh -managed=true -domain=${ASERVER_HOME} -template=soadomai
   ntemplateExtESS.jar -template_name=soadomaintemplateExtESS


   ./unpack.sh -domain=${MSERVER_HOME} -overwrite_domain=true -templa
   te=soadomaintemplateExtESS.jar -app_dir=${ASERVER_HOME}
   ```

2. On SOAHOST2, pack and unpack the domain:

   ```
   source envMidTier.sh

   cd $ORACLE_COMMON_HOME/common/bin


   ./unpack.sh -domain=${MSERVER_HOME} -overwrite_domain=true -templa
   te=soadomaintemplateExtESS.jar -app_dir=${APPLICATION_HOME}
   ```

3. On SOAHOST1, start the ESS managed server:

   ```
   source envMidTier.sh

   cd $MSERVER_HOME/servers/wls_ess1/logs


   nohup $MSERVER_HOME/bin/startManagedWebLogic.sh wls_ess1 http://
   admin.packt.com:7001 > wls_ess1.out &
   ```

4. On SOAHOST2, start the ESS managed server:

   ```
   source envMidTier.sh

   cd $MSERVER_HOME/servers/wls_ess2/logs


   nohup $MSERVER_HOME/bin/startManagedWebLogic.sh wls_ess2 http://
   admin.packt.com:7001 > wls_ess2.out &
   ```

5. Validate that the following URLs are accessible:

   `http://soahost1.packt.com:8021/EssHealthCheck`

   `http://soahost2.packt.com:8021/EssHealthCheck`

   `http://soa.packt.com:7777/EssHealthCheck`

Configuring the WebLogic proxy plug-in

Follow these steps to configure the WebLogic proxy plug-in:

1. Navigate to `http://admin.packt.com:7001/console`.

2. Log in as the **weblogic** user.

3. Navigate to **soa_domain** | **Environment** | **Clusters** | **ESS_Cluster** | **Configuration** | **General** | **Advanced**.

4. For **WebLogic Plug-In Enabled**, set the value to **yes**.

5. Save and activate the changes.

6. Restart the **wls_ess1** and **wls_ess2** managed servers.

Congratulations! You have successfully installed Oracle SOA Suite 12*c* in a two-node cluster!

URL References

All relevant URLs are consolidated in the following table as a reference:

URL	Description
`http://admin.packt.com:7001/console`	WebLogic Server Administration Console
`http://admin.packt.com:7001/em`	Enterprise Manager Fusion Middleware Control
`http://soa.packt.com:7777/soa/composer`	Oracle SOA Composer
`http://soa.packt.com:7777/integration/worklistapp`	Oracle BPM Worklist
`http://osb.packt.com:7777/servicebus`	Service Bus Console
`http://osb.packt.com:7777/sbconsole`	Redirects to Service Bus Console
`http://soainternal.packt.com:7777/wsm-pm`	WSM Policy Manager Validation

URL	Description
`http://soa.packt.com:7777/soa-infra`	SOA Infrastructure
`http://soa.packt.com:7777/sdpmessaging/userprefs-ui`	The User Messaging Preference UI
`http://soa.packt.com:7777/integration/services/IdentityService/identity?WSDL`	Identity Service Web Service
`http://osb.packt.com:7777/sbinspection.wsil`	Oracle Service Bus WSIL Servlet
`http://soa.packt.com:7777/EssHealthCheck`	ESS Health Check

Startup and shutdown command reference

This section lists the various startup and shutdown commands that can be run from the command line, in addition to the location of the primary log file of the service being started:

- For OHS: Replace ohs_1 with the name of the OHS instance:
  - Startup:
    ```
    source envWebTier.sh
    $MSERVER_HOME/bin/startComponent.sh ohs_1
    ```
  - Shutdown:
    ```
    source envWebTier.sh
    $MSERVER_HOME/bin/stopComponent.sh ohs_1
    ```
  - Log file:
    ```
    source envWebTier.sh
    cat $MSERVER_HOME/servers/ohs_1/logs/ohs_1.log
    ```
- For AdminServer
  - Startup:
    ```
    source envMidTier.sh
    cd $ASERVER_HOME/servers/AdminServer/logs
    nohup $ASERVER_HOME/bin/startWebLogic.sh > AdminServer.out &
    ```

- ○ Shutdown:
  ```
  source envMidTier.sh
  $ASERVER_HOME/bin/stopWebLogic.sh
  ```

- ○ Log file:
  ```
  source envMidTier.sh
  cat $ASERVER_HOME/servers/AdminServer/logs/AdminServer.out
  ```

- For managed servers:
  - ○ Startup: Replace wls_soa1 with the name of the managed server:
    ```
    source envMidTier.sh
    cd $MSERVER_HOME/servers/wls_soa1/logs
    nohup $MSERVER_HOME/bin/startManagedWebLogic.sh wls_soa1
    http://admin.packt.com:7001 > wls_soa1.out &
    ```

  - ○ Shutdown: Replace the highlighted text with the name of the managed server:
    ```
    source envMidTier.sh
    cd $MSERVER_HOME/bin
    ./stopManagedWebLogic.sh wls_soa1 http://admin.packt.
    com:7001
    ```

  - ○ Log file: Replace the highlighted text with the name of the managed server:
    ```
    source envMidTier.sh
    cat $MSERVER_HOME/servers/wls_soa1/logs/wls_soa1.out
    ```

- For Node Manager (AdminServer):
  - ○ Startup:
    ```
    source envMidTier.sh
    cd $ASERVER_HOME/bin
    nohup ./startNodeManager.sh > nm.out&
    ```

  - ○ Shutdown:
    ```
    source envMidTier.sh
    $ASERVER_HOME/bin/stopNodeManager.sh
    ```

  - ○ Log file:
    ```
    source envMidTier.sh
    cat $ASERVER_HOME/bin/nm.out
    ```

- For Node Manager (MidTier):
    - ° Startup:
      ```
      source envMidTier.sh
      cd $MSERVER_HOME/bin
      nohup ./startNodeManager.sh > nm.out&
      ```
    - ° Shutdown:
      ```
      source envMidTier.sh
      $MSERVER_HOME/bin/stopNodeManager.sh
      ```
    - ° Log file:
      ```
      source envMidTier.sh
      cat $MSERVER_HOME/bin/nm.out
      ```

- For Node Manager (WebTier):
    - ° Startup:
      ```
      source envWebTier.sh
      cd $MSERVER_HOME/bin
      nohup ./startNodeManager.sh > nm.out&
      ```
    - ° Shutdown:
      ```
      source envWebTier.sh
      $MSERVER_HOME/bin/stopNodeManager.sh
      ```
    - ° Log file:
      ```
      source envWebTier.sh
      cat $MSERVER_HOME/bin/nm.out
      ```

Summary

Installing a highly available Oracle SOA Suite 12*c* cluster is a little more tedious than a traditional single-node installation, and even the EDG should be considered as merely a guide.

This chapter focused on one of the more commonly used architectures and provided concise and direct instructions to help you avoid the lengthy installation documents from Oracle.

The steps involved include:

- Downloading the Software
    - Downloading Oracle Fusion Middleware 12*c*
    - Downloading Oracle Java
    - Downloading Oracle Web Tier 12*c*

- Ensuring proper installation prerequisites
    - Ensuring hardware requirements
    - Setting up a load balancer
    - Setting up a hostname
    - Preparing a filesystem
    - Configuring an operating system
    - Verifying a temp and SWAP space
    - Creating operating system accounts
    - Configuring operating system prerequisites
    - Creating custom environment scripts
    - Unzipping software

- Installing Java and Infrastructure
    - Installing Java and Infrastructure on MidTier
    - Installing Java and Infrastructure on WebTier
    - Running the Repository Creation Utility
    - Creating a new domain
    - Starting Node Manager in Admin Server domain home
    - Creating the boot.properties file
    - Starting the Admin Server
    - Creating the domain directory for managed servers on MidTier
    - Starting Node Manager in the MidTier domain directory
    - Modifying the Node Manager ports for MidTier
    - Modifying the upload and stage directories to absolute paths
    - Starting the WSM managed servers

- Configuring WebTier
    - ° Installing OHS on MidTier
    - ° Installing OHS on WebTier
    - ° Extending the domain with OHS
    - ° Propagating the extended domain to WebTier
    - ° Updating the OPSS JPS configuration on WebTier
    - ° Starting the Admin Server
    - ° Starting Node Manager on WebTier on port 5558
    - ° Configuring OHS

- Installing Oracle SOA Suite
    - ° Installing Oracle SOA Suite
    - ° Creating Oracle SOA Suite Database schemas
    - ° Configuring SOA schemas for transaction recovery
    - ° Extending the domain with Oracle SOA Suite
    - ° Configuring the default persistence store for transaction recovery
    - ° Propagating the domain to the domain directories and machines
    - ° Configuring Oracle HTTP Server for Oracle SOA Suite
    - ° Configuring the WebLogic Proxy PlugIn
    - ° Configuring the Oracle File Adapter for Oracle SOA Suite
    - ° Configuring the Oracle FTP Adapter for Oracle SOA Suite
    - ° Configuring the Oracle JMS Adapter for Oracle SOA Suite

- Installing Oracle Service Bus
    - ° Installing Oracle Service Bus
    - ° Extending the domain to include Oracle Service Bus
    - ° Configuring the default persistence store for transaction recovery
    - ° Propagating the domain to the domain directories and machines
    - ° Configuring the WebLogic proxy plug-in

- Installing Oracle Enterprise Scheduler
    - ° Extending the domain to include Oracle Enterprise Scheduler
    - ° Configuring the default persistence store for transactoin recovery
    - ° Propagating the domain to the domain directories and machines
    - ° Configuring the WebLogic proxy plug-in

Index

Symbols

A

B

E

ECIDs 123-125
Enterprise Deployment
    Topology (EDG) 363, 365
Enterprise Scheduler Service (ESS)
  consoles, discovering 329, 330
  dead database connections, tuning 356
  default persistence store, configuring for
      transaction recovery 410
  domain, extending 409, 410
  domain, propagating to domain directories
      and machines 411
  ESS data source, tuning 355
  ESS WLST commands, using 356
  incompatibility 333
  installing 409
  job 331
  job definition 331
  job request 331
  job set 332
  job type 331
  purge policy 333
  request dispatcher 332
  request dispatcher, tuning 355
  request processor 332
  request processor, tuning 355
  schedule 332
  specialization 332
  starting 333, 334
  stopping 333, 334
  terminology 330
  troubleshooting 352-354
  tuning 352-354
  tuning, for optimal performance 355
  WebLogic proxy-plugin, configuring 412
  work assignment 332
  work shift 332
environment
  preparing 40
  setting up 41
ESS WLST commands
  environment variable, setting 356
  job definitions, managing 357
  job requests, managing 359
  job requests purging, WLST used 360
  schedules managing, WLST used 358

WLST offline, connecting to 356
Event Delivery Network
  monitoring 145, 146
Event Engine
  administering 226
  configuring 226
Execution Context ID (ECID) 119

F

failover 363
Fusion Middleware Control
  about 17, 157-161
  accessing 26
  administrative functions, performing 19
  composite, deploying 87, 88
  composite, redeploying 89
  composite, undeploying 89
  console, navigating with navigator 29
  consoles, discovering 20-26
  dashboard, presenting 27, 28
  functionality 18, 20
  Service Bus 27
  SOA Infrastructure 27
  used, for deploying SOA composites 87

G

Global Transaction Retry settings
  configuring 168, 169

H

High availability (HA) 363
Human Workflow Service Engines
  administering 210
  components and applications 210
  Human Task Service component address,
      managing 213
  human workflow data, migrating from test
      to production 221-225
  multiple authentication providers,
      configuring for human
      workflow 219, 220
  Organizational Users and Groups 214-217
  users and groups, mapping to application
      roles 217, 218

Workflow Task Configuration, managing at runtime 211

I

import.py script
downloading 104
URL 104
infrastructure problems, troubleshooting
about 273
BeanInstantiationException 279
DeploymentException 276
FabricInvocationException 277
logging, extending 274, 275
logs, using 275
MDSException 278
OSB Instance Error 278
SOAPFaultException 276
StackOverflowError 275
thread dumps, using 280-282
Unable to allocate additional threads error 277
unable to extend lob segment 279
infrastructure properties
composite lazy loading, configuring 164, 165
configuring 161-163
infrastructure thread pool, configuring 166, 167
Server profiles, managing 163, 164
infrastructure resources
configuring, for developers 233
custom XPath, setting up 236
Provide Role Based Access, providing to SOA Infrastructure 233, 234
Read-Only MDS database accounts, creating 234-236
infrastructure, shutting down
about 51
command line, using 51
console, using 53
WLST, using 54
infrastructure, starting up
about 42
command line, using 42
console, using 44
WLST, using 46

infrastructure thread pool
configuring 166, 167
installation, prerequisites
about 369
Filesystem, preparing 371
hardware requirements, ensuring 370
hostname setup 371
load balancer, setting up 370
operating system, configuring 371

J

Java and Infrastructure, installing
about 377
Admin Server, starting 384
boot.properties file, creating 383
Domain Directory, creating for Managed Servers on MidTier 384
new domain, creating 380-382
Node Manager ports, modifying for MidTier 385
Node Manager, starting in Admin Server domain home 382
Node Manager, starting in MidTier Domain Directory 385
on MidTier 377
on WebTier 378
Repository Creation Utility (RCU), running 378, 379
Upload and Stage Directories, modifying to absolute paths 386
WSM Managed Servers, starting 386
Java EE applications
listing 30, 31
Java Message Service (JMS)
about 118
destinations, monitoring 149, 150
Java Naming and Directory Interface (JNDI) 65
JCA adapters
administering 187
configuring 187
reference bindings, configuring 190, 192
reference bindings, managing 190-192
Service Bindings, configuring 187-189
Service Bindings, managing 187-189
JDK 322, 323

[PACKT] enterprise
PUBLISHING
professional expertise distilled

Thank you for buying
Oracle SOA Suite 12c Administrator's Guide

About Packt Publishing

Packt, pronounced 'packed', published its first book, *Mastering phpMyAdmin for Effective MySQL Management*, in April 2004, and subsequently continued to specialize in publishing highly focused books on specific technologies and solutions.

Our books and publications share the experiences of your fellow IT professionals in adapting and customizing today's systems, applications, and frameworks. Our solution-based books give you the knowledge and power to customize the software and technologies you're using to get the job done. Packt books are more specific and less general than the IT books you have seen in the past. Our unique business model allows us to bring you more focused information, giving you more of what you need to know, and less of what you don't.

Packt is a modern yet unique publishing company that focuses on producing quality, cutting-edge books for communities of developers, administrators, and newbies alike. For more information, please visit our website at www.packtpub.com.

About Packt Enterprise

In 2010, Packt launched two new brands, Packt Enterprise and Packt Open Source, in order to continue its focus on specialization. This book is part of the Packt Enterprise brand, home to books published on enterprise software – software created by major vendors, including (but not limited to) IBM, Microsoft, and Oracle, often for use in other corporations. Its titles will offer information relevant to a range of users of this software, including administrators, developers, architects, and end users.

Writing for Packt

We welcome all inquiries from people who are interested in authoring. Book proposals should be sent to author@packtpub.com. If your book idea is still at an early stage and you would like to discuss it first before writing a formal book proposal, then please contact us; one of our commissioning editors will get in touch with you.

We're not just looking for published authors; if you have strong technical skills but no writing experience, our experienced editors can help you develop a writing career, or simply get some additional reward for your expertise.

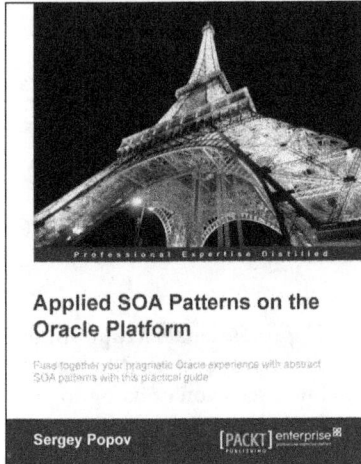

Applied SOA Patterns on the Oracle Platform

ISBN: 978-1-78217-056-3   Paperback: 572 pages

Fuse together your pragmatic Oracle experience with abstract SOA patterns with this practical guide

1. Demonstrates how to approach the Big Problem, decompose it into manageable pieces and assess the feasibility of SOA methodology to build the entire solution using real-life examples.

2. Explores out the links between SOA Principles, Open Standards and SOA Frameworks with clear standards implementation roadmaps.

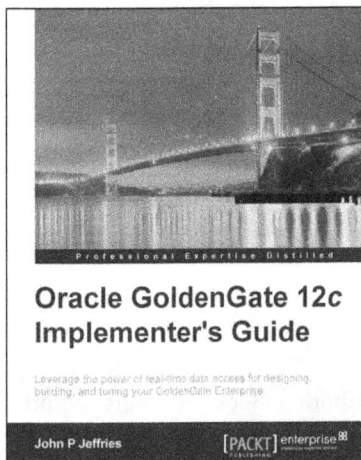

Applied SOA Patterns on the Oracle Platform

Fuse together your pragmatic Oracle experience with abstract SOA patterns with this practical guide

Sergey Popov   [PACKT] enterprise ✕

Oracle GoldenGate 12*c* Implementer's Guide

ISBN: 978-1-78528-047-4   Paperback: 422 pages

Leverage the power of real-time data access for designing, building, and tuning your GoldenGate Enterprise

1. Orchestrate the rich features of GoldenGate 12c and exploit the performance-enhancing features and manageability in your Enterprise environment.

2. Master data integration techniques to empower your organisation's readiness to migrate to cloud technologies quickly and easily.

3. An easy-to-follow step-by-step guide full of hands-on examples that offer a solid foundation of real-time data integration and replication in heterogeneous IT environments.

Oracle GoldenGate 12*c* Implementer's Guide

Leverage the power of real-time data access for designing, building, and tuning your GoldenGate Enterprise

John P Jeffries   [PACKT] enterprise ✕

Please check **www.PacktPub.com** for information on our titles

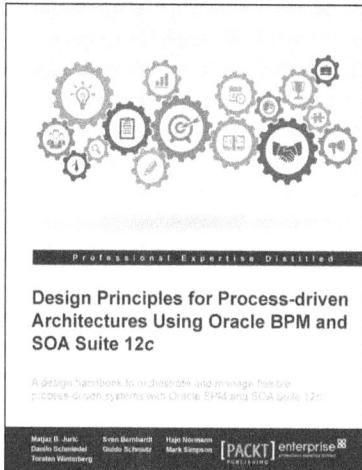

Design Principles for Process-driven Architectures Using Oracle BPM and SOA Suite 12*c*

ISBN: 978-1-84968-944-1   Paperback: 444 pages

A design handbook to orchestrate and manage flexible process-driven systems with Oracle BPM and SOA Suite 12*c*

1. Learn key principles to model business processes with BPMN and BPEL, and execute them in an SOA environment.

2. Use best practices for composite applications, including service design and human interactions, and apply them in your daily projects.

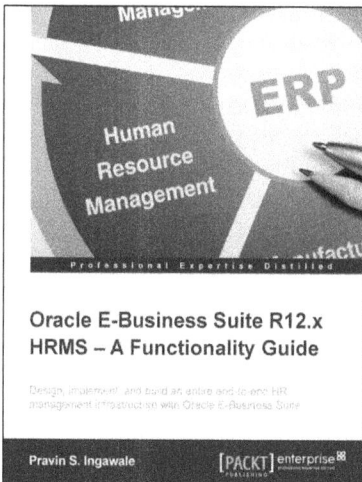

Oracle E-Business Suite R12.x HRMS – A Functionality Guide

ISBN: 978-1-78217-738-8   Paperback: 222 pages

Design, implement, and build an entire end-to-end HR management infrastructure with Oracle E-Business Suite

1. Learn about concepts such as system administration, work structures, and people management in Oracle Apps HRMS.

2. Learn to automate the key HR functions in Oracle Apps HRMS.

3. A step-by-step guide to creating your own set of implementation rules and to help you in following the best practices in the industry to deliver the best solution to customers.

Please check **www.PacktPub.com** for information on our titles

www.ingramcontent.com/pod-product-compliance
Lightning Source LLC
Chambersburg PA
CBHW080133220326
41598CB00032B/5049